PLACES
WHERE
TEACHERS
ARE
TAUGHT

John I. Goodlad
Roger Soder
Kenneth A. Sirotnik
Editors

PLACES
WHERE
TEACHERS
ARE
TAUGHT

Jossey-Bass Publishers

San Francisco • Oxford • 1990

PLACES WHERE TEACHERS ARE TAUGHT
by John I. Goodlad, Roger Soder, and Kenneth A. Sirotnik, Editors

Copyright © 1990 by: Jossey-Bass Inc., Publishers
350 Sansome Street
San Francisco, California 94104

&

Jossey-Bass Limited
Headington Hill Hall
Oxford OX3 0BW

Library of Congress Cataloging-in-Publication Data

Places where teachers are taught / John I. Goodlad, Roger Soder,
Kenneth A. Sirotnik, editors.—1st ed.
p.   cm.—(The Jossey-Bass education series) (The Jossey-
Bass higher education series)
Includes bibliographical notes and index.
ISBN 1-55542-276-4 (alk. paper)
1. Teachers—Training of—United States—History. 2. Education—
Study and teaching (Higher)—United States—History. I. Goodlad,
John I. II. Soder, Roger, date. III. Sirotnik, Kenneth A.
IV. Series. V. Series: The Jossey-Bass higher education series.
LB1715.P53 1990
370'.7'30973—dc20   90-38687
CIP

Manufactured in the United States of America

The paper in this book meets the guidelines for
permanence and durability of the Committee on
Production Guidelines for Book Longevity of the
Council on Library Resources.

JACKET DESIGN BY WILLI BAUM

FIRST EDITION

Code 9071

A joint publication in
The Jossey-Bass Education Series
and
The Jossey-Bass
Higher Education Series

Contents

Preface xi

Acknowledgments xv

The Editors xvii

The Contributors xix

**Part One: Teacher Education: A Contemporary
Perspective on the Past**

1. Connecting the Present to the Past 3
 John I. Goodlad

2. Recurring Themes and Variations 40
 Robert A. Levin

**Part Two: Evolution of Teacher Education:
Institutional Perspectives**

3. Abiding by the "Rule of Birds":
 Teaching Teachers in Small Liberal Arts
 Colleges 87
 Charles Burgess

4. The Evolution of Normal Schools   136
    Richard J. Altenbaugh, Kathleen Underwood

5. Teaching Teachers in Private Universities   187
    Barbara Beatty

6. Teacher Education and Leadership in Major
    Universities   236
    Irving G. Hendrick

**Part Three: Evolution of Teacher Education:
State Perspectives**

7. The Influence of Bureaucracy and Markets:
    Teacher Education in Pennsylvania   287
    Linda Eisenmann

8. Centralization, Competition, and Racism:
    Teacher Education in Georgia   330
    Kathleen Cruikshank

Part Four: Perspective on the Future

9. Beyond Reinventing the Past: The Politics of
    Teacher Education   385
    Roger Soder, Kenneth A. Sirotnik

    Index   413

Preface

Why bother with the case histories of a handful of places where teachers are taught? The answer, of course, is well known and worth repeating: Historians are concerned *about* the future; hence, they are concerned *with* the past. Gaining some purchase on the past helps us get back to the future. As in any empirical study, of course, this is an interpretive process. Human beings make history. Human beings interpret history. Interpretations become history and are reinterpreted by others. And historical analysis often has a history of its own that needs to be understood in the context of the endeavor. Such is the case for the present work.

Background

This book is one of three growing out of an inquiry initiated by the Center for Educational Renewal of the University of Washington. Created in September 1985, the center announced three sets of activities: A comprehensive study of the conditions and circumstances of educating educators for the nation's schools; a study of other professions, to search for exemplars for the education of educators; and the development of school-university partnerships for purposes of simultaneously improving schools and the education of those who work in them. The first two of these enterprises were completed in 1990 with publication of three books. The third is likely to continue into the future for as long as the inquiry itself does.

There has not been in the past quarter century a detailed description of what takes place in the college and university settings where teachers are educated. Yet teacher education is, once again, at the forefront of the educational reform agenda, as it was in the early 1960s. We have difficulty comprehending how anything can be improved significantly unless its present situation is thoroughly understood by those seeking change. Consequently, we decided to provide some of the missing knowledge regarding current conditions and circumstances, and analyses of where and how improvements might be effected. We set out to study in considerable depth a small, representative sample of the different kinds of colleges and universities that prepare teachers, special educators, and principals.

Two of us brought to this demanding task experience with a similarly comprehensive inquiry into a small sample of elementary and secondary schools. We had learned from this earlier study the importance of putting at the outset the demanding conceptual work that ultimately gives direction to the data-gathering process and then disciplines the later collating, analyzing, and drawing of conclusions—processes characterizing the followup to such an effort. By September 1987, we were ready to print questionnaires for the faculty members and students in our sample and to begin the arduous task of conducting hundreds of hours of interviews with individuals in the colleges and universities and the surrounding schools where students were placed for observation and practice teaching purposes. The sample and sources of data are described in Chapter One.

Meanwhile, it had become increasingly clear to us that our efforts to describe and understand present conditions and circumstances would be enormously enhanced by understanding of the evolution up to the present of each of the colleges and universities we chose to study. The documents sent to us from each institution included information on their histories. But this clearly was insufficient. Equally clear was the realization that we could not piece together from secondary sources the requisite historical context and perspective. Consequently, we decided to recruit a small group of educational historians to develop a condensed case history of each college and university in our sample. What followed from this decision is described in Chapter One.

As stated earlier, this inquiry into the education of educators, launched in 1985, produced three books. The first grew out of our early efforts to define a mission for the education of educators—a mission based on what those who work in our schools do and should do. We realized that this mission must be in large part a moral one. Seeking to understand and define it, we wrote papers and commissioned additional ones, the whole comprising *The Moral Dimensions of Teaching* (1990).

The second book grew out of our recognition that a historical perspective would shed light on current conditions affecting the education of educators. *Places Where Teachers Are Taught* not only provides that perspective but also adds substantially to the rather limited information previously available on the evolution of teacher-preparing institutions.

The third book, *Teachers for Our Nation's Schools*, published simultaneously with this one, seeks to integrate the whole: The conceptual bases of teaching as a profession, including the moral dimensions of these bases; the historical perspective that helps us see some of the implications of the legacies of the past; and the data-based inquiry into present practices, problems, issues, and shortcomings to be addressed. *Teachers for Our Nation's Schools* includes recommendations designed to rectify or alleviate a good many of these shortcomings.

Overview of the Contents

This volume is divided into four parts. In Chapter One of Part One, John Goodlad sets the contemporary context for the discussion of the evolution of teacher education; Robert Levin then considers recurring themes and variations of that evolution in Chapter Two.

In Part Two, the evolution of teacher education is discussed from institutional perspectives. Charles Burgess (Chapter Three) addresses teacher education in small liberal arts colleges; Richard Altenbaugh and Kathleen Underwood (Chapter Four), normal schools; Barbara Beatty (Chapter Five), private universities; and Irving Hendrick (Chapter Six), major universities.

In Part Three, teacher education is considered from a state perspective. Linda Eisenmann discusses the influence of bureaucracy and markets on the development of teacher education in Pennsylvania (Chapter Seven); Kathleen Cruikshank treats the interrelated themes of centralization, competition, and racism in her discussion of teacher education in Georgia (Chapter Eight).

In Part Four (Chapter Nine), Roger Soder and Kenneth Sirotnik consider the implications of their coauthors' findings, in discussing the politics of teacher education.

Seattle, Washington　　　　　　　　John I. Goodlad
August 1990　　　　　　　　　　　Roger Soder
　　　　　　　　　　　　　　　　　Kenneth A. Sirotnik

Acknowledgments

We are deeply grateful to the Spencer Foundation for providing financial support. A timely grant covered costs of two
meetings with the educational historians to plan successive stages
of the project, their visits to the twenty-nine sites, the preparation of the case histories, and, subsequently, of the chapters
that follow.

Our thanks go also to three historians of education who
assisted us in the early stages: Patricia Albjerg Graham, dean
of the Harvard University Graduate School of Education; Karl
Kaestle of the University of Wisconsin; and David Tyack of
Stanford University. With their counsel we developed a short
list of competent individuals; from it we invited those who later
developed the case histories and joined with us in writing this
book.

Another educational historian, Jurgen Herbst of the
University of Wisconsin, also counseled us in the selection of
colleagues and then prepared three of the institutional case
histories. William R. Johnson of the University of Maryland,
Baltimore County, met with our entire group at the critical
juncture of determining a structure for the book. The fact that
he and Jurgen Herbst were then writing chapters for another
book—on teachers and teacher training in the twentieth and
nineteenth centuries, respectively—helped persuade us not to
duplicate their efforts in the present volume. As matters turned
out, their two chapters in *American Educators: Histories of a
Profession at Work* (1989) proved to be very useful references in

the writing of *Teachers for Our Nation's Schools*. We express thanks and appreciation to both.

The logistics involved in arranging for visits, communicating with our authors, and so on, was handled through the Center for Educational Renewal, first by Kathleen Olson and then by Joan Waiss. We are grateful to both for managing so much of the support necessary to the success of any complex activity. Others on the staff of the center became involved in various ways—particularly Paula McMannon and Michael Reed. We extend to them, and to all others not named who took part in one way or another, our deep appreciation. Our sincere thanks go also to Jordis Young for her careful editing of the manuscript.

We will long remember the extraordinary cooperation of dozens of people in the twenty-nine colleges and universities we visited. We particularly sought out individuals carrying with them a good deal of institutional history, some still active and some now retired. Without all of them, a large part of what we announced in 1985 would not have come to fruition.

J.I.G.
R.S.
K.A.S.

The Editors

John I. Goodlad is professor of education and director of the Center for Educational Renewal, University of Washington. Born in Canada, he has taught at all levels, from kindergarten through graduate school. He served from 1967 to 1983 as dean of the Graduate School of Education, University of California, Los Angeles. He holds a B.A. degree (1945) in history and an M.A. degree (1946) in history and education, both from the University of British Columbia; a Ph.D. degree (1949) from the University of Chicago in education; and honorary degrees from nine universities in Canada and the United States.

Goodlad's research interests are in educational change and improvement and have been reported in more than twenty books and hundreds of other publications. An extensive study of schooling resulted in *A Place Called School* (1984).

Roger Soder is associate director of the Center for Educational Renewal, University of Washington. He attended the University of Chicago and did graduate work at the University of Washington. His sustained inquiry into an array of professions has brought to the center's work a useful perspective on the education of educators. Soder's research interests continue to focus on the ethics and politics of rhetoric.

Kenneth A. Sirotnik is professor and chair of the Area of Policy, Governance, and Administration, College of Education, University of Washington. Previously, he spent a number of years as senior research associate in the Graduate School of Education at the University of California, Los Angeles (UCLA), teaching, writing, and participating in many educational research studies. Sirotnik's interests and publications range from topics in measurement, statistics, evaluation, and technology to issues of educational policy and local school improvement and change.

Sirotnik received his B.A. degree (1964) in mathematics, M.A. degrees (1966 and 1967) in measurement and statistics— the first in the field of education and the second in psychology—and his Ph.D. degree (1969) in education measurement, statistics, and evaluation, all from UCLA.

The Contributors

Richard J. Altenbaugh is associate professor in the Department of History, Northern Illinois University. He received his B.A. degree (1970) from the University of Pittsburgh in history and his M.Ed. (1974) and Ph.D (1980) degrees from Pittsburgh in the history of education. Altenbaugh has published articles in *Labor History, History of Education Quarterly, Urban Education,* and *Theatre Journal,* among others. His books include *Education for Struggle: The American Labor Colleges of the 1920s and 1930s* (1990) and *The Teacher's Voice: A Qualitative Analysis of Teaching in Twentieth-Century America* (forthcoming, with others).

Barbara Beatty is assistant professor of education at Wellesley College, where she helps coordinate the teacher preparation program and teaches courses on pedagogy and on education and social policy. She received her A.B. degree (1968) from Radcliffe College in Romance languages and literatures and her Ed.M. (1973) and Ed.D. (1981) degrees from the Harvard Graduate School of Education, in administration, planning, and social policy. She is the author of various publications on the history of teaching and teacher education and is writing a book on the history of early childhood education, child rearing, and child care.

Charles Burgess is professor of the history of education at the University of Washington, where he is also adjunct professor of history and a fellow at the Institute for the Study of Educational Policy. He received his B.A. degree (1957) from the University of Oregon in history and his M.S. (1958) and Ph.D. (1962) degrees from the University of Wisconsin in history and history of education, respectively. He was a postdoctoral fellow (1967–68) at Harvard University.

Kathleen Cruikshank is completing a doctorate in curriculum and instruction at the University of Wisconsin, Madison. Her major research interests are in curriculum history, curriculum theory, and the involvement of teachers past and present in their own professional development. She received her B.A. degree (1967) from Colorado College in philosophy and her M.A. degree (1968) from the University of Washington in German language and literature.

Linda Eisenmann is assistant director of the Mary Ingraham Bunting Institute of Radcliffe College, a multidisciplinary research center for women scholars, artists, and writers. She has taught the history of education and women's history at Wellesley College, Bowdoin College, and Harvard University. She received both her B.A. (1975) and M.A. (1977) degrees in American literature, from Connecticut College and Georgetown University, respectively, and her Ed.M. (1981) and Ed.D. (1987) degrees in the history of education from the Harvard Graduate School of Education. Her current research interests include the intersection of gender issues and teacher education.

Irving G. Hendrick is professor of education and dean of the School of Education at the University of California, Riverside. He received his A.B. degree (1958) in history and his M.A. degree (1960) in education from Whittier College, and his Ed.D. degree (1964) in the history of education from the University of California, Los Angeles.

Robert A. Levin is a doctoral candidate in history at Carnegie-Mellon University and a consultant to the Cape Elizabeth, Maine, public schools and the Educational Testing Service. He has taught history, government, and English in the

Brookline, Massachusetts, public (middle and high) schools and others, served as an intermediate school principal in Gorham, Maine, and directed the teacher education program at Bradford College in Massachusetts. He holds an A.B. degree (1972) from Brandeis University in sociology and an M.A.T. degree (1973) from Brown University.

Kathleen Underwood is associate professor of history at the University of Texas, Arlington, where she also directs the Women and Minorities Research and Resource Center. She received her B.A. degree (1969) from the University of Colorado, Boulder, in history and her M.A. (1976) and Ph.D. (1982) degrees, both from the University of California, Los Angeles, in history. She has written a book, *Town Building on the Colorado Frontier* (1987).

PLACES
WHERE
TEACHERS
ARE
TAUGHT

PART ONE

Teacher Education:
A Contemporary Perspective
on the Past

1

Connecting the Present
to the Past

John I. Goodlad

Successive cycles of educational reform are as certain as the succession of the seasons. The diagnoses and proposals of one era resurface in the next, usually devoid of critical comparative analysis. The language of reform following publication of *A Nation at Risk* (1983) was surprisingly similar to that following the launching of Sputnik (1957) a quarter century earlier. Yet there was little reference to the historical source material constituting the literature of criticism of the earlier era.

Five years after release of *A Nation at Risk,* the Carnegie Foundation for the Advancement of Teaching published a study of teachers' views of the so-called first wave of school reform.[1] They gave the movement low marks. It is not surprising that they were particularly critical of limited teacher involvement in a top-down movement and of general failure to address problems most directly concerning them. Simultaneously, policymakers driving school reform were endeavoring at their meetings to figure out why the wave was flattening out short of the targeted beaches. How helpful it would have been, at the outset, to have read House's *The Politics of Educational Innovation*[2] and Sarason's *The Culture of the School and the Problem of Change,*[3] both addressing the earlier reform era, for an understanding

3

of how teachers and schools resist change thrust upon them. Educational reform is characteristically ahistorical.

The call for reform in teacher education is as repetitive as that for reform of schools—in diagnoses and proposals as well as cycles.[4] As a consequence, whether our interest be in the fate of recommendations made frequently during the past or in that of unusual ones, there is rarely much in contemporary discourse to help us predict the consequences of reforms' reappearance. For example, with the idea of clinical appointments in teacher education resurfacing today, it would be useful to seek understanding of why Conant's proposal for clinical professors went nowhere.[5] Perhaps it is the nature of reform to look ahead with hope undiminished by sobering lessons from the past.

Tyack observes that educational historians have largely neglected teachers and teaching.[6] They have largely neglected teacher education, too. There are encouraging signs that these important topics will attract greater scholarly attention in the future.[7] History offers the opportunity of ". . . 'meta-analysis', by which I mean stepping back from a particular period."[8] Stepping back suggests two potentially useful possibilities: stepping back in time and stepping back in place, in order better to see the meaning, consistency, and context of seemingly related phenomena. Regarding the education of educators for the schools, this is much more easily said than done.

The difficulty arises in large part out of the great extent to which historians, in trying to tell coherent stories of the past, must depend on biography and autobiography. Very few teachers or teacher educators ever caught the attention of first-rate biographers—further evidence, presumably, of the low status of schoolteaching. Teachers, particularly male teachers, were more likely to attract the scorn of storytellers in creating stereotypes such as the hapless Ichabod Crane. It is not surprising that the available histories of individual lives tend to be narrow, necessitating a search for other kinds of documents in any effort to portray the teacher education enterprise at a particular time. There is rich source material in various forms for autobiography: diaries, letters, annual reports, and reflections of the kind sometimes written by educators in their declining years. Again, however, these often suffer from undue narcissism and narrowness of perspective. Nonetheless, biography and autobiography—"the poor man's history," as Raymond Carver described it[9]—have proved useful in seeking a picture of what it was like to teach in a rural school circa 1880 or to be a female faculty member in a small college or university.

Getting a historical perspective on teacher education is even more difficult, because to do so one needs institutional biographies. The histories of individual institutions exist, but one finds here, too, a kind of narcissism, often reflecting the writer's long-term love affair with a college or university or a blatant public relations effort to publicize both the institution's golden anniversary and a current drive to attract more gold from alumni. Once again, the audience for the historian's efforts to place in perspective the course of a university's development, let alone its attention to teacher education, is modest.[10] Yet the reform of teacher education—reform necessarily involving colleges and universities—is a recurring topic of debate, debate deserving a much better historical perspective than has been available to date.

Studying the Education of Educators

It is often said that history informs the present. As stated in the preface, several colleagues and I set out to learn as much as possible about present conditions and circumstances of educating educators in a representative sample of colleges and universities. We recognized at the outset the diversity represented by the 1,300 or so institutions in the United States that prepare teachers. Yet we also recognized that these colleges and universities fall into broad types. We adapted the Carnegie classification scheme in settling on six types, recognizing that there is much variation within each type. We then consulted a map dividing the United States into eight census regions and selected a state from each. These eight states—California, Oklahoma, Colorado, Iowa, Illinois, Pennsylvania, Massachusetts, and Georgia—together contain 30 percent of all teachers practicing in the United States. From these states, we selected thirty colleges and universities, weighting the sample somewhat toward both public institutions and the regional universities that produce the largest proportion of teachers. One university declined our invitation too late for us to find a suitable substitute. This left us with a sample of sixteen public and thirteen private institutions.

In the public category, we selected four major research universities, five major comprehensive universities, and seven regional universities and colleges. Those in the first of these groupings often are referred to as "flagship" and usually are named "the University of [state name]." These contain many graduate programs, professional schools, and extramurally funded research projects and almost invariably have the highest entry standards for public undergraduate and graduate education in the state. Major comprehensive universities closely parallel the flagship institutions but generally have somewhat lower extramurally funded research budgets. Commonly, they are named "[state name] State University." Regional universities and colleges usually are named according to the region of the state represented (for example, eastern or central) and are designated "[region plus state name] University or College." They are predominantly undergraduate, with some graduate studies, several professional schools, such as business, education, and nursing, and a small number of extramurally funded research activities. Entry standards are almost always lower than for the above two types of institutions. Many were once normal schools and teachers' colleges, and they still prepare rather large numbers of teachers.

In the private category, we selected five major comprehensive universities, four regional comprehensive universities, and four liberal arts colleges. Major private universities, like their public flagship counterparts, offer both graduate and undergraduate programs, maintain professional schools, and frequently rival their public counterparts in extramurally funded research programs. Their entry standards usually are high. The regional comprehensive private universities and colleges usually have a substantial undergraduate tradition and offer professional preparation at both graduate and undergraduate levels. These generally serve the teaching, business, nursing, welfare, and technical needs of the immediate community and region. Most have lower entrance standards than do the major comprehensive institutions. Private liberal arts colleges are primarily undergraduate. Many offer within the baccalaureate program the courses required for state certification to teach. Often, they began with the mission of preparing teachers for the schools and ministers for the churches. Their entry standards vary widely.

Prior to selecting the sample, we had spent several months conceptualizing the study and determining the kinds of information likely to be useful in providing a reasonably accurate picture of how educators are prepared in these twenty-nine colleges and universities.[11] We also looked into conditions and circumstances in a dozen other professions—more into some than others—for whatever useful lessons might be derived from such inquiry. By late summer 1987, we had translated our conceptualization into a set of rather specific expectations for the adequate conduct of the teacher education enterprise and the kinds of data we would need in order to determine the degree to which these expectations appeared to be met on each campus.[12] We then designed a process for gathering the necessary information from available documents, from questionnaires to be answered by students and faculty members, from observations of institutional life and teacher education activities in cooperating schools and school districts, and from interviews with presidents, provosts or academic vice-presidents, deans, students, and professors in the arts and sciences as well as in education, supervisors of teacher education, cooperating teachers, and other school personnel. In addition, selected individuals at each site arranged for our visits and assisted us in getting additional data from an institutional survey. By early fall 1988, we were in a position to begin the tasks of collating these several bodies of data and analyzing them for the purpose of drawing conclusions.[13]

Before gathering the data during the 1987–88 academic year, we concluded that every possible effort should be made to get some perspective on the evolution of each institution. We discovered that routine publications provided a considerable amount of information regarding founding purposes; growth (such as from a normal school to a regional state university); critical junctures such as those caused by wars, depressions, prosperity, and demographic changes in the college-bound population; and other areas. Also, various kinds of institutional histories often were available—many of them of the self-serving kind described above. In our initial inquiries to people at each institution, we secured the names of individuals—many of them retired—who were, in a sense, living historians with rich memories of what they perceived to have happened in the life of a college or university over a period of several decades.

It appeared to us that we would be remiss in not going beyond the information already in our hands and the additional historical data that would come to us naturally during upcoming visits to each institution. Consequently, we sought and obtained a small grant from the Spencer Foundation for purposes of assembling in a meeting several educational historians to discuss the feasibility and potential usefulness of a study focused on the development over time of the education of educators in the twenty-nine colleges and universities in our sample. Not only would such a study enrich our contemporary analysis, we reasoned, but also it would have considerable value in its own right. Those assembled not only agreed but also volunteered to conduct mini case histories of the evolution of teacher education in the institutions, each selecting from three to five campuses. We concluded the meeting by developing a dozen core questions designed to serve as an initial framework for collecting data during the relatively brief time each individual would have available for his or her part of the overall inquiry.

Following this meeting, my colleagues and I in the Center for Educational Renewal wrote a proposal for the funds required in order to proceed. Unfortunately, we missed the fall 1987 meeting of the board of the Spencer Foundation and so faced a delay of several months—and, indeed, uncertainty as to whether our request would be approved. Several members of the group found it necessary to move forward with other commitments. On receiving the good news of approval early in February 1988, we hastened to find not only replacements but also the additional people needed to cover the entire sample. In the preface, we express our appreciation to all those who accepted our invitation and those who assisted us in the selection process.

Even though the academic year was by now well advanced, we could not, for several reasons, postpone visits and data gathering to the next year. Our colleagues in the study were forced to proceed with very tight schedules. All of the case studies were in our hands by late summer. All were reproduced and sent to each participant prior to a meeting held in October 1988. At that meeting, we revisited much of the agenda of the earlier meeting, held more than a year before—especially the question of how best to organize the individual case histories into a useful manuscript.

Three possibilities resurfaced: to organize (1) by institutional types (for example, liberal arts colleges), (2) by states, or (3) by themes (for example, the impact of the growing role of research in American colleges and universities). While the questions identified in the earlier meeting proved to be only marginally useful, the experiences of studying documents, visiting campuses, and interviewing selected groups and individuals had been powerfully informative and educative, and several themes of compelling power had emerged. We concluded that the twenty-nine mini case histories constituted a unique resource that should not be partially lost to the logic of an organizing structure but that we would be shortchanging both this resource and readers in simply presenting the twenty-nine individual accounts.

Consequently, we decided on an approach designed to make maximum use of the case histories, facilitate discussion of commonalities and differences, and remind each author of the themes appearing to recur so frequently in the histories of the teacher education enterprise on each campus. Grouping by types appeared to sustain these virtues, but we were not convinced that the original classification into six categories was entirely satisfactory. We also agreed that reading all twenty-nine case histories had revealed some powerful themes that transcended these types. We concluded that the distinctive involvement of each state was sufficiently influential in the development of teacher education on college and university campuses to warrant special attention.

The titles of succeeding chapters indicate the discussion and considerable postmeeting reflection. The absence of introductory chapters on the history of teacher education in the nineteenth and twentieth centuries is not an oversight. Although the writers of the case histories gathered contextual information shedding some light on the conditions and circumstances of teacher education generally during these periods, this was not their charge. Nor did the time available permit this larger effort. The writing of nineteenth- and twentieth-century histories of the education of educators is a task beyond what we set out to do—a task almost unavoidably apart from and, at best, supplementary to the one reported here. Also, the effort probably would only have duplicated similar chapters for a book on the history of teaching being prepared under the auspices of the American Educational Research Association—chapters written, incidentally, by two of the educational historians who participated in our work.[14] We seriously considered two opening chapters of the kind described but, after considerable discussion, abandoned the idea.

The classification scheme followed in choosing the twenty-nine colleges and universities resulted in some difficulties that we sought to resolve. For purposes of historical analysis, our sample of institutions appeared to fall more readily into four rather than six categories. We retained the private liberal arts colleges as a group of four: Berry College (Georgia), Bucknell University (Pennsylvania), Coe College (Iowa), and Mills College (California). A second, rather natural grouping embraced all those public institutions with normal school backgrounds and a dominant teacher education function early in their history: Central State University (Oklahoma), Chicago State University, Fitchburg State College (Massachusetts), Fort Valley State College (Georgia), Illinois State University, San Francisco State

University, the University of Northern Colorado, the University of Northern Iowa, and West Chester University (Pennsylvania). Then we lumped all of the private universities into a third cluster: Boston College (Massachusetts), Boston University (Massachusetts), California Lutheran University, Drake University (Iowa), Emory University (Georgia), Mercer University (Georgia), the National College of Education (Illinois), Roosevelt University (Illinois), and the University of Denver (Colorado). This left us with doctoral-granting, research-oriented public universities as the fourth group: Georgia State University, Oklahoma State University, Pennsylvania State University, Temple University (Pennsylvania), the University of California, Berkeley, the University of Georgia, and the University of Illinois.

Although Fort Valley State was not founded as a normal school, we placed it in this cluster because of the early and continuing dominance of teacher education. Until relatively recently, the National College of Education focused on teacher education, with a history sufficiently similar to that of former normal schools to justify placement in this category, even though it is a private institution. At the time of our visits, the college was negotiating a possible move to a new site and considering changing its name to National University, and so we placed it in the private university cluster as well.

It is obvious that the groupings are very arbitrary and that the variation within each is substantial, with the liberal arts colleges most clearly and reasonably constituting a group of believably alike institutions. Yet each of these is uniquely different from the others. The University of Northern Colorado has granted the doctor of education degree since the 1920s, but its history and relatively modest research resources persuaded us that it belonged in the second category. Similarly, the private university cluster ranges from institutions just barely warranting the description "university" to major research universities of national standing. And, whereas the University of California, Berkeley, is regarded as one of the world's leading research universities, some of the others in this category are just becoming accustomed to research as a major mission.

Four chapters emerge out of this clustering, then: "Abiding by the 'Rule of Birds': Teaching Teachers in Small Liberal Arts Colleges"; "The Evolution of Normal Schools"; "Teaching Teachers in Private Universities"; and "Teacher Education and Leadership in Major Universities." Of course, the central focus of each chapter is teacher education, but, to avoid some awkwardness, we have eliminated "teacher education" from the titles. Although teacher education is the subject of this book, its conduct and fate depend heavily on the evolution of the entire institution.

Charles Burgess, author of Chapter Three, developed all four histories and so draws solely on his own case materials. This is not so with the other chapters and authors. Richard Altenbaugh and Kathleen Underwood visited and wrote case histories on several but not all of the colleges and universities dealt with in Chapter Four. Some of the case materials on which their chapters depend were developed by others in our group. Such is true also for Chapters Five and Six. Both Barbara Beatty and Irving Hendrick draw from some case histories other than those they wrote. The camaraderie and sense of shared mission that developed in the October 1988 meeting of the group served us well later when cross-checking with fellow authors became necessary or desirable.

Another outcome of this highly productive meeting was agreement on a set of topics to be commonly addressed. Most obvious among these are such matters as the founding missions of the institutions, levels of certification offered, and whatever contextual information (location, proximity to other colleges and universities, population served, and so on) could add richness and understanding. To the degree possible, we sought in Chapters Three through Six a common effort to describe the programs offered and the changes effected over the years, the ideals driving preparation programs, and the laboratory facilities available, including the use of laboratory schools. It would be important, we agreed, to describe outside forces shaping the institutions and their programs: religious affiliations, enrollment crises caused by wars and other major social factors, certification and accreditation requirements, competition with other institutions, and so on. Each author would 'endeavor to determine the preservice, in-service, and graduate constituencies served and relationships maintained with surrounding schools. It was apparent to us that each institution's teacher education program has been shaped by powerful internal forces: tension between arts and sciences faculty members and those in education, the rapid growth of a research emphasis, financial crises brought about by rapid decline in enrollment, and so on. We concluded that the generally local character of the teacher education enterprise is pervasive and warrants careful analysis. Similarly, the struggle for professional recognition of teaching and teachers must be dealt with. Clearly, too, we would want to describe how certain common elements played themselves out similarly but differently between and across institutions.

Some of these topics loomed so large in our discussions that they appeared to warrant separate chapters. However, it was difficult to choose some over others, and we recognized the complexity of addressing them all. Further, we reasoned, doing so might well divert us from our desire to use to the full the rich primary-source materials at hand. The obvious importance of the state context in shaping teacher education programs brought us to the conclusion that there should be a chapter or chapters seeking to view institutional development from the perspective of state relationships, context, and impact. All six of the institutional types included in our initial sampling design were represented by the six colleges and universities selected in Georgia. Our attention then turned north to Pennsylvania, where we had studied four colleges and universities, each representing a different type. Linda Eisenmann and Kathleen Cruikshank had each studied three, in Pennsylvania and Georgia, respectively, and agreed to write Chapters Seven and Eight.

In this outline, we see considerable fruition of our stated desire to maximize the case histories as our unique contribution to further understanding of the emergence of teacher education in the United States. We see also our considerable recognition of the state role in shaping this emergence. In the list of common topics, we recognize the importance of addressing some elements commonly in seeking to provide a historical perspective on the institutional development of teacher education.

By the time of the October 1988 meeting, my colleagues in the center and I had completed visits to all twenty-nine institutions to conduct our interviews. We also had at our disposal the field reports of the second team of associates who had visited all twenty-nine. Further, as members of the two teams, we had spent many weeks in a process of synthesizing our field notes around the propositions regarding the education of educators that had guided our research methodology in the first place. (See the preface for further discussion of this background information.)

In this synthetic process, we drew on a vast body of data and impressions gathered during our visits and by mail and telephone. The result was a rather thick description of prevailing conditions and circumstances regarding the education of educators at each institution, with considerable additional description of the college or university context. Included in each was at least a sketch of the historical development of the institution, its department, school, or college of education, and its preservice effort in teacher education. All but one (William Johnson, invited to the meeting as a consultant) of the educational historians had visited from two to five campuses and written a mini case history on each. Everyone present had read all twenty-nine of these case histories.

Needless to say, my immediate colleagues and I in the center had derived from our discussions and reading some rather strong preliminary conclusions regarding persistent themes running through the rich body of data. We were looking forward to the opportunity to either strengthen or question these preliminary conclusions through the analysis of the questionnaire data, a phase of work still lying ahead. The meeting with the several educational historians offered another opportunity to further validate or cast doubt on our conclusions to date.

In this meeting, we stayed away from a deliberate, systematic validation effort. Instead, we counted on a more spontaneous, informal process through which a colleague would volunteer a hypothesis or tentative conclusion beginning to emerge from the case material. This occurred frequently, not only in the part of the discussion directed to topics to be addressed commonly but also in our endeavor to agree on an outline of a manuscript reporting our work. But we stopped short of listing a set of impressionistic conclusions regarding contemporary conditions on which we might seek to agree. We left the meeting with the understanding that I would attempt to develop such a set, and this I try to do in the concluding section of this chapter.

A first draft of this chapter was in the hands of each author prior to his or her writing a subsequent chapter. There was no accompanying expectation that each author would use what follows as an outline. Rather, the intent was to alert each writer to the proposition that the following generalizations about contemporary conditions and circumstances of teacher education appear to characterize the enterprise. Their conclusions might be different, however. Mine emerged from visiting all twenty-nine settings and reading the case histories prepared by our group of historians.

Diversity and Commonality

One striking feature of higher education in the United States is overarching and all-encompassing. This feature is best described by the word *diversity*. Visitors from abroad find this characteristic to be both fascinating and perplexing. The huge volume of data regarding higher education continually being gathered speaks to this diversity in student population, size of the faculty and student body, costs of attending, religious affiliation, rural or urban setting, types of programs offered, and more.

Yet one does not probe very far into this diversity without coming upon some very obvious similarities: the go-and-stop rhythm of quarter or semester structural arrangements, the generally didactic instructional mode, student assignments and tests, course credits, the distinctive contours of the student-teacher relationship, and so on. These similarities surface whether one walks into a high-rise urban campus abutting busy streets and sidewalks or red-brick bungalows set back from the mowed lawns of a campus quadrangle. Reading the bulletins of University X and University Y does not prepare one for the similarities and differences encountered in a visit.

Approximately 1,300 of these colleges and universities prepare teachers. It is not surprising that one finds that unique institutional characteristics spill over into the conduct of teacher education programs. No two are identical. Yet one can describe in broad strokes some persistent similarities: the dual demands of general and professional curricula in those preparing teachers at the undergraduate level, a substantial psychological orientation for prospective elementary school teachers, subject matter majors for high school teachers, a block of time set aside for student teaching, heavy reliance on teachers in the schools (cooperating teachers) for the day-to-day guidance of student teachers, and so on. Yet look a little more deeply, and marked variations in the specifics become apparent. The more things appear the same, the more deeply one must look to find the differences invariably present.

Future teachers at Coe College identify closely with the ambience of the college as a whole. Preparing to teach uses up one's electives and adds a dimension not shared by other students. A student coming to Boston University with the expectation of preparing to teach, however, immediately finds a home in the school of education and then partakes of the larger context. The teacher education programs of the two very unlike institutions differ in structure courses, readings, and much more. Yet one still finds in both the so-called foundation courses in history or philosophy or sociology of education, methods courses, visits to schools prior to student teaching, and, of course, student teaching itself. Expanding one's perspective to include a broader sample of institutions, one sees the education of educators to be marked by some common features that take on unique characteristics within the context of a particular time and place.

Although institutional context has always played a significant role in creating diversity, institutional context itself is conditioned significantly by outside forces, particularly war or peace and economic prosperity or depression. Talk of raising standards declines in the face of declining enrollments. Entrepreneurial programs created in periods of economic recession are easily cut off (often with claims of enhancing academic standards) during periods of surging enrollments. The impact of changing external circumstances is apparent in the changing fortunes of teacher education over time. Yet not all programs have been shaped in similar ways during these cycles. This shaping is in part a product of institutional size and location, of private or public affiliation, of internal leadership, and of licensing and accreditation. In this last regard, teacher education has experienced both the benefits of protection and the limitations of prescription. Again, no two programs for the education of educators, even in colleges or universities in the same state, have been shaped in precisely the same fashion and form.

Teasing out the theme of "the same but different" over time would require extensive forays into other themes of equal significance. Most of these emerged during the first of our visits to colleges and universities undertaken during 1987–88 by my several colleagues and me. They reemerged and took on increasing significance during each subsequent visit on our itinerary. A few themes were added early on, but none faded from view. Instead, their pervasiveness became increasingly clear and, it seemed to us, of increasing importance in our effort to describe and understand the teacher education enterprise in our diverse, representative sample of colleges and universities in the United States.

In the next section of this introductory chapter, I identify several of the major themes and seek to describe how they are being played out both commonly and uncommonly in the colleges and universities we studied. In Chapter Two, Robert Levin draws on the twenty-nine case histories in such a way as to provide considerable insight into the evolution of these and other themes over time.

Some Emerging Themes

Stability and Instability. A substantial proportion of the colleges and universities in our sample began with the education of teachers as a major or even central mission. Such was the founding mission of normal schools, even though not all students enrolled intended to become teachers. The small liberal arts colleges stated the initial dual mission of preparing teachers for the schools and ministers for the churches. Although both types of institutions (most of the former normal schools have now become regional universities) continue to prepare teachers, few claim this function as a top priority.

Commonly, the principals or presidents of the early normal schools and the presidents of other types of colleges and universities stayed on in their posts for many years. Not infrequently, they established a close, supportive relationship with their selected heads or chairs of teacher education, a relationship that often proved to be enduring. With both individuals committed and with relatively long periods of stewardship, teacher education enjoyed relative stability—a condition frequently prevailing into the twentieth century.

Very little of this stability is evident today. The proliferation of colleges and universities, together with increased mobility for purposes of enhancing personal opportunity, enormously expanded career choices. Presidents of small colleges moved on to become presidents of larger, more prestigious ones. Chairs of small departments became deans of schools or colleges of education. Until rather recently, however, these presidents and deans tended to stay on in their new positions and not look for still greener pastures beyond. Significant numbers of university presidents had been deans of education, a career shift occurring much less frequently today. Consequently, they understood and tended to be supportive of schools and colleges of education. In general, their replacement by individuals coming from medicine, law, and the arts and sciences spelled less support for teacher education.

Our conclusion, from perusing documents, visiting colleges and universities, and interviewing a wide array of individuals on each campus, is that two kinds of instability prevail relative to the focus of our interest. First, a revolving-door syndrome among top administrators is disturbingly apparent. The close, long-term relationship between the president and chair or dean of education has virtually vanished. Second, partly because of this situation and partly because of mixed signals from political and accrediting arenas, schools of education are in limbo, waiting for directional signals or for still another shoe to fall.

In several of the institutions visited, the president was either in his or her first or last year, was in acting or interim status, or chose not to be available for an interview because of current instability in tenure. The position of provost or academic vice-president was equally uncertain or unstable. Current searches for one or more deans usually were under way. Several education deans were either acting or in their first or last year. Some informed me of their unannounced but pending departure; several inquired as to job opportunities elsewhere. One institution was still reeling from having had two deans the previous year after several previous years of tumult. One faculty group reported having had a new dean virtually every year over a period of years and a current dean known to be a candidate for other positions. In several institutions, half or more of the major administrative positions from deanships on up were occupied by persons in acting or interim status. How refreshing it was to encounter individuals who had been in their present posts for years and firmly stated their intention of staying there!

With just a few exceptions, recent calls for reform in teacher education, accompanied by new state legislation and revisions in licensing and accrediting requirements, have had a destabilizing rather than stabilizing effect on program planning and renewal by faculty groups. The attitude frequently expressed is that there is little point in taking the initiative when anything accomplished by a working party will be undone by legislative action or the state department of education or both. A more cynical attitude expressed is that the specifications and requirements handed down at least guarantee some programmatic coherence, whereas none would reveal the inability of the faculties in education and the arts and sciences to negotiate agreements.

The calls for excellence and for leadership begin to sound more than a little hollow. Then, as we shall see in subsequent discussion, to this instability must be added the effects of institutional loss of and search for the kind of identity that would make the status of teacher education clear, if not secure. Our inquiry to date into the education of educators in selected colleges and universities convinces us that the reconstruction needed reaches far beyond the oft-repeated clichés of more general education, elimination of education majors, and more extensive internship with mentors. Some historical awareness of the general decline of teacher education in colleges and universities may help us understand not only what is needed today but also how to move from where we are to what would be significantly better.

The Search for Institutional Identity. One no sooner yearns for the good old days than one is put straight: There were no good old days. Yet, considering present circumstances, it is difficult to believe that there were not, once, better times for teacher education and teacher educators. Such as these were, they had to do with institutional mission and its impact on the status of teacher education programs and those responsible for them.

The transition from normal school to regional state university and from teaching to research together appear to have contributed significantly to the insecure status of teacher education and faculty members connected with it on today's college and university campuses. There are two important dimensions to this transition: a decline in status of the unit labeled "Education" and a corresponding decline in status for teacher education commensurate with the advance of the institution to higher standing as a research-oriented university.

As stated above, the education of teachers was central to the normal schools and early liberal arts colleges. Rapid expansion of higher education during the twentieth century increased the options for people wishing to teach, making it easier and increasingly attractive for liberal arts colleges to emphasize their "liberal," nonvocational character. More and more, the provision of education courses and student teaching became a service function, ensuring a teaching certificate as a kind of employment insurance if wanted or needed. Many liberal arts colleges that enrolled 50 percent of their students in teacher education programs as recently as thirty to forty years ago today enroll fewer than 20 percent. Some prepare teachers no longer.

The progression of normal schools to teachers' colleges, to state colleges, and then to regional state universities not only increased the size and status of the arts and sciences departments but also added professional, semiprofessional, and technical colleges. Many initially small private universities grew and expanded in similar fashion. Teacher education was not so much pushed aside as it was overshadowed. It became one of several competing functions rather than central.

In our visits and interviews, we found presidents and provosts almost invariably identifying the arts and sciences or the business school as central. Rarely was the school of education or teacher education cited as a top priority. Even in places only recently removed from teachers' college identification, other fields and specialties received top billing. More often than not, the normal school beginnings and history were passed over quickly in pamphlets and bulletins. Older faculty members in the department or school of education spoke nostalgically about the good old days when teacher education stood tall in an institution that proclaimed this function on its masthead. One president stood out in his clear appreciation of a state mandate requiring that his university—not long ago a place of national renown for in-service teacher education—once more stress the education of first-level teachers. It was not uncommon for academic administrators to view the decline of teacher education on their campuses virtually as evidence of a rite of passage signifying a coming of age for their institutions.

For two decades following the end of World War II, nearly all colleges and universities, whether public or private, experienced dizzying expansion. There was little or no need to share scarce resources; most fields flourished with or without overt approval or sanction. Suddenly, they faced decline and the need to cut back. Evidence to support differential budgetary attrition for departments and colleges of education grew as we visited more and more campuses. At first, we believed that what we heard from deans and professors of education was just another part of a growing picture, perceived but not fully accurate, of prejudicial treatment. Increasingly, however, we learned from others, including some presidents and provosts, that there had been an overreaction—that, indeed, budget cuts often had not been equitably executed. In most such settings, budgetary restorations had not yet caught up with the growth in both graduate and undergraduate teacher education enrollments now being experienced. It appeared that the more successful the school or college of education in advancing faculty research productivity, the less the likelihood of its placing teacher education at the head of its list of priorities. As universities advance in status, we conclude, the status of teacher education declines, not only within the institution as a whole but also within the school or college of education, which is, in turn, of rather lowly status on most campuses.

It is clear from our data not only that teacher education declined in significance and prestige as normal schools and small colleges evolved to university standing but also that the morale of professors of education suffered accordingly. These faculty members, once involved in the dominant institutional function and secure in their central role, even if not fully respected by their academic colleagues, found themselves increasingly on the periphery. It is interesting that the negative views of professors in the arts and sciences on small campuses, particularly of liberal arts colleges, were more likely to be addressed toward education professors and the field of education generally than toward their own colleagues in the education department. Frequently, we were told that this particular college or university was blessed to have such good people, particularly when the quality of programs and people elsewhere is so bad. A familiar sentence comes to mind: "Some of my best friends are [fill in the blank]."

It becomes increasingly clear that the vicissitudes of teacher education on college and university campuses, particularly during the last three decades, cannot be explained and accounted for easily; they certainly cannot be understood apart from a closely related part of a complex, puzzling picture—that of the place of teachers and public school teaching in the history of American life and thought. Why, for example, have so many of the colleges and universities in our sample downplayed their teacher education and lower school roots simply by ignoring them? And why did some presidents, provosts, and academic deans view attrition in teacher education as evidence of a maturing campus?

From Teaching to Research. One needs to have only a modest acquaintance with higher education to be aware of the degree to which research dominates university life. The pecking order of major universities depends almost entirely on the size of their extramurally funded research budgets and the visibility of their faculty as evidenced by publications based on their research. Visibility built on research activity and publication in prestigious journals provides both career mobility and comforting assurance of being wanted. Current estimates of what it costs in salary, laboratories, equipment, and the like to entice highly visible professors in the sciences from University X to University Y run into the millions of dollars per individual. The perks often include little expectation of teaching beyond the mentoring of doctoral-level students who join the professor in his or her research. Scholarly work provides such a professor with airline tickets (accompanied by honoraria) to the rest of the world. A colleague may be recognized as a gifted teacher, but such a reputation will not carry far beyond the local campus and certainly will not provide equal mobility and monetary rewards.

Although most major universities have taken steps in recent years to provide greater recognition and rewards for teaching, professors only rarely are promoted because of their teaching record—and then only if research productivity attains some minimal level. Although the criteria for promotion almost invariably include research, teaching, university service, and professional contributions (such as holding office in a professional organization), contributions in all three of the non-research categories fall short of substituting for lack of productivity in the first. This situation is not likely to change significantly, in either the long or the short term.

No matter how one argues that research enhances teaching (and a good case can be made), it is hypocritical not to recognize the degree to which the dominance of research endangers other university functions, not only in those universities where it is clearly the norm but also in other college and university settings where it is fast becoming the fashionable expectation. The most devastating consequences were apparent in many of the regional public and private universities that only recently had been teachers' colleges or dominantly teaching institutions. Here, we often found an aging faculty initially employed with the expectation that teaching was the most valued activity, whether in education or the arts and sciences departments. But the word was out (usually attributed to a newly appointed provost or academic vice-president rumored to be supported by the president): All future promotion decisions will be heavily dependent on research productivity.

Pinning down precisely what this message conveyed proved to be very difficult. Usually, a faculty member's definition, such as three articles a year in refereed journals, brought out disagreement from colleagues regarding the specifics but not the general expectations. A visit with the administrator identified as the source of the message almost always brought forward a softer view and a looser definition, such as "scholarly work" or evidence of "a mind at work." Meanwhile, however, it was not uncommon to find a faculty committee charged with setting the criteria. In one instance, such a committee had developed a point system: four points for an article in a refereed journal, three points for an invited article in a major journal, two points for an article in a regional or state journal, and one point for authorship of a published committee report—with these awards cut in half for co-authorship! If all of the professors published at even half the level expected or rumored to be expected, there would be a need for thousands of journals in addition to the thousands already serving the academic community.

The impact of this growing academic fashion on teacher education has been severe and is becoming more so. The impact in institutions already in or nearly in the circle of prestigious universities is clear: Teacher education not only ranks low among university priorities, it is marginal in the school or college of education. Teaching teachers is a highly demanding activity, requiring a great deal of time and energy. Securing a research grant enables a professor to opt out, if he or she happens to be involved at all. A senior professor spoke feelingly of the previous semester's rigors: For the first time in years, she had taught an undergraduate teacher education class. She was not about to do it again—ever. Students here in such classes spoke of there being outstanding, nationally recognized professors in the school of education, but they had no association with them. One is reminded of Harry Judge's prototypical dean who spoke proudly of studying but not preparing teachers in his school of education.[15]

Whereas professors in the schools of education of major research universities are able to move into research projects and graduate teaching, such options are largely missing in the regional universities. Nonetheless, the message regarding scholarly productivity is coming down ever more strongly in the latter group of institutions, but research is to be an add-on to the traditional expectations of teaching and service. Not only are the teaching demands heavier than in the major research-oriented universities, there are commonly not the resources and assistance necessary to the writing of proposals and the conduct of research; there are not role models to serve as mentors to aspiring young professors. When more established scholars are brought in to serve as models, they usually come with higher salaries and reduced teaching loads, creating resentment among those whom they are expected to inspire.

On one hand, then, teacher education in the major universities is turned over to doctoral-level students and a variety of part-time and adjunct instructors, clearly conveying the message that the enterprise is of minor importance. On the other hand, in the regional universities, where most teachers are prepared, faculty morale is lowered because the activities from which they formerly derived personal rewards and satisfaction no longer appear to lead to professional recognition. None of this is lost on students in teacher education programs. They generally do not see themselves as central to university function and faculty purpose.

Ironically, this increasing identification of schools and professors of education with the academic rather than the professional functions and symbols of university life has not commonly enhanced their image relative to the arts and sciences and most of the other professional schools. Even on some campuses with nationally recognized schools of education, both administrators and arts and sciences faculty members whom we interviewed viewed educational research as second-rate and expressed the view that professors of education should get on with the business of preparing teachers. Confronted by the question of how they would then get promoted, the interviewees usually remained silent or simply shrugged. But several suggested the need to bring research in education and the preparation of teachers into closer juxtaposition.

Only in our four liberal arts colleges as a group were circumstances markedly different from those characterizing most of the colleges and universities in the other groups. These, too, expect scholarly work, but more in the context of keeping up with one's field than in that of advancing knowledge for its own sake. Further, the definition of appropriate scholarly activity is tempered considerably by liberal arts traditions and the place of the humanities in them. It is interesting that even some education courses were viewed as having a legitimate place in advancing these traditions. Of course, good teaching and concern for students were seen as primary—a view that is quite compatible with the views of many faculty members engaged in teacher education, not only in liberal arts colleges but also in many of the other colleges and universities in our sample.

The dilemmas posed in the above account of the accelerating rise of research and accompanying decline of teaching in most of the colleges and universities we studied will not easily be resolved. Surely we want this nation's teachers to be educated by scholarly, caring individuals who value their teaching and do it well. But the observable direction of higher education in the United States at this time is certainly not toward ensuring such a situation. There are some movements designed, initially at least, to inject into the arena some corrective measures. But these currently lack the conviction and momentum necessary to redirection. Meanwhile, other initiatives, frequently conducted in the name of higher standards and professionalism, are eroding the traditional role of colleges and universities in the education of educators for our schools. Both sets of forces are addressed again in the concluding chapter of this volume.

Fragmentation. As recently as three decades ago, there were relatively common cores of professional preparation for both elementary and secondary school teachers, with considerable overlapping of the two. I recall, for example, while traversing the country as a member of James B. Conant's team investigating teacher education, consistently encountering required courses in history or philosophy of education (or some of both in an introductory course on American education), educational psychology, and general methods of teaching, and a solid block of student teaching for elementary school teachers. Secondary school programs broke up the block, usually with courses in academic majors. Further, this ordering was usually the curricular sequence. Commonly, too, professors teaching the sequence of courses supervised students in the field.

Although this pattern is still discernible today, fragmentation has largely obfuscated it. Courses in the history and philosophy of education usually exist as options along with other alternatives, if they exist at all. There are likely to be different courses in subdivisions of educational psychology for various levels and groups of future teachers. Further, the particular program in which a student is enrolled determines the degree to which he or she observes in the field and participates there in school and classroom activities.

On a large campus, identifying all the programs for teachers offered and all the units through which they are conducted is a challenge. The school or college of education is only one such unit. It is not uncommon for students in one unit never to encounter those in another and never to take the same courses. Usually, students take courses that are required only for a particular program, most of which can be taken in any order. Further, undergraduates preparing to teach often enroll at any time in education courses without seeking admission to a program or announcing their intention to become teachers. Admission frequently is not sought until close to the time of declaring for student teaching. What keeps many students on a prescribed course of studies is the tight schedule that results from meeting requirements for both graduation and certification as a teacher. These two sets of specifications often extend college attendance well beyond the usual eight semesters or twelve quarters of anticipated enrollment.

One does not generally find, then, on college and university campuses a process through which students planning to teach are socialized together into the teaching profession. Where one finds anything resembling a cohort group experiencing some kind of deliberate formal and informal socialization, it almost always is in a small program or in a segment such as early childhood education, physical education, special education, music education, or the like—a segment barely or not at all connected with any other segment, let alone a common socialization process experienced by all. There may well be several dozen such segments scattered across a large university campus.

Even though professions such as law and medicine are marked by distinctive specialties with little in common, socialization into these professions plays a large part in the education of both lawyers and doctors. Lawyers study certain common cases; doctors take common foundation science courses. There are certain common rituals retained and honored year after year in schools of law and medicine. And there are not on any campus a half dozen units outside the school of law or medicine engaged in the professional education of future lawyers and doctors.

Yet schoolteachers, much more than either lawyers or doctors, come together as workers in institutions that are heavily dependent on arrangements presumably carried out collegially by faculty groups. Many students of school reform see these institutions failing precisely because faculty groups are not able to establish the infrastructure and relationships necessary for school renewal and the restructuring demanded by profound social disjuncture and changing student demographics.

The hope in the late 1980s for the educational reform movement launched several years earlier lay in site-based management and teacher empowerment. Yet little was being said about the fact that the teachers who were to effect school renewal shared very little in common from their teacher education years. Their segmentation into specialties resulted not only in the fragmented socialization process described above but also in a narrow vision of role—as a teacher of pupils in the primary grades or of social studies or English. We found it to be almost impossible to get from students during hundreds of hours of interviews a vision of responsibilities extending beyond the classroom. Clearly, they were ill prepared to address issues pertaining to balanced curricula and tracking or other aspects of school organization. Yet the rhetoric of school reform during recent years carries with it the expectation that teachers will take on problems pertaining to schools as comprehensive entities. Is it reasonable to expect this widely diverse group of individuals—sharing little by way of values and ideals, knowledge, and skills—to come together naturally and cohesively in a process of fundamental school improvement? I think not.

Nonetheless, I believe—as do many others—that any near approximation of the schools that we need and envision depends precisely on what is currently unreasonable to expect. Working toward making this expectation reasonable appears to be the sensible thing to do. The revitalization of teacher education, requiring as it must the simultaneous revitalization of schools as places where teachers are taught, constitutes a critical agenda.

Discontinuities. A reasonable expectation for teacher education programs is that they be oriented toward a conception of what education and teaching ideally are and what schools are for. A further reasonable expectation is that this conception be shared and continually examined by the faculty group responsible for each program—not just the tenure-track professors but everyone, including cooperating teachers. These expectations would be evidenced in the presence of cohesive programs geared to this philosophical conception and ongoing processes of planning and evaluation.

These expectations may be reasonable, but we are forced to conclude that they are being fulfilled at an acceptable level in very few settings. Where they are being approximated—and we found few such places—the number of teachers being produced is small, preservice teacher education is being undertaken as the prime function of the department or school of education, and virtually every member of the faculty is involved. Frequently, too, faculty members are housed in close proximity to one another; they usually converse, both formally and informally, on almost a daily basis. Rarely were there individuals disengaged from the teacher education enterprise, unless they were on leave for purposes of research, travel, and other forms of professional development. Even in these settings, however, others participating in the program, such as cooperating teachers in the schools, rarely were brought into the dialogue and planning.

The common pattern differed markedly from the above. If existing programs had at one time been planned by a responsible faculty group, the process had virtually disappeared by the time of our visits. Many faculty members expressed excellent ideas for the conduct of teacher education but frequently admitted that there were no vehicles for putting their ideas into action. Indeed, many confessed to an absence of collegial dialogue. Our second visitation team, usually appearing on the scene two weeks after the first, reported that faculty members frequently expressed their satisfaction with discussions with the first team. This confirmed our impression that serious dialogue around the problems and issues of education and teacher education was missing or scarcely present in more than a few of the settings. The larger the institution, the greater the number of programs, and the more varied the activities of faculty members, the greater the likelihood of our finding faculty members going about their individual pursuits cut off from one another and not engaged in discourse directed to program renewal. But then, this is the individualism so often fostered by the norms of academe, especially the reward structure.

It is not surprising that programs tended to comprise collections of courses, various field experiences, and student teaching—each part separated from the others, each part frequently taught by different people with little or no communication among the key actors. On the negative end of this segmentation, we found a director of teacher education simply lining up the courses most closely appearing to meet state requirements and checking to make sure that each was assigned to an instructor. Student teaching assignments were arranged by another person—not a member of the tenure-track faculty. On the positive end, small clusters of faculty members assumed responsibility for a cluster or block of courses—as, for example, the "methods" courses for future elementary school teachers. It was more common than uncommon to find cooperating teachers who did not have the faintest glimmer of program goals or of whether any such existed. In several settings, students were on their own in seeking out cooperating teachers willing to take them on, sometimes still desperately seeking placements just as their student teaching quarter or semester was beginning. Even in places where all of the pieces appeared to be efficiently organized and under the careful coordination of one administrator, the hoped-for philosophical cohesion and continuing dialogue among a responsible faculty group were almost consistently missing.

These findings, sketched here only in broad strokes, lead us to a better understanding of why research so consistently reveals the stubborn persistence of long-standing school and classroom practices. Cooperating teachers—not necessarily picked because of their outstanding talents and not initiated into a coherent teacher education program that they helped plan—simply induct student teachers into their ways of teaching and dealing with pupils. Teachers teach as they were taught in schools and colleges and pass these ways along to others. It is not reasonable to believe that beginning teachers, just graduated from programs characterized by discontinuities and just recently apprenticed in ordinary classrooms, will deviate significantly from the norm—a norm deemed by many researchers and reformers to fall far short of being satisfactory.

The Knowledge-Practice Tension. There has not been for many years—and perhaps never has been—so much discourse about teaching as a profession, professionalism, professionalization, and professional schools of education as there is today. A professional school of education is, presumably, one that goes beyond merely passing along knowledge about education to the comprehensive induction of neophytes into what it means to teach and be a teacher. Graduates of such a school behave as professionals, adhering to certain norms of conduct and belief and guided by specialized knowledge in their decisions. A strong professional school is always at or near the center of productive tensions between practice and professional norms. Practice moves continuously and rapidly toward reflection of these norms, which, in turn, evolve, expand, and renew.

Unfortunately, the tension between professional norms relative to teaching in schools and the practices exhibited in these schools is limp. The necessary connections for increasing the desired tensions are largely missing. I briefly discuss two examples.

The first arises directly out of the discontinuities discussed above. The most abrupt discontinuity occurs when the neophyte teacher enters the student teaching phase of a program. Suddenly, this beginner is thrown not only into the norms of practice but into a situation demanding quick recourse to survival techniques—techniques almost invariably provided by the cooperating teacher. They are taken on because they appear to work; there is little time or inclination to ponder alternatives. Frequently, what appears to work runs counter to the teaching practices—commonly taught in the abstract—favored in campus courses. Sometimes the practices encountered in the classroom are mandated by the district.

We found situation after situation where students reported sharp differences between what they were taught in courses and what they experienced in classrooms. Professors and cooperating teachers spoke freely of such dissonance. But the position taken by most students and faculty members was that they must conform to school and district expectations. They could (and would, they frequently said) do things differently in their own classrooms later. Only occasionally did we find a setting where university-based and school-based faculty members worked as a team, both effecting the transition from college classes to school classrooms and sharing norms. More often than not, ongoing school practices, not cutting-edge theory and knowledge, drove the behavior of neophyte teachers at the critical stage of their first significant immersion.

A second finding makes the first more serious. More and more, states are seeking ways to assess demonstrable teaching competence prior to certifying beginning teachers. In Georgia, for example, first-year teachers are visited and observed by selected individuals on several occasions over the year. A major expectation is that they demonstrate their knowledge of and skill in lesson planning and the execution of a plan. The trained evaluators bring into the classrooms a predetermined conception of a plan and its execution.

The reaction to this requirement on the part of college and university teacher educators was almost uniformly negative, ranging from criticism of its minimal nature to characterizations of it as an "abomination." What most troubled my colleagues and me was the degree to which the planning of a unit of learning and teaching had infiltrated teacher education programs. While some students were pleased with experiencing the state's expectation, most were critical of repeated exposure to it in successive classes. Other learnings viewed as being more important were being shortchanged. It appeared to us that the weakest programs were being more shaped by this requirement than were the stronger ones.

Instead of a fresh stream of knowledge and ideas flowing down into the ponds of practice, the demands of extant practice were determining the curriculum in many instances.

We would be aghast if a medical school admonished young interns to do as the hospital does when faced with decisions of practice. Law schools certainly are aware of the bar examination and respond when their students do poorly on some part of it, but their curricula are not closely geared to it. Practices such as those we observed in Georgia and programs geared to the entry-year requirement drive quality down, not up. My colleague Roger Soder concluded from this and similar instances that competition drives down quality when outcomes are held constant (in this case, the same certificate and same salary regardless of program demands, as long as graduates satisfy the specified state requirement).

States have a responsibility to assure their people that persons coming through teacher education programs are literate, and the states are well within appropriate bounds of authority and responsibility in setting licensing requirements. States endanger quality and make a mock of professionalism when they take it on themselves to specify the curricula to be followed. College and university boards of trustees, administrators, and faculty members are derelict in their responsibilities when they sit idly by—as they usually do when teacher education programs are being savaged by state edict—while institutional autonomy is seriously eroded. The fact that they rarely become aroused over just one more familiar intrusion into the curriculum of teacher education is another sad reflection on the low status of this enterprise and the long road yet to be traversed in the making of teaching a profession and schools of education professional.

The Urban Problem. One would like to believe that some relief is in sight for the much-documented problems of urban schools through the infusion of new teachers. But the picture is gloomy. The urban colleges and universities where we hoped to find rigorous, innovative programs preparing teachers for the demands of urban teaching for which their forerunners often were ill prepared were, for the most part, disappointing. Faculty members generally were reluctant to place student teachers in other than the "safest" classrooms, which meant that they commonly located placements in the suburbs. Only occasionally did we find significant proportions of minority students preparing to teach. When we did, the institutions were academically among the weakest; teacher education was geared to preparing for survival and not imaginative teaching. The percentage of minority students in the teacher education programs of the strongest urban colleges and universities almost invariably was lower than the percentage of minority students in the institution as a whole. If a minority student gains admission to a relatively good college or university, why become a schoolteacher?

Recruitment efforts, to the degree visible, were disappointing. Historically black colleges were not attracting white students even when this kind of integration clearly would solve quite inexpensively some of the problems with access to higher education of a given region. Urban institutions once white or integrated but now black in student populations showed no sign of once again achieving integration. Recruitment programs designed to reach down into secondary schools for minority recruits into teacher education were virtually nonexistent.

The problems of educating teachers for urban schools and building a corps of minority teachers will neither go away nor simply be resolved by the passage of time. They are getting worse fast and will not be corrected without Herculean efforts that must include substantial outlays for student recruitment and financial support. But a more disturbing and potentially dangerous cancer lurks. Some of the most thoughtful, concerned black professors with whom we talked see racial prejudice running deep: It is all right in the eyes of white citizens for white teachers to teach black students, but it is not all right for black teachers to teach white students. This road of bigotry and prejudice is long and much traveled.

Concluding Observations

In the contexts of the conditions and circumstances so frequently coming to the forefront in our visits to twenty-nine colleges and universities, the agenda for reform in teacher education so often advanced now and over many years before appears pallid. One cannot argue with the repeated proposal to provide more general education courses for teachers; however, the gains from so doing will be marginal until we confront and deal with the question of what constitutes an exemplary general education for teachers and of how to ensure that the very best scholar-teachers will teach it. Although we would want all students to have the best general education, the consequences of an illiberal education for teachers are far-reaching. Surely there are undergraduate curricula for teachers worthy of the designation "pre-ed" in the same sense that there are appropriate "premed" curricula. Since schoolteachers are the only ones among us charged with inculcating into the young the defined subject matter, such a pre-ed curriculum might well become recognized as the most liberating and, therefore, the best one for all.

Similarly, the requirement of an academic major for high school teachers begs the central issue. Future teachers must learn their subjects twice—once as students and once as teachers of the subjects. "More student teaching" or "apprenticeship with a mentor" begs a host of issues. Do we really want future teachers to learn more of the ways of current teaching in schools? Recent research on school practices suggests quite the opposite. Indeed, we found one carefully thought out program in which the plan deliberately reduced student teaching to meet minimal certification requirements in the belief that less is better. More field-based experiences for teachers are likely to be beneficial only under conditions of close supervision, critical inquiry into current practices, and, ultimately, residencies in exemplary, renewing schools. Such conditions are chimerical. Turning imagined conditions into real circumstances will be exceedingly difficult.

It would be impolitic, imprudent, futile, and irresponsible to challenge the research role of universities. Similarly, it would be foolish to question the importance of teachers' knowing more and more about learning and how best to promote it. But the clear retreat from teacher education of professors in major research universities does not encourage me to believe that the joining of educational knowledge and practice lies just ahead on the road to professionalizing teaching. The loud blowing of bugles in the name of research on campuses now shaking themselves loose from the embarrassing coils of their teacher education beginnings poorly serves students, schools, and, therefore, this nation. The current appeal to college and university presidents to strengthen their commitments to teacher education is timely and worthy.[16] But it will sound hollow if not backed soon by actions that place the education of educators at the forefront of institutional mission and near the top of budgetary priorities.

The history of the teacher education enterprise in representative colleges and universities in the United States is not one of our most gratifying and uplifting sagas. Some of what has evolved is described on preceding pages. More follows in another volume, *Teachers for Our Nation's Schools*. Succeeding chapters in this volume help us to understand some of the commissions and omissions that contributed to the conditions and circumstances prevailing today. Perhaps they will help us understand some of the commissions and omissions necessary to a future saga that will be looked back upon with greater pride and satisfaction.

Notes

1. Carnegie Foundation for the Advancement of Teaching, *Report Card on School Reform: The Teachers Speak* (Princeton, N.J.: Carnegie Foundation for the Advancement of Teaching, 1988).

2. E. R. House, *The Politics of Educational Innovation* (Berkeley, Calif.: McCutchan, 1974).

3. S. B. Sarason, *The Culture of the School and the Problem of Change*, rev. ed. (Newton, Mass.: Allyn & Bacon, 1982 [originally published 1971]).

4. Z. Su, *Teacher Education Reform in the United States (1890–1986)*, Occasional Paper no. 3 (Seattle: Center for Educational Renewal, College of Education, University of Washington, 1986).

5. J. B. Conant, *The Education of American Teachers* (New York: McGraw-Hill, 1963).
6. D. Tyack, "The Future of the Past: What Do We Need to Know About the History of Teaching?" in D. Warren (ed.), *American Teachers: Histories of a Profession at Work* (New York: Macmillan, 1989), p. 409.
7. See, for example, G. J. Clifford and J. W. Guthrie, *Ed School: A Brief for Professional Education* (Chicago: University of Chicago Press, 1988). To considerable degree, this book is testimony to the neglect of what they sought to do, in that Clifford and Guthrie cite so few secondary sources in their historical account of schools of education in ten major research-oriented universities. Clearly, the terrain they covered had not been much traveled by others.
8. Tyack, "The Future of the Past," p. 3.
9. R. Carver, *Where I'm Coming From* (New York: Atlantic Monthly Press, 1988), p. 380.
10. Today, Lawrence Cremin is able to recount with wry amusement his feelings and those of his co-authors in contemplating, years ago, the disparity between sales of their history of Teachers College and the large inventory of books: L. A. Cremin, D. A. Shannon, and M. E. Townsend, *A History of Teachers College, Columbia University* (New York: Columbia University Press, 1954).
11. We set out to describe the processes of educating teachers, special educators, and principals. Usually, here and in other descriptions of this Study of the Education of Educators, we refer to all three groups as either educators or teachers and to the education of educators as teacher education.
12. For further description of this conceptualization, see J. I. Goodlad, "Studying the Education of Educators: Values-Driven Inquiry," *Phi Delta Kappan*, 1988, *70* (Oct.), 104–111; and R. Soder, "Studying the Education of Educators: What We Can Learn from Other Professions," *Phi Delta Kappan*, 1988, *70* (Dec.), 299–305.
13. For further information regarding selection of the sam-

ple, designing the data-gathering process, gathering information, and so on, see K. A. Sirotnik, "Studying the Education of Educators: Methodology," *Phi Delta Kappan,* 1988, *70* (Nov.), 241–247.

14. The observations and generalizations presented in the remainder of this chapter emerged and strengthened during visits to the twenty-nine colleges and universities constituting the sample used in a Study of the Education of Educators (see the preface). They are documented in the Technical Report Series of the Center for Educational Renewal and in the final report emerging from the study, *Teachers for Our Nation's Schools* (San Francisco: Jossey-Bass, 1990).

15. H. Judge, *American Graduate Schools of Education* (New York: Ford Foundation, 1982).

16. See "The Letter: 37 Presidents Write . . . ," *Bulletin* (American Association for Higher Education), 1987, *40* (3), 10–13.

2

Recurring Themes
and Variations

Robert A. Levin

In the first part of this chapter, I elaborate on six of the themes in the historical evolution of teacher education presented by Goodlad in Chapter One, with brief examples from the case-study institutions. The themes are (1) stability and instability in leadership and authority; (2) changing institutional identity; (3) lack of coherent professional socialization; (4) a disconnected curriculum; (5) lack of constructive tension between knowledge and practice; and (6) lack of commitment to urban education. In the second part, I discuss other themes identified by historians in the Study of the Education of Educators that have influenced the historical evolution of teacher education, including gender, race, class, populism, and trends in educational philosophy and school practice.

This chapter is a bridge between Goodlad's introduction to this volume and the more in-depth studies of institutional types and venues that follow. Its tone is intended to be one of proposition rather than proof. Its objective is to raise questions that bear on one central theme: purposefulness in the enterprise of educating educators. Goodlad paints a picture of teacher education mired in external and internal struggles, evolving away from a coherent purpose or set of purposes, and avoiding key normative issues regarding what subsequent generations of teachers should value and perceive as their role. On balance, the histories that this volume's authors gathered support more often than they contradict Goodlad's view.

The Goodlad Themes

The significance of Goodlad's themes is apparent throughout the twenty-nine historical cases researched for the study. As he demonstrates in Chapter One, these themes are interrelated. For example, transitions in leadership are often related to changes in an institution's mission or identity. Similarly, failure to influence students' professional identity and role beyond the classroom is a predictable outcome of curriculum fragmentation and the dizzying proliferation of disconnected education degree programs. For that reason, and also to make the most accurate use of the twenty-nine case histories, whose findings and emphases varied, I have chosen to regroup Goodlad's themes into three categories and to address them each in turn. These categories are issues of stability and status; the curriculum, program structures, and practitioners; and diminishing commitments to urban education.

I illustrate each issue with examples from clusters of case studies, and I apologize in advance for any slights or injustices resulting from telling less than an institution's complete story, as well as for any instances in which the cited researcher would have reported on his or her findings differently.

Issues of Stability and Status

Goodlad argues that leadership and status in teacher education have through the decades been eroding in American colleges and universities. This erosion has been characterized, he says, by three troubling trends: (1) The mission of preparing teachers has become overlooked, indeed denigrated, as universities and, indeed, schools of education themselves "mature" by emphasizing graduate programs, research, and more prestigious fields; (2) a parallel decline has occurred in tenure of education deans, their pull with presidents and provosts, and

the number of university leaders with personal roots in or
commitments to professional education; and (3) state governments and, more recently, blue-ribbon commissions have in-
truded on the education professoriate's ability to set its own
agenda and stand guard over its own standards. Goodlad considers these factors "destabilizing" to growth and renewal in
the education of educators, and in particular he cites the inex-
orable march of normal school–teachers' colleges away from
their founding missions in order to become more respected
universities.

The twenty-nine places abound in historical data about
institutional identity and the increasingly (if not originally)
marginal status of teacher education. Two public institutions
with nineteenth-century normal school roots—San Francisco
State University[1] and the University of Northern Iowa[2]—serve
as initial examples.

San Francisco State Normal School was established by
the state legislature in 1899. Constitutionally, it was considered
part of the state's public school system until 1947, after which
the state colleges (as distinct from the universities) came under
the supervision of the state superintendent of public instruction within the state department of education. "It is little wonder," Irving Hendrick observed, "that the education of teachers stood at the very heart of what the institution was about."[3]
California's normals spent only fourteen years as teachers' colleges before they became state colleges in 1935, representing
what Hendrick called a "modest change in mission" with the
introduction of liberal arts majors and, by the end of World
War II, some business and vocational degrees as well. Between
1945 and 1949, however, when secondary teaching credentials
and master's degrees were added and the postwar demand for
higher education was in full swing, San Francisco State's enrollment grew from 737 to 3,865 students. Not only was the
institution's identity evolving, but the nature of relationships
between education and the liberal arts faculty began an evolution of its own, away from the smallness and shared mission of
a teacher-preparing place. By 1954, President J. Paul Leonard
singled out "training for all phases of work with children and

youth"—school-based and other—as just one of four goals of the college. Education was one of nine divisions of the college through the 1950s, and, while it was still the largest, its enrollment had finally dropped below 50 percent of the student body. A historian, Glenn S. Dumke, became in 1957 the first president without a professional education background—a pattern familiar elsewhere, as stated by Goodlad.

"Maturing" affected the San Francisco State faculty in several ways. Hendrick's interviews suggested that, in the 1950s and 1960s, "from a liberal arts faculty point of view, their subjects [were no longer] seen . . . as service courses in the preparation of teachers, [but] as worthwhile majors in their own right," allowing those departments to "establish professional reputations of their own." Hendrick found that by the 1980s, despite various top-level administrative commitments to teacher education and to San Francisco State being "the best at what it does, there seems to be a prevailing feeling now that this is impossible. The strongest and most prestigious institutions seem to serve as models for the rest."[4] Thus, the current School of Education reportedly seeks to recruit and promote faculty members with research and publishing records who may also obtain extramural funding. In terms of relative budget status, the School of Education receives some special consideration— a 14:1 student-faculty ratio when the campuswide average is 20:1 and the business school ratio is 21:1. On the other hand, the nursing program is budgeted at an 8:1 ratio, which shares with the School of Education "the costly nature of courses involving intense clinical experiences."

The Iowa State Normal School at Cedar Falls, dating from 1876, followed an evolution similar to that of San Francisco State, but on a very different timetable and apparently with more bitter feelings along the way. Its founding president envisioned, from the beginning, a school that would "aspire to collegiate and professional status," as Jurgen Herbst found.[5] Unlike many normals in this study—especially in the East and Midwest—students were not required to commit themselves to a career in teaching to gain admission, although they were required to student-teach, and a "model school" opened in the

1880s that remains a significant operation today. Teachers' college status came in 1909, well before that of San Francisco State, but formal state college status, in 1961, trailed that of San Francisco by nearly three decades. The student teaching requirement for all students survived until 1960.

It is not evident from the case studies why the mood at Northern Iowa, as described by Herbst, more obviously fits Goodlad's gloomy portrayal of the declining status of teacher education than does the former normal school at San Francisco. Looking back to 1961, Herbst was told that "the single-minded commitment of administration and faculty to teacher education gave way to emphasizing the liberal arts, and graduate work diverted resources from the training of classroom teachers to research in educational and industrial technology. Divisions arose within the faculty . . . accentuated in 1967," when the institution became the University of Northern Iowa, and left faculty in the 1980s still "divided on the future course of the institution."[6] Some veteran faculty members felt that a distinctive national reputation for academic programs, and what is now the Price Laboratory School, had enabled the teachers' college to rank with the elite of Columbia and George Peabody teachers' colleges. As Goodlad found at several of the twenty-nine institutions—particularly those that became regional universities from a normal school past—there is apparently a great sense of loss of the mission that was but is no longer. Other regional institutions, however, such as two in Oklahoma (Oklahoma State and Central State), seem to have evolved more gently and traveled less far afield from their early teacher-preparing function.[7]

It seems important at least to hypothesize about the apparently different natures of seemingly similar evolutions in these two places. San Francisco State's evolution to a general-purpose college occurred much sooner; therefore, institutional missions may have had more time to blend and compromise than they did at Northern Iowa. San Francisco also earlier on perceived a special role for itself as an urban commuter campus for diverse student interests—an additional source of pride and sense of purpose beyond its normal school roots. Evolution and reform, too, seem to have been more state-driven, and over a longer period of change, in San Francisco, with several other state colleges in the same boat at the same time—not so much the case in Iowa. Finally, budget compromises—again as spin-offs of a state-driven formula—may be clearer, better understood, and perhaps even perceived as fairer and more reasonable than priorities set at Iowa, whether or not the facts match the impressions.

A brief comparison of two private universities in the 1970s and 1980s, Emory[8] and Drake,[9] offers another apparent contrast in how institutions have traveled the path away from undergraduate teacher education and toward a graduate and research focus, with skepticism about the quality and desirability of education departments in the air.

Emory University discontinued its Division of Teacher Education in 1970, naming educational psychologist James Miller as chair of the new Division of Educational Studies. This occurred after a twenty-year period of intense creative activity in teacher and administrator certification programs, clearly related to market forces, demographics, and federal funding. With 90 certified teachers in the undergraduate class of 1967 and 101 more in the upcoming junior class, by 1984 that figure had dropped to eleven. The education faculty refocused its efforts more in the direction of research and its doctoral program, although not with "unanimity [or] universal enthusiasm," according to Miller. An undergraduate concentration was mounted in educational studies—"for the study of education as a social institution." While relationships with school districts continued to be fostered through master's degree programs, a small undergraduate certification function was also maintained. At the same time, education gained a new and higher status in the university's organizational structure—from a division "of" the College of Arts and Sciences to a division "in" Arts and Sciences, including enfranchisement on university committees. The impression is that the education faculty took its own initiatives on the basis of a keen awareness of the scent in the wind at Emory.

Drake University abolished its College of Education in

1986, establishing a Department of Teacher Education sub-
sumed within the College of Arts and Sciences, along with a
new Graduate School of Education and Human Services, which
controls certain aspects of undergraduate certificate candidates' programs. The impression is that the undergraduate education faculty took it on the chin, finding, as Herbst reported,
"little comfort in their association with colleagues in the Arts
and Sciences. Their morale [was] not of the best." [10]

Again, the historical material in the study does not and
probably could not explain with authority how and why some
teacher education programs faded with their boots on and were
given a decent memorial in a positive, restructured program,
while others trailed off in unresolved bitterness. It may also be
that Goodlad's essential point here—that instability and decline
have come to characterize the programs most likely to affect
how teachers operate in our nation's classrooms—stands whether
an institution evolved that way happily or sadly. It is hard to
avoid the impression that few will mourn for education faculties' hurt feelings or entertain their nostalgia for the good old
days. (Goodlad, in fact, questions how good the old days were;
his work elsewhere suggests that better old days in teacher education might have facilitated more democratic and innovative
public schooling by now.[11]) The real question seems to be the
extent to which the community of scholars cares a whit about
mass democratic education for the nation's children, beyond
slinging barbs at the schools and/or education faculties. Professors in all fields, including education, share responsibility for
the state of learning in society, both in school and out of it. If
presidents, provosts, and deans continue on the path seen by
Goodlad without considering this shared responsibility, it will
be to our mutual peril.

All of which leads to another element of Goodlad's concern: state regulation. Goodlad cites the views of the education
professoriate as he encountered them, grousing about the
fruitlessness of generating innovative programs when the current climate—and this is not new—seems prone to slapping another set of seemingly rigid requirements on resistant but relatively powerless college faculties. It is easy to substantiate,

although not so easy to historically trace the roots of, this "state versus teacher preparers" sentiment; it came up repeatedly, although not without dispute, in published and personally recalled statements from state and private institutions in the study over various decades. A Bucknell professor in the 1980s called Pennsylvania's department of education "a devilish outfit" that was "blindly bureaucratic and political with no interest in promoting creative intelligence in the field."[12] Emory University in 1948 listed twenty-five undergraduate education courses and seventeen graduate courses on its books, right under the names of its three and one-half education faculty members. A subsequent chairperson suggested that this apparent fantasy must have had something to do with satisfying state regulators that all the appropriate courses were in place, though several might in fact meet together, or not be offered every year.[13]

Other institutions seemed not to suffer from state education department requirements—even to thrive on them. The close relationship between rising entry standards for teachers in the first half of this century and the growth and prominence of normal schools–teachers' colleges nationwide is the most obvious example. A much more controversial example dates to the late 1960s and 1970s—the era of "competency-based teacher education," driven by state mandates and federal grants and still very much visible today in certification programs and the state authorization for those programs. The National College of Education in Evanston, Illinois, was apparently on the leading edge of competency-based programs in Illinois and by the 1970s was labeled by the state certification board as the best private teacher-preparing institution in the state.[14] The University of Georgia joined forces with its state department in 1967 to initiate the Georgia Educational Models program, explained by Cruikshank as "a highly behavioristic project" that "applied selected performance specifications" first for elementary teachers and then to other certificate programs. National recognition came for the first time to the state's education programs, Cruikshank found, with those involved traveling nationally, disseminating reports, and so on—all on substantial federal grant monies. "The growth which accompanied this achievement was phenomenal. During 1967–68, 103 new faculty appointments were made," she reported.[15]

Since the first normal schools nearly a century and a half ago, the state was teacher preparation, and teacher preparation was the state. Often the principal players moved back and forth from school district to campus to state department of education. Calls for higher or different standards for teaching certificates often generated debate, but the histories in this study are not clear as to when or whether a "state versus professoriate" rift became a new or growing part of the landscape.

Here, too, faculty concerns must be viewed in context and with a second look. The medical and legal professions have often been criticized for turning the public trust into windfall profits and for a less than egalitarian approach to the delivery of professional services. Professional educators may, in fact, be publicly accountable to an opposite extreme, eroding their flexibility to set their own agendas (and charge their own rates!), especially in the area of teacher certification requirements and programs. But the historical record suggests to me, more often than not, that state regulators come from the ranks of educators (collegiate and elementary-secondary) and that drafting specific and specialized regulations may be more seductive to us than we would readily admit.

As a director of teacher education in 1989, I joined a roomful of colleagues from public and private institutions in Massachusetts at a planning session on how to respond to sweeping new certificate requirements from the state department of education. In one breath, group members decried the state's claim to know what really ought to constitute requirements for an early childhood certificate or a middle school certificate, whether severe or moderate learning disabilities are separate fields, and so on. With the next breath, however, it was clear that folks in the room could not agree on the fine points of these matters, although many felt deeply enough about their positions that it was clear how specifically they would write the regulations if they could. Furthermore, it had been many of our colleagues, as appointed or invited representatives to various state committees, who had promulgated the controversial regulations in the first place—committees that were still holding open hearings to obtain further public and professional reactions. So I suggest that the issue is more complex than "they" doing it to "us." I do believe that there is a broad concern, alluded to by Goodlad, that room to innovate must be protected under whatever accountability system prevails. Whether that room exists, in the various states and in the twenty-nine places, is not yet clear.

Goodlad's other concern about evolving instability is the gradual decline of the long-tenured, influential education dean, at the same time that presidencies of former teachers' colleges have gradually passed out of the hands of folks rooted in public education or teacher preparation. This is evident in many of the twenty-nine places, as discussed above with the examples of San Francisco State and others, and no doubt contributes to education programs' struggles for budgets, recognition, and flexibility for mounting new programs.

The problem is not unique to shorter-term deans in recent times. Arthur Wilde directed and was dean of Boston University's education programs for twenty years, from their inception as a department in 1914 through the creation and growth of the School of Education starting in 1918. Today's embattled deans may take some solace from Wilde's efforts. For one, the university insisted that each school be economically self-sustaining each year, making growth and experimentation a risky business. Wilde felt that his services to the community and his planning efforts were significantly compromised under these conditions. Furthermore, approximately 30 percent of his 1923 budget went to paying rent to the College of Business Administration for education's facilities (since it had none of its own yet), and when education did obtain a home, its quarters were "noisy and dirty" ones—in the Mechanics Building! On a more substantive note, the liberal arts dean and faculty opposed and voted down Wilde's initial petition to mount a four-year education degree program in the 1930s; Wilde asserted that the liberal arts folks "had little or no confidence" in the School of Education and that they said so "more or less publicly."[16]

On the revolving-door and diminished influence of deans, too, the histories as gathered for the study are suggestive but not conclusive. Some deans stayed on through the demographic decline of the 1970s and early 1980s, slashing programs and losing budget shares but maintaining programs and influence as enrollments warranted. Temple University seems to be one such example,[17] with a counter example out in the suburbs at West Chester University, where deans were replaced by "coordinators" as teacher education lost power and prestige—although there was evidence in the late 1980s of a turnaround.[18]

In summary, the trends identified by Goodlad toward instability and loss of status in education programs are clear and historically documented, although not without ambiguity, as well as some contradictory or partially contradictory evidence. Vibrant and healthy practitioner certificate programs at research institutions such as Georgia State and Boston Universities suggest a plus side on issues of status and stability, even amid divided priorities in the faculty. Other institutions, including some mentioned above, seem to exemplify the downside.

Curriculum, Program Structures, and Practitioners

Goodlad found what he called fragmented and discontinuous curricula and program structures in his visits to the twenty-nine departments and schools of education in 1988–89. He based these findings on two basic assertions.

First, the professional education curriculum lacks focus beyond the mechanics of the classroom, failing to address normative issues about how schools function in a larger societal context and failing to socialize students as a professional cohort group on such issues as tracking, conceptualizing a whole curriculum, and critiquing predominant and alternative practices in age groupings, grading, and other policies. "We found it to be almost impossible," Goodlad writes in Chapter One, "to get from students during hundreds of hours of interviews a vision of responsibilities extending beyond the classroom." In short, the course rubric "Foundations of Education," once thought to have been a staple of teacher education (even though it may have dealt only minimally or abstractly with the above issues), has been nearly abandoned or reduced to an elective or a survey-style lecture course. His second assertion bears on this problem, as well.

That second assertion is that certification and degree programs have proliferated to such a degree that education faculty members across program boundaries do not meet or plan collaboratively, exacerbating the values problem and preventing the faculty from determining either a philosophical conception of what the institution stands for or an ongoing process of planning and evaluation within the education school as a whole. Even within a single certification or degree program, especially at large institutions, Goodlad found such discontinuities, so that "programs tended to comprise collections of courses, various field experiences, and student teaching—each part separated from the others, each part frequently taught by different people, with little or no communication among the key actors." These discontinuities inevitably corrode the quality of university–school district collaboration.

Normative Issues. The problem of a non-values-driven curriculum—one might say, failing to educate students liberally about their professional role and responsibilities, in particular on key normative issues of democracy in schooling—has long historical roots, depending on one's notion of appropriate values for teachers to hold. Two points are central here. First, the teacher education program pie has historically been three-fourths "academic" or "general education" in nature—and even the normal schools' traditional argument that they taught academic subjects with a professional educator's bent is now open to question.[19] This means that we were not educating critically thinking, equity-oriented, socially conscious teachers—the heart of what Goodlad really means—except to the extent that professors, textbooks, and instructional strategies in the basic academic disciplines sought to do so.

Second, the professional education curriculum per se—

foundations, psychology, methods, and so on—rapidly became oriented toward values opposed to the ones Goodlad prefers. These were the values of sorting and classifying children for purposes of efficient mass schooling and ease of entry into the existing economic structure, exemplified by the growth of standardized testing and distinct vocational programs to at least the 1920s,[20] and curriculum and instruction driven by frequent assessment of microskill attainment—the latter a tradition dating to the earliest common schools, given a great boost by the competency-based education movement in the late 1960s and 1970s. Undergirding this particular values orientation of schooling have been rigid grouping practices—by grade levels, perceived ability, presumed job future, handicapping condition, and even behavior—that eloquent but drowned-out voices have been decrying since at least the turn of the century.[21] Lagemann may have said it best: "One cannot understand the history of education in the United States during the twentieth century unless one realizes that Edward L. Thorndike won and John Dewey lost. The statement is too simple, of course, but nevertheless more true than untrue."[22]

To test these statements against evidence from the twenty-nine places, we should look at what we were able to learn historically about their required programs of study. The evidence suggests that the statements are accurate, but the twenty-nine historical case studies provide only sketches of actual curriculum content, goals, and emphases. Much work remains for other projects in this area.

Virtually all of the nineteenth-century normal school programs in the study followed the familiar pattern of offering first a remedial, elementary-grades curriculum to their potential teachers and then, as standards were raised into the twentieth century, a basic academic curriculum in high school-level subjects. In her paper on West Chester University,[23] Eisenmann cites a 1910 study of Pennsylvania's normals that found that 77 percent of students' time was "spent in courses which duplicate the high school curriculum." Considering that a good part of the remaining 23 percent would have been credits for observation and practice teaching, it is clear that very few credits were even available for the kind of professional course work Goodlad finds missing today. High school graduation became an admissions requirement for Pennsylvania normals in the 1920s, after which they staked a familiar claim to distinctiveness from both high schools and colleges in that "the purely academic side of the curriculum would give way" to subject matter courses taught with an eye toward the knowledge and skills that future teachers would need in grade school classrooms.[24]

What evidence is there that programs at the twenty-nine places had a particular values orientation? Herbst described the Illinois Normal University (now Illinois State) in the 1890s as a "gateway for . . . American Herbartianism," a philosophy of education from German psychologist Johann Herbart (1776–1841). "The Herbartians introduced new concepts, such as apperception (that new knowledge was learned and understood best when it could be related to what was already known and familiar to the child) and the culture-epoch theory and the correlation of studies (that the subjects of the curriculum should be organized and integrated around historical periods). They placed great emphasis on the child's interest as a key factor to be considered in the learning process"[25] as well as on a specified lesson-plan structure to implement this approach to its best advantage.[26] It is not clear how Illinois Normal geared either its curriculum or its own instructional methodology to its interpretation of Herbartianism. The University of Denver is another institution in which "Herbartian methodology was [reportedly] central to the curriculum in 1900," although here, too, additional research would be needed to understand exactly what that meant.[27]

Illinois Normal moved into the first decades of the twentieth century with new programs for teachers of kindergarten, manual and household arts, agricultural and commercial subjects, drama, and music, also familiar patterns in the expansion of normal school curricula. Denver, at the same time, was reportedly offering a greater emphasis on psychology by 1911, following the other major trend of education curriculum. The Deweyan notions of this period about learning theory and vocationalism—that a child-centered, activity-based curriculum would help to equalize differences in learning style and traditionally defined "intelligence"—simply did not seem influential in the twenty-nine histories.

Further evidence of how manual training became synonymous with vocationalism and the working class comes from the case of Fitchburg Normal School (now Fitchburg State College).[28] Barbara Beatty writes:

> The program of which [founding principal John G.] Thompson was proudest . . . and the innovation for which Fitchburg became nationally renowned, was the manual training school and Co-Operative Industrial Course. . . . Though not intended solely as vocational training, but as a kind of manual exercise and hand practice considered to be good for all students, manual training was perceived as education for students from lower-class backgrounds for whom academic study was not appropriate, and became associated with the industrial and vocational education movements.[29]

Fitchburg Normal in 1908 established a campus model junior high school designed to provide a practical education for students who did not plan to attend high school. Students built school furniture and handled many office functions. "For Thompson," Beatty reported, "the new school was evidence of the realization of the progressive ideal of joining school and life"[30]—but clearly not what Dewey had in mind in his lab school at the University of Chicago at nearly the same time.

Another variation on the vocationalism theme was exemplified by Pennsylvania State University, among others, where "Home Economics had always provided an enormous portion of School of Education enrollments [until it] split off into its own School in 1949, taking with it the program in Home Economics Education."[31]

These examples help to explain historically why normative questions about democratic schooling and the teacher's role in critiquing the school as a whole have not made the teacher education curriculum hit parade.

There is, however, at least some validity to the normal schools' claim of a distinctive, coherent academic-professional curriculum, and even to a certain sensitivity to the sociology of rural schools and the problems of teaching in remote areas. Although the focus and scope of the twenty-nine case studies do not permit me to draw proof from them, a separate study offers help.

Keene and Plymouth (New Hampshire) state normal schools in 1938 required six credits in science for elementary candidates, three in "nature" and three in "general science." Nature "is given [so] teachers may . . . help children to secure an acquaintance with . . . their nature environment . . . and appreciation of the wonders and beauties of the world in which they live." Topics included "study and care of plants including trees; life story of common insects, good and bad; the common birds, their usefulness and ways of protecting them; . . . weather and sky. The vital importance of the field excursion as a method . . . in every grade is stressed and illustrated." General science included upper-grade material not specified in the course catalogue, including "its values for rural children, and the learning and teaching problems involved in realizing these values under conditions imposed by rural school organization."[32]

New Hampshire normals' four-credit sociology requirement for elementary candidates considered how "family and neighborhood groups, racial relationships, divorce, delinquency, 'defectives,' poverty and crime . . . are related to education within and without the school." A two-credit requirement, "Rural School Problems," addressed "grouping of pupils," including "the place of group and of individual instruction" and "handling a heterogeneous group of children as one class," "alternation of work," "utilizing educative experiences in the rural environment; . . . caring for the physical needs of children [and] making school management and the care and decoration of the school plant educative."[33]

These program descriptions suggest a level of purposefulness and coherence that was often missing in teacher education before or since. The stereotypical plethora of teachers' college "methods" courses for elementary candidates—of reading, math, social studies, language arts, or you name it—seems to be a development of the 1950s and 1960s, not long before the 1963 Conant Report and other books blasted the fragmentation, redundancy, and alleged "mindlessness" of the professional education curriculum. This conception of a teachers' college curriculum shows signs of creeping into New Hampshire's program after World War II but does not appear fullblown until well into the 1960s; it had been substantially dismantled by the late 1970s, at least at Keene.[34]

Again, the current, available research does not allow as clear an understanding of the values expressed in such courses as would be desirable. For example, what position did the "Rural School Problems" course take on the effects, ethics, and social and educational consequences of certain grouping practices? Often in studying the history of teacher education, one gets the feeling that the topics covered are as agreed upon as motherhood and apple pie, but critical differences of opinion regarding those topics may have been blunted, much as survey courses in many fields tend to blur normative issues. We simply need more solid evidence in this area.

Program Proliferation and Discontinuities. We have already seen some of how quantitative-oriented child psychology and vocationalism led to larger and more varied education curricula in the first half of this century. The last straw in program proliferation was surely the beginnings of graduate degrees in various administrative and supervisory specialties, which date from the first decades of this century in regional and national institutions alike. There have been several growth spurts in this trend—in psychology and administration during the pre–World War II period; in administration, supervision, and guidance in the postwar period, as states began to require master's degrees for some teachers and teacher specialists; and with a vengeance from the 1960s to the present in dozens of special-needs areas, early childhood education, and an unprecedented variety of post-master's and doctorate specialties in every manner of research and practice. Two cases—Boston University, with a long history, and Georgia State University, with a short one—are illustrative.

As with many others of the twenty-nine institutions, Boston University's first expansion of education programs beyond a pedagogy course or two occurred through a Saturday lecture series, and eventually extension courses, for local educators. Begun in 1898, this programming followed an unsuccessful request from the school superintendent of the nearby town of Waltham that Boston University offer classes at the high school to train teacher aides. By 1910, the university was offering twenty-two extension courses to 149 area teachers, generally in content areas such as Latin, Greek, German, and English. Thus, the university responded to a community demand, while at the same time helping its faculty to survive on slave wages by opening up moonlighting opportunities through the extension program. During the same period, some 70 percent of Boston University's undergraduates were entering teaching (there was, as yet, no teacher education program there), while the total undergraduate enrollment was static. Embarking on a formal teacher education program seemed to be one way of attracting students, including women, who were welcome and sought after by Boston University from its founding.[35] Thus, after some consideration, a Department of Education was voted in during the 1912–13 academic year, with Dean Wilde appointed for the fall of 1914. Its bachelor's degree-granting School of Education opened four years later.

The school's initial degree-seeking students were graduates of two-year normal school programs who would take almost entirely liberal arts requirements for their junior and senior years.[36] Programs proliferated early, "demonstrat[ing] the trend toward specialization [that] would characterize" the school.[37] They included religious education, high school "commercial science," and recreational leadership (for the Boy and Girl Scouts and so forth); by 1919, a separate School of Religious Education opened, and at about the same time, an in-service master's program for Boston secondary school teachers began. The extension enrollment was up to 1,370 by 1922. A cooperative nursing education program was added in 1924; in 1929, the school incorporated the Sargent School of Physical Education in Cambridge, thus doubling the School of Education's size (though Sargent, too, split off administratively soon thereafter).

By the 1930s, the first full four-year program for teacher education, competing with the normal schools, came into being. Extension enrollment was up to 4,000. Also in the 1930s came the Educational Clinic for testing and evaluating children with learning problems and conducting research on reading instruction and curriculum. Nearly 3,000 children were evaluated in the first six years, with tutoring services provided to nearly 600. A new Division of Teaching Aids trained educators in audiovisual equipment use, developed a large film library, and sponsored an annual visual education conference. (These developments are discussed in the following section.) The 1960s and 1970s saw significant new growth in the School of Education, especially in urban and special education programs. Boston University's role in Boston's school desegregation case from the mid 1970s will be discussed in the section on urban education.

Boston University's School of Education took an enormous blow during the 1970s, a period of declining school enrollments and the disappearing teacher job market; enrollment plunged from 7,000 to 1,500. Enrollments at the close of the 1980s remained modest by comparison to the boom times—320 undergraduates and 800 graduate students—but the undergraduate numbers were up substantially from the early 1980s. There were eleven undergraduate specializations and many more at the graduate level, distributed among four divisions: administrator and policy studies, curriculum and teaching, developmental studies and counseling, and special education.

Neither these data about Boston University nor what follows about Georgia State prove that students and faculty from various programs barely recognize each other in the elevator or fail to plan coherently in the ways noted by Goodlad. Beatty characterized Boston University's school today as not of a single philosophical orientation. What distinction there is between eclecticism and lack of focus or purpose was clearer to Goodlad's team that conducted extensive surveys of current faculty, students, cooperating schools, and programs than it was to the historians who looked for long-term trends in the evolution of twenty-nine places.

Georgia State University's story, while shorter, is dramatic. Georgia State College of Business Administration formed a Department of Education in 1958, but it was in 1967, two years before it became Georgia State University, that a School of Education was established with a faculty of 12. Within three years, the faculty stood at 102. Within twenty years, according to university documents, the College of Education had become the third-largest education degree-granting institution in the United States, with 70 percent of its programs in graduate education (thirty-seven programs to choose from) and also a postmaster's education specialist degree (choice of twenty-eight) and the doctorate (choice of twenty-six across eight departments). Generating just 13 percent of all credit hours taken at the university, the College of Education by 1986 was responsible for 56 percent of the doctorates and 41 percent of the master's degrees granted by the entire university, as reported to the National Council for Accreditation of Teacher Education (NCATE) in that year. Education dean Jerry Robbins's figures in 1988 indicated that more than 50 percent of the university's extramural funding came to the College of Education, which enrolled at that time approximately 3,400 students—some two-thirds in school-oriented programs and one-third (and growing) in nonschool education programs. Faculty recruitment from the beginning was for a graduate faculty that would also mount undergraduate programs.[38]

Interviews with veteran faculty members, department chairs, and deans painted a picture of strong departmental missions in certain departments at certain times. For example, Joanne Nurss came from Emory to Georgia State in 1969, initially in educational psychology and then as head of the early childhood department, before becoming an associate dean in 1974. At the time, there were no public kindergartens any-

where in the southeastern states, and there was a new four-
teen-state effort to create them and to determine their goals.
Nurss organized conferences and attended governors' meetings, and she reports that "Regionally, Georgia State would have
been seen very much as a leader" in this effort.[39] Sherman
Day, the college's second dean and "about the eighth person
hired here," arrived in 1967 and became chair of the counseling department, on whose faculty he still serves. He chaired a
faculty of ten at the time that tried as part of its mission to
educate "whole counselors," bringing together students with
school and nonschool career interests, hoping to broaden school
districts' view of the skills and role of the counselor. He was
also committed to creating a cohesive cohort group of entering
students to build a professional culture. "We didn't want people to come in and say, 'What's available at 5:00 Tuesday night?'"
and instead tried a "law school approach" of keeping an entering class together in course work, having peers learning from
each other, and trying to build on camaraderie despite having
a nonresidential school. This apparently was not and is not the
norm in the College of Education programs, as suggested in
Goodlad's overview of discontinuities in the twenty-nine places.

Asked about philosophies and guiding principles linking
departments in the College of Education, its dean suggested,
"Eclectic is the kindest term I can put on it. . . . I think that's
one of our shortcomings."[40] A senior foundations professor
suggested that *eclectic* is preferable to *dictatorial* as an intellectual framework for higher education. A former dean suggested that the college had stood for "traditional progressivism" in the Atlanta education community. Another senior faculty
member suggested that the curriculum and instruction department from its inception was concerned with materials and
methods but "did not deal with goals, philosophies, or values
of schooling," although there were variations in this respect
among different subject field specialties within the methods
faculty.

Georgia State, then, exemplifies some of the huge constraints on purposefulness facing an institution whose lifeblood
is the part-time, in-service educator seeking an advanced de-

gree in a highly diversified college of education with a large, diverse, and fragmented faculty. When push comes to shove, the common denominator for succeeding as a young faculty member at such an institution is not helping to promote a particular mission or set of values but the old familiar—produce research, bring in extramural funding. As for pulling together as departments or a whole college for program evaluation and renewal, some of this no doubt has occurred, but the course catalogue tends to leave an impression that proliferation is the major form of renewal. Just as examples, two sets of full-semester courses leave that impression: In Early Childhood, we find "Diagnosis of Reading Difficulties," "Correction of Reading Difficulties," "Reading Comprehension and Written Composition in Early Childhood," "Literature for Young Children," "Reading, Writing, and Language for Young Children," and "Language Arts for Young Children." And in Special Education, we find "Characteristics and Identification of the Gifted," "Curriculum and Methods for Teaching the Gifted," "Methods for Teaching the Gifted and Their Parents," and "Program Development for Gifted Education."

Education Faculty, Practitioners, and the Knowledge-Practice Tension. The most striking historical paradox in this inquiry surrounds Goodlad's next assertion: that there is no consistent interplay between new knowledge and classroom practices, either within school districts or between districts and colleges of education. There is a renewing kind of "tension" between the frontiers of what is known and the frontline implementing of day-to-day practice that Goodlad sees present in medicine and law but absent in education. He blames part of the problem on the conservatism of state regulators and their trivial pursuit of telling schools and colleges how to prepare student teachers (an issue addressed above) and part on a nearly complete lack of productive, substantive communication between college supervisors and school-based cooperating teachers regarding the student teaching experience. "Professors and cooperating teachers spoke freely of such dissonance," which always seems to stick the unsuspecting student teacher in a crossfire, Goodlad noted in Chapter One. "But the position taken by most students and faculty members was that they must conform to school and district expectations. . . . Only occasionally did we find a setting where university-based and school-based faculty members worked as a team." Those of us who have taught student teachers surely recognize the crossfire.

Here is the historical paradox. The whole point of educating teachers in normal schools and in the regional colleges that they became was to provide a work force for the surrounding public schools. Most of the twenty-nine historical case studies cited long-standing, close, and warm ties—and some revolving doors—between education faculties and school personnel in the early decades, when schools and teachers' colleges shared a common administrative structure in some states. Even in more recent times, school districts typically have eagerly sought graduates of the institutions that they knew and loved best to fill new openings. And these have been times in which, as has been established, college faculty and leadership positions have gone decreasingly to men and women with direct ties to elementary and secondary classrooms and increasingly to career professors and researchers. Not more than one or two of the twenty-nine histories mentioned friction or hostility between the education faculty and the school districts at any point in the past, and they often emphasized friendly relations, ease of student teaching placements, and the desire of in-service faculty and administrators to return to the campus for advanced degree work. Most of the major education programs today would be dead without an eager constituency of their own local public school personnel to take graduate courses. Several examples of this have already been cited in this chapter; more could be found in nearly all of the twenty-nine cases.

Now we can assume, if only from our own experiences as teacher educators, that some rough edges in professor-practitioner relations have been blurred or simply not taken into account in these histories. Nonetheless, what is going on here?

My wife recently taught me that when my son and his friend are puttering along happily at enjoyable but independent games in the same room, one calls that "parallel play."

Parallel play is supposed to be quite healthy as long as everyone gets along and no one's interpersonal skills suffer long-term atrophy. In a similar vein, a junior high teacher colleague of mine uses the maxim "go along, get along" to characterize the nonprofessional culture of his faculty. One can argue about whether the state is a sufficiently independent entity to be able to force teacher educators and cooperating school districts indefinitely to educate newcomers in a certain way, thus making school-college dialogue moot. What seems less arguable is that colleges of education and school districts choose to operate in parallel play—congenially rather than collegially[41]—and that such has been the predominant model of school-college collaboration through most of this history.

Congeniality enables foundations and methods teachers to cover their material and school-based cooperating teachers to engage interns in "reality" without any required dialogue between the two. As Goodlad found, reality has a tendency to win out because it relates most closely to surviving the training period and initial years on the job and because it does not threaten long-standing school-university peace. Congeniality also seems to characterize those graduate programs in which the professors present knowledge or perspectives that would substantially alter school practice if the students took it seriously. Many elementary and secondary practitioners consider large segments of professors' agendas rather quaint and out of touch with what is really going on. To what extent does needed dialogue actually take place, and what impact does it have on schoolchildren?

There is, in fact, no evidence from the twenty-nine historical documents that such dialogue was part of the ongoing structure of any college of education in the study. That does not mean that it did not take place; the historians did not delve into curriculum and instructional practices beyond evident trends and major institutional and program developments, and, no doubt, individuals have grappled with these matters all along. Furthermore, a number of the twenty-nine places have or have had "laboratory" or "demonstration" schools on or tied to the campus, designed in theory to address the knowledge-practice tension; their story goes beyond the work of this study, although present knowledge suggests that it would not contradict Goodlad's basic arguments.[42] What some of the twenty-nine histories do contain is some promising swipes at the problem that suggest how collegiality is possible, what has been done, and, as Goodlad states, what seems to be missing in most places today.[43]

Boston University's School of Education, under deans Jesse B. Davis and Donald D. Durrell in the 1930s and 1940s, set out to create research- and knowledge-based divisions and programs that would serve and involve local educators and children beyond teaching courses. The Educational Clinic and Division of Teaching Aids, mentioned above, were products of what Beatty suggests was a conscious plan

> to create innovative yet practical responses to the increasingly specialized needs of schools. . . . Durrell was a believer in team learning and team teaching, and he formed an educational team which worked actively to promote new programs that would "make a difference in schools." Along with School of Education graduates Helen Sullivan and Linwood Chase, Durrell and other faculty members spent time in classrooms testing their ideas about the psychology of learning and reading instruction, and writing and lecturing about their results. In the process, they formed a large informal network of educational practitioners who were knowledgeable about and involved in the School of Education's programs.[44]

The Atlanta Area Teacher Education Services (AATES) was a post–World War II joint venture of six school districts and six colleges and universities, including the University of Georgia and Emory University, "in a collaborative effort to upgrade the qualifications of practicing teachers, many of whom did not possess baccalaureate degrees and formal preparation to teach."[45] Although AATES achieved no institutionalized, structural change in the relationship of schools to colleges, two developments—"a renaissance of arts in [some] schools" inspired by the University of Georgia's Lamar Dodd and a collaborative longitudinal child study directed by Lynn Shufelt of the AATES and co-led by Goodlad—were short-term models of change.[46] A key to both was the building of a cohort group, a point made earlier by Sherman Day of Georgia State, to critically examine particular instructional and institutional issues over an extended period of time. In the mid 1950s, with AATES still going strong, Emory University's Division of Teacher Education mounted a master's degree program in administration inspired by the same notion of a cohort group addressing key issues in a seminar format. Structurally, it was not a school-university partnership, since participants came as individuals taking a course of study, not as representatives of school districts committed to institutional renewal; but it was an attempt to build a graduate program around a notion of practitioners as partners in an ongoing effort of inquiry and reflection.[47]

As a final example, Richard Altenbaugh offered the following historical comment on the National College of Education (NCE) faculty:

> The main intellectual characteristic of [NCE] education faculty has been their ability to bridge theory to practice; this reflected the largely service orientation of the college. For example, teachers in the Baker Demonstration School have always maintained appointments and teaching assignments in the regular departments. And all faculty have public school roots, and continue to remain in close contact with the schools. [They] maintain membership in national organizations, such as the National Council of Teachers of Mathematics and the International Reading Association, [and] edit the *Journal of Reading Behavior*. . . . Much of [the faculty's recently emphasized] research focus remains as applied research, often touching on ethnographic studies.[48]

These, and no doubt additional, untold stories from the twenty-nine and other institutions suggest criteria for meaningful school-university collegiality that receive much more detailed discussion in the cited literature on the knowledge-practice tension. Relatively young networks committed to such partnerships now have "branches" around the country under the general leadership of people such as Theodore Sizer at Brown University and John Goodlad at the University of Washington. If successful, they hold out the promise of achieving what "laboratory" schools apparently did not—genuine laboratories for pedagogical dialogue and institutional renewal.

Diminishing Commitments to Urban Education

The final teacher education theme advanced by Goodlad in Chapter One is the failure of teacher education programs to address the needs of the nation's many deteriorating urban school districts. What Goodlad called "the urban problem" has several dimensions, including (1) a reluctance of education faculty to place student teachers in other than "safe" suburban classrooms; (2) a lack of minority students preparing to teach; (3) unsuccessful recruitment efforts by institutions across racial lines by both predominantly white and predominantly black education programs; and (4) racism, with black teachers often unwelcome in white districts—and, one could add, white teacher candidates avoiding predominantly black districts. The 1987 National Survey of Students in Teacher Education Programs, analyzed by Nancy Zimpher, characterized the 93 percent white, predominantly female and rural-suburban undergraduate teacher candidate as of "limited horizons" and "cultural insularity," traveling less than 100 miles from home to attend college and planning to return to within 50 miles of home to teach.[49] (This situation has a long history, of course, which is touched on in the next section.)

Two of the twenty-nine histories are of predominantly black institutions: Fort Valley State College, a historically black college, and Chicago State University, an urban institution that once denied admission to blacks but now serves them primarily. While data on matters of race are limited in the other twenty-seven cases, available evidence tends to support Goodlad's view, especially his observation that, while many urban universities serve substantial numbers of black and other racial minority students, a relatively much smaller percentage of those students have chosen the college of education. Furthermore, several education programs reported that their competitive disadvantage with respect to the prestige of other fields left them with less than an intellectually scintillating band of undergraduates—a statement presumably applied equally to white and minority students.

A veteran College of Education leader at Georgia State University, which is located in downtown Atlanta, said that one important aspect of the university's mission has been equity and opportunity for black degree candidates. This leader observed that

"One of the pieces of data that is not publicly released is that black graduates of Georgia State do extremely well" by comparison to all graduates and by comparison to black graduates of other Georgia institutions, data "we don't capitalize on" out of sensitivity to the possible reactions of some other institutions. In the College's early years, all applicants were admitted conditionally, that is, a system of open admissions. "Standards" came more to rule the admission process, and although a transitional support program exists for undergraduates, no such program exists for graduate students—which our observer feels is damaging to this aspect of the College's mission, in that there has been a reduction in black enrollment.[50]

Barbara Beatty offered the following observations in her study of the Jesuit institution Boston College and its School of Education:

By the turn of the century, the majority of students in the Boston Public Schools were from Irish Catholic backgrounds, and Irish Catholics made up the bulk of the teaching force. . . . The tendency of Boston College graduates to teach in the Boston Public Schools was so well established . . . that it was as if the College were a private Catholic normal school for the city. A common pattern was for Boston College undergraduates to teach in Boston, return to Boston College to get a graduate degree, and then become administrators in the system. Numerous principals and head masters in Boston were Boston College graduates, as were four of the city's superintendents in the first two-thirds of the twentieth century.[51]

Recent surveys reveal a marked change in where graduates of the School of Education today obtain positions. Unlike male liberal arts graduates of past years . . . most female and male education graduates in the late 1970s and 1980s got teaching jobs in suburban public schools around Boston and New England. There is anecdotal evidence suggesting that this was not a new pattern for women, however, as female graduates of Boston College's Intown Summer and Graduate School programs in the past (before women were admitted to the main campus) may also have taught primarily in suburban school systems, in part because Boston's public normal school trained most of the female teaching force for the Boston Public Schools. Though Boston College requires some urban student teaching experience, large numbers of student teachers are placed in suburban school systems such as Waltham and Natick, and it is in these and similar systems that many graduates find work.[52]

Colleges of education may, of course, play other kinds of roles in urban education. One example, touched on above, was the Boston University School of Education's role in the court-ordered desegregation of Boston's public schools starting in the 1970s. Education dean Robert Dentler, appointed to that post in 1973, was named a court-appointed master and helped develop both a busing plan and a still-operating higher education partnership that pairs colleges with individual schools. Boston University maintained its commitment to the multicollege partnership program throughout the 1980s, encouraged by President John Silber, placing it in the care of Silber's special assistant, Robert Sperber, former superintendent of the neighboring Brookline Public Schools.

Mercer University Atlanta, soon after its establishment in the early 1970s, began a prison-based baccalaureate degree program, which by 1988 was serving students in several state and federal prisons in the Atlanta area—a contribution to urban education apparently unique among the institutions in this study.[53]

The Goodlad Themes: An Afterword

It appears that the priorities and reward structures of colleges of education and those of school districts have evolved quite far apart from each other since the days when heads of teacher education were called "principals" and their ties were to the public schools. It is interesting that this, it appears, was not entirely a twentieth-century phenomenon. In his recent contribution to the American Educational Research Association's volume on the history of teaching, Jurgen Herbst summarized the normal schools' efforts up to the turn of the century as "The Nineteenth-Century Record: Retreat from Teaching." While several factors of normal school history led Herbst to this judgment, the essence of it was "they wanted to shake their traditional status of precollegiate institutions and to take on the prestige and the work of colleges and universities."[54]

For this and other reasons, to be highlighted below, it becomes clear that American schools and colleges of education for well over a century have been ambivalent about the nature of a "professional" or "renewing" agenda in elementary and secondary education. Their shortcomings today in the areas emphasized by Goodlad are traceable directly to this historical ambivalence about their mission. A commitment to engage teachers and administrators in a mutually renewing examination of knowledge and practice fades in and out of the education school picture like radio reception of a distant station late at night.

Additional Themes Identified in the Study

This brief concluding section links several other historical themes in the evolution of colleges of education to those presented by Goodlad in Chapter One. These are themes emphasized by my colleagues and myself as we prepared the twenty-nine institutional case histories for the Study of the Education of Educators.

This chapter has been an inquiry into focus and purposefulness in the teacher education enterprise, which has appeared out of focus and ambivalent about purpose. Issues larger than professional teacher preparation itself—gender, race, class, populism, and the evolution of public school practice generally—are in some ways causes of certain Goodlad themes. One issue—race and racism—forms a dramatic backdrop to this entire story inasmuch as elementary, secondary, and higher education continues to reflect the predominant segregation of the larger society, and matters involving equity and urban education too often continue to go unaddressed. While my own research in the study does not equip me to address the richness of this theme, Kathleen Cruikshank's work on the state of Georgia (Chapter Eight) offers critical insights.[55] The other themes are divided into three groups: (1) populism and class, (2) gender, and (3) "how teachers taught."

Populism and Class. Illinois Normal School (Illinois State), from its opening in 1857, "attracted a large number of serious, idealistic, though not always well prepared, students from the state's rural areas and small towns. Many of them were the children of first generation immigrants," Herbst noted, considering a career that could be a step "up on the social and economic ladder." Its founders "viewed the Normal University [as] a people's university open to young men and women from all walks of life."[56] The normal school was, in fact, the state's only university until 1867. Its original curriculum was mandated to include agricultural chemistry and animal and vegetable physiology, along with civic education; this demonstrated "rather clearly that Illinois legislators and schoolmen desired to emphasize the intimate connection [between the normal and] the state's principal economic concern."[57] As it turned out, at Illinois and other normal schools, a relatively low percentage of students completed their studies or intended to make teaching a life's work, or even temporary work. The normal school requirement that students commit themselves at entry to teach in the public schools proved unenforceable.

Although Illinois Normal's leaders conceived its broader-than-teaching mission to be distinct from that of the Massachusetts normals, it was not completely so. In terms of curriculum, Fitchburg Normal (Fitchburg State) surely pursued a narrower focus in its early years, but Fitchburg has played a similar historical role in attracting students from modest to moderate means who are often the first generation in the family to complete college, as well as a role of offering classical studies to the community through its public lecture series.[58] One is tempted to paint such institutions with a broad "populist" brush, as Keene (New Hampshire) State College historian James Smart did in emphasizing the traditional teachers' college's role as a "people's" institution.[59] (Normal schools and teachers' colleges have traditionally maintained free or very modest tuition and, in Keene's case, even free books and fees for many decades.) Consider Beatty's thoughtful critique:

> Fitchburg was, and remains, career-oriented. Students in its liberal education programs today take

some courses that other institutions would consider professional education. In this sense its curriculum in some ways resembles the shop math and
practical English courses of the "Fitchburg Plan"
co-operative industrial arts program of the early
part of the century. And like students in this earlier program, one wonders about the mobility of
Fitchburg graduates. Geographically, at least, most
Fitchburg students come from the Fitchburg region and return to the region to work and live.
Fitchburg is a "hometown school." What effects
attending Fitchburg has on students' social mobility is another question. The College is aware of
the lower-income background of its students, many
of whom are the first in their families to attend
college. A mission statement in the catalogue . . .
notes the College's "particular concern for those
of low and moderate economic means," and the
College's commitment to prepare them "to live and
make a living." For many students, undoubtedly
teacher education programs at Fitchburg provide
a means of upward social mobility, as education
did for millboys . . . at the turn of the century.
But with the association of elite education and the
liberal arts, the emphasis on careerism and practicality at Fitchburg also raises larger, hard questions about the role of different types of teacher
education in American society.[60]

Among other things, Beatty implies that a kind of teacher
education designed to help upwardly mobile students "live and
make a living" may not be the same critical-thinking-oriented
teacher education urged by Goodlad. It would be unfair, of
course, to paint Fitchburg's program as less aggressively "professional" than others, especially considering that its history
turned up the only overt report of a conflict in which local
school officials considered Fitchburg's 1960s and 1970s educa-

tion faculty just too progressive and pushy for their taste.[61] But Beatty's questions are pressing ones.

Northwest Georgia's Berry College, dating to approximately 1902, was committed to educating the rural poor, for "boys and girls learning the needed lessons to fit them for life, to lift them into the glory of young manhood and young womanhood."[62] Founder Martha Berry wanted a boarding school in order to do this uplifting away from rural parents who might not respect book learning. These ideals were extended to the institution that grew into a junior college in 1926 and a four-year college in 1930.

So it was that mobility or, as Beatty wonders about, lack of mobility was an agenda in many ways larger than what institutions valued about philosophical or pedagogical issues in education.

Gender. The twenty-nine histories are sprinkled liberally with discussions of colleges' and education programs' constituencies and missions with respect to gender. Several of the twenty-nine are or were single-sex institutions; normal schools and teachers' colleges, generally coeducational from their founding, were always predominantly female (overwhelmingly so in the early decades), and, as we have seen, that pattern holds true across all institutional types today in programs for initial teacher certification. Conversely, administrator certification programs in all institutional types have a century-long tradition of male domination, though the percentages have shifted more than in the initial teacher certification programs. Normal school administrators even before the turn of the century worried about "low status" in their institutions if they could not attract male students. This latter fact suggests why the gender issue matters.

If teacher education curricula have failed, as Goodlad argues, to instill the values of broad-based, liberal, critical thinking into a teacher's professional repertoire, one might well consider that females in these institutions were originally supposed to be anything but movers and shakers in the school setting.

For example, it is commonly understood that normal schools were located by states in far-flung areas in order to bring improved common schools, as well as higher education opportunities, to rural areas. Many of the twenty-nine places were purposely kept away from communities with "city influences," "bad elements," social distractions, or just plain concentrations of employed or unemployed men, in order to make sure that young ladies learned to become and remain ladies. It goes without saying that their principals, professors, and employers were, in the vast majority of cases, men. Teaching as a job in which one implements top-down orders has a rich historical tradition.

Submissiveness was surely not the only point of all this. San Francisco's State's Ritual of Teachers Guild Service, which survived until the faculty voted it out in 1929, was designed "to consecrate women in the high calling of serving children . . . with all the tenderness and dedication they could muster."[63] Some graduates were no doubt inspired by the formal affair created by Frederic Burk and held in Berkeley's Greek Theater, in which verses such as the following were solemnly recited:

The breadth and depth and height of woman's work
To guard and nurture children; for the joy
To call that work a privilege; that thus
We come to make the kingdom in our heart
A very paradise wherein our love
Is sweeter for our work, and all our work
Is better for our love.[64]

One should not make too much of quaint customs, or even of gender employment patterns in education, as "proof" of a historical leaning away from a certain professional orientation to teacher education. There are at least two dangers in doing so. First, women have, in fact, been innovators, movers, and shakers in teaching and curriculum development over the decades, in some places and times; if they had not been, since most teachers have been women, public schooling would have got nowhere in all these decades, instead of making those strides it has made. If criticism is due to the "system," and thus to many women, for the current state of schooling,, then women must also receive the credit for many advances in curriculum and instruction. Second, pooh-poohing the "relationships" side of professional and personal decision making is a common male mistake, as Carol Gilligan pointed out to the late Larry Kohlberg.[65] If loving children is an inappropriate normative starting point for the teaching profession, we are all in deep trouble.

Still, there is something suspicious here when schools are viewed as lockstep and resistant to change, teacher education is viewed as pedestrian and not addressing the real issues, and the history of both has roots in the protection and "appropriate" channeling of women. At least some connection seems self-evident.

How Teachers Taught. This chapter concludes as it began, questioning how education professionals conceive of purposefulness in what they do. The institutional representatives that Goodlad's team interviewed generally said that the college of education is in no position, or does not choose, to disrupt existing practice in the grades. Thus, student teaching, the capstone of a candidate's entry into the profession, the scale by which candidates measure what they have been taught and conceive of what is possible, is generally geared to the status quo.

That being the case, it is worth our time to recall that two major studies of the 1980s—one historical,[66] one on current practice[67]—documented that teaching has been and continues to be conceived of as telling the kids what they are supposed to know, grading them over a narrow percentage scale of how much they got, and moving on. Both studies also documented significant "minority" behaviors—historically, Cuban estimated, perhaps 25 percent of classrooms, consistent across time and place—in which some innovation, some notion of knowledge transformed into practice and practice informing knowledge, prevailed. Professors should not be too smug about this, since similar research on college teaching could well yield an even more gloomy picture of teacher attitudes and instructional practices. That is the point: We teach as we were taught. Colleges, as the capstone of a student's education, may carry the strongest influence over future teachers' conceptions of how to teach. This certainly pertains to arts and sciences courses, since they compose the bulk of teacher preparation credits. Our own house at the college level is hardly in order.

The Study of the Education of Educators, including this volume on history, leaves us with a sense of century-long unfinished business. As a profession, we have scored about 25 percent on making knowledge and practice cohabitable.[68] It is not our understanding that in a profession, scores are allowed to be that low. We would surely fire our doctor, accountant, or lawyer for a batting average like that.

Notes

1. I. G. Hendrick, *Historical Case Study: San Francisco State University* (Seattle: Center for Educational Renewal, College of Education, University of Washington, 1988).
2. J. Herbst, *Historical Case Study: University of Northern Iowa* (Seattle: Center for Educational Renewal, College of Education, University of Washington, 1988).
3. Hendrick, *Historical Case Study: San Francisco State University*, p. 1.
4. Hendrick, *Historical Case Study: San Francisco State University*, p. 21.
5. Herbst, *Historical Case Study: University of Northern Iowa*, p. 5.
6. Herbst, *Historical Case Study: University of Northern Iowa*, p. 2.
7. I. G. Hendrick, *Historical Case Study: Oklahoma State University* (Seattle: Center for Educational Renewal, College of Education, University of Washington, 1988); I. G. Hendrick, *Historical Case Study: Central State University* (Seattle: Center for Educational Renewal, College of Education, University of Washington, 1988).

8. R. A. Levin, *Historical Case Study: Emory University* (Seattle: Center for Educational Renewal, College of Education, University of Washington, 1988).

9. J. Herbst, *Historical Case Study: Drake University* (Seattle: Center for Educational Renewal, College of Education, University of Washington, 1988).

10. Herbst, *Historical Case Study: Drake University*, p. 12.

11. J. I. Goodlad, *A Place Called School* (New York: McGraw-Hill, 1984); J. I. Goodlad, F. Klein, and Associates, *Looking Behind the Classroom Door* (Worthington, Ohio: Charles Jones, 1974); J. I. Goodlad and R. H. Anderson, *The Non-Graded Elementary School* (New York: Teachers College Press, 1959).

12. C. Burgess, *Historical Case Study: Bucknell University* (Seattle: Center for Educational Renewal, College of Education, University of Washington, 1988).

13. Levin, *Historical Case Study: Emory University*.

14. R. J. Altenbaugh, *Historical Case Study: National College of Education* (Seattle: Center for Educational Renewal, College of Education, University of Washington, 1988).

15. K. Cruikshank, *Historical Case Study: The University of Georgia* (Seattle: Center for Educational Renewal, College of Education, University of Washington, 1988), p. 108.

16. B. Beatty, *Historical Case Study: Boston University* (Seattle: Center for Educational Renewal, College of Education, University of Washington, 1988).

17. L. Eisenmann, *Historical Case Study: Temple University* (Seattle: Center for Educational Renewal, College of Education, University of Washington, 1988).

18. L. Eisenmann, *Historical Case Study: West Chester University* (Seattle: Center for Educational Renewal, College of Education, University of Washington, 1988).

19. W. R. Johnson, "Teachers and Teacher Training in the Twentieth Century," in D. Warren (ed.), *American Teachers: Histories of a Profession at Work* (New York: Macmillan, 1989).

20. James D. Anderson points out that black normal schools of the mid to late nineteenth century were confronting

the issue of vocationalism in the curriculum, although vocationalism is commonly discussed as a twentieth-century development. See, for example, J. D. Anderson, *The Education of Blacks in the South, 1860–1935* (Chapel Hill: University of North Carolina Press, 1988).

21. See, for example, J. Dewey, *The Child and the Curriculum: The School and Society* (Chicago: University of Chicago Press, 1956); Goodlad, *A Place Called School;* Goodlad, Klein, and Associates, *Looking Behind the Classroom Door;* Goodlad and Anderson, *The Non-Graded Elementary School;* J. Spring, *The Sorting Machine Revisited* (New York: Longman, 1989); J. Oakes, *Keeping Track* (New Haven: Yale University Press, 1985); A. Gutmann, *Democratic Education* (Princeton, N.J.: Princeton University Press, 1987); H. Rugg, *The Teacher of Teachers* (New York: Harper & Row, 1952); C. A. Grant and C. E. Sleeter, *After the School Bell Rings* (Philadelphia: Falmer, 1986).

22. E. C. Lagemann, "The Plural Worlds of Educational Research," *History of Education Quarterly,* 1989, *29* (2), 185–214.

23. Eisenmann, *Historical Case Study: West Chester University.*

24. Eisenmann, *Historical Case Study: West Chester University.*

25. J. Herbst, as cited in D. Warren (ed.), *American Teachers: Histories of a Profession at Work* (New York: Macmillan, 1989), p. 226.

26. See, for example, J. Spring's discussion of Herbartianism, *The American School 1642–1985* (New York: Longman, 1986); and W. S. Monroe's standard work, *Teaching-Learning Theory and Teacher Education* (Urbana: University of Illinois Press, 1952).

27. K. Underwood, *Historical Case Study: University of Denver* (Seattle: Center for Educational Renewal, College of Education, University of Washington, 1988).

28. B. Beatty, *Historical Case Study: Fitchburg State College* (Seattle: Center for Educational Renewal, College of Education, University of Washington, 1988).

29. Beatty, *Historical Case Study: Fitchburg State College,* p. 8. Beatty's references for this passage are D. Kirkpatrick,

The City and the River, vol. 2 (Fitchburg, Mass.: Fitchburg Historical Society, 1971–1975); P. J. Ringel, "The Introduction and Development of Manual Training and Industrial Education in the Public Schools of Fitchburg, Massachusetts, 1893–1928," unpublished doctoral dissertation, Teachers College, Columbia University, 1980.

30. Beatty, *Historical Case Study: Fitchburg State College,* p. 9.
31. L. Eisenmann, *Historical Case Study: Pennsylvania State University* (Seattle: Center for Educational Renewal, College of Education, University of Washington, 1988), p. 25.
32. R. A. Levin, "Preparing Elementary Teachers: The University of Pittsburgh and Keene State College in Historical Perspective," doctoral dissertation in progress, Carnegie-Mellon University, 1991.
33. Levin, *Preparing Elementary Teachers.*
34. Levin, *Preparing Elementary Teachers.*
35. Beatty's *Historical Case Study: Boston University* reported that Boston University "was the first university to award a Ph.D. to a woman, and a number of women who were to be influential in the growth of women's higher education and professional development attended Boston University in the period before the turn of the century" (p. 3).
36. In *Historical Case Study: Boston University,* Beatty noted, "The new school thus reversed the order of what was becoming accepted as the standard division of teacher education into two years of general education followed by two years of professional education, as Wilde noted in his first annual report" (p. 7). I consider this historically significant in the evolution of teacher education because it is different. For nearly a century since the establishment of bachelor's degree programs for teachers, there has been a virtual lockstep sequence to the course of study. This is not to say that Boston University's plan was better, but colleges have universally experienced freshmen and sophomores who lack much understanding of or commitment to the rationale for studying certain introductory subject matter. It is at least possible that teacher can-

didates, with a decent high school background followed by some preprofessional course work and exposure to teaching and the school curriculum, might return to the liberal arts classrooms renewed and more focused on what they need to learn and why. Furthermore, education seminars dealing with normative and structural issues about schooling might make a stronger impression on such "returning" students; these courses are too often wasted on young underclassmen.

37. Beatty, *Historical Case Study: Boston University*, p. 7.
38. R. A. Levin, *Historical Case Study: Georgia State University* (Seattle: Center for Educational Renewal, College of Education, University of Washington, 1988).
39. Levin, *Historical Case Study: Georgia State University*, p. 6.
40. Levin, *Historical Case Study: Georgia State University*, p. 13.
41. The "congeniality/collegiality" framework suggested by Roland Barth has become a basis for staff development programs offered by such educators as Jon Saphier, Matthew King, and Irwin Blumer.
42. Levin, *Preparing Elementary Teachers.* Also, two helpful articles about what laboratory schools have and have not accomplished are W. Van Til, *The Laboratory School: Its Rise and Fall?* (Terre Haute: Indiana State University and the Laboratory Schools Administrators Association, 1969); J. I. Goodlad, "How Laboratory Schools Go Awry," *UCLA Educator,* 1980, *21* (2), 46–53.
43. Many individual principals, teachers, superintendents, and teacher educators and even some researchers have addressed these concerns energetically and successfully for a long time. Most, no doubt, do so in relative anonymity. However, the national curriculum councils of social studies, science, mathematics, and so on, the Association for Supervision and Curriculum Development, and others have been perhaps the most significant institutionalized forces in promoting collegiality of knowledge and practice. Their memberships tend to run approximately 75 percent elementary and secondary practitioners and 25

percent university people. The subject-specific organizations are large and are active nationally and regionally, although it would be unusual for their memberships to surpass even 10 percent of teachers nationwide who teach that subject. Perhaps one measure of education's professional resistance to collegiality is, in fact, the relatively small percentage of classroom teachers who join and participate, despite the national and regional visibility of the organizations, as well as the research community's significant but uneven involvement. In addition to the excellent monthly journals of these organizations, the following are among the helpful books available: R. S. Barth, *Run School Run* (Cambridge, Mass: Harvard University Press, 1980); A. R. Tom, *Teaching as a Moral Craft* (New York: Longman, 1984)—do not miss the appendix, which is Tom's detailed syllabus for the "Secondary Professional Seminar, Spring 1981, Washington University"; K. A. Sirotnik and J. I. Goodlad (eds.), *School-University Partnerships in Action* (New York: Teachers College Press, 1988).

44. Beatty, *Historical Case Study: Boston University*, p. 13.
45. J. I. Goodlad and F. Jordan, "When School and College Cooperate," *Educational Leadership*, 1950, 7 (Apr.), 461–465.
46. Goodlad, as cited in Sirotnik and Goodlad, *School-University Partnerships in Action*.
47. Retired Emory faculty member Newton Hodgson, who came to Atlanta as an AATES fellow based at Emory, discussed this program during an interview with the author.
48. Altenbaugh, *Historical Case Study: National College of Education*, p. 17.
49. N. L. Zimpher, "1987 National Survey of Students in Teacher Education Programs: Preliminary Findings" (AACTE Research About Teacher Education Project), paper presented at the American Educational Research Association Annual Meeting, New Orleans, Apr. 1988.
50. Levin, *Historical Case Study: Georgia State University*, p. 7.

51. B. Beatty, *Historical Case Study: Boston College* (Seattle: Center for Educational Renewal, College of Education, University of Washington, 1988), p. 16.

52. Beatty, *Historical Case Study: Boston College,* p. 19.

53. R. A. Levin, *Historical Case Study: Mercer University Atlanta* (Seattle: Center for Educational Renewal, College of Education, University of Washington, 1988).

54. J. Herbst, "Teacher Preparation in the Nineteenth Century," in D. Warren (ed.), *American Teachers.*

55. It also appears that histories of higher education have focused separately on either predominantly black or predominantly white institutions. Cruikshank's chapter in this volume should encourage more new work on historical commonalities and differences between black and white institutions, leading to greater understanding of how to address some of the issues raised in this study by John Goodlad.

56. J. Herbst, *Historical Case Study: The Illinois State University* (Seattle: Center for Educational Renewal, College of Education, University of Washington, 1988), p. 5.

57. Herbst, *Historical Case Study: The Illinois State University,* p. 6.

58. Beatty, *Historical Case Study: Fitchburg State College.*

59. J. G. Smart, *Striving: The History of a Small Public Institution* (Canaan, N.H.: Phoenix, 1984).

60. Beatty, *Historical Case Study: Fitchburg State College.*

61. Beatty, *Historical Case Study: Fitchburg State College.*

62. C. Burgess, *Historical Case Study: Berry College* (Seattle: Center for Educational Renewal, College of Education, University of Washington, 1988), pp. 1–2.

63. Hendrick, *Historical Case Study: San Francisco State University,* p. 3.

64. Cited in Hendrick, *Historical Case Study: San Francisco State University,* p. 4.

65. C. Gilligan, *In a Different Voice* (Cambridge, Mass.: Harvard University Press, 1982).

66. L. Cuban, *How Teachers are Taught* (New York: Longman, 1984).

67. Goodlad, *A Place Called School*.

68. Many observers have cautioned us about the unique problems inherent in trying to apply "knowledge" to a relatively artistic field such as teaching, by comparison to fields with more technical knowledge bases, while at the same time criticizing those egghead educational researchers who speak only to each other, never to practitioners. Among the many eloquent statements of this sort, see, for example, J. Schwab, "The Practical: A Language for Curriculum," in I. Westburg and N. J. Wilkof (eds.), *Science, Curriculum, and Liberal Education* (Chicago: University of Chicago Press, 1978).

PART TWO

Evolution of
Teacher Education:
Institutional Perspectives

3

Abiding by
the "Rule of Birds":
Teaching Teachers
in Small
Liberal Arts Colleges

Charles Burgess

In 1950, the size of the average university student body in
America was just 1,460. The world of higher learning still
echoed John Henry Newman's view of the university at its best:
It was an intimate family devoted to learning, "an alma mater,
knowing her children one by one, not a foundry, or a mint, or
a treadmill."[1] The four institutions featured in this study are
of average size by the standards of the 1950s. A spirit of Newman's alma mater still touches the air at all four—Berry College, near Rome, Georgia; Mills College, in Oakland, California; Coe College, in Cedar Rapids, Iowa; and Bucknell
University, in Lewisburg, Pennsylvania.

The four small independent colleges whose stories are
here sketched return us to a premultiversity world—a world of
higher learning still connected, however tenuously, with the
medieval ideals of alma mater and communitas and the "aca-

demic village" of Jefferson's dreams. They invite us to listen
with a new ear to John Ciardi's concern about size:

> Some rule of birds kills off the song
> in any that begin to grow
> much larger than a fist or so.
> What happens as they move along
> to power and size? Something goes wrong.[2]

Educational and social lives intertwine at these small residential colleges. Willy-nilly as much as by intent, students and
faculty greet one another in many moods, in many settings beyond the classroom. A sense of academic interconnectedness
still lives among the faculty. Students can still feel the texture
of learning's seamless robe. Governance has a peculiarly direct
immediacy. No bureaucracies intervene and complicate. These
collegiate qualities of wholeness and intimacy deserve under-
scoring for the special educational effects they have on faculty
and students alike.

Ralph Waldo Emerson once maintained that there was
ultimately no history: only biography. In an Emersonian sense,
the institutional records of these four colleges are not histories
so much as they are biographies—collections of life records left
by determined individual pioneers, dedicated preachers and
teachers, altruistic and egoistic men and women who possessed
a keen sense of posterity. A solitary individual's decision could
reap success for a college; one individual's failure could cause
a local calamity. However uneven their talents, all members of
the community influenced collective outcomes. Biographies recorded the collegiate pulse over time.

Berry College

Berry College, its campus nestled on a 28,000-acre rural
estate in northwest Georgia, makes the Emersonian point about
the significance of biography. The marks of its founder, Martha Berry (1866–1942), still give the campus a distinctive character. By all accounts, Martha Berry was a remarkably ener-

getic and able woman, single all her life and single-mindedly dedicated to the welfare of poor children and youth in her rural neighborhood, contagiously confident in herself and her educational mission, and, over all the years of her work, an educational pioneer who displayed great talent for reaching the hearts of youth and the pocketbooks of the charitable. Her notions of history and biography had Emersonian overtones. "I never can think of Berry as an institution," Martha Berry once reflected. "To me it is boys and girls learning lessons to fit them for life, to lift them into the glory of young manhood and young womanhood."[3]

The year 1902 is commonly given as the date of the founding of Berry College. In that year, Martha Berry opened a Boys' Industrial School, a boarding institution for local poor, rural white boys. The original charter for the school declared the Boys' Industrial School to be dedicated to "moral, industrial, and educational uplift," and it set afoot ideas that later became features of her college as well.[4] An early innovation that became a trademark of the institution was student uniforms. Blue shirts and overalls were worn by the boys. In 1909, when the Martha Berry School for Girls opened on the campus, the girls dressed in "long skirts, gathered waists, white collars and cuffs."[5]

Mandatory student work became another fixture of institutional development. Every uniformed student was expected to work on the campus according to a fixed weekly schedule in return for room and board and, in some cases, tuition as well. On Sundays—and regularly until Berry students had their own on-campus chapel—they went to church in nearby Rome, attending the services of a different denomination each week, in keeping with the school's avowedly nondenominational character.[6]

Martha Berry determined to minister to the mountain people. Their superstition and poverty, their ignorance of the Christian promise, and the meager prospects of their children's lives all moved Berry. Already, in 1900, she had opened a Sunday school for the mountain children in the nearby Possum Trot Church. Her Sunday school became a day school.

Soon she tucked a second, a third, and a fourth day school into the local hillsides. Berry, called "the Sunday Lady of Possum Trot," at first tried to stagger her schools' schedules and manage all four herself. She was grateful, however, when others came to her aid and joined her in teaching the Scriptures and helping children "learn how to use their talents and resources better." [7]

The founding of the Boys' Industrial School and the Martha Berry School for Girls came with Martha Berry's conviction that day schools could not compete with local attitudes, with parents who had no respect for "book larnin'" and who thought schooling a waste of time. No matter how diligent the teacher, day school students seemed to make only meager headway against such discouraging attitudes. Berry concluded that boarding schools were needed to provide effective instruction and supportive supervision around the clock.

The local poor students could scarcely be expected to pay cash for boarding school education—but they could be asked to offer their labor. To finance their learning, Berry students agreed to build their own dorms and classrooms, plant and harvest crops for the schools, build barns and outbuildings, care for the mules and farm machinery, raise poultry, tend and milk the cows, blaze trails and lay roads on the campus, cut trees for lumber and firewood, cook their own meals, do their own laundry—in short, Berry students agreed to make the institution as self-sufficient as possible. Spiritual development overlaid training in home economics, industrial and agricultural arts, animal husbandry, masonry (including brickmaking), carpentry, handicraft, weaving, and the three R's. Spires were placed on the barns, chicken coops, and other buildings as well as on the chapels "so the students would lift their eyes and hearts to God as they worked." [8]

To improve her services to the mountain people, Martha Berry gradually expanded her operation. In 1916, she opened a Mountain School for older boys. In 1917, the corporate charter was amended, with the legal name of the institution changed to the Berry Schools. Five years later, the Berry Schools gained accreditation from the Southern Association of Colleges and

Secondary Schools. In 1926, when she established Berry Junior College, she moved for the first time beyond the elementary and secondary levels. Two years later, Berry Junior College was also accredited by the Southern Association. Finally, in 1930, Berry College itself, the four-year institution, was established.[9] Martha Berry directed the college, as she had the other Berry schools, with those ideals that had inspired her pioneering venture at Possum Trot Church. When she died in 1942, a forty-year era in the history of Berry College closed.

An Interval of Uncertainties (1942–1956). Martha Berry's death clouded the prospects for Berry College for well over a decade. She had completely dominated the student body and faculty with the power of her presence. She had possessed the charisma of Leader; and the dominant majority of the Berry student bodies and faculty had grown comfortably dependent on her maternal leadership. With her, anything had seemed possible. After her death, no new leader could be found to replace her.

She left behind a college that had grown steadily in enrollment, but one that had remained only marginally collegiate in the eyes of important critics. The air of the lower schools clung to it. By 1939, she had obtained for her college the approval of the Georgia State Department of Education, the University of Georgia system, and the American Association of Colleges. But official accreditation eluded her. In 1936, the Southern Association of Colleges and Secondary Schools noted reproachfully that "much of the spirit of the high school" permeated Berry College. Too many students aspired to major in business, to the neglect of agriculture and industrial arts—fields in which the institution claimed to be a specialist.[10] Academic programs were considered unsteady and improperly integrated with professional studies. College accreditation had become increasingly important to institutional health—if not survival—but, because of the conditions at Berry College at the time of Martha Berry's death, collegiate accreditation eluded the college for another fifteen years.

Between 1942 and 1956, a total of six presidents came

and went in a sputtering attempt to guide and upgrade Berry College and its lower schools. It was a time of deep institutional rifts between those who clung devotedly to the lower school, *in loco parentis* pattern set by Martha Berry and those impatient to change, to do what must be done to bring the institution up to mid-twentieth-century academic and professional standards. In the near paralysis of the struggle between nostalgia and reform, it was ironically a time best suited for caretaker presidents. Those who tried to be activists were usually disappointed. Activists were likely to be found wanting for one or another reason and encouraged to resign—if they had not already found some pretext to leave.

Admittedly, however, much needed to be done. From the vantage point of presidential perspective, it was clear that nothing less than a change of the Berry image was needed. For more than half a century, the Berry Schools, including Berry College, had won a deservedly warm spot in the hearts of locals as a unique haven for poor children and youth. The uniforms, work expectations, and worship had set Berry apart. Among Martha Berry's many benefactors, Henry Ford had invested massively in the Berry Schools to promote just these features. Ford's praise had been limitless. "These are the greatest schools in the world," he declared.[11] Even before World War II, however, many of those noble features of the lower schools had somehow become impediments to Berry College. That which had won applause for the schools earned scorn for the college.

Formidable adversaries, both on and off campus, greeted each of the first six presidential successors to Martha Berry. Collectively, however, these administrators somehow helped maneuver Berry College to the brink of a new era. James Armour Lindsay (1946–1951), for example, introduced important changes during his problem-ridden tenure. He lifted faculty morale—and reduced the rate of faculty turnover—by forming the Faculty Council. Until that time, the faculty had been treated like lower school teachers, expected to obey directives, prepare course outlines, and submit their weekly lesson plans. For the first time in Berry's history, the faculty became, at least on paper, a formal part of the policy-making machinery. Lindsay laid the foundation of student government by creating the Inter-Society Council, composed of all presidents of all organized student groups. Faculty-student relations were improved in an atmosphere of increased active responsibility for both groups. Other "transitional" presidents in this period presided over the complicated decisions to exchange the traditional boys' bib overalls for blue shirts and denim jeans at a time when the overalls had become less an on-campus benefit than an off-campus stigma and object of ridicule in nearby Rome (1944), to establish a campus nursery school (1951), to close the historic Possum Trot Elementary School (1954), and to eliminate the pioneering Martha Berry School for Girls (1955).

But the shadows of uncertainty, frustration, and dependency lingered over the campus. After resigning as Berry president in 1955, Robert S. Lambert detected a crippling effect in even that most sacrosanct tradition: the student work requirement. He complained that

> Democracy is not practiced on campus. The students have little to say about conditions because they all work for their board and only about half of them pay very nominal tuition. Thus, although they are deeply appreciative for that opportunity and evince a marvelous loyalty, independent thinking is not encouraged.[12]

All the while, the stigma of collegiate nonaccreditation continued to bruise Berry morale. Fewer capable students sought admission to the college, and growing numbers of Berry students sought transfers to accredited institutions. Teacher education at Berry was increasingly threatened by the policy of some Georgia school systems to hire teachers only from accredited institutions. Accreditation was assiduously, even desperately sought. Under Martha Berry's first six presidential successors, Berry College failed to win accreditation. But the stamp of official acceptance had finally come within reach.

Accreditation and Beyond (1957–1970). "He built this institution from nothing." The faculty member was reminiscing about John Raney Bertrand, president of Berry College (1956–

1980).[13] Another faculty member, with a grumpy edge to his respect, remembered Bertrand as "an almost enlightened despot." In their own ways, both professors praised Bertrand for bringing an important season of solid administrative leadership back to Berry College. For nearly a quarter century, Bertrand presided with distinction over the fortunes of Berry College.

At the time of his arrival in late 1956, the years of curricular and programmatic upgrading at Berry College were about to bear fruit; the years of the college being caricatured as another incarnation of the Possum Trot School were about to be left behind. In 1957, a few months after John Bertrand assumed office, the Southern Association of Colleges and Secondary Schools accredited Berry College.

Within the campus community, accreditation brought a euphoric relief that added impressively to the affection and loyalty that Bertrand already enjoyed. It was clearly the time for him to open the floodgates and wash away the last remnants of the "old" Berry image. It was finally time, as one observant Berry graduate had long been urging, "to talk about what Berry is now instead of going over those worn-out stories of the early days."[14]

In 1962, a new Berry charter hinted broadly of the far-reaching changes that Bertrand and the trustees had in mind for Berry College. The new charter declared that the purpose of the college was to "offer educational programs to meet the needs of young men and women to increase their effectiveness as persons, citizens, practitioners of the arts, sciences, and professions . . . to aid worthy and qualified young people to educate themselves for necessary work." The charter further suggested "that the college and school should be Christian in spirit and democratic in procedure."[15] The prospects for novelty in the permissive, participatory, and open wording of the new charter were plain to all who knew Berry history.

Berry College was poised to become another type of institution. Until the early 1960s, Berry students had been southern, poor, white, rural, and Protestant. They boarded on campus and worked for their board and room, if not for their tuition as well. They were required to attend chapel services twice a week. They all wore uniforms. Under the hand of Bertrand and the Berry board of trustees, the new charter set the tone for breathtaking changes. In the year of the charter, uniforms were suddenly done away with, an honor system was expanded, and in other ways students were given more responsibility to manage their affairs. Students no longer needed to be southern, poor, rural, Protestant, or white. Students from affluent families were now able to gain admission. An equitable racial, religious, and regional mix of students was for the first time fostered.[16] Chapel attendance and the campus work program both became voluntary. Students who worked (and the vast majority continued to work, out of deference to tradition if not out of economic necessity) were now paid in cash instead of simply being given credit toward their college expenses.[17] In the wake of these innovations, the academic qualifications of Berry students also rose.

Faculty cohesiveness reached new heights in the 1960s. Building especially on the work of James Lindsay, Bertrand further empowered the faculty as well as students. There was a feeling, one professor recalled, "of everyone working together to make faculty governance work." The president hired able and aggressive new faculty members and gave department heads more autonomy. Faculty needs and curricular development began to depend more heavily than ever before on faculty judgment. It was a decade of tremendous transformation and growth. The letter as well as the spirit of the 1962 charter was fulfilled in the 1960s. The decade brought decentralized authority and student and faculty empowerment, with students and faculty alike credited with maturity of judgment. Across the board, as the 1970s dawned, Berry College had become more academically dynamic and "democratic in procedure."

The Emergence of the Modern College (1970 to the Present). During the first dozen years of his tenure, Bertrand had consistently encouraged the faculty and students to develop creative independence and increase their participation in the affairs of the institution. Campus morale ran high through

the 1960s. But a fiscal emergency in the early 1970s undermined many of the gains of the previous decade. According to
faculty recollections, Bertrand made a serious miscalculation
when faced with the crunching demands of austerity. He appeared to be reverting to an anachronistic authoritarian style.
Without involving the faculty to its satisfaction, his budget cuts
constricted the curriculum and services and adversely affected
faculty pay raises.

A belligerent mood infiltrated the faculty. A committee
was formed to seek legitimate input to the budgeting process
and to explore the possibilities of collective bargaining. Charges
of salary discrimination were raised. The National Labor Relations Board became involved. In his struggle with the faculty,
Bertrand finally saw even the student body turn on him. In a
1979 formal student ballot, Berry students resoundingly voted
"no confidence."

John Bertrand had promoted the development of an independently intelligent faculty and a more maturely able student body. He had presided over the transformation of Berry
College into a more dynamic and democratic institution. He
knew the words to the song of faculty-student involvement, but
according to his critics, he never learned the music. One faculty member mused, "I don't think he knew what to do with
what he'd created." Bertrand resigned in 1980, after a quarter
century of heralded accomplishments at Berry.

Since 1980, Gloria M. Shatto, a member of the board of
trustees that received Bertrand's resignation, has served as
president of Berry College.[18] The change in leadership restored campus stability, if not morale. A new emphasis on research and publication challenges the earlier, more exclusive
concentration on teaching and service. Faculty members are
now divided about the new accent on publishing. Some see it
as timely, if not overdue; others lament the passing of the days
when colleagues had time to help one another with pedagogical projects. "Now you almost have to publish," one dis-
gruntled faculty member observed. "But still you have to teach
fifteen hours as before."

The dramatic cumulative changes at Berry since World

War II have brought it ever closer in line with the nation's small independent colleges. Still, Berry College keeps a firm grip on its uniqueness. Teaching and service continue to be honored; and, in intangible ways, Berry remains loyal to its rich tradition. Students, faculty, and staff evince a special pride in the origins and stature of their college. Some still even recite the old motto—"Not to be ministered unto, but to minister"— although it no longer rings with the "missionary zeal" of the Martha Berry era.[19] Today, the more evocative mottos are the confident declarations that "Berry Works" and "Berry Cares." A remarkable sense of the union of heart, head, and hand has survived nearly a century of crises and triumphs.

Teacher Education at Berry College. From the outset at Berry, education had clear spiritual and utilitarian objectives. The ties among work, worship, and learning were exemplified daily in word, deed, and sign. The telling sight of stately spires on chicken coops and school buildings alike silently testified to the union of heart, head, and hand. In the early years at Berry, agricultural and mechanical trades, industrial arts, and home economics were the likeliest careers for Martha Berry's boys and girls. Even then, however, Berry graduates also served as teachers in the Berry Schools and other local mountain schools. Martha Berry promoted teacher education both as a worthy objective of schooling and because of its "multiplier effect." She—and her successors—recognized that a good Berry-educated teacher could reap benefits for Berry as well as for adjacent communities.[20]

Traditionally, teacher education at Berry College overshadowed other professional programs. In the beginning, teacher preparation shared the professional stage with agriculture and home economics. More recently, it has been in the fore, followed by business administration. Until the 1980s, approximately one-half of each Berry College graduating class became teachers. While the current percentage of teachers now hovers closer to one-quarter of each class, teacher education remains an undisputedly major program at Berry College.

From the beginning, the significance of teaching as a career was brought home to the Berry faculty and students in special ways. Berry was always "a teaching place." Along with the Boys' Industrial School and the Martha Berry School for Girls, elementary education continued in the Possum Trot School. In 1916, the Foundation School served the older boys. With the establishment of Berry College, the Berry Schools (attended by the children of Berry faculty and staff as well as local youngsters) encompassed learning from the first grade through the baccalaureate degree. While the Possum Trot Elementary School was discontinued in the 1950s, it was in effect replaced in 1977 by the Lilly Endowment Early Childhood Education Center, with a nursery school, kindergarten, and primary program. The Early Childhood Education Center later became the Berry College Laboratory School (kindergarten through fifth grade). In 1964, meanwhile, the boys' school became Berry Academy, covering the middle school and high school years. In 1971, the academy became coeducational, and it served as a college preparatory institution for another dozen years before closing its doors. Today, the Laboratory School continues as the on-campus link between Berry College and the world of schoolteaching.

The fortunes of professional education and liberal arts at Berry College are productively linked. But their relationship over time has not been static. It has been and continues to be dynamic. Until little more than half a century ago, vocational training in agriculture and mechanics joined teacher preparation in constricting the liberal arts idea to little more than the three R's. As Berry College rose to its feet, professionalism presided over a waning vocationalism, and a liberal arts ideal began to stir. In the late 1980s, the liberal arts approached stage center. "Yes, we seem headed in that direction now," said one arts and sciences professor. "You might say," he added with a smile, "that Berry is now at least a 'semi-liberal arts college.'" While emphases shift, many observers steadfastly see Berry College much as Martha Berry beheld it. For them, Berry College is not an institution at all. It is still students "learning needed lessons to fit them for life, to lift them into the glory of young manhood and young womanhood."

Mills College

The 1850s were inauspicious times for general educational advance in California, and they were downright inhospitable to women's educational interests.[21] The decade was scarred with crime and vigilantism. The Gold Rush was petering out, its free-spending, male-dominated transient population being overtaken by a more stable population of frugal, self-reliant families in towns and countrysides. The shift of the decade from transients to "permanent folks" was punctuated by lawlessness, social turbulence, and mid-decade depression. At the dawn of the decade, women composed only 8 percent of the California population, and there were no educational facilities exclusively for females. In the unsteady days of 1852, however, the Young Ladies' Seminary, which was to become Mills College, opened its doors.

Located in the pioneer town of Benicia, then the capital of California, the fledgling seminary was managed by an all-male board of trustees during its first three years.[22] Nonsectarian but Christian (and Protestant), the seminary opened in response to a sensed local need "for the higher education of the daughters of the pioneer families of California without the necessity of making the long ocean voyage to New York and severing family ties."[23]

From 1855 to 1865, the management of the Young Ladies' Seminary was in the capable hands of Mary Atkins. Featuring arts, letters, languages, ornamental studies, health and physical exercise, and moral and religious instruction, Atkins's quest for well-rounded educational attainments was to become a fixture of Mills College history. She gained a singular reputation as one who treated "her great family of scholars as if they were her own children—feeding them abundantly, providing clean dormitories for them, training them gently into habits of order and neatness. They reverence her very much as the early Holyoke scholars used to revere Mary Lyon, and love her as girls love their mothers," noted a local reporter.[24]

Atkins, a graduate of Oberlin College, the first coeducational college in America, not only nurtured the seminary for a decade, she also secured her own successors: Cyrus T. Mills and his wife, Susan T. Mills. In 1863, Atkins had visited the Punahou School in Honolulu to meet its directors, Dr. and Mrs. Mills, and urge them to visit Benicia. Two years later, impressed with "Miss Atkins's Seminary," the couple agreed to guide the fortunes of the institution. In 1865, the seminary for the education of young ladies became the Mills Seminary-College. One historian of Mills College, without wishing to minimize the work of the original trustees, noted that these three figures—Mary Atkins, Cyrus Mills, and Susan Mills—were the "spiritual founders" of Mills College.[25]

"Dr. Cyrus Taggart Mills and Lady," two experienced missionaries and educators, one from Williams, one from Mount Holyoke, slowly and consciously began to convert a successful secondary school into a women's college that could measure up to the best comparable institutions on the Atlantic seaboard and serve as a "Vassar of the Pacific Coast." In 1870, they moved Mills Seminary-College from the town of Benicia to its present location in the foothills of Alameda County, then a large rural acreage. Colleges at their best, after all, were bucolic. As one Mills student rhapsodized, it was unalloyed joy to be "transported from the limits of the circumscribed town to God's great, beautiful out-of-doors, to the freedom and joy of the hills."[26] In 1885, one year after Cyrus Mills died, the institution was chartered as Mills College. The first collegiate class graduated four years later.

The seminary lingered alongside the college through most of Susan Mills's remaining widowed years. She herself became president of Mills College in 1890, and for the next nineteen years she sustained and nourished many of the ideals that had guided her and her husband since their Punahou days nearly a half century earlier.

In 1909, the year of Susan Mills's resignation as president, the modern Mills College was aborning. By then, firm decisions had been made to close the seminary and put an end to college preparatory work.[27] The sense of the seamless robe of collegiate learning had been established. The ideals of liberal studies had begun to permeate the curriculum.

The Reinhardt Years. In 1916, Aurelia Henry Reinhardt succeeded Luella Clay Carson (1909–1914) and Hettie Belle Ege (1914–1916) as president of Mills College. A native of San Francisco, Reinhardt had done her undergraduate work at Berkeley before embarking on graduate studies at Yale and at Oxford University. The first California woman to receive a doctorate from Yale University, she served twenty-seven eventful years as president of Mills College, resigning in 1943. In 1917, as a hint of her ambitions for her institution, Reinhardt secured the admission of Mills College to the Association of American Universities and Colleges. Mills College also became a charter member of the American Council on Education.[28]

The profession of teaching ranked high with Reinhardt. Her notion of an ideal faculty included a devotion to teaching on their part and a supportive attitude toward Mills students who aspired to be schoolteachers. Indeed, she tried to inspire her faculty with a vision of liberal studies integrated with nearly every worthy work outside the campus. Traditional learning was at the center, located on the campus. But in her eyes, its vitality hinged on its connectedness with the issues of the world and the needs of independent maturity and socially responsible living.

Horace Mann and Mary Lyon, remembered by Reinhardt as "two of the most important prophets, preachers, and workers for education in our democracy, brought together at the same moment in time the needs of children and women."[29] Mann and Lyon had declared schooling to be an avenue to liberation for both groups. Under President Reinhardt, Mills College continued that tradition of liberation.

President Reinhardt wanted her faculty and students to see educated women as more than the keys to the survival of the United States as a democracy. She maintained that all of humanity needs "women, educated women, women who vote, women prepared for a profession, but," she added, the human family also "needs women, as comrades, wives, mothers of the race." With so many essential roles to play, the educated woman is "an incalculable influence if she will have it so." She challenged her Mills colleagues to give its women the Promethean gifts of fire and light. Men had already felt the pain and the joy of Prometheus, the "wrath and violence" that accompanied his gifts of fire and light. So, too, "woman feels her new powers and possibilities with the pain of ineptitude, uncertainty, and misgiving." But unlike man, Reinhardt declared, "She shall learn to use them some future day without the payment of wrath and violence."[30]

No exclusionary curricular purist, Reinhardt was avowedly "progressive" and open to new subjects of study. In adding new options for Mills students, she insisted only that they meet three conditions. New subjects could qualify if they could be related to "existing departments of college study," to the "emerging professional demands of the modern woman," and to the aim of improving the "preparatory schools of the country." The robe of learning could grow; but it must remain without divisive seams. Reinhardt charged all members of the Mills community to honor one another as mutually supportive friends of learning.[31]

The study of education prospered under Reinhardt. She placed herself at the head of the Department of Education and formed a School of Education made up of representatives from "all departments which offer work contributing to the training of teachers for the public elementary and high schools."[32] In the 1920s, the *Mills College Catalogue* featured the School of Education as if it were central to the mission of the institution. In that decade, too, summer school for teachers began to be a regular feature of each academic year. Reinhardt herself once enrolled as a student and attended the teachers' classes faithfully.[33] Soon general and, as Reinhardt beheld them, "golden" summer sessions were operational.

Having surrounded herself with able and independent faculty members, Reinhardt found that her sense of the future of Mills College did not always win uncritical faculty acceptance on the campus. She preferred to call her faculty members "colleagues" and professed to work cooperatively with them, but as her biographer put it, "the memories of relations between the executive and the teaching force are highly contradictory."[34] Her agenda was not always shared by her faculty. Reinhardt won a few and lost a few. She would have preferred, for example, to continue the practice of mandatory chapel. But in 1933, she acquiesced and let chapel become a voluntary activity.

At other times, in the face of defiance, the resourceful Reinhardt could find ways to hold to her course. The Department of Child Development, established in 1930, stands as a case in point. Reinhardt had wanted the Departments of Education and Psychology to work together to develop a synthesis of material on physical, mental, and social development; and she further urged the department faculties to incorporate the Nursery School (or Children's School, as it became popularly known) as part of their synthesis. But she could get the departments neither to cooperate with one another on her project nor to integrate. Even interdepartmental cooperation with the Children's School had been elusive. For a while, the school was housed in Education, then in Psychology.[35]

Convinced that such a developmental synthesis was imperative for the Mills education program, Reinhardt bypassed the Departments of Education and Psychology. She hired Lovisa C. Wagoner away from Vassar and had her establish a Department of Child Development to synthesize developmental material. Wagoner, who had received her doctorate at Iowa and had taught at Berea before going to Vassar, was also placed in charge of the Nursery School. Unable to gain departmental cooperation, Reinhardt in this instance simply created a new department.[36]

Wagoner's first years as head of the Department of Child Development were rocky. Neither she nor her department was hospitably received by the Departments of Education and Psychology; but she built her department steadily over a score of years and, with dedicated ability and an amiable facade, overcame the inevitable jealousies and resentments. Psychology remained rather aloof from the new enterprise, preferring the cadence of its own drummers; but Education finally became cooperative with Child Development when the state of California decided to offer early childhood credentials. The first nursery school diplomas were announced in the 1933–34 academic year.

Teachers Made, Teachers Born. The Children's School soon came to epitomize the best in teacher preparation at Mills College. To the delight of parents, faculty, and observers, children learned joyfully through spontaneous play in programs "based on profound respect for, and understanding of, the way children naturally develop and learn."[37] The Children's School and its trinity of concerns for physical, mental, and social development thus became a major public relations feature for Mills College. It loosened donor purse strings, and no one wanted it hindered or impeded. Edna Mitchell, former head of the Department of Education, astutely noted, "When people see the children and the Children's School it makes an enormous difference in how they feel about Mills College. A warmth, affection, and new interest in the campus almost inevitably appear."[38] Faculty members come in and just "hang around," one professor observed. "If there are complaints, it's that the hours are too short. With the art program, the string quartets, and other quality activities the Children's School is pretty heady stuff!" In 1988, members of the Music Department (with three of their children in the school) put together a fund-raising music program for the Children's School.

The school survived its share of near disasters; and, under the leadership of Frances Ruth Armstrong, it gained firm footing. Through the critical first days of uncertainty, then during the long years of dislocations and organizational juggling after Wagoner's retirement, the Children's School under Armstrong's direction became a "steadying force" on the campus. Armstrong, an English major who came to Mills as a student and stayed to bring sustained applause to the Children's School for nearly a quarter century, ably directed the school from 1952 (even when Kraemer was its titular head) to 1974. "She took the state-required Education courses, not because she needed them, but just to get legitimated," one colleague recalled wryly, adding, "She was the kind of teacher who is born, not made."

In the late 1980s, the Children's School remained a central feature of the Department of Education and a public relations gem, along with a Mills College/Oakland Unified School District Teacher Training Center and Demonstration School at John Swett Elementary School in Oakland.[39]

Teacher Preparation at Mills College. Teacher preparation, from the days of Susan Mills (1890–1909) to the presidency of Mary Metz (1981–1990), has been an unquestionably important part of the Mills College program. Modest programs for limited teaching opportunities sufficed at first; but by the late 1980s, Mills College prepared teachers for every level from early childhood through the community college. Teacher preparation, however, has not been without its campus detractors. Members of the college faculty "have at times shown their scorn for educationists," one arts and sciences professor admitted.

Once again, as in the case of Berry College, size worked in the interests of education. As one professor noted, "Mills is manageable. Things are on a human scale here." During the late 1960s and early 1970s, size had played a major role in keeping Mills College a "haven of serenity" in the shadow of the riot-riddled Berkeleys of America.[40]

Size makes possible a familiarity of the sort that enables members of the education faculty to be measured by their personal merits. The phenomenon of size seems to be centrally at work, separating professors from their specialties, weighing specialties in one set of scales and individual worth in another set. "One knows the gossip about every department in a place this size," laughed one professor. And the gossip about the Department of Education is good news.

The Mills education programs remind one anew of the incalculable debt that twentieth-century educational reform owes to innovative spirits at small private institutions. Faculty members exude a confidence in their ability to improvise, to experiment, to do what makes sense for teachers-to-be. They are demonstrably proactive. And they are supported and appreciated by a college that smiles on teachers and frowns on educationists.

Coe College

The Midwest—American heartland. To this region, nourished by the Mississippi River and its tributaries, settlers came from widely differing origins to fashion a unique kinship of experiences. Season by season, migrants and immigrants learned the rituals of survival in their ever unpredictable and sometimes hostile land. They developed a deep loyalty to their adopted region, but one fractured at critical intervals by an unshakable pride in diverse origins and faiths. In adapting their local and territorial identities to the fixed demands of the plains, they fashioned the bonds of a peculiar unity. Midwesterners understood and took pride in their distinctiveness.

Willa Cather was one of those who saw midwesterners as a breed apart. Herself a child of the plains, she could feel the rumbling tempo of the land even through the window of a train as it flashed across the state of Iowa. From the vantage of an observation car seat, she and a companion watched Iowa's

> never-ending miles of ripe wheat . . . country
> towns and bright-flowered pastures and oak groves
> wilting in the sun. . . . The dust and heat, the
> burning wind, reminded us of many things. We
> were talking about what it is like to spend one's
> childhood in little towns like these, buried in wheat
> and corn, under stimulating extremes of climate:
> burning summers when the world lies green and
> billowy beneath a brilliant sky, when one is fairly
> stifled in vegetation, in the colour and smell of
> strong weeds and heavy harvests; blustery winters
> with little snow, when the whole country is stripped
> bare and grey as sheet-iron. We agreed that no
> one who had not grown up in a little prairie town

could know anything about it. It was a kind of freemasonry, we said.[41]

The great plains country generated a "personal passion" that no outsider could experience. The "passion" wore many faces in Iowa. Politicians as different as Herbert Hoover and Henry Wallace and crowd pleasers as diverse as Buffalo Bill Cody and Billy Sunday claimed Iowa as home. The enigmatic painting *American Gothic* was the plains-inspired work of Iowan Grant Wood. Germans, Scandinavians, and Bohemians, Catholics, Lutherans, and Presbyterians—along with other and less prominent communal groups of Iowa settlers—found something of Cather's passion there. Their towns and grain mills rose as testaments to the present; their churches and schools lent a sense of posterity.

But successful institution building required more than the passion of the plains. Coe College, in Cedar Rapids, demonstrated the point. Coe spent its childhood as an institutional waif in a land where the temperature might shift fifty degrees or more in a day, at a time when enthusiasm for educational institutions blew hot one moment, cold the next. Desperate to keep or find benefactors, the waif unabashedly changed its name time and again. From its first days in 1851, it answered to the name of the Williston Jones School, the School for the Prophets, Cedar Rapids Collegiate Institute, Parsons Seminary, and Coe Collegiate Institute. Thirty years later, in 1881, it stood on wobbly but determined legs as Coe College. In an era when major American church groups were busily christening more than 500 educational institutions across the land, Coe had been one of their scrawny Presbyterian gamins. But while more than 80 percent of the ill-conceived new institutions died in infancy, Coe endured. It learned the laws of survival on the plains. It knew how to plead for alms that it might continue its quest of Veritas Virtusque—"Truth and Moral Excellence." A generation of financial woes had given young Coe College an ingenuous candor and a vital feistiness to match its lofty vision. That blend of traits proved essential.

Coe's Beginnings. In 1851, the original cradle of Coe College was a Presbyterian parsonage in Cedar Rapids. The Reverend Williston Jones in that year dedicated his parlor to the preparation of a small band of young men for eastern seminary studies. But his boys needed money as sorely as learning if they hoped to go "back East." So in 1853, Jones became a fund raiser, traveling to New York to seek help from congregations in a state noted for religious enthusiasms. At one church fund raiser, Daniel Coe, a Catskill farmer, sat in a pew listening to Jones plead for $1,500 in student aid. After the service, Coe offered to give Jones money if he would start an Iowa seminary of his own with the money rather than use it to ship lads off to eastern institutions. Coe, "an unlettered mountain deacon," added two conditions to his gift. He stipulated that Jones was to buy a farm to provide work that could offer self-support to Iowa's "poor pious boys." He also insisted that the new institution be "made available for the education of females as well as males."[42]

By the time of the Coe donation, the Williston Jones School, sometimes called the School for the Prophets, had already become the Cedar Rapids Collegiate Institute. In 1852, Knox College had sent David Blakely to take charge of the Jones school and transfer the classes from the Jones parsonage to the local Presbyterian church building, changing the school's name in the process. When Jones returned with the good news of Coe's largess, the trustees accepted Coe's conditions and further agreed that "The teachers to be Employed shall possess Evangelical piety; and the reading of the Sacred Scriptures and prayer shall be regarded as one of the daily Exercises of the Institute; and the Students shall be Enjoined to attend some Church on the Sabbath."[43]

Then silence fell. The board failed to obtain a suitable site. Cedar Rapids Collegiate Institute suspended operations. There was no money to be had. A "panic" rumbled through the region in 1857. An even greater threat proved to be the popular new high school in Cedar Rapids, completed in that same year. The townspeople demonstrably favored their high

school over the competing secondary-level Presbyterian institute. In 1859, the railroad came to Cedar Rapids, further
draining off whatever surplus capital that the institute might
have gained. Then the Civil War diverted potential backers'
attention from the languishing school. The Cedar Rapids Collegiate Institute lived only on paper. It continued to be a corporate entity, and it continued to clutch the Daniel Coe donation. But it was a phantom institute.

In 1866, rising at the chance to get some of the Lewis B.
Parsons estate money, the trustees renamed the Cedar Rapids
Collegiate Institute. It became Parsons Seminary. Still actually
an academy, the coeducational seminary announced its aim to
give students "a thorough education in all branches of study
both solid and ornamental. Religious or biblical (not sectarian)
instruction will occupy a prominent place."[44] But many sub-
scribers were delinquent with their promises. Even the Iowa
City presbytery reneged on its promises. The coveted "Parsons
Legacy" never materialized. Once again the enterprise failed.
The seminary closed after sputtering through 1870.

In 1875, Daniel Coe indirectly provided a second inspi-
ration to the beleaguered Iowa institution. His son-in-law came
to reclaim the apparently defaulted Coe donation. His presence bestirred the presbytery as nothing before had, for by
now the money had been spent. Land had been acquired and
improvements begun. Half a building, called "Main Hall," stood
on eighty acres of Coe-money property near Cedar Rapids.
Feeling the threat posed by Coe's son-in-law, the presbytery
prompted the trustees to try again to open a "school of high
order," promising not to renege again. It did not take the
trustees long to decide that they would rename their venture
after Daniel Coe. In 1875, the Coe Collegiate Institute came
into being.

For six years, the Coe Collegiate Institute survived as a
combined secondary school and college. Under the direction
of Robert A. Condit, 40 pupils—some of them no more than
eight years old—attended the institute the first year. Soon a
department of "technology" was being planned, along with a

kindergarten; and a conservatory of music actually opened. In 1877, the "Academic Department" reported 113 students, and the "Department of Music" counted 78 students.

In 1879, the first graduates received diplomas. It was clear by then that Coe Collegiate Institute should become a college. The growth of public schools called for a college in the region, not another preparatory school. The Iowa synod reluctantly agreed to support a Coe College "on the seemingly impossible condition that the . . . Institute be presented to the synod completely free of debt." T. M. Sinclair, a local industrialist who at that time was vice-president of the institute, stunned the synod by personally liquidating the debt. In 1881, Coe College was incorporated.[45]

The Quest for an Academic Agenda. The early presidents of Coe College operated without a clear educational philosophy. They steadfastly wanted learning to be moral. They also wanted Coe to survive. Without being unduly limited by a precisely defined mission, the presidents could try novel curricular goals from time to time. President Marshall thus linked public relations to the awarding of the Ph.D. degree. In 1893 and 1894, six prominent local men were so honored. The degree program suddenly ended. In 1895, still under Marshall, Coe awarded the bachelor's degree in civil engineering—to one student. For a few years, there was a bachelor's degree in philosophy.

In the twentieth century, local pressures increased to make the college more "practical." The Cedar Rapids press led in the cry for colleges to offer business, mechanical, and technical courses. Coe president William Wilberforce Smith (1905–1908) liked what he heard. He established a Department of Education in 1906. But his tenure was shortened by his unpopular interest in converting Coe into a junior college. His successor, John A. Marquis (1909–1920), fared much better by trying to combine the liberal arts collegiate model with the technical school model. He ushered in an era of expansion, groundbreaking, and construction and, in 1919, presided over the absorption of nearby Leander Clark and Western Colleges into Coe College.[46] When he became president in 1909, Coe had twenty-two faculty members; when he left in 1920, Coe had sixty-two faculty members teaching nearly 600 regular college students. He established a Domestic Science Department and, in 1913, gained accreditation from the North Central Association of Colleges and Secondary Schools, an accreditation that has been continuous. In the same year, he oversaw the final demise of the academy preparatory school.[47] Coe was no longer in the secondary school business.

Marquis was the answer to the dream of the Cedar Rapids press. He encouraged vocational courses at Coe "wherever he could," even seeking an extension division to provide "technical and scientific subjects for men working in factories and stores." The training of athletic coaches became one of his most enduringly popular programs. He wanted and got a form of higher education that was "useful and practical" during his tenure.[48]

It was Harry Morehouse Gage (1920–1941) who first brought to Coe College an articulate sense of the aims of a liberal arts college. He worked to capitalize on Coe's religious heritage by linking it with the tradition of liberal studies and developing a faculty made of "genuine scholars and able teachers." President Gage told that Board in 1925: "The mission of Coe is intellectual and spiritual. . . . No complications of educational problems, no additions of vocational studies . . . no pre-vocational emphasis should . . . divert us from this purpose of a liberal arts college."[49] Gage did not try to undo the vocationalisms at Coe so much as he worked to restore a respected, secure place for the humanities. He also gained a reputation as one who was fiercely loyal to his faculty. The tensions between a president who wants a full dormitory and a faculty that wants higher academic standards were largely foreign to Coe during the years of Gage's presidency. He improved faculty quality with careful appointments, developed a sabbatical leave policy, and gained trustee approval to rule that Coe teachers must have some postbaccalaureate training. Still, in 1940, as Gage entered his last year at Coe, only eighteen of sixty-three faculty members held the Ph.D. degree. But the quality of instruction across the campus won plaudits. Through all his years at Coe, Gage offered his faculty what one of its members called a "sheltering presence." Even in the depths of the Depression, Gage sustained an ideal of "our Coe Family" that eased the pain of salary cuts.

Resigning in 1941 to become president of Lindenwood College for Women in suburban St. Louis, Gage was remembered as "one of the most consistently capable educators to serve the college."[50] He retired from Lindenwood in 1946 and returned to live in Cedar Rapids. No one could have anticipated it at the time, but the Coe faculty would once again profit from Gage's "sheltering presence."

The next seventeen years at Coe saw a parade of four acting presidents and four presidents. Coe once again became buffeted by ideological crosscurrents. Many who experienced the 1950s at Coe remember the decade as the nadir of the institution in the modern era.

By 1960, however, the institution seemed healthier than ever before. The first critical step to rejuvenation came when the trustees successfully implored Harry Morehouse Gage, who was living in retirement in Cedar Rapids, to serve as acting president until a permanent appointment could be made. For two years, Gage ministered to the faculty, restored amicable internal relations with the trustees, and settled the bewildered student body. A former chair of the board of trustees recalled Gage's role as pivotal, one that "no other man could have filled, whatever his executive capabilities. What was needed at that moment was a calm, experienced pilot to whom the board, the faculty, student body and alumni could look with complete confidence and assurance that a sure course would be steered through disturbed waters. How well he filled that position needs no words of description."[51] One professor put it more simply; "Gage saved Coe College."

Another "golden age" returned with the presidency of Joseph E. McCabe (1958–1970). The Coe collegiate fortunes, on a roller coaster since the days of Daniel Coe's donation, had survived the devastations of the 1950s. In the Gage-McCabe years, Coe's fortunes reached a new lofty peak. Next to Gage, said one appreciative professor, "McCabe was the greatest thing to happen to Coe." Said another, "He brought class to Coe" and restored its present liberal arts cast. McCabe eliminated courses in typing and bookkeeping and oversaw the establishment of a standard program in business administration. Under his leadership, a foreign language requirement for graduation was reestablished. College Board examinations were required for admission. McCabe turned Coe back toward the liberal arts and applied liberal arts and scuttled the misguided plans of the 1950s for job training at Coe.[52] He helped Coe recover, as he put it, from the "institutional amnesia" that had for so long separated the college from its history and purpose.[53]

But his reforms scarcely survived his tenure. Infidelity to the liberal arts tradition began anew in the 1970s when liberal arts requirements were waived. Students at Coe College picked a major and amassed credits. Beyond that, free choice reigned. Majors had no upper limits, and prerequisites were largely abandoned. Overspecialization and premature specialization ran unchecked for over a decade. "At the time we thought it was right to let eighteen-year-olds pick their own curriculum," said one professor, adding ruefully, "but we made a mistake." In the 1980s came the return of what a faculty member called "a semblance of the liberal arts tradition." Along with the restoration of "order," Coe also underwent a reduction in force. By the late 1980s, the college seemed once again to have survived through "interesting times." But references to the need for more "creative retrenchments" continued.

The Place of Teacher Preparation. Since the late nineteenth century, Coe College has prepared students for elementary and secondary teaching. Teacher preparation at Coe "has enjoyed a history almost as old as the college itself."[54] Pedagogy found its first home as part of the Department of Philosophy and Political Science as an applied liberal art. Courses in pedagogy were offered, first, "as a part of the regular collegiate work equal in interest and value to the collateral courses in other departments," and, second, they were intended "to present a practical study of the history and science of education for such students as may intend entering the teacher's profession."[55] By academic year 1899–1900, the college catalogue noted that its courses in pedagogy enabled students to gain certificates and diplomas from the state board of examiners. At the same time, Coe reaffirmed its belief "that the History and Science of Education is worthy of the same intelligent study that is accorded to other subjects found in the curriculum."[56]

When the Department of Education was established in 1906, the task of teacher preparation attained an independent identity. In 1928, under C. Harve Geiger's hand, formal practice teaching was inaugurated. Geiger, then a newly appointed professor of education and psychology, secured the cooperation of "members of the Cedar Rapids public school system" to establish supervised practice teaching as part of the Coe program.[57]

In principle, the Coe faculty has consistently united the liberal arts with teacher preparation courses. A Coe College Teacher Education Committee, composed of faculty from representative liberal arts departments and the Department of Education, symbolizes the partnership approach. The Teacher Education Committee, along with the Education faculty, the college administration, and the Academic Policies Committee, maintains an all-campus interest in teacher preparation. No other professional programs at Coe are so intimately linked to the tradition of arts and sciences. Music, business administration, and physical education are under less thorough cooperative oversight.

Personality, individual agency, charisma—whatever one might call a system in which a program is known by the person who runs it—has always been a critical consideration at Coe College. Over the years, education faculty members generally enjoyed student trust and prestige across the campus. By the late 1960s, education was the largest department on the campus.

Business administration now produces the most student credit hours at Coe. Its popularity with students deeply concerns many faculty, some of whom continue to fear a return to the mentality of the 1950s at Coe. The business program is considered strong. Those who are troubled by it seem not to be embarrassed by it. Ultimately, as one of the more pragmatically resentful professors sighed, "it's the hand that feeds us." High enrollments in a given professional program might not, in and of themselves, earn prestige across the college faculty community; but to earn credit for institutional solvency has its compensations.

None of the interviewed arts and sciences faculty members chose to comment on the historic insecurity of the liberal arts tradition itself at Coe. Nor did they mention their constituency. Coe College, once called a "poor man's college," has always served a city and region of widely diverse peoples. Roughly nine out of ten Coe students received financial aid in the late 1980s. In 1986, family income of Coe students averaged approximately $25,000.[58]

Coe students and their families are fairly evenly divided between those who would prefer Coe to be more academic and those who want economic practicality above all else. In 1963, a Danforth Foundation committee reported on a persistent Coe demographic, citing a sharp split between those students whose values match those of the nation's leading liberal arts colleges and those students whose traits run in other directions.[59]

Joseph McCabe tended to agree with the Danforth report. "One very good thing for Coe came out of the Great Depression in the early thirties," McCabe declared in his memoirs. "Sons and daughters of the leading families in town attended Coe, along with students from the less favored classes. Czechs, whose parents were mostly Democrats, were now in college with students whose parents ran the town, and were for the most part Republicans. This heady mix of kolaches and blue stockings is typically Cedar Rapids and typically Coe."[60] It was a mix of the sort that was unlikely to permit any clear victor in the competition between liberal and technical studies. It produced, rather, a dynamic relationship between career development and the ideals of lifelong learning, a productive relationship, however nettlesome it might have been to the partisan educator.

The unique student-faculty mix of the Coe community provides a haven for its teacher educators against an outside world seemingly inclined to treat the peculiar abilities of small colleges as nonexistent.

Bucknell University

Nineteenth-century church leaders routinely became educational reformers without inviting the advice of the business-minded. In pre–Civil War America, various denominational groups regularly kept their frenzied college-building enthusiasms beyond the reach of cautious bookkeepers. Between 1800 and the Civil War, the leading Protestant denominations set up hundreds of new colleges and simply charged them on their Virtue cards. Inspired church leaders set the gospel-spreading institution afoot; thereafter, they commonly left it to God (and other benefactors yet to be identified) to figure out how to sustain their new school. Through it all, an implicit assurance prevailed that religious conviction promised economic solvency.

Church-related colleges formed in the early nineteenth century had a straightforward and dramatic mission: to "make America completely Christian." The Baptists, along with especially the Methodist Episcopalians and the Presbyterians, enthusiastically endorsed this mission. According to Baptist perceptions, new colleges would produce educated Baptist ministers to guide the established eastern states, save the western hinterlands, fill the foreign mission fields, and, in the process, ensure a better education for their own children. New colleges were "intended to be a great Baptist enterprise—of the Baptists, by the Baptists, but, happily, not exclusively for the Baptists."[61] All Christians would benefit. Baptist clergymen gave their congregations a vision of worldwide conversions led by American Protestants. In return, congregations gave the clergymen the seed money.

When their unchecked zeal for college building did occasionally pay a handsome return, it seemed further to blur distinctions between an inspired desire to do good and economic know-how. As Finley Peter Dunne's fictitious Mr. Dooley told Mr. Hennessy, "Fortchnitly, Hinnissy, a rayformer is seldom a business man. He thinks he is, but business men know diff'rent. They know what he is. He thinks business and honesty is th' same thing. He does indeed. He's got thim mixed because they dhress alike." In the confusion of sincerity with solvency, the casualty rate for colleges built by the church reformers ran high. But church leaders, unlike business leaders, could fix their attention on the nobility of striving, win or lose. Temporal failures in Christian service could make deferred rewards all the sweeter. According to Mr. Dooley, even those church-related colleges that fell victim to the vagaries of the frontier brought welcome news to the church reformers. "Nawthin' th' clargy likes so much as a sad fact," said Dooley.[62]

Whatever the case, those church-inspired institutions that survived became happy facts and made lasting contributions to higher learning in America. One such survivor was Coe College, which we have already considered. Another was the University at Lewisburg, later to become Bucknell University.

The Baptists and the University at Lewisburg. On February 5, 1846, the University at Lewisburg, in Pennsylvania, became the 100th college chartered in the United States. Located on a Lewisburg knoll in the fertile Susquehanna River Valley, the new school was called a "university" to reflect the grandeur of Baptist dreams for the school. It came into being as part of a denominational impulse that included setting up Sunday schools, distributing Bibles, and spreading a literature of Baptist and Protestant Christianity across the land.

Stephen William Taylor resigned his faculty position at Hamilton College in New York to direct the fortunes of the new university for its first five years. Without the title of president, it was nonetheless he who defined the character of the institution, drafted its first charter, established its first curriculum and textbooks for a "classical program," wrote its first bylaws, and shelved the first books in its library. He brought piety and learning to bear on the University at Lewisburg before returning to New York to become president of another Baptist institution, Madison University (the forerunner of Colgate). A century later, an observer of Bucknell's long career concluded that without Taylor, "it is almost certain that our University would never have existed."[63]

In 1851, Howard Malcom (1851–1857) became the first president of the university. One year later, he established the Female Institute as part of the university. His overall plans were in general agreement with the expressed views of Francis Wayland, then president of Brown University and the nation's leading Baptist educator. As did Wayland, Malcom rejected the notion of education as an elitist undertaking, calling it an enterprise open to all. Again as did Wayland, Malcom rejected the curricular limits called for in the Yale Report of 1828 and found more utility in the University of Virginia's Rockfish Gap Report (1818).

Through the 1850s, the university seemed off to a promising start. Then civil war threatened to undo the gains of more than a decade. Inflation brought financial distress. There was reasonable concern about the likelihood of a Confederate Army invasion of the Susquehanna Valley. (The university class of 1863 was involved in the Union military to the extent that there was talk of canceling the commencement exercises that year, but a sufficient number of the university's young men returned to Lewisburg in time for the rite to proceed as planned.) By the war's end, the university had an endowment but wallowed in financial embarrassment.

In 1867, the University at Lewisburg made a momentous decision to divest itself of its Department of Theology. Lewisburg and Crozier Theological Seminary, in nearby Upland, agreed that Crozier would thenceforth provide the program of theological studies for both institutions. Thereafter, under the presidency of Justin Rolph Loomis (1858–1879), the University at Lewisburg determinedly set its face against professional courses. In 1869, Loomis did establish a "Preparatory Department" to offer a two-year course leading to admission to the Classical Program of the institution and an "English Academy" to prepare students "either for admission to the Scientific Program of the College or for teaching in the public schools." (At a time before methodological instruction in pedagogy had become a fixture of preservice education, Loomis did not think of teacher preparation as professional training.) Although a graduate of Brown University, Loomis proved to be no fan of Francis Wayland and "narrow utility." He was pleased to declare, in 1876, that his university had "resisted the temptation to organize professional schools, which [might] be entered with very little preparatory study."[64]

The cumulative effects of war, the ideas of Francis Wayland, the utilitarian impact of the Morrill Act, and Charles Eliot's "elective plan" at Harvard took their toll on the Lewisburg school under Loomis's hand. In the 1870s, the enrollment picture clouded. The college, the preparatory and academic departments, and the Female Institute all suffered. By 1879, the college had skidded from seventy-four students to forty-four, the preparatory and academic departments fell from sixty-four to twenty-four, and the Female Institute slipped from ninety-eight to sixty-five. Insistent voices began to call for a "New Education" at the institution.

Building Bucknell University. When David Jayne Hill (1879–1888) became president, a new era, if not a new education, began at the Lewisburg school. Himself cast in the Loomis mold, Hill resisted calls for an "elective system" at the University at Lewisburg, standing closer to the examples of Yale and Princeton. He preferred an "old" education. But the new era came when Hill secured a handsome pledge from a former trustee, William Bucknell, of Philadelphia. In 1881, Bucknell agreed to give the institution $50,000 on a matching-pledge basis provided that the governing structure of the institution would be reorganized. Reorganization and the raising of the matching funds elevated the university from the pit of insolvency once again. One year later, Bucknell became chair of the board of trustees and "paterfamilias" of the university. He placed $100,000 in the general fund and established a $25,000 kitty for scholarships and prizes. Buildings rose at his bidding: a chapel, an observatory, the East Hall, a chemical and physical laboratory, and other structures. In 1888, the University at Lewisburg was renamed. Bucknell University came into being.

The "founding years" at Bucknell University were synonymous with the presidency of John Howard Harris (1889–
1919). Major outlines of the modern Bucknell University were
drawn in the Harris years. Harris skillfully linked the original
ideals of the University at Lewisburg with the aims of the modern Bucknell University. He was a striking figure, an innovator
who all the while clung to the style of the old-school administrator, combining the roles of "pastor, teacher, administrator,
and counselor acting *in loco parentis.*"[65]

By the early twentieth century, swelling enrollments of
Bucknell students also had several new professional options.
They could elect to work for a bachelor of science degree and
escape the classical language requirement. They could enroll
in a Department of Law or a Department of Medicine. Teacher
preparation continued to be a prominently featured choice,
reaching independent status as a Department of Education in
1916. Home economics was launched in 1912, and five years
later, a four-year program led to the bachelor of science degree in "household economics." Engineering, meanwhile, became the brightest star in the Bucknell galaxy of professional
programs. By 1902, Bucknell offered a four-year program
leading to the baccalaureate in civil engineering. Over the next
seven years, in addition to civil engineering, students could elect
chemical engineering, electrical engineering, and mechanical
engineering.

During the presidency of Emory William Hunt (1919–
1931), Bucknell took the Harris curriculum on a shakedown
cruise and reassessed some collegiate professional options. Not
all of Harris's innovations endured. Law and home economics
lost departmental status. Departments of physical education and
psychology came into being. Summer school became a firmly
rooted fixture, dominated by courses for teachers and teachers-to-be, and at first considered "just as revolutionary" as the
Department of Education.[66] Then, in the gathering gloom of
the Depression, Homer Price Rainey (1931–1935) reorganized
the faculty and took drastic steps to keep Bucknell afloat in the
tides of rising debts and declining income.

In 1933, Bucknell University opened Bucknell Junior

College in nearby Wilkes-Barre. Intended to be an integral part of Bucknell, the new junior college was expected to be self-supporting while feeding upper-division students into the main campus at Lewisburg. On paper, it looked like a source of black ink for the parent institution. A cadre of members of the Bucknell faculty was dispatched to the new school, where the professors taught lower-division courses and recruited new students for Bucknell. The set-up costs provoked financial headaches, but the junior college soon began to make Rainey's judgment look sound. Before long, indeed, the new college was offering four years of collegiate work. In 1947, having served well beyond its original purpose as a Depression measure to strengthen Bucknell, the one-time junior college was chartered as Wilkes College and given its independence.

Arnaud C. Marts (1935–1945) succeeded to the presidency of Bucknell and, without moving to Lewisburg in this period, served as a fine-tuner of a faculty-dominated institution. He commuted for a decade. "Marts would spend about one day a week on the campus," as one professor recalled. "He whisked in on Wednesdays for chapel, faculty meetings, and other incidental business, then left. Somehow, it all worked remarkably well!" Few remember ever seeing Marts's wife. One professor asserted flatly, "Marts's wife never did come to Bucknell!"[67] (But Phi Beta Kappa did. In 1940, a chapter opened on the Bucknell campus.) Marts's low-profile but popular administration was accompanied by a carefully groomed enhancement of faculty and departmental leadership. When authorized to fill vacancies, for example, it was the departments that hired new faculty, not the trustees or the president. A decentralized approach to university governance gained a foothold and developed faculty initiative. Marts gained a reputation as a master of the art of delegating authority.

After a decade of decentralized operations, or "splendid anarchy," as one faculty member thought of it, the 1950s called out for collective stocktaking. President Merle M. Odgers (1954–1964) urged his faculty colleagues to realize that they had reached a historical "traffic circle." Odgers saw four roads open to Bucknell. First, the institution could make a run at the pace-setting urban universities. Bucknell could stress multiversity growth, add more autonomous schools, and ape the major trend of the decade. Second, Bucknell could grow without any institutional direction, just following the market trends of the moment. "In this type of institution, for example," Odgers observed, "the enrollment for a degree in Commerce and Finance outstrips the number enrolled for a Bachelor of Arts degree." A third road would lead the institution back to a position of academic purism in which it divested itself of all professional training and featured only the arts and sciences. There was also a fourth road—the one that Odgers preferred. His choice superficially appeared "to resemble the third and it does offer all of the advantages of the third without its disadvantages." The fourth road involved some professionalism while maintaining the centrality of the direction, mission, and purpose of the arts and sciences. Without "divorcing ourselves from preparation of those who expect to enter upon careers in engineering, teaching, medicine, or business, we would insist upon integrating this training with the liberal arts." After holding up three other options, Odgers bade his colleagues hold to their present course.[68] In the quarter century since the Odgers tenure, Bucknell has continued to prefer that "fourth road."

Teacher Preparation at Bucknell. The aim of teacher preparation was once so intimately linked to the Classical Program at the University at Lewisburg as to be distinguished from professional studies. Indeed, "from her first commencement Bucknell sent out teachers." It remained in harmony with the heart of the curricular objectives of the pre–William Bucknell years and required no special training. "In those days," according to one Bucknell skeptic of earlier practices, "a teacher was a teacher born, a teacher by divine right, a teacher by instinct, a person who imbibed and absorbed knowledge, and by a sort of intellecutal photosynthesis transformed it into usable material which he transmitted to his pupils by any means or methods he happened to choose."[69]

Gradually, however, the idea of specific course work for prospective teachers took root. In 1888, the year William

Bucknell's name was given to the university, he invited John Harris to spend a Sunday with him. At that meeting, Bucknell and Harris, chief benefactor and president-elect, discussed the "increasing demand for men and women of College grade to teach in the public schools." The two men agreed that Bucknell University "could aid in this work by giving some courses in Education." They concluded that the institution "should cultivate friendly relations with the State Normal Schools and admit their graduates to suitable courses."[70] The prospects of promoting education pleased Harris, who "was as eager to find professional or vocational occupations for graduates of Bucknell as he was to persuade students to enter Bucknell for collegiate training."[71] For a few years, he even tried his own hand at teaching courses on the history, philosophy, and psychology of education.

By 1900, the course offerings in education found a home in the newly formed Department of Philosophy. (The departmental program included, in addition to courses in education, courses in psychology, philosophy, ethics, and theism.) The Bucknell catalogue advised that "Graduates of Bucknell University receive State teachers' certificates in Pennsylvania, after three years of experience in teaching. The courses in education and methods of teaching, including Child Psychology, the History, the Psychology and the Philosophy of Education, are helpful to those intending to teach. . . . No extra charge is made for the courses in Education."[72] Bucknell also set up a protean teacher placement service, calling it a "registry" of Bucknell graduates who intended to teach. The registry was designed to bring prospective employers and teachers together.

The program of 1902–03 continued without changes of note until 1916. In that year, Harris set up a separate Department of Education under the direction of his dean, Llewellyn Phillips, "perhaps the most loved and revered man that has ever taught in Bucknell University."[73] The "increasing rigidity of state requirements" necessitated a department dedicated exclusively to teachers.[74] The required course list continued to lengthen in the 1920s. For four years beginning in 1924, in addition to the program training regular Bucknell students to be teachers, a special two-year course enabled normal school graduates to obtain college degrees. Again, in 1924, there appeared a four-year program leading to the degree of bachelor of science in education. Students who worked for the B.S. in education were required to take twenty-four hours in education and psychology for certification. Bachelor of arts students, meanwhile, took eighteen hours of education to be certified.

In 1925, in an attempt to improve on its already satisfactory relations with local schools, Bucknell launched its own summer session Demonstration School, with 26 pupils, 2 critic teachers, and 7 student teachers. Gradually, the Demonstration School grew. By 1930, 200 pupils were being overseen by 13 faculty members. In a comparison with the "cooperative plan" in which student teaching was farmed out to local schools, the Demonstration School was found superior "in that it is entirely under the control of the college, and it is possible to give student teachers large freedom."[75]

The explosive interests in teacher preparation also helped bring into being a Bucknell Education Club, formed in 1925. Club members sponsored addresses by distinguished educators primarily from Pennsylvania, the middle states, and New England. A year later, the club launched the *Bucknell Journal of Education* and sponsored the first annual Bucknell Conference on Education. The conferences aimed to "bring to the students of Bucknell who were looking forward to teaching, something of the atmosphere of education out in the field, and also to bring to teachers and administrators in the field, opportunities for discussion of problems vital to the profession."[76] A half century of professional educators in Pennsylvania regularly reserved the dates of the annual Bucknell Conference in their calendars.

The dynamic growth in education in the 1920s owed much to the imaginative leadership of Frank G. Davis. In word and deed, Davis reminded his colleagues and students that a teacher prepared at Bucknell should bear a distinguishing mark: A Bucknell teacher should be readily identifiable as a person who had learned how to "professionalize" a cultural education.[77] It was Frank Davis, also, who was centrally responsible for launching the Bucknell Junior College in 1933. Even through its rough financial start, the junior college paid off in prestige for Bucknell. Regional administrators applauded Bucknell. The people of Wilkes-Barre applauded Bucknell. It was a widely acclaimed success. "To see the junior college evolve into an independent four-year college was a triumph for Bucknell University, most assuredly," said one faculty member, "and, to a considerable extent, it was a triumph of the Bucknell Department of Education." Frank Davis and his colleagues in education became educational alchemists. Every endeavor they sponsored seemed to turn into gold for Bucknell. They filled the region with Bucknell-trained professional leaders and well-wishers.

The Bucknell administration delighted in its education department and appreciated its role of state leadership and its handsome contributions to institutional prestige and solvency. At the same time, the remarkable developments in teacher preparation at Bucknell seemed to be thrusting the institution in an unexpected direction. Having achieved an enviable standing in education, the Bucknell administration felt that "it had to emphasize its technical training in the field of education, whether it wished to do so or not." As one observer noted, "It was an interesting turn of fate."[78]

The position of education on the campus remained secure and productive throughout the Davis era. But in 1949, when he asked the faculty to approve a four-year curriculum in elementary education leading to a bachelor of science degree in education, he seemed to have gone too far. A quarter century of muffled arts and sciences dubiety over the successes of education surfaced—but it was by no means merely a matter of petty jealousy. Many of the Bucknell faculty who themselves applauded the good work of their Department of Education were firmly convinced that their institution should never enter the methodological and pedagogical thickets of elementary teacher preparation. If there was any legitimate home for preparing elementary teachers, they argued, it was in normal schools, not in self-respecting colleges and universities. "There was quite a stink about it," said one professor who was there. The faculty minutes, however, were completely sanitized. They noted only that on May 25, 1949, the faculty approved the Davis proposal.

Something else seems also to have been at work. The paths of the professionals and the liberal arts faculty had begun to diverge rather sharply. At mid century, teacher educators at Bucknell were becoming increasingly conscious of their "professionalism." They began to make sharper distinctions between the imperatives of professional loyalty and the dated restraints of academic loyalty. At the same time, Bucknell arts and sciences faculty members were coming into their own, gaining a wider—an "East Coast" or even national—reputation for their institution. Their own self-esteem, their self-image, was on the rise in the postwar era. With renewed self-esteem came a determination to strengthen institutional loyalty and to assert the primacy of the liberal arts over the professions. Bucknell faculty members rededicated themselves to service as the trusted bearers of culture from the days of the Academy in Athens. As inheritors and keepers of Western university ideals, they pledged anew to confront all philistinisms unflinchingly. Professional education and the liberal arts have for some time been cool but cordial companions at Bucknell.

The "Rule of Birds" in Retrospect

As one professor put it, teacher education is a "natural" for liberal arts colleges. At these four small institutions, size is the servant of civility and the key to quality. Independent of one's departmental affiliation, individual excellence is acknowledged and honored. Residential students and faculty at the liberal arts college come to know one another in ways forever barred to members of a multiversity or commuter campus. These small colleges form communities in which men and women of letters, scientists, artists, professionals, and students interact face to face in widely varied settings. Idealism is healthy and open-eyed, with a diminished likelihood of confusing abstractions for real things. Above all, these colleges are historically "teaching places" where academic and professional teacher preparation naturally blend as harmonious pursuits. The "rule of birds" applies at Berry, Mills, Coe, and Bucknell.

The "rule" varies at these four institutions. At Berry and Coe, the professional faculties look more dutifully to the external professional bodies. They acknowledge a sense of vulnerability to those external forces that influence so much in teacher preparation. Theirs is a rather fatalistic helplessness to resist the will of either the major universities in their state, their respective state departments of education, or national accrediting agencies. They see themselves as pawns in the world of teacher preparation, liable at any moment to be damaged by decisions tailored to suit the behemoth institutions in their states. Only Berry has attained accreditation from the National Council for Accreditation of Teacher Education (NCATE); and only at Coe is there a tinge of apologetic wistfulness in the decision not to seek it.

At Mills and Bucknell, meanwhile, the professional faculties evince feistiness in their dealings with external educational agencies. Mills and Bucknell representatives were outspokenly opposed to seeking professional accreditation. Teacher educators at these two institutions are predisposed to resist decisions that seem professionally ill-advised either to themselves or to their cross-campus colleagues. While the professional faculties at all four institutions fare well with their administrations, the professionals at Mills and Bucknell also seem to share more fully the academic faculty's notions of restraint and reasonableness in teacher preparation. Across these two campuses, there seems to be a clearer sense of a uniqueness in the mission of professionals at a liberal arts institution. While interdepartmental teacher education committees at Berry and Coe represent to locals the presence of a cooperative institutional spirit in teacher preparation, it is by the very absence of such steering committees at Mills and Bucknell that the arts and sciences faculties testify to their faith in their professional colleagues.

At all four institutions, the academic and professional faculties tended to identify external education agencies as the source of the evils of American education. In the estimation of the academic faculties, the special havens of the educationists were found in the Department of Education in Washington, D.C., the departments of education in their own states, and the state and national accrediting agencies. (The professional faculties regularly added to this list the education units at the influential flagship institutions in their states that quietly influence state department and accreditation agency decisions.) Characterized as mindless bureaucrats all—weaned on heavy diets of redundant education courses in techniques and strategies and innocent of academic competencies, overloaded with information about how to teach and knowing scarcely anything about what to teach—the educationists gave professional education a deservedly bad name. Educationist rules for teacher preparation and for the management of public schools amounted to attacks on learning itself.

At each of our four institutions, the local professional faculty were seen as somehow different. They were exempted from the scorn and contempt heaped on educationists in general. The academic faculties saw their professional colleagues as uniquely able and personable and more becomingly modest in making claims for professional preparation. They were beheld as scholars in the field of education who regularly saw to it that their students aimed first for academic competencies. They were commonly either considered to be the institution's frontline defense against the alien educationists or thought of as respected but beleaguered fellow teachers forced to make the best of a series of bad decisions handed down from some distant bureaucratic headquarters. The academic faculty seemed determined to maintain an ecumenical attitude toward professional teacher preparation on campus, whether out of conviction or convention. Many tangible evidences of support by conviction were evident. The Laboratory School at Berry, the Children's School at Mills, the education faculty's resistance to professional course proliferation especially at Bucknell and Mills, the farming out of methods courses to the various academic departments, the good public relations won by the institution for placing competent new schoolteachers in nearby communities—these and similar signs of respect for the work of their professional cohorts were repeatedly applauded by members of the academic faculties. All of the faculty members—academics and professional alike—were, after all, fellow teachers.

But the future of these liberal arts colleges as "teaching places" is uncertain. Pressures to publish have invaded all of these institutions. Grounds for promotion and tenure are beginning to read more like those at the flagship university than at a liberal arts college "teaching place." At each campus, few faculty members defended the new policy. Most spoke negatively of the new stresses on research, their views ranging from dubiety to unequivocal opposition. But it seemed inescapably clear that the research-and-publication imperatives were being enforced and that they threatened to dilute the historically important focus on teaching at these institutions.

Birds and campuses that grow too large no longer sing melodiously, as John Ciardi implied. Many concerned faculty members at these four institutions fear that the mandate to publish might have an effect similar to that of excessive size. If a small liberal arts college apes the multiversity's penchant for research, will it any longer have a song to sing?

Notes

1. J. H. Newman, *The Idea of a University* (Garden City, N.Y.: Image Books, 1959), p. 165.
2. J. Ciardi, "The Size of Song," in J. Ciardi, *Selected Poems* (Fayetteville: University of Arkansas Press, 1984), pp. 47–48. Reprinted by permission.
3. Quoted in T. Byers, *For the Glory of Young Manhood and Womanhood—Yesterday, Today and Tomorrow*, Vol. 1 (Mount Berry, Ga.: Berry College, 1963 [mimeographed]), p. viii.
4. Byers, *For the Glory of Young Manhood and Womanhood*, p. 9.
5. H. T. Kane. *Miracle in the Mountains, with Inez Henry* (Garden City, N.Y: Doubleday, 1956), p. 118. The uniform idea came to Martha Berry as a way to avoid embarrassment for students who might lack the wherewithal to dress

as finely as others. Uniforms were modified over the years but remained the standard student dress throughout Berry's life. By the 1960s, however, the uniforms themselves became sources of concern. Since their abandonment in that decade, they have been donned only for special occasions.

6. From the origin of the Boys' Industrial School and on to the years of Berry College, a Protestant version of non-denominationalism prevailed. In 1962, however, after United States citizens had for the first time elected a Catholic to the presidency, the charter supplanted references to Protestantism with the simple note that the Berry "college and school should be Christian in spirit and democratic in procedure." Byers, *For the Glory of Young Manhood and Womanhood,* p. 10; see also Kane, *Miracle in the Mountains,* p.130.

7. See, for example, Berry Women's Club, *Berry Trails: An Historic and Contemporary Guide to The Berry Schools* (Mount Berry, Ga.: Berry Women's Club, 1977), p. 54.

8. Berry Woman's Club, *Berry Trails,* p. 53; Kane, *Miracle in the Mountains,* pp. 67–68.

9. With the accreditation of Berry Junior College in 1928, its graduates entered Berry College in 1930 and enabled the college to hold its first commencement in 1932.

10. E. H. Pendley, *Sixty Years of Education for Service: An Account of the Administration of Berry College and Mount Berry School for Boys* (Mount Berry, Ga.: Berry College, 1963 [mimeographed]), p. 12.

11. E. H. Pendley, *A Lady I Loved* (Mount Berry, Ga.: Berry College, 1966), p. 43.

12. Pendley, "Sixty Years of Education for Service," p. 73.

13. This observation and other unattributed comments in this section of the chapter came out of confidential conversations with various members of the Berry community. John Bertrand had been the dean and director of the Max C. Fleischmann College of Agriculture at the University of Nevada, Reno, before coming to Berry. He had also served

as a naval officer. His Ph.D. degree was obtained at Cornell University.

14. Pendley, *A Lady I Loved*, p. 132.

15. Byers, *For the Glory of Young Manhood and Womanhood*, p. 10.

16. In a memorandum to the Graduate Steering Committee, April 4, 1973, Inez A. Edge reported that the faculty was no longer exclusively Protestant. In addition to sixty-two Protestant faculty members, four were Catholic, four were Greek Orthodox, one was Buddhist, and one was Jewish. Berry College voluntarily admitted its first black student in 1964.

17. It is still a matter of pride at Berry to have an Assured Work Opportunity Program that "assures every full-time resident Berry student an on-campus job regardless of financial need. In a four-year time approximately 93 percent of Berry students work on campus at least 10 hours per week." From "The Height of Opportunity: Berry College," a trifold mailer brochure for prospective students, 1988.

18. Shatto, an economist, received her Ph.D. degree at Rice University and came to Berry with wide-ranging experience in teaching and administration. She had served as a Berry College trustee since 1975.

19. Byers, *For the Glory of Young Manhood and Womanhood*, p. 10. Byers considered the loss of missionary zeal to be the greatest change at Berry over the years.

20. See, for example, "Basic and Advanced Teacher Education Programs," institutional report submitted to the National Council for Accreditation of Teacher Education, Department of Education and Psychology, Berry College, Georgia, 1987, p. 6.

21. V. A. Stadtman, *The University of California, 1868–1968* (New York: McGraw-Hill, 1970), p. 11.

22. R. A. Keep, *Fourscore and Ten Years: A History of Mills College* (San Francisco: Taylor and Taylor, 1946), p. 2.

23. Keep, *Fourscore and Ten Years*, p. 13.

24. Keep, *Fourscore and Ten Years,* p. 22.
25. Keep, *Fourscore and Ten Years,* p. 13; see also E. O. James, *The Story of Cyrus and Susan Mills* (Stanford, Calif.: Stanford University Press, 1953).
26. Keep, *Fourscore and Ten Years,* p. 58.
27. The last seminary class exited in May 1911. See *Mills College Catalogue,* 1911–12.
28. Keep, *Fourscore and Ten Years,* p. 146.
29. A. H. Reinhardt, "Education—A Challenge to American Women," *Mills Quarterly,* 1937, *20* (May), 7.
30. Reinhardt, "Education," p. 11.
31. Keep, *Fourscore and Ten Years,* p. 146; G. Hedley, *Aurelia Henry Reinhardt: Portrait of a Whole Woman* (Oakland, Calif.: Mills College, 1946), p. 110.
32. *Mills College Catalogue,* 1920–21, pp. 15, 29.
33. She was not an uncritical participant. Reacting to one lecturer who spoke Educationese, Reinhardt wrote in her diary, "vacuous." Quoted in Hedley, *Aurelia Henry Reinhardt,* p. 138.
34. Hedley, *Aurelia Henry Reinhardt,* p. 11.
35. F. R. Armstrong, "Children's School," *Mills Quarterly,* 1961, 43 (May), 5–7.
36. The details of this incident and other unattributed comments in this portion of the chapter came out of confidential conversations with various members of the Mills College community.
37. M. Watson, "Changes Made at Children's School True to Traditions," *Mills Quarterly,* 1979, *62* (Nov.), 13. At times, the interests of the Children's School served as a weapon used by the early childhood advocates who opposed increasing the college investment in teacher preparation for the public schools.
38. Letter from Edna Mitchell to Mary S. Metz, president of Mills College, Mar. 4, 1986.
39. "The Mills College/Oakland USD Partnership, and the designation of John Swett as a Demonstration School, is based on the 'Key School' concept as defined by John Goodlad." *Partnership Handbook: Mills College/Oakland*

Unified School District, John Swett Demonstration School (n.p., n.d. [1988]), p. 4.

40. E.-J. P. White, "Three Wise Men: Dr. Robert J. Wert at Mills, 1967–1976," *Mills Quarterly*, 1987 (May), p. 14.

41. W. Cather, *My Ántonia* (Boston: Houghton Mifflin, 1918), p. iii.

42. G. H. Douma and C. C. Stepanek, "Coe College: An Informal History, 1851 to 1941," *Coe College Courier*, 1951, *52* (Dec.), 9.

43. E. M. Eriksson, *Cedar Rapids Collegiate Institute and Its Founders, 1853–1866: An Account of the Beginnings of Coe College* (Cedar Rapids, Iowa: Coe College, 1928), p. 18.

44. E. M. Eriksson, *Parsons Seminary and Its Founders, 1866–1875: A Chapter in the History of Coe College* (Cedar Rapids, Iowa: Coe College, 1929), p. 17.

45. Douma and Stepanek, "Coe College," p. 11; see also E. M. Eriksson, *Coe Collegiate Institute and Its Founders, 1875–1881: An Account of the Immediate Predecessor of Coe College* (Cedar Rapids, Iowa: Coe College, 1930). Condit, who stayed on at Coe until 1906 as a professor of ancient languages and literature, provided more than a link of continuity between the institute and the college. "In every sense of the word," noted Eriksson, "he was a founder of the Institute and of Coe College" (p. 103).

46. *Institutional Evaluation of the Program of Teacher Education*, prepared for the Iowa State Department of Public Instruction (Cedar Rapids, Iowa: Coe College, 1965), p. 1.

47. E. M. Eriksson, "A Period of Expansion Under President John A. Marquis" (typescript, 1928).

48. Douma and Stepanek, "Coe College," pp. 19–20.

49. Douma and Stepanek, "Coe College," p. 21.

50. Douma and Stepanek, "Coe College," p. 21.

51. R. K. Watters, *A Venture of Faith: Harry Morehouse Gage and the Gage Years at Coe* (Cedar Rapids, Iowa: Development Office, Coe College, 1977), p. 13.

52. See J. E. McCabe, *A Coe College Memoir* (n.p., Parthenon Press, [1984]).

53. McCabe, *A Coe College Memoir*, p. 127.

54. *The Program of Teacher Education: Coe College,* prepared for the State Department of Public Instruction (Cedar Rapids, Iowa: Coe College, 1969), p. 9.

55. *Annual Catalogue of Coe College for the Eighteenth Year: 1898–1899* (Cedar Rapids, Iowa: Coe College Press, 1898), p. 25.

56. *Annual Catalogue of Coe College for the Nineteenth Year: 1899–1900* (Cedar Rapids, Iowa: Coe College Press, 1900), p. 27.

57. E. M. Eriksson, "The Era of Greatest Progress Under Harry Morehouse Gage" (typescript, 1931), p. 25. Twice during the 1940s, Geiger was called on to serve Coe as an acting president while the trustees chose a new president.

58. Figures taken from "Priority: Student Financial Aid," in *Investing in Excellence: The National Campaign for Coe College, Cedar Rapids, Iowa* (Cedar Rapids: Development Office, Coe College [1987]), p. 23.

59. "Studying the Means and Ends of Liberal Education at Coe" (report of the Danforth Foundation Workshop Committee, July 1963), p. 21.

60. McCabe, *A Coe College Memoir,* p. 10.

61. J. O. Oliphant, *The Rise of Bucknell University* (East Norwalk, Conn.: Appleton-Century-Crofts, 1965), pp. 4–6.

62. F. P. Dunne, *Mr. Dooley on Ivrything and Ivrybody* (Mineola, N.Y.: Dover, 1963), pp. 192, 220.

63. Oliphant, *The Rise of Bucknell University,* p. 25.

64. Oliphant, *The Rise of Bucknell University,* pp. 113, 114.

65. Oliphant, *The Rise of Bucknell University,* p. 193.

66. L. E. Theiss, *Centennial History of Bucknell University: 1846–1946* (Williamsport, Pa.: Grit, 1946), p. 350.

67. This and the following unattributed comments emerged from confidential conversations with various members of the Bucknell University community.

68. Paper of Merle M. Odgers in faculty minutes, Oct. 21, 1957.

69. M. L. Fox, "The Evolution of Education at Bucknell," *Bucknell Journal of Education,* 1926, *1* (Nov.), 3.

70.   J. H. Harris, *Thirty Years as President of Bucknell with Bac-calaureate and Other Addresses* (Washington, D.C.: W. F. Roberts Press, 1926), p. 7.

71.   Oliphant, *The Rise of Bucknell University*, p. 220.

72.   *Bucknell University Catalogue*, 1902–1903, p. 61.

73.   M. L. Fox, "The Evolution of Education at Bucknell," *Bucknell Journal of Education*, 1927, *1* (Jan.), 1.

74.   *Memorials of Bucknell University, 1919–1931: The Administration of Emory William Hunt* (Lewisburg, Pa.: Bucknell University Press, 1931), p. 63.

75.   *Memorials of Bucknell University*, pp. 65, 66.

76.   *Memorials of Bucknell University*, p. 67.

77.   Fox, "The Evolution of Education at Bucknell," p. 2.

78.   Theiss, *Centennial History of Bucknell University*, p. 350.

4

The Evolution of
Normal Schools

Richard J. Altenbaugh
Kathleen Underwood

In 1891, William T. Harris, U. S. commissioner of education, stated, "Let us hope that the time is not far distant when an untrained teacher will be considered a greater absurdity than an untrained doctor or lawyer."[1]

However, Harris's statement did not reflect the historically diffuse nature of teacher preparation. The first formal, institutionalized effort appeared with the normal schools. Yet the normal school concept remained loosely defined, producing many variations. This soon led to something other than teacher training, relegating the education of educators to a subordinate role within its own institution. There was a disparity between rhetoric and reality—that is, in spite of a lofty notion of teacher training as an institution's mission, the way the general public, students, and the faculty perceived the normal school shaped it more.

What follows is a sample of normal school histories drawn from ten studies from across the nation, including private and public institutions as well as rural and urban examples. The first section establishes the historical context of the larger normal school movement. The next section relies on the case studies to provide generalizations about teacher training and compares them to the broader normal school experience. That section is 'structured around founding mission, pedagogical ideals, programmatic approaches, external forces, constituencies, internal forces, and institutional niche. Three representative vignettes provide more focused views of the evolution of the normal schools.

History of the Normal School Movement

Until the advent of the normal schools, no concrete sense of teacher competency, let alone teacher training, existed. During the colonial period, teacher ability ranged from bare literacy to college education. However, while scholastic standards varied in each community, religious orthodoxy remained immutable. Although the earliest proposal for teacher preparation appeared in 1789, with many following in the 1800s, the first documented school for the training of teachers opened under private auspices in Concord, Vermont, in 1823. Samuel Hall, a preacher with some teaching experience, founded this school as well as similar institutions throughout New England. Other private ventures that emerged were the New Harmony Community School founded in Indiana in 1826 by James Neff and one established in Lancaster, Massachusetts, by James Carter. In 1834, New York state subsidized a short-lived semipublic approach, manifested through state-aided seminaries and academies, which merely grafted teacher preparation onto the existing curriculum. The Lancaster, or monitorial, plan, imported from England, likewise contributed to teacher education. For all its shortcomings, Joseph Lancaster's system of mass education encompassed instructional manuals, pedagogical techniques, and teacher training. The Philadelphia Model School, inaugurated in 1818 as a "teachers' school," represented an "adjunct of the Lancasterian system" and served as the prototype for the city training school. Finally, the widespread use of teachers' institutes preceded, as well as paralleled, the formation of the normal schools. Henry Barnard, credited with inaugurating this innovation in 1839, applied the institute concept to prospective as well as practicing teachers, labeling it an "Itinerating [sic] normal school agency."[2]

The common school movement represented the most important factor in the formalization of teacher training, as manifested in the public normal schools. Public school enrollment increased rapidly from 3,350,000 in 1850 to 5,000,000 ten years later. In Massachusetts, which had one of the most comprehensive public school systems, the number of students jumped by more than 50 percent between 1840 and 1860, creating a shortage of qualified teachers, which no existing institutional form appeared capable of supplying. Public normal schools not only filled this institutional void but also defined teacher competence.

It has been well chronicled how Horace Mann founded the first public normal school, with Cyrus Peirce serving as its principal. The public normal school pioneered the training of female teachers. "A new kind of school, a new kind of profession, the principle of taxpayer support and a new vocation for women: these innovations were represented at the Lexington Normal School opened on a rainy July day in 1839." However, Massachusetts received criticism from all quarters, which foreshadowed later attacks on teacher education, generally belittling the professional preparation of teachers and arguing that existing academies and high schools appeared capable of the task. Peirce also experienced frustration with this new venture: "He was particularly chagrined to find that some of his students did not even want to become teachers, and others did not have the necessary ability."[3]

The evolution of the normal school reflected a dynamic situation. Rather than pedestrian, one-dimensional institutional development, Jurgen Herbst points to a variety of complex factors, stressing regional variations, American response to imported pedagogical ideals, social class perceptions, and rural and urban differences. In particular, he uses these variables to compare New England normal schools with their midwestern counterparts.[4]

The New England public normal school concept, for the most part, followed the European model. Henry Barnard, Calvin Stowe, and Charles Brooks studied teachers' seminaries in Europe and promoted them in this country. Following the century-old Prussian example of knowledge plus pedagogy, the original normal school notion consisted of four basic components: a "review of the branches of knowledge"; the "art of teaching"; the "subject of the government of the school"; and a "practice," or model, school.[5] The normal school functioned as a new type of school designed for one purpose—to train teachers. Early proponents "believed that normal schools and their students belonged to the world of the common school, not to the sphere of secondary or collegiate education."[6]

Variations of this model soon became evident. Massachusetts founded two other normal schools at Barre (later Westfield) and Bridgewater, locating them at strategic sites to address the demand for rural elementary teachers. A fourth opened in Salem in 1854. The last, like its Lexington counterpart, admitted only female candidates. Westfield and Bridgewater enrolled both female and male students and acquired other characteristics. The "Westfield approach" emerged in the 1850s and 1860s, departing from its sole mission of training elementary teachers. It tended to be more academic, broadening its curriculum offerings and adding another year to the program of study; this resulted in a two-year sequence that introduced college preparatory work and opened the door to the training of teachers for the high schools. Critics saw this as a tendency "to betray the elementary school teacher, and to scuttle the old Massachusetts normal school." Bridgewater adopted a more balanced strategy, combining "the training of elementary school teachers with the new departures in the science of education, school administration, and the training of high school teachers." Herbst adds a cautious note, however:

> It was to prove difficult and, as it would turn out, impossible to keep the goals in balance. Eventually, the new dispensation of scientific pedagogy and training for high school and administrative positions would dominate the field. But for a time the Bridgewater tradition defined as a combina-

tion of instruction for classroom teaching and
preparation for advanced career goals successfully
competed with the Westfield idea for the loyalties
of the normal school pedagogues.[7]

The normal school's means of training teachers lacked
intellectual coherency as well, at least at first. The founders of
the early schools were weak on pedagogical theory, since most
were ministers or politicians rather than educators. They saw
the need for morality, literacy, and a modicum of factual
knowledge but demonstrated little interest in fostering creativity, imagination, or independent thought in children. "They
wanted the United States to become a politically stable nation
of thrifty, virtuous, hard-working citizens and saw the public
schools as instruments for promoting that goal." They never
intended that normal schools would become institutions of
higher learning. An elementary teacher simply did not require
a liberal education: "It was enough that the teacher should have
a sound knowledge of the subjects taught in the elementary
school, be virtuous, industrious, dedicated to work, and obe-
dient to superiors."[8] Character training therefore superseded
intellectual concerns at the normal schools. The school founded
at Oswego, New York, in 1866, with its reliance on Pestalozzi's
"object lesson," appeared to be the only exception. The "Oswego Method" dominated normal schools until 1880 and was
replaced by Herbartianism, which emanated from the Illinois
Normal University, for the remainder of the century. Progressivism prevailed during the first half of the twentieth century.[9]

The midwestern and western normal experience departed markedly from the New England example, assuming a
guise more in concert with American culture. Early normal
schools represented adaptations or extensions of American
secondary schooling.[10] As the common school movement spread,
public school leaders and college educators joined ranks. Unlike the case in New England, the lines between postelementary
schooling and the normal schools became blurred. Western
public education catered to a predominantly homogeneous, rural
constituency; schooling did not function as a mechanism of so-

cialization for a heterogeneous, urban population as it did in the East. All levels of schooling served as part of an educational continuum, with colleges not necessarily ministering to an established elite. Herbst, echoing a Turnerian interpretation, puts it this way:

> On the prairie farm under western skies the class-bound perceptions of a European past began to dissolve. State superintendents of common schools and college presidents took turns in each other's positions and jointly worked to establish educational institutions from the primary schools to the colleges.[11]

The acceptance and success of normal schools had little to do with their presumed purpose of teacher training. Local communities supported and promoted them because they were viewed as secondary schools: "In their curricula and functions they did not differ from private academies and public high schools. Toward the end of the century, they came to resemble colleges."[12] Therefore, the transition of the normal school from a single-purpose to a multipurpose institution began, in many cases, with its inception in the Midwest and West.

Normal school experiences in Minnesota and Wisconsin corroborated this pattern. The student profile of Winona Normal School—Minnesota's first such institution, founded in 1858—revealed significant variation in attendance. Between 1860 and 1900, female students composed 85 percent of the student body, with 75 percent coming from rural areas of the state. More significantly, 24.1 percent of the students claimed "owner-entrepreneur," "manager," "small business," and "highly educated" backgrounds. Although these figures did not compare with the Massachusetts normal schools, which amounted to 40.2 percent for the "owner-manager" and "artisan" classes, the distribution of Minnesota's normal students defied the typical frontier occupation-status pattern, causing George Bates to conclude, "Despite the school's declared educational objectives, certain parents might send their children for other reasons which sometimes might be incompatible with their stated purposes."[13] Parents sent their children to normal schools to receive a "higher education." Such was the case in Wisconsin. In 1865, the state legislature founded two normal schools, one at Platteville and the other at Whitewater. The normal school resuscitated the former community's ailing academy and fulfilled the latter's long desire for a "public high school." "That citizens," according to Jeff Wasserman, "regarded an academy or high school as more important than a professional school for training teachers was apparent from the start."[14] Thus, many students enrolled at these institutions who had no intention of becoming teachers. Furthermore, as that state's public high schools became more prominent and began to incorporate elementary teacher training into their curricula, the normal schools responded by upgrading their admissions policies, concentrating on the preparation of secondary teachers and acceptance of high school graduates. This altered their relationship with not only the secondary school system but also the University of Wisconsin. Wasserman explains:

> As the normal school curriculum expanded to include subjects of a more advanced nature, it more closely resembled the curriculum of the Madison institution. It was just a matter of time before Wisconsin's normal schools became feeder institutions to the University; by the 1890s, it was common for normal graduates to enroll on the Madison campus as juniors.[15]

This compelling generalization about the Wisconsin normal metamorphosis has broader, more pragmatic, implications:

> In every instance, it adjusted its goals and reflected realistic alternatives rather than impossible ideals. In this capacity, it helped to shape the modern educational system. Teacher education remained on the periphery of the normal school's work.[16]

Therefore, the midwestern and western normal school seldom, if ever, assumed a single purpose, rapidly becoming a "people's college."

Nineteenth-century normal schools bequeathed an ambivalent legacy. On the one hand, they democratized higher education in the Midwest and West.

> Normal schools, rather than the land grant universities, were the pioneers of higher education for the people. Almost everywhere the state universities and agricultural and mechanical colleges were developed at a central location or state capital, whereas the normal schools were scattered to the small country towns across the prairies.[17]

On the other hand, their contributions to teacher training remained uneven. In 1860, only eleven modest normal schools existed nationwide. The southern states made no provisions for teacher training, except for teacher institutes. By 1898, the number of public normal schools had jumped to 166, graduating 8,188 students; private institutions numbered 165, graduating 3,067.

Normal school enrollment grew from 10,000 in 1870 to 70,000 in 1900, when estimates indicate that the majority of elementary teachers had received at least a modicum of normal school instruction. However, normal schools experienced a high dropout rate, particularly in the Midwest and West. The demand for instructors exceeded the supply, causing students to leave school to secure positions. Estimates were that only seven percent of the students who matriculated graduated each year. Rural schools continued to employ many teachers who possessed merely an elementary school background, occasionally supplemented by some teacher institute experience.

The normal school system supplied no more than half of the public school teachers in some states. In Massachusetts alone, more than 60 percent of the teachers claimed no formal training of any kind. As we have seen, the midwestern and western normal school never assumed a pure form, focusing more on academic preparation than on professional training. "The very name of one of Illinois's first and greatest teacher education institutions, Illinois Normal University, nicely symbolizes the later attempt to stand between the pure normal school and the state university."[18] Illinois Normal, "the Bridgewater of the West," maintained the tradition of training elementary teachers as well as administrators and secondary instructors.

In the South, normal schools did not appear until the 1870s, and black normal schools suffered from blatant racism. The demand for teachers grew with the post–Civil War proliferation of common schools. In Virginia, where the state "liberally provided for the higher education of her sons," the State Female Normal School, founded in 1884, represented a manifestation of the legislature's "provision . . . for the education of her daughters"—that is, white female teachers for the public schools. By 1900, southern black students' needs remained neglected because of a shortage of teachers, with one black teacher for every ninety-three school-aged children; the annual demand numbered 7,000 teachers. White southerners refused to teach black children. "Hence the proper training of an adequate supply of black teachers was a necessary first step toward successful expansion of common schooling for black children."[19]

The concept of the black normal school represented a southern phenomenon. However, it appeared ill-defined and lacked systemic characteristics—that is, black teachers often received their training at institutions that were not purely "normal" in origins or practice. This may be explained by the fact that normal school efforts appeared to be generated or sponsored by a variety of sources. When the federal government founded Howard University in 1867, the Normal and Preparatory Department served as one of the original components in its charter, in addition to medicine, theology, law, and agriculture. Philanthropic and religious associations established the Baltimore Colored Normal School in 1864 and Hampton Normal and Agricultural Institute in Virginia in 1868. Individuals also formed institutions such as the Miner School in Washington, D.C., in 1852. Finally the state governments played a role.

Virginia created the Virginia Normal and Collegiate Institute (Petersburg) in 1881–82, "for the higher education of the colored youth of the State and with special reference to the training of teachers." In 1877, North Carolina statutes provided for the formation of normal schools "for the teaching and training of young men of the colored race." An 1879 amendment authorized female admissions. In 1881, the legislature established normal schools at Fayetteville, Salisbury, Plymouth, and Goldsboro to train teachers for the "colored schools."[20]

James Anderson presents a revisionist argument that white, northern philanthropists and the early-twentieth-century transformation of teacher education profoundly shaped this effort. The General Education Board (GEB), formed in 1902 and subsidized by white northerners, imposed its influence on southern education by sponsoring industrial efforts, embodied in the Hampton-Tuskegee model. Since the South provided only modest public support for black education, responsibility for black teacher training fell on private institutions, which relied on a classical, liberal arts curriculum. The philosophical conflict over teacher education appeared inevitable, focusing on which model—industrial or liberal arts—would prevail. Many private black institutions, with the exception of southern church-supported black schools, became "Hamptonized."[21] This philosophical and programmatic transition from liberal arts to industrial education reversed that of midwestern normal schools, which quickly shed vocational matters (for example, teacher training) for academic concerns.

Industrial education therefore became the foundation of black normal institutions. Philanthropists hoped to train industrial teachers who "would socialize black children to be common laborers and servants in the South's caste economy." The GEB began in 1911 to create county training schools, thus pursuing its "interest in the development of industrial and manual training in black rural schools through state departments of education in general and particularly through the preparation of teachers in county training schools." Each county facility operated seven elementary grades and three years of secondary and normal school courses. "By 1917, all former slave states, except Missouri and West Virginia, had one or more county training schools."[22] By the 1930s, the GEB and the John F. Slater Fund had subsidized such ventures with $1,488,678 and $1,208,475, respectively.

The GEB and the Slater Fund made several demands in exchange for their financial support. Principally, the "school property must belong to the state, county, or district, and the county training school must be recognized as part of the local public school system." In 1917, these same philanthropists created a "suggested" curriculum guide, following the Hampton-Tuskegee example. Teacher preparation required agriculture, gardening, cooking, sewing, housekeeping, canning, and similar tasks. "The academic subjects in the teacher training course did not go beyond what was required for a first grade county teachers' license, which was very little beyond the subjects of the common school course."[23]

In spite of these efforts and financial inducements, the teacher training schools never achieved much success, because their proponents ignored the broader changes in teacher certification and education. "With higher standards for certification paralleling the development for professional standards, the job opportunities in teaching for county school graduates diminished proportionately." Attendance at the county programs always remained anemic: "The low enrollment occurred in large part because Blacks who aspired to be teachers searched for a higher quality of academic education than was offered in the county training schools." By the 1930s, the majority of black students attended four-year private colleges and universities. However, while 75 percent of southern black high school teachers possessed at least a bachelor's degree, only 9 percent of Black elementary instructors claimed similar academic backgrounds. Nevertheless, the county training schools played a role in the southern education system: "In 293 of 916 counties in 15 southern and border states, the county training school was, for Blacks between the ages of 15 and 19, the sole source of public secondary education in 1933."[24] Unfortunately, this opportunity came at the price of social control. After 1935, they rapidly disappeared, phased out in most cases but occasionally converted to public high schools.

After 1900, teacher preparation continued to be diffuse, albeit more formalized. Private normal schools declined sharply, because they could not compete with the publicly supported schools that charged little or no tuition. In addition to the normal schools, university "chairs of pedagogy" and the "college for teachers" concept emerged. Colleges and universities began in 1880 to establish chairs of pedagogy to meet the growing need for secondary-level teachers. This appeared largely self-serving and an outgrowth of the aggressive competition for students: "In terms of sheer enrollment, teacher education may have accounted for more than half of higher education growth between 1870 and 1930." Since the focus of high school training remained discipline based, the academic integrity of university education never seemed threatened, but this also represented a gender concern. "As colleges had hesitatingly discovered in the later 19th century, women wanted higher education—not only to prove they could study without expiring under the strain but also prepare for the rapidly growing profession of high school teaching."[25] As a result, universities satisfied enrollment needs, academic integrity, and gender issues in one fell swoop. By 1892, 31 universities claimed "chairs of didactics," and 114 colleges and universities enrolled students in "teachers' courses." This grew to the hundreds by the 1930s.

A new institutional form also appeared in 1887: the New York College for the Training of Teachers. Distinct from the normal schools, it sought a professional aura—"a college for the training of teachers, an institution to which graduates of normal schools and colleges may go for their purely professional training, as intending doctors and lawyers go to schools of medicine and law."[26] Headed by Nicholas Murray Butler, it became Teachers College in 1892; grafted onto Columbia University, it shaped "educational theory and practice beyond the wildest dreams of its founders. One of the peculiar contributions of this institution was the preparation of educational leaders and normal school instructors."[27] Thus, it did not earn notoriety for its undergraduate teacher training program, especially since it had none after 1926.

Normal school educators consciously moved to adopt the "professional course and to reject the education of elementary teachers as their primary task." Normal school principals first met on a national basis in 1859; this later evolved to the American Normal School Association. A committee report delivered to the 1872 association meeting in Boston proposed a tiered approach with specialized institutional functions—an idealized state configuration. As the committee's report envisioned it, a university school, or faculty, of education should serve as the crown. Next, every state should devote one higher normal school to the training of high school and elementary instructors, as well as preparing city and county school superintendents. Following this, elementary county normal schools should train rural elementary teachers. Finally, every county should sponsor teacher institutes. Herbst ominously concludes:

> As far as the American Normal School Association was concerned, training teachers for the rural elementary schools had decidedly gone out of fashion. Now the future lay with the creation of an educational professional elite. The preparation of high school teachers, normal school instructors, and superintendents was the goal. The new city and county normal schools, according to this scheme, would replace the old, but now upgraded, normal schools. They would offer a program similar to that of the Boston normal school.[28]

As the United States evolved to an urban society, teacher training likewise shifted from the training of rural to urban instructors. In 1852, Boston became the first municipality to train female candidates, establishing the Girl's High and Normal School; but by 1854, high school work already overshadowed the normal school features. This led the Boston School Committee to separate the two schools eighteen years later. The normal school became Teachers College of the City of Boston in 1924, later Boston State Teachers College, and finally Boston State College. Unlike its rural counterparts, that city's normal school required two years of high school preparation prior to the one-year program. This was expanded in 1892, revealing a more academically oriented emphasis. New York City followed Boston's lead in 1856 with the Daily Normal School for Females. Following the Civil War, many other large cities established their own training schools, usually consisting of departments attached to the public schools. By 1914, every city with a population of at least 300,000 maintained normal schools or training classes in connection with their public school systems, often integrated with the academic program of the city high schools.[29]

The university concept of teacher training, rather than the normal idea, dominated the scene during the twentieth century, and Teachers College, the bastion of Progressivism, served as the most influential institution. For William Johnson,

> Its history represented the triumph of the university school of education with its research emphasis. If not all universities prepared students exclusively at the graduate level, the Columbia model was one to which many aspired. Viewed in this way, the history of twentieth-century teacher training can be seen as a series of institutional displacements, with normal schools becoming state teachers colleges, then multipurpose liberal arts colleges, and now, in many instances, regional state universities.[30]

Normal schools actually began this transition well before the turn of the century. According to McFadden Newell's extensive 1900 survey of normal school curriculum guides, the state normal school of New Hampshire devoted only 25 percent of its program to pedagogical subjects. This compared favorably with the Midwest, where Illinois State Normal University reserved only 23 percent of a three-year course for professional studies. As Johnson concludes, "By 1900, then, it would appear that concentration on academic training was the norm, not the exception, among American normal schools."[31] They began to raise admission standards, requiring high school diplomas, and to extend the program of study.

The New York State Normal College at Albany first required high school graduation in 1890; it was followed by Massachusetts in 1894. By 1900, the proportion of high school graduates among those matriculating in 38 of the largest schools reached an average of 26 percent. The "treason" of the normal schools, as Herbst labels it, became a trend. After 1920, two- and three-year normal schools evolved to four-year teachers' colleges. While the nation had 46 teachers' colleges and 137 state normal schools in 1920, these figures shifted profoundly in only thirteen years to 146 and 50, respectively. The number of city normal schools declined from 33 in 1920 to 16 in 1933. By 1940, the term *normal school* had become obsolete. Consequently, the entire history of the American normal school experience spanned a mere century. As Charles Harper stresses,

> The Middle-West took up the work of converting normals into teachers colleges and pushed the transition with energy. The West and South followed quickly, but the East was rather badly handicapped as most normals east of the Alleghenies had surrendered to the colleges and universities their right to prepare high school teachers.[32]

Teachers' colleges served 180,000 teachers per year, furnishing about 56 percent of the public school teachers. "Of the 150 teacher's colleges and normal schools belonging to the American Association of Teachers Colleges, 31 were offering work for the master's degrees in 1939."[33] State teachers' colleges likewise experienced a short life, since by the 1960s they had begun to evolve into multipurpose state colleges or state universities, which granted liberal arts and other degrees as well as education degrees. The percentage of women's faculty positions shrank because of this transition, peaking at 67.3 percent in public normal schools in 1920 and 65.9 percent in state teachers' colleges in 1910.

A variety of external and internal forces generated this transformation. Normal schools began to deemphasize teachers' education because of local support for a more varied educational opportunity, as we have seen. Politicians and bureaucrats likewise tinkered with their state systems of education to ensure an efficient allocation of resources and to upgrade certification standards. Also, the formation of the North Central Association of Colleges and Secondary Schools (NCA) in 1896 pressured high schools to accept only college-trained teachers. Normal schools responded to these new standards by expanding their facilities, developing into teachers' colleges. It was further rationalized that training elementary and secondary teachers together might raise the status of the formerly lower-paid group. This reflected broader changes, emanating from within the profession.

By the end of the nineteenth century, few educators regarded elementary teaching as a career in itself. The new departures in the science of education, school administration, and the training of high school teachers marked a trend toward pedagogical experts based at universities, stimulating the transition in the role of the normal school. Concurrently, many normal school faculty members and administrators believed that the teaching of academic subjects conferred a higher status. Moreover, the nineteenth-century emphasis on the personal character and moral training of teachers resulted in a failure to germinate a more substantive and legitimate body of technical knowledge worth bequeathing to subsequent generations of teacher trainers. Because of their identification with the common schools, the early Massachusetts normal schools concentrated on a short period of intensive training, "something like a protracted teachers' institute."[34] Their western counterparts, largely because of their higher education kinship, initiated a relatively long curriculum, with three years as the standard by 1870. Finally, Johnson gives us a glimpse of another, related reason. In an analysis of the Maryland State Normal School, he points to the fact that its faculty suffered from persistent inbreeding and concomitant incompetence. Therefore, in some cases, normal schools lacked intellectual vitality and settled into a complacent immutability; "the normal faculty were unable (or unwilling) to reorganize the school."[35] An intellectual drift away from professional training to an academic thrust appeared natural and easiest.

This inertia fed a growing apathy in teacher training at the normal schools, leading them toward the university notion of teacher preparation: "University schools of education became the dominant model because they entered a pedagogical and professional vacuum."[36] Ironically, university schools of education have consciously distanced themselves from training and serving classroom instructors, with many completely abandoning undergraduate preparation. Further, the university research agenda has produced little useful knowledge for the practitioner or scholarship respected by members of traditional academic disciplines.

Arthur Powell points to one brave educator's cynical remarks in 1946 about Harvard's endless philosophical and administrative squabbles over research versus practice, characterizing "research and the training of 'educational technicians and "petit" functionaries' as disastrous retreats from the main business of teacher education. The field of education already suffered from too much trivial research and too many high-salaried but ignorant 'educators.' "[37] Therefore, because the normal schools followed the university pattern, teacher preparation did not fare well; and from the case studies examined here, this is exactly what happened. An important caveat is necessary: The tenuous nature of teacher education in general and at the normal schools in particular did not reflect the limitations or flaws of any particular institution. Rather, as Powell concludes about Harvard's experiences, "programmatic gyrations mirrored the uncertainties of American education [more] than they revealed failures of institutional vision."[38] Thrifty taxpayers, legislators, and parents often preferred academics over teacher training; ambitious students saw normal schooling as a stepping-stone to an occupation other than teaching; and pretentious normal school pedagogues wanted the prestige of preparing educational professionals instead of training lowly elementary teachers.

Generalizations from the Case Studies

The normal school concept remained loosely defined, in large part because, as we have seen, it had to answer to several constituencies. In an attempt to understand the normal school concept, case studies of several former normal schools were undertaken. The institutions examined include West Chester (Pennsylvania) State University, Illinois State University, Chicago State University, the University of Northern Iowa, the University of Northern Colorado, Central State University (Oklahoma), Fitchburg (Massachusetts) State College, Fort Valley (Georgia) State College, San Francisco State University, and the National College of Education (Illinois). Many points of comparison exist among the case studies that permit generalizations about normal schools and their evolution. At the same time, these institutions remain disparate enough that the vagaries within the teacher training enterprise can also be viewed.

With few exceptions, all of the schools studied here began in the last quarter of the nineteenth century, a dynamic time when massive immigration from Europe filled eastern cities and settled the upper Great Plains. The completion of the transcontinental railroad in the late 1860s encouraged the relocation of native-born Americans to the West. This tremendous population redistribution placed pressure on public school systems throughout the country; as noted earlier, these systems never had enough teachers to staff the classrooms. It also placed pressure on state legislatures to provide adequately trained teachers.

These schools shared more than their inception dates. Their chief common characteristic was that they began as normal schools and/or had teacher training as a dominant mission from the first day students enrolled. That original mission changed over time, and teacher education now plays a less important role. Several of these schools have become multipurpose universities, offering a wide range of liberal arts and professional courses. This transition often generated internal conflict, most often between the liberal arts and education faculties. Like all institutions of higher education, the schools studied here had to compete for financial support and for students. These schools not only served their preprofessionals but also maintained long traditions of in-service and extension courses that reached out to teachers already in the classroom.

The study sample reveals points of contrast as well. Programs varied in their emphasis and in who they trained—rural, elementary, and/or secondary teachers and, in some cases, administrators. One factor that provides contrast, and that may be tied to region, has to do with institutional niche. In some instances, such as Fitchburg and West Chester, the institution functioned as one of several state-funded normal schools. However, in the states of Iowa, Colorado, and Oklahoma, there existed only one publicly funded teacher training school in the early years. This meant that in terms of state budgets, these normal schools faced competition from the state university and/ or the agricultural and mechanical school but not from other normal schools. In Colorado and Iowa, it also gave the leaders of these schools a highly visible role. Race also represents an issue that might provide a point of comparison, but because the study sample included only one black school, it is impossible to make an assessment. Moreover, that institution, Fort Valley, defied easy comparisons. Although it provided normal school training and graduated teachers, in reality it was an elementary and high school until the late 1930s.

Mission. By definition, teacher training remained central to the founding mission of each of these normal schools whether the school began as a local academy, as did West Chester, or as a university, as did Illinois Normal. For many of the schools, teacher training continued to be the primary mission until the Second World War, although not without pressure from the liberal arts. Still, for Illinois Normal and Fort Valley, teacher training represented only one, albeit the most important, of several missions. At Illinois, the goal was to offer instruction in agriculture, mechanical arts, and traditional academic areas; at

Fort Valley, teaching was also mixed with education for future farmers.

Each of these schools experienced an erosion of its founding mission, marked by the declining importance of teacher training and the increasing importance of the liberal arts in particular and such other professional training as business administration and nursing. All of the case studies, like the broader normal school movement, followed the evolution outlined above—that is, from state normal schools to state teachers' colleges (usually in the first two decades of the twentieth century), then state colleges, with liberal arts growing in importance and graduate programs (in the 1940s), and finally to multipurpose universities (in the 1960s). Not all of these schools made such changes at precisely the same time, but a pattern did emerge. This evolution depended on such factors as administrative leadership, institutional competition for tax dollars and students, and student demands for program expansion.

Modification of certification, marked by greater state control, accompanied the changing status of teacher training institutions. By 1900, most states had determined several levels of teacher certification, although in many areas, particularly in the South and the West, testing to determine certification level rested primarily in the hands of county superintendents. As teacher training institutions, normal schools became closely tied to state certification regulations and to the state departments of public instruction. Clearly, state-funded teacher education would be expected to graduate teachers who could meet state certification guidelines. The influence of the state on the evolution of these normal schools will be fully treated later.

Pedagogical Ideals. Except for Illinois Normal, none of these schools served in the vanguard of teaching theory, although several had experimental components. Because of its long history, West Chester experienced several pedagogic models, including both Lancasterian and Pestalozzi, but probably the most innovative in the early years was the National College of Education. Founded in 1886 as "Miss Harrison's

Kindergarten Training School," the school identified with Progressive education. Influenced by Dewey's ideas, the school centered on the child. A second school that adopted an innovative program was Fitchburg, with its focus on manual training. Introduced as a course offering in 1897, the Co-operative Industrial Arts Program was firmly in place within a decade. Later called the "Fitchburg Plan," manual training attracted a large number of male students to the school. Colorado State Normal School also gave emphasis to manual training when it instituted a sloyd course (a system of manual training developed from a Swedish model) in the late 1890s.

Otherwise, the philosophical and theoretical approach of these institutions followed a pragmatic bent. High levels of government funding in the 1960s encouraged institutions of higher education to design programs, especially in special education. San Francisco State's program with exceptional children continues to attract would-be teachers who want to major in such special fields as teaching mentally retarded, visually or orthopedically handicapped, emotionally disturbed, and gifted children. In a similar vein, Colorado State College trained students for vocational rehabilitation. Moreover, Colorado State received federal funding to augment the training of students to teach on Indian reservations.

Programmatic Approaches. For most state-funded normal schools, a two-year program leading to a diploma and certification was common in the beginning. Today, all these schools offer at least a bachelor's degree, most offer the master's, and three have doctoral programs.[39] The fact that they started with similar programs and have similar programs today masks the wide variation that existed in the intervening century. For example, both Iowa State Normal School (in 1909) and Colorado State Normal School (in 1910) moved quickly to become teachers' colleges, albeit not without challenges, particularly from their state universities; West Chester and Fitchburg did not achieve similar status for another two decades, a delay more in keeping with the national pattern, where the 1920s mark the shift from two- and three-year programs to the four-year teacher training college. In fact, as West Chester was awarding its first bachelor's degree, Colorado State Teachers' College offered its Ed.D. degree, and Fort Valley was still primarily a high school. In terms of specific normal programs, Iowa State Normal possessed one of the most ambitious. It offered a two-year course for students interested in elementary teaching, a three-year course for those aimed at high school teaching, and a four-year course for principals and superintendents. Fitchburg too had more than the required two-year elementary course. Students there could enroll in a third-year advanced course, in which they taught and received a small salary. Students who already had teaching experience could graduate with a normal school degree after completing a one-year program. Fitchburg also offered a kindergarten course. Similarly, Colorado's normal school followed this pattern of offering additional courses in the third and fourth years. Other normal schools expanded more slowly. San Francisco State, for example, did not lengthen its program until the 1920s.

Once normal schools achieved the designation as state teachers' colleges, they solidified their third- and fourth-year programs and offered the bachelor's degree, most often in science.[40] Graduate programs represented another important feature of the state teachers' college. Colorado State College offered its first master's degree in 1912, Fitchburg in 1935.

A central component of most normal institutions was the model school, where students could observe the properly functioning classroom. Over time, many of these model schools were replaced by "training" or "demonstration" schools where students could gain practical skills through participation. Model schools also doubled as preparatory schools for students whose skills did not permit them immediate entry into the normal course. At Oklahoma Normal School, many of the students who matriculated had first enrolled in the model school. The same was true at Iowa State Normal School. In some sense, Fort Valley itself was a model school-preparatory school, because it had grades one through eight as well as the normal course. To a large degree, model schools gave way to "student teaching" as state laws required "real" experience in order to graduate with certification. Yet, in some cases, the demonstration school brought prestige to the institution. At Colorado State Normal, the model school provided the faculty with opportunity for research. In contrast, the National College of Education has remained steadfast in its commitment to incorporating the latest data or to implementing the best pedagogy, serving as a model for teachers. Malcolm Price Laboratory School at Iowa State Teachers College, established in 1944, has an international reputation, and the continuing prestige of this school promotes Iowa as a center for teacher education. San Francisco State's Frederic Burk School served until the 1960s as a demonstration center for student teachers.

External Forces. Three external forces stand out as important influences on normal school development: the state, with its control over funds and its ability to determine certification standards; accreditation agencies, such as the North Central Association (NCA) and the National Council for Accreditation of Teacher Education (NCATE); and larger social forces, such as depression and war.

State legislators and administrators played tremendous roles in determining the structure and program of teacher training institutions. One obvious way they exerted such influence was through appropriations. State-supported colleges and universities vied for limited public funds, requiring strong advocates to prevent their programs from being dismantled and/ or awarded to other schools. Another way that the state influenced teacher training was through certification. Since the mid nineteenth century, the trend has been toward ever increasing requirements for various levels of certification and toward the power to certify coming to rest in the hands of the state. The main question is, as one state superintendent of public instruction put it in 1882, "How shall we secure a better class of teachers for the common Schools?" This question remained a recurring one to state legislators and school administrators in the late nineteenth century, and it continues to be so today. The answer usually focused on two aspects: First, certification should be made more strict, and, second, teachers should have "a spe-

cial training. . . . They should be taught . . . how to teach."[41]
By the late nineteenth century, these two aspects became inter-
twined.

As certification became more complicated, teachers sought
training to meet new standards; in turn, as such training became available, certification requirements escalated. Not until
the twentieth century, however, did special training become a
prerequisite to certification in most states. In 1911, Colorado
required six weeks in a teacher training school for everyone
seeking a third-class certificate. Thus, over time, certification
became both more protracted and more exacting. What began
as a function and power of local boards, and then county superintendents, came to rest more firmly in the hands of state
boards of education. Not only did the locus of power change,
the requirements for certification became more refined. Once
state boards were established, they and the state superintendents of public instruction played powerful roles in the certification procedure. Tests became standardized to avoid what
one administrator termed "partiality or prejudice."[42]

Not only did state boards push for changes in certification, they also gave increasing importance to the concept of
formal training, particularly normal school training. As one
western superintendent stated in 1880, "normal training or a
teachers' NORMAL SCHOOL" was a necessity if the state was
to "secur[e] a better class of teachers."[43] As control by state
boards increased and as more normal schools appeared, potential teachers found it desirable, if not necessary, to seek some
sort of formal training. Moreover, those who completed the
normal school program received higher and more prestigious
levels of certification. In many states, they could forgo any sort
of testing; in others, they could seek life certification more
quickly. Graduates of teacher training institutions never had
trouble finding employment until the Great Depression. At the
same time, however, graduation from the normal school did
not bestow the prestige on teachers that completion of medical
or law school afforded the graduates of those institutions.

Accreditation agencies exerted a powerful force on all
educational institutions, and teacher training schools were no

exception. Colorado State Teachers College, for example, took great pride in being the first teachers' college recognized by the Association of American Universities. Since its inception in 1954, NCATE has been one of the more important gateways for teacher training institutions to gain and maintain accreditation. To this day, preparation for periodic visits from NCATE (and other accrediting agencies) represents a major undertaking for college faculty members. A negative review can damage a school's reputation. It can also spark reform.

NCATE gave the teacher education program at Chicago State University provisional accreditation in 1962 and full status five years later. However, after a visit in 1972, NCATE labeled the program the "worst imaginable" and placed it on probation.[44] The college faced the possible forfeiture of its NCATE accreditation after a subsequent review in 1975. NCATE demanded sweeping changes by then. The stakes were high; the loss of accreditation would have obliterated Chicago State's Division of Teacher Education and its graduate program. The faculty and administrators scrambled to ensure the program's accreditation. They embarked on a comprehensive plan, raising academic standards for teacher education majors, revising the laboratory teaching experience, and implementing new graduate programs attuned to the advanced training of teachers. Not content with these reforms, in 1974 the university reorganized its structure, converting its former divisions into the College of Arts and Sciences and the College of Education and adding two new colleges, Nursing and Business and Administration. The College of Allied Health was added in 1977. The efforts proved successful. NCATE granted full and unconditional accreditation for elementary and secondary teaching, counseling, and school principal programs in 1975. A year later, NCA awarded the university full and unconditional accreditation.

NCATE also threatened teacher training at the University of Northern Colorado. After a 1980 visit from NCATE, the school lost accreditation for several of its programs. Another review in 1981 raised additional questions. The negative report from NCATE (and other accrediting agencies) prompted a major restructuring of the University of Northern Colorado's program.

Thus, teacher training institutions have always walked a tightrope, trying to attract students to maintain and increase enrollments, to please state legislatures, to enjoy continued tax support, and to maintain the standards outlined by various accreditation groups. And they have had to walk that tightrope amid larger social forces.

The Great Depression and three wars, in the 1940s, 1950s, and 1960s, profoundly altered the course of action in the study's teacher training institutions. The key issue for all schools of higher education during the Depression was declining funds. Although enrollments dropped in the late 1920s and early 1930s, the number of students never generated as much concern as state funding, or the lack thereof. As schools competed for a declining resource, programs shrank and the faculty went without pay. West Chester and other teachers' colleges in Pennsylvania faced challenges from Pennsylvania State University concerning who would train high school teachers. Since job opportunities also declined, it became almost impossible to justify continuing to train teachers. The Depression threatened the very existence of Chicago State, where student enrollment dropped as early as 1930. A 50 percent budget cut slashed the faculty and further reduced enrollment. The school discarded its elementary and high schools, while a local junior college absorbed another building. Rumors abounded about the normal school's imminent demise, and the board debated the issue. With an oversupply of teachers, the last thing that some board members wanted was to subsidize the training of more teachers.[45]

The Second World War represented a major catalyst for change for almost all of the country's teacher training institutions. At first, they faced declining enrollments as young men enlisted; they also had to deal with a declining number of faculty members, as they too enlisted or were drafted. To compensate for the loss of tuition dollars and state appropriations and to fill empty dormitories, some institutions signed military contracts to provide specific training. Fitchburg, for instance, furnished training for army and navy aviation cadets and participated in a cooperative nursing education program. Colorado State Teachers College obtained training contracts from the U.S. Army Air Force to train clerks. It made a similar contract with the Army Air Force, which called for housing 800 students. The trustees readily accepted, believing, as one trustee stated, that the arrangement "would not only materially help the college during the war period when enrollments were depleted, but also would contribute to the morale of the city of Greeley."[46] In all cases, the schools departed from teacher training, at least temporarily.

Much more important than military training contracts, the GI Bill and its provisions for the education of veterans changed the teacher training institution. Enrollments swelled in the postwar years, and colleges and universities faced wide-ranging problems, such as shortages in housing and faculty. A more fundamental challenge came from student demands for a broadened program. At San Francisco State, where enrollments soared from 737 in 1944 to 3,865 in 1949, student demands for a broader curriculum resulted in the creation of a master's degree in education. At Colorado State College of Education, enrollments in the fall of 1948 were three times what they had been in 1944.[47] The GI Bill also brought many more men to the campuses of teacher training institutions, and with them came demands for programs other than education. These demands provided much of the impetus for an increased focus on liberal arts and for the multipurpose universities that emerged in the early 1960s.

The Korean and Vietnam wars also affected these college campuses, although in very different ways. In the early 1950s, these schools again faced decreased enrollments and abandoned dorms as men received their draft notices; again, administrators responded by seeking government training contracts. Also, the student unrest that characterized many campuses during the 1960s was noticeably absent from state teachers' colleges, except at San Francisco State.

Constituencies. Women generally dominated enrollment at teacher training institutions. A report by the U.S. commissioner of education for 1898–99 revealed that women outnumbered men at all the schools in the study sample. Fitchburg had the largest ratio of women to men—14:1; at Oklahoma, the ratio remained much smaller—1.3:1.[48] Men were most likely to matriculate at institutions that also offered agricultural and mechanical arts; nevertheless, even at Illinois Normal, women outnumbered men by two to one. This is not to say that men did not matriculate at normal schools; they did. For men, however, attendance at a normal school served as preparation for further education. However, in at least one case, the proportion of women at the institutions studied here has increased. Fitchburg's industrial arts program, inaugurated in the early 1900s, encouraged the enrollment of more males, but such programs remained uncommon. The GI Bill, as noted earlier, served as the catalyst that prompted men to enroll in teachers' colleges. Since then, the expanded programs that have accompanied changes in the various colleges' offerings have continued to draw men to these campuses. This trend represents part of a century-old process.

Cyrus Peirce's complaint that his students lacked the necessary ability to become teachers has been echoed by normal school directors since the 1830s; the complaint remains constant to the present. Every institution found that a large percentage of its students, regardless of gender, appeared unqualified for any sort of college work and thus had to first enroll in the preparatory departments. There is no question that students at Fort Valley needed remedial work. Few had any education beyond the elementary level. At the more traditional normal schools, many of the students were in preparatory rather than college-level courses. The 1898–99 report of the commissioner of education revealed that at Chicago State, 52 percent of the student body enrolled "below" the normal course. At Iowa State Normal School, the proportion unprepared for the normal course was 16 percent, and at Colorado State Normal School it was 34 percent. These figures may well be underestimated, because the competition for students was so fierce that some normal schools admitted students who did not have the necessary skills to complete their normal programs.[49] Such practices lowered the academic standards at many teacher training institutions.

Peirce's complaint that students "did not even want to become teachers" has also been repeated over time. While it would seem that, because the schools studied here were teacher training institutions when they began, all the students who enrolled would have been in teacher preparation courses, that was not necessarily the case. At Illinois Normal University, other programs of study were also available. As these normal schools evolved first into state teachers' colleges and then into state colleges, more and more liberal arts courses became available. Many students, especially those who lived near the colleges, came for those courses rather than the teacher training curriculum that formed the original mission of such institutions. Other students used the normal school as a "junior college," completing its program as a step toward enrollment at a state university. To ensure that students who entered the normal department would actually teach, Illinois Normal not only required that they pledge their intent to teach for three years after graduation; students also had to report their employment, whatever it was, to the state superintendent of public instruction. Signing a pledge to teach and signing a contract with a school district were two different matters. Records at Illinois indicate that only 30 percent of the alumni during the 1860s spent any time in teaching. A study of the career paths of graduates of Colorado State Normal School reveals a stronger commitment to teaching. There, 91 percent of the graduates staffed classrooms at one point or another in the five years following commencement. Gender helps to explain the discrepancy in these figures. Women graduates were much more likely than men to enter classrooms immediately after graduation.

One very important way that teacher training schools have expanded their constituencies is by providing such wide-ranging services as extension programs, branch campuses, in-service seminars, and summer programs. At Iowa State Normal, for example, a service component was established at the turn of the century, with a summer school begun in 1897 to serve the teachers in ungraded rural schools. Two years later, the school offered courses in continuing education to assist experienced teachers who wanted to expand their skills. In 1913, these continuing education courses were formalized into extension services, and study centers were established throughout the state. These centers provided one-day in-service institutes that emphasized methods, again aimed primarily at those teachers who worked in rural schools. In 1917, Iowa initiated branch campuses for summer school, likewise seeking to reach teachers who wanted additional training but who might be unable or unwilling to move to Cedar Rapids for the summer. Other schools followed similar strategies. Colorado State Normal School first offered summer courses in 1904 and extension courses in 1908. In 1918, the summer courses became a summer quarter—a move that made attendance even more attractive. The institution expanded in the late 1940s to include off-campus teaching centers. Such services continued to grow until the late 1970s.

Internal Forces. Internal factors can play vital roles in shaping the direction of any institution, including a teacher training school. At the normal schools studied here, one important internal factor has been the effect of the evolving mission. When teacher training was the central focus, the faculty clearly perceived the institution's roles as pedagogy and teaching methods, which reflected a noble commitment. For example, during the Great Depression, faculty members at some of these schools remained although they were not receiving any salary. As research came to play a more dominant role in the post–World War II years, competition for prestige, power, and pay developed between "teaching faculty" and "research faculty." Moreover, as the missions of these institutions downplayed teacher training, morale in the education departments declined. However, at schools such as Northern Colorado, where teacher training has been given a renewed importance, faculty spirits are better.

A second internal factor has been leadership. Especially in the early years, several of these institutions claimed forceful principals or presidents, determined to make their respective schools extraordinary in the field of teacher training; to a great extent, each achieved success: Frederic L. Burk at San Francisco State, Zachariah X. Snyder at Colorado State Normal School, Homer Horatio Seeley at Iowa State Normal School, and John G. Thompson at Fitchburg. Presidents can have a deleterious effect on institutional direction and morale as well. At the University of Northern Colorado, for example, presidents since the late 1970s have faced several crises, including charges of plagiarism, battle lines drawn between the colleges of liberal arts and education, the loss of accreditation for certain programs, and economic retrenchment that resulted in the firing of tenured faculty members, an action that brought sanctions from the American Association of University Professors (AAUP). While an extreme example, the case of the University of Northern Colorado points to the tremendous impact that administrators can have on the institutions they lead.

Institutional Niche. Almost from their founding, teacher training institutions have been competing with other institutions of higher education for state funds and for the training of teachers and administrators for secondary schools. Most state legislatures expected that the normal schools and later the teachers' colleges would be primarily responsible for training teachers for elementary grades, and in many cases for rural schools. In this design, teachers for the high schools would receive their education at a liberal arts institution, most likely the state university or the agricultural and mechanical college. Private liberal arts institutions also had a stake in training secondary teachers.

There are some marked exceptions to this division of teacher training responsibilities: Illinois Normal, Fort Valley, and, of course, the National College of Education. At the same time that state legislators and administrators of state universities clearly saw that normal schools would fill the elementary teacher niche, principals and presidents of those same schools sought to broaden their scope. From the founding of the American Normal School Association in the early 1870s, normal school administrators had strategies for increasing the prestige and power of their institutions. They raised entrance standards, often requiring a high school diploma to matriculate, and they extended the programs, especially with regard to preparing high school teachers and school administrators. Iowa State Teachers College came under attack in 1909 for just such assertive programming. The school was accused of "exceeding its franchise." According to the charge, it duplicated other state institutions, employed too many teachers, and paid them too much! In other words, it neglected its mission to focus solely on training teachers for rural schools. One explanation for such an attack was that once the school became a college, it came under the control of the same board that controlled Iowa State and the University of Iowa. Concerned about duplication, the board in 1912 ordered that all professional education courses (those that high school teachers and principals would most likely take) and liberal arts courses be eliminated from the teachers' college. Protests from the state universities must also have played a part in the board's ruling; it was rescinded in 1913. Colorado State Teachers College faced similar fights over who should train secondary teachers, successfully retaining that right after several battles in the state legislature.

The mission of training teachers for the elementary schools began to change by the late 1890s—earlier if the actions of the American Normal School Association are considered. Competition for students and for public funding resulted in program development and, ironically, greater emphasis on the liberal arts. Thus, by 1960, when most of these schools had evolved into multipurpose universities, the original teacher training mission had long been eclipsed by liberal arts and various professional schools. This general picture of the evolution of normal schools, however, will be more finely focused in the three vignettes that follow: the University of Northern Colorado, San Francisco State University, and Fitchburg State College. Although all three trace their origins to the 1890s, each provides a perspective on that continuing evolution. The University of Northern Colorado has recently been designated the primary teacher training institution in that state; San Francisco State remains but one of several state universities competing for funds in the California system; and Fitchburg State College aspires to become a multipurpose university.

Vignettes from the Case Studies

University of Northern Colorado. Like most state normal schools, Colorado State Normal School was established as Colorado's population increased, demanding more teachers. Educators had called for the creation of such an institution as early as the 1870s, when it became clear that the state university in Boulder provided little in the way of pedagogy. The state legislature did not fund the school until 1889, and then only with the understanding that the town of Greeley, where the school would be built, would supply the land and most of the necessary funds. The creation of a separate normal school met with much opposition, especially from citizens of towns where other institutions of higher education already existed: Boulder, Fort Collins, and Denver. Nevertheless, Colorado State Normal School opened for classes in the fall of 1890, with an enrollment of seventy-six; the following spring, twelve students received diplomas.

Teacher training represented the school's primary mission until the early 1950s, when programs in liberal arts and business began to attract more students. The changing names of the school reflected the move away from its original mission: In 1910, it became Colorado State Teachers College; in 1935, Colorado State College of Education; in 1957, Colorado State College; and in 1970, the University of Northern Colorado. Recent restructuring of higher education in Colorado has once again altered the former normal school's mission. Concern about duplication of programs among state-supported institutions of higher education, combined with worries about teacher preparation, has resulted in a renewed mission for this school. The

University of Northern Colorado has been designated as the "primary teacher training" institution in the state.[50]

Like many other dynamic educators of the turn of the century, Zachariah X. Snyder, the school's second president, expressed dissatisfaction with a two-year teacher training school. Determined to make the normal school into a "real" college and to challenge the grip that the liberal arts colleges had on the training of secondary teachers, Snyder expanded the traditional two-year degree first to a three-year program (in 1904) and then to a four-year course (in 1907). Then, because of the school's more stringent course work for high school teachers, Snyder persuaded the state legislature in 1910 to promote the normal school to a college: Colorado State Teachers College. Two years later, the master's degree was offered. These changes brought the school into direct competition with existing colleges for attracting students.

Under Snyder's lead, Colorado State Normal School (CSNS) became nationally known among teacher training institutions, and Snyder, too, developed a national reputation through the success of the school and through his participation in the National Education Association (NEA). Snyder was in the mainstream of contemporary educational theory, including Herbartianism. Like G. Stanley Hall and others, he believed in the importance of child study, arguing in a paper to the NEA in 1904 that "the laws of evolution are found operating in the processes of education of a child."[51] In that vein, he instituted kindergarten training at CSNS. During his tenure at the school, the faculty grew tenfold, from four in 1891 to forty-seven in 1915. In the same period, the student body also increased dramatically, from 76 to 653.

Colorado State Normal School initiated several programs in its first two decades that ensured its success. In 1908, it set up an extension division in response to a strong demand from teachers "for the opportunity to do work outside the college." Programs were designed for individuals and for groups "to suit teachers who are working under various conditions. Those in the country and isolated parts of the state must work alone, but those in the cities, towns and villages prefer to work in groups."[52] Correspondence courses also brought help to teachers already in the classroom. The school also introduced sloyd—the Swedish system of manual arts—into the curriculum, encouraging normal school students to both learn it and learn how to teach it. A model school, started in 1892, provided students the chance to observe teaching and to practice what they learned. It also gave the faculty the opportunity to try out new pedagogies. Ever an experimenter, Snyder also promoted "the new spelling"; catalogues of the school in the 1910s provide evidence of his commitment.

The summer school, begun in 1904, was also immensely successful at Colorado State Normal School. That program was financially self-sustaining from the beginning. In the first year, 110 students enrolled in courses taught by a small number of the regular faculty. By 1910, enrollment had increased sixfold, and almost all the faculty remained to teach the short summer term. Students were drawn to summer school by the desire to further their progress toward degree completion. They were also attracted by the expertise of the faculty. Not only did the regular faculty stay on to teach the summer term (indeed, many of them had twelve-month contracts), prestigious faculty from other institutions of higher education vied to teach at Greeley and to enjoy the pleasure of a Colorado summer. G. Stanley Hall, for example, came the first summer and returned several times. For the 1922 summer term, faculty members were drawn from Harvard, Columbia, Stanford, Yale, the University of Michigan, and the University of Minnesota.[53]

The school has continued its dependence on extension programs almost to the present. In 1949, for example, Colorado State College of Education (CSCE) named three full-time faculty members to administer the program to provide better in-service training and to assist teachers with temporary or limited certificates to become permanently certified. To reach teachers throughout the state, off-campus teaching centers were established. The program became increasingly important as elementary school enrollments began to swell in the early 1950s.

For the first three decades, students who enrolled at Colorado's teacher training institution were primarily female and from Colorado's eastern slope. Like the students who enrolled in Wisconsin normal schools, these were daughters of rural America, daughters whose fathers were businessmen and artisans. By the 1920s, the school began to attract students from states bordering Colorado, particularly for its summer program, which offered additional training in a picturesque setting. Not until after World War II did the gender composition of the campus change as veterans flocked to the campus on the GI Bill.

The decade of the 1970s proved to be particularly troublesome for the University of Northern Colorado (UNC) as a series of crises brought unwanted attention. One focus of concern on the campus was the split between liberal arts and education regarding the quality of the graduate work in education, as the faculty of liberal arts charged that the college of education's programs were "weak" and that it was "too easy" to earn a graduate degree in education.[54] Faculty in the college of education accused those in the college of liberal arts of jealousy. A second area that engendered a great deal of criticism was an extension program that centered on military bases. As part of this massive program, some faculty members were able to travel a great deal and to augment their salaries, which caused a rift within the faculty between those who participated (and traveled and got much larger salaries) and those who did not. A third crisis emerged in June 1980, when UNC lost NCATE accreditation for several programs. A second negative report the following June raised additional questions about the quality of teacher training at UNC.

These crises naturally affected the image of the University of Northern Colorado, and enrollment suffered. Controversy at UNC did not subside when a new president was named in 1981. Robert C. Dickeson moved quickly to confront the various problems of declining enrollment and charges of inept or corrupt programs. His methods, however, were not particularly subtle. Several programs were eliminated, restructured, or absorbed into other departments. The number of faculty was, at that time, directly tied to enrollment, and as enrollment dropped, the university faced faculty cutbacks. In early August

1982, forty-seven faculty members, thirty-seven of whom had tenure, had their appointments terminated because of "program exigency." That action provoked the AAUP, which placed the University of Northern Colorado on its list of censured institutions, where it remains today.[55] The university's actions, especially the firing of tenured colleagues, clearly angered and frightened many faculty members. The residue of this action still hangs over the university. Some faculty members are bitter, others relieved that things seem to be settling down; among those hired since 1982, there is a sense that "it probably was a good thing."

Although other teacher training institutions were later established in other parts of the state—at Gunnison and Alamosa—the school at Greeley has always been the most important among these teacher training schools. But from its beginning, Colorado State Normal School had to compete with the University of Colorado at Boulder and Colorado A & M at Fort Collins (now Colorado State University), and that competition has only become more stiff over the past decade.

In 1985, in a period of severe economic decline, the Colorado legislature overhauled postsecondary education, giving tremendous power to the Colorado Commission on Higher Education. That appointed body was charged with rewriting the mission for all public institutions of higher learning in the hope of eliminating overlapping programs. As part of the state's House Bill 1187, the University of Northern Colorado's mission was restated: "The university shall be the primary institution for undergraduate and graduate teacher education in the state of Colorado." Thus, in 1988, as the University of Northern Colorado laid plans for its centennial celebration, it found itself ironically back at its origins—Colorado's foremost teacher training institution.

San Francisco State University. San Francisco State Normal School, as part of the public school system in California, had the education of teachers "at the very heart of its program."[56] As with most teacher training schools, the mission of the school has expanded over the years, but at San Francisco State, teacher training has remained an important factor.

San Francisco State was established as a teacher training institution in 1899 with the usual two-year course. In 1921, it became a teachers' college and offered a bachelor's degree. During the 1920s, the training course for elementary teachers was gradually lengthened to three years. In 1935, the school became San Francisco State College, and liberal arts began to play an increasingly important role. That trend continued through the 1940s and 1950s, and by the 1960s the power of teacher education had diminished. The college inaugurated a general education program in the mid-1940s and offered its first M.A. degree program in 1949.

San Francisco State Normal School thrived under the leadership of its first president, Frederic L. Burk. Burk was well educated, with a doctorate in psychology from Clark University, where he had studied with G. Stanley Hall. Under Burk's leadership, San Francisco State became one of the most important normal schools in the nation, and he hired a faculty that had made or would make educational history: Frank F. Bunkder, Percy E. Davidson, Henry Suzzallo, David Rhys Jones, and Carleton Washburne. He built an institution that also achieved an international reputation for its work in teacher education.

In 1935, when all teachers' colleges in California dropped the word *teachers* from their names, San Francisco State College assumed the characteristics of a liberal arts college, providing for study in fields other than teaching. By the end of the Second World War, the college offered programs in liberal arts and vocational training in business, industry, homemaking, teaching, and public and social service. As normal schools have almost always done, the school offered a course of study for students who wished to continue their studies at a university.

Almost from the earliest days of the school, San Francisco State became known for its work in the education of exceptional children, providing training for teachers wanting to work with, among others, mentally retarded, visually handicapped, speech-defective, and gifted children. Moreover, the prominence of these programs and the faculty who directed them, combined with substantial success in winning external support, has given San Francisco State a reputation that compares favorably to that of many larger, research-oriented universities.

San Francisco State's School of Education also received recognition for its Frederic Burk School, a demonstration school for student teachers. Although it had widespread support from both the academic community and the constituency it served, it could not withstand the financial cuts that were made when Ronald Reagan was governor. A kindergarten and child-care center, also under the direction of the School of Education, have been more successful. Students both observe and participate in the operation of these facilities.

One of three tax-supported normal schools when it opened in 1899, San Francisco State has always had to compete for state support. Moreover, like all other California institutions of higher education, San Francisco has had to acknowledge the "flagship" status of the Berkeley campus of the University of California, with powerful and influential lobbyists and alumni. The loss of the prestigious Frederic Burk School provides evidence of that competition for money.

In California, as in most states, teacher education program policies have been heavily influenced by the state legislature and, in the case of California, by the Commission on Teacher Credentialing. Teacher education and certification policy is determined by an interlocking directorate made up of university teacher educators, state department of education bureaucrats, and officers of professional accrediting bodies. Such external control on programs severely limits San Francisco State's control of its curriculum.

As with almost all normal schools, women composed the majority of the student body. For example, between 1899 and 1930, only fifty-nine men ever attended the school, and only women held the office of student body president. Since the 1950s, the student body has included increasing numbers of men. San Francisco State has always attracted students from the city and nearby communities. At present, these students are middle-class, many work to support dependents, and a high proportion of the College of Education students are part-time students.

As at many former normal schools, the shift first to liberal arts and then to a multipurpose university caused dissension at San Francisco State. The long-standing trust and homogeneity between faculties and administrators gave way during the early 1960s to a formal organization of the faculty. Initially, a faculty council was formed in 1961, evolving into a faculty senate and then an academic senate. Faculty in education and in the liberal arts sensed that times were shifting and that teacher education would no longer dominate. Such a shift cheered the liberal arts faculty, whose subjects had been seen as service courses rather than as worthwhile majors.[57] The shift alarmed the education faculty as its members lost prestige within their own institution.

The Master Plan for Higher Education, approved in 1960, has been a major influence on San Francisco State, and it shows the continuing dominance and influence of the University of California, the state's favored institution. Traditionally, the missions of the state schools, such as San Francisco, have included those programs that Berkeley and the other university campuses do not want to emphasize. For example, Berkeley at first fought having the state teachers' colleges become state colleges because of the competition for students, especially in the 1930s. After the Second World War, however, Berkeley stopped challenging the state colleges, and those institutions began to provide some professional- and master's-level work. Nevertheless, many at San Francisco State believe that the master plan served the universities by permitting them more selective admission policies and by excluding the state schools from awarding Ph.D. degrees.[58]

Fitchburg State College. Fitchburg Normal School owed its origins to the city superintendent of schools, Joseph G. Edgerly, who began a municipal teacher training program in 1893. Local boosters supported the school and successfully petitioned the Massachusetts Board of Education to take over the school as part of the state system of normal schools. Once that occurred, students at Fitchburg followed the state's guidelines for teacher education. The design of the normal school was "strictly professional," to prepare pupils "for the work of organizing, governing and teaching the public schools of the state."[59] By 1900, the program offerings had increased. In addition to the two-year elementary course outlined by the state, students at Fitchburg could enroll in a third-year advanced course, in which they taught and received a small salary. Students who already had teaching experience could graduate with a normal school degree after completing a one-year program. Moreover, Fitchburg offered a kindergarten course.

Fitchburg has experienced the same metamorphosis as most normal schools, but it has undergone those changes more slowly than most. Not until 1932, some forty years after its initial founding, did it become Fitchburg State Teachers College. It awarded its first bachelor of science degree in education that year, and three years later it offered the master of arts degree. Since the late 1940s, general education requirements have expanded. New programs in engineering, business administration, and liberal arts have been added, and in 1960, it became Fitchburg State College, again lagging behind its counterparts in other parts of the country. Accordingly, the proportion of students in teacher education had declined. Presently, the school offers three degrees: bachelor of arts, bachelor of science, and bachelor of science in education. It is not surprising that the current president is said to have aspirations for university status for Fitchburg.

While adhering to state-mandated courses, Fitchburg's program also contained a broader agenda. The school's first principal, John G. Thompson, wanted the students exposed to general culture, and he developed a lecture series that brought in scholars from nearby universities and colleges. At the same time, Thompson was a progressive educator whose motto was "learn by doing." Students at Fitchburg enrolled in at least twelve weeks of full-time practice teaching, for example. They virtually ran the school: cooking, cleaning, doing carpentry, and printing the school's catalogue. Such work defrayed expenses for many students.

Manual training represented Fitchburg's most innovative program, and one that would earn it a national reputation. The school offered its first course in 1897, and by 1908 the campus included a manual training school: the School of Practical Arts. Local students who had no intention of attending high school could attend shops for working with wood, textiles, leather, metal, and clay. They participated in many aspects of manufacture and sales. Known as the "Fitchburg Plan," this manual training attracted a large number of male students to the school. Like its chief proponent, Principal Thompson, the manual training program was evidence of the progressive ideal of joining school and life. Fitchburg's legacy in industrial education continued almost to the present. As recently as the 1960s, the dean of the college was a graduate of the industrial arts program.

Fitchburg has always been a regional school, drawing almost all of its student body from nearby communities. Indeed, its selection as one of Massachusetts's normal schools was made in large part because of its location. Moreover, the development of the manual training program was related to the machine-tool industry in Fitchburg. As a result, many of the students have come from working-class families, although among female students, socioeconomic background appeared more varied as the daughters of merchants and professionals enrolled. Although designated as a coeducational institution, it remained predominantly female until the industrial arts program was initiated, when more male students attended. It has drawn mostly first-generation students from its region. As at almost all teacher training institutions, the proportion of students preparing to teach at Fitchburg has declined over time, particularly since the 1950s. In 1982, for example, only 20 percent of the student body majored in education. At present, however, the trend seems to be reversing.

Fitchburg has always had to compete for students, programs, and funds. Unlike the normal schools at Lexington and

Bridgewater, which became models for normal schools in other regions, Fitchburg can make no such claims. Its manual training program brought it fame, but otherwise it remains as one of several colleges and universities in the Massachusetts system of higher education.

Concluding Comments

The case studies discussed here permit several generalizations about the evolution of teacher training institutions in the United States. Although historians remain skeptical about using the past to predict the future, these examples also provide some tentative insights into what the next decade or two might hold for teacher education. The normal school experience presents to us a mixed legacy at best and a pessimistic one at worst.

Teacher training functioned as the central mission of all normal schools and as an organizing focus until the Second World War, when other curricula, particularly liberal arts, came to dominate. But encroachment on the teacher training mission by liberal arts dates almost to the founding of many normal schools. Ambitious school leaders, determined to provide more than training for elementary and/or rural teachers, quickly introduced programs that would lead to a bachelor's degree. By the 1920s (much earlier for some), many state normal schools had become teachers' colleges, offering a bachelor's degree. Many also had created programs to train high school teachers, which brought them into competition with private liberal arts colleges and state universities. The teacher training mission has also been affected by the several constituencies that normal schools have served, among them state legislators, students, professional educators, and, more recently, accreditation agencies. Each of these constituencies exerted pressures on the normal school to accommodate their own interests. For example, the tremendous increase in college enrollments following the Second World War further eroded the teacher preparation mission, as former normal schools responded to the demands of predominantly male students for programs in liberal arts and other professions. Once they became multipurpose institutions, the former normal schools confronted pressures from internal forces vying for programmatic control. Thus, teacher training has often assumed a defensive posture, even within its own institutions.

Still, normal schools have made significant contributions to teacher preparation by training thousands of instructors since the mid nineteenth century. Most entered the classroom, albeit for varying periods of time. Some taught for only a brief period before entering other professions or, more likely for women, marriage; others stayed in the classroom for decades. More important, these teachers, because of their normal school or teacher's college background, seemed to be better prepared than their counterparts who simply passed a county examination. Of course, the curricula varied from campus to campus, but teachers who spent even a modicum of time at a teacher training institution surely gained some confidence in their pedagogical abilities.

Women have not always fared as well. They almost always made up the majority of the student body at any teacher training institution. Teaching, after all, served as one of the few prestigious occupations open to women. Before the Second World War, men trickled into these institutions, but after the war, they flooded into them. By then, the schools no longer centered solely on teacher preparation, with the male students often enrolling in other programs. Therefore, as the institutions became more multipurpose, they also grew more masculine—in both students and faculty.

Normal schools once served as institutional leaders in establishing teacher competency and training. Later, and in response to demands from various constituencies, they followed the university model. More recently, the dictates of state regulations and recommendations of policy makers have set the course. This was not due to an institutional metamorphosis alone. This analysis of teacher education has broader social implications, as Clifford and Guthrie conclude:

Most nineteenth-century physicians and lawyers learned their trade through apprenticeships. Teachers, too, had not rushed to enroll in the normal schools; most were content to learn their poorly paid and often briefly practiced craft on the job. In the next century, however, state requirements filled the teachers colleges and universities with students, just as the growing prosperity of their parents enhanced the appeal of the medical schools for aspiring physicians, and the rise of modern corporations created lucrative new opportunities for ambitious lawyers. Emulating law and medicine, education schools made efforts to recruit more "raw A.B.'s" to graduate pedagogy programs but were frustrated by teaching's low salaries and the larger society's willingness to secure teachers cheaply.[60]

Within this context, normal schools served neither as victims nor as villains. Rather, they responded to the social forces affecting teacher education by shaping what we have today.

This brief summary leaves unanswered the question of the future status of teacher education at former normal schools; that simply is not the task of this chapter. However, what we have learned is that a school's commitment to teacher training depends on the same constituencies discussed earlier: taxpayers, parents, students, lawmakers, faculties, administrators. In view of this reality, the prognosis is mixed. At institutions such as the University of Northern Colorado, where a new mandate focusing primarily on teacher education has been inaugurated, enthusiasm appears high; at other institutions, such as the National College of Education, the future seems unclear.

Further, reformers have renewed hope in teacher education throughout the country. They have translated this optimism into reinvigorating the curriculum with the idea that teachers will enter the classroom better able to educate. Teacher preparation alone, however, cannot resolve the education crisis in the United States. If the past is any guide, teacher education will not hold much promise until state and federal politicians and educational policy makers recognize that more bureaucratic structure, greater teacher regimentation, and expanded student testing do not result in better education for America's youth.

Notes

1. J. P. Gordy, *Rise and Growth of the Normal School Idea in the United States* (Washington, D.C.: U.S. Government Printing Office, 1973), p. 12.
2. W. S. Elsbree, *The American Teacher: Evolution of a Profession in a Democracy* (Westport, Conn.: Greenwood Press, 1970), pp. 32–45; J. P. Gordy, *Rise and Growth of the Normal School,* p. 12; C. F. Kaestle (ed.), *Joseph Lancaster and the Monitorial School Movement: A Documentary History* (New York: Teachers College Press, 1973), pp. 9, 47–48; P. H. Mattingly, *The Classless Profession: American Schoolmen in the Nineteenth Century* (New York: New University Press, 1975), pp. 61–72. See M. L. Borrowman (ed.), *Teacher Education in America: A Documentary History* (New York: Teachers College Press, 1965), p. 15: "So far as teacher education is concerned, the belief in a highly technical program, for which immediate practical results provide the highest justification, developed largely within the normal-school tradition." Barnard is quoted in McF. A. Newell, "Contributions to the History of Normal Schools in the United States," in *Report of the Commissioner of Education, 1898–1899,* vol. 2 (Washington, D.C.: U.S. Government Printing Office, 1900), p. 2293; see also the discussion on p. 2327 of the Philadelphia Model School.
3. K. E. Melder, "Woman's High Calling: The Teaching Profession in America, 1830–1860," *American Studies,* 1972, *13* (Fall), 19–32; Newell, "Contributions to the History," pp. 2268–2269; J. Herbst, "Teacher Preparation in the Nineteenth Century: Institutions and Purposes," in D. Warren (ed.), *American Teachers: Histories of a Profession at Work* (New York: Macmillan, 1989), p. 219.

4. J. Herbst, "Nineteenth-Century Normal Schools in the United States: A Fresh Look," *History of Education,* 1980, *9,* 219–227.
5. Gordy, *Rise and Growth of the Normal School,* pp. 43–44.
6. Herbst, "Nineteenth-Century Normal Schools," p. 221.
7. J. Herbst, *And Sadly Teach: Teacher Education and Professionalization in American Culture* (Madison: University of Wisconsin Press, 1989).
8. P. Woodring, "The Development of Teacher Education," in K. Ryan (ed.), *Teacher Education: The Seventy-Fourth Yearbook of the National Society for the Study of Education* (Chicago: University of Chicago Press, 1975), p. 9. Also refer to Herbst, "Nineteenth-Century Normal Schools," p. 221; and Gordy, *Rise and Growth of the Normal School,* pp. 120–142.
9. Woodring, "The Development of Teacher Education," p. 10; Gordy, *Rise and Growth of the Normal School,* p. 66.
10. Elsbree, *The American Teacher,* p. 145; C. A. Harper, *A Century of Public Teacher Education* (Washington, D.C.: National Education Association, 1939), p. 73.
11. Herbst, "Nineteenth-Century Normal Schools," p. 223.
12. Herbst, "Nineteenth-Century Normal Schools," p. 226.
13. G. E. Bates, Jr., "Winona Normal School Student Profile, 1860–1900," *Journal of the Midwest History of Education Society,* 1979, *7,* 10–21. The Massachusetts statistics are from an earlier time period but reflect a similar stage in institutional development. See R. M. Barnard and M. A. Vinovskis, "The Female School Teacher in Ante-Bellum Massachusetts," *Journal of Social History,* 1977, *10* (Mar.), 332–345.
14. J. Wasserman, "Wisconsin Normal Schools and the Educational Hierarchy, 1860–1890," *Journal of the Midwest History of Education Society,* 1979, *7,* 1–9.
15. Wasserman, "Wisconsin Normal Schools," p. 5.
16. Wasserman, "Wisconsin Normal Schools," p. 7; Borrowman, *Teacher Education in America,* p. 19.
17. Herbst, "Nineteenth-Century Normal Schools," p. 227.
18. Elsbree, *The American Teacher,* pp. 312–314, 319, 330;

Woodring, "The Development of Teacher Education," p. 3; Barnard and Vinovskis, "The Female School Teacher in Ante-Bellum Massachusetts," p. 334; Harper, *A Century of Public Teacher Education*, pp. 72, 111–112; Borrowman, *Teacher Education in America*, p. 20; Herbst, *And Sadly Teach*, p. 193. A comparative study carried out a decade and a half later found that in Pennsylvania, 50 percent of the teaching force had graduated from a normal school and 13 percent from a college; in Georgia, the figures were 46 percent and 13 percent, respectively; in Colorado, 32 percent and 27 percent; and in Illinois, 18 percent and 28 percent.

19. The legislative resolution is quoted in Newell, "Contributions to the History of Normal Schools," pp. 2344–2345; J. D. Anderson, *The Education of Blacks in the South, 1860–1935* (Chapel Hill: University of North Carolina Press, 1988), pp. 110–113; Harper, *A Century of Public Teacher Education*, pp. 95–96.

20. Newell, "Contributions to the History of Normal Schools," pp. 2417–2419, 2423, 2426–2427.

21. Anderson, *The Education of Blacks in the South*, pp. 114, 136.

22. Anderson, *The Education of Blacks in the South*, pp. 134, 137–138, 140.

23. Anderson, *The Education of Blacks in the South*, pp. 140, 144.

24. Anderson, *The Education of Blacks in the South*, p. 145.

25. Gordy, *Rise and Growth of the Normal School*, p. 105; G. J. Clifford and J. W. Guthrie, *Ed School: A Brief for Professional Education* (Chicago: University of Chicago Press, 1988), p. 126.

26. Woodring, "The Development of Teacher Education," p. 4; Elsbree, *The American Teacher*, p. 320.

27. Elsbree, *The American Teacher*, p. 321.

28. Herbst, *And Sadly Teach*, pp. 194–195, 206, 208.

29. Elsbree, *The American Teacher*, pp. 153, 329–330; Newell, "Contributions to the History of Normal Schools," p. 2447; Herbst, *And Sadly Teach*, p. 183.

30. W. R. Johnson, "Teachers and Teacher Training in the Twentieth Century," in Warren, *American Teachers,* p. 243. Clifford and Guthrie, *Ed School,* pp. 4–5, refer to these as "beacon schools of education."

31. Johnson, "Teachers and Teacher Training in the Twentieth Century," p. 16; Newell, "Contributions to the History of Normal Schools," pp. 2295–2297, 2363. This estimate is based on the number of courses and number of classes attended weekly.

32. Woodring, "The Development of Teacher Education," pp. 4–5; Elsbree, *The American Teacher,* p. 325; Harper, *A Century of Public Teacher Education,* pp. 105, 137–138; Herbst, *And Sadly Teach,* p. 231.

33. Harper, *A Century of Public Teacher Education,* pp. 152–153.

34. Johnson, "Teachers and Teacher Training," p. 24; Woodring, "The Development of Teacher Education, pp. 4–5; W. Learned and others, "Purpose of a Normal School," in Borrowman, *Teacher Education in America,* pp. 192–199; Harper, *A Century of Public Teacher Education,* pp. 109, 129, 140–141.

35. Johnson, "Teachers and Teacher Training in the Twentieth Century," p. 24; Herbst, *And Sadly Teach,* pp. 222–224.

36. Johnson, "Teachers and Teacher Training," p. 25.

37. A. G. Powell, *The Uncertain Profession: Harvard and the Search for Educational Authority* (Cambridge, Mass.: Harvard University Press, 1980), p. 230; Clifford and Guthrie, *Ed School,* p. 49.

38. Powell, *The Uncertain Profession,* p. 287.

39. Those three are Illinois, Colorado, and Iowa.

40. Few retained the two-year elementary course; Oklahoma was an exception, offering this course well into the 1900s.

41. *Fifth Biennial Report of the [Oregon] Superintendent of Public Instruction* (Salem, Ore.: Superintendent of Public Instruction, 1882), pp. viii–ix.

42. *Thirteenth Biennial Report of the [Oregon] Superintendent of*

Public Instruction (Salem, Ore.: Superintendent of Public Instruction, 1892), p. 225.

43. *Fourth Biennial Report of the [Oregon] Superintendent of Public Instruction* (Salem, Ore.: Superintendent of Public Instruction, 1880), p. 53.

44. To exacerbate matters, graduates of Chicago State were flunking the National Teacher Education exam at an alarming rate.

45. Chicago State was tuition free.

46. Colorado State Teachers College, Board of Trustees, executive committee minutes, Dec. 8, 1942.

47. In 1964, enrollment at Colorado State College was 4,900, an increase of 800 percent in two decades.

48. The ratio at Chicago was 3:1; at Colorado, 2.7:1; at Iowa, 2.3:1; and at West Chester, 1.7:1. *Biennial Report of the U.S. Commissioner of Education, 1898–99* (Washington, D.C.: U.S. Department of the Interior, 1900), pp. 1818–1829.

49. *Biennial Report of the U.S. Commissioner of Education,* pp. 1818–1829.

50. Colorado Commission on Higher Education, *Colorado Statewide Master Plan for Postsecondary Education, 1987–1988 thru 1991–1992* (Denver: Colorado Commission on Higher Education, 1988), p. 46.

51. Z. X. Snyder, "Educational Creed," *NEA Addresses and Proceedings,* 1904, p. 105.

52. "The Summer Quarter, Preliminary Announcement," Colorado State Teachers College *Bulletin,* 1922, pp. 9–10.

53. "The Summer Quarter," pp. 9–10.

54. "Reins Passed to 'Managerial' President as U. of Northern Colorado Tries to Forget Public Embarrassments," *Chronicle of Higher Education,* Oct. 14, 1981, pp. 5–6.

55. "Academic Freedom and Tenure: University of Northern Colorado," *Academe,* May–June 1984, p. 1a.

56. I. Hendrick, *Historical Case Study: San Francisco State University* (Seattle: Center for Educational Renewal, College of Education, University of Washington, 1989).

57.   G. S. Dumke, in San Francisco State University, "Events and History Notebooks," Department of Special Collections/Archives, as cited in Hendrick, *Historical Case Study: San Francisco State University.*

58.   E. A. Dunham, *Colleges of Forgotten Americans,* as cited in Hendrick, *Historical Case Study: San Francisco State University.*

59.   *Catalogues and Circular (1895–96),* quoted in Guinder as cited in B. Beatty, *Historical Case Study: Fitchburg State College* (Seattle: Center for Educational Renewal, College of Education, University of Washington, 1988), p. 4.

60.   Clifford and Guthrie, *Ed School,* pp. 163–164.

5

Teaching Teachers in Private Universities

Barbara Beatty

When proposing that a department of education be established at Boston University in the early 1900s, Dean William Marshall Warren warned of the "peculiar dangers" of training students for teaching "even under university conditions," although he thought that Boston University could "safely and advantageously increase its work in Education."[1] This combination of caution and opportunism historically characterized the attitude of many private universities toward teacher education. With some exceptions, they were reluctant to fully embrace teacher education but willing to avail themselves of its potential benefits.

The linked themes of reluctance to embrace teacher education, its low status compared to that of the traditional academic disciplines, the need to generate tuition, and service to schools converged in the evolution of teacher education in the private universities in this study. To better understand these dynamics and their impact on the education of educators, this chapter examines the evolution of teacher education in nine private universities. Differences and similarities among these institutions and the history of teacher education in private universities are discussed generally. The founding missions, programs, pedagogical ideals, and student bodies of these nine

187

places where teachers were taught are then described in brief individual case studies and analyzed in the context of some of the internal and external forces that shaped teacher education in these private universities.

The nine places selected for this study include three major national and six comprehensive regional universities. (Specific sampling criteria and procedures are discussed in Chapter One.) Some of the "most distinguished" private graduate schools of education described in recent studies by Harry Judge and by Geraldine Clifford and James Guthrie were not included in this sample, in part because they are not places that traditionally have prepared large numbers of classroom teachers. Their influence is felt in these nine places, however, particularly in the major national universities.[2]

The major national universities studied were Emory University in Atlanta, Georgia, and Boston University and Boston College in Massachusetts. The six regional universities were the University of Denver in Colorado; Drake University in Des Moines, Iowa; the National College of Education in Evanston and Chicago, Illinois; Roosevelt University in Chicago; California Lutheran University in Thousand Oaks, California; and Mercer University in Atlanta, Georgia.

The Nine Places: Differences and Similarities

Some of the most striking differences among these nine institutions were geographical. Even the major national universities were responsive to their varied environments and reflected the character of the suburbs, cities, and parts of the country in which they were located. For the regional institutions, these local variations were even more marked. Sometimes this local character was apparent in the architectural symbolism or situation of the campus. Roosevelt University's downtown campus, for instance, is centered in the Auditorium Building, now a national historical landmark, a masterpiece of late-nineteenth-century urban architecture designed by Dankmar Adler and Louis Sullivan. Boston College is located on "the Heights," one of the choicest pieces of real estate in the

Boston area, which the Jesuits successfully wrested from Boston's Yankee aristocracy.

In the regional institutions in particular, this local character was represented in the student body, which varied in ethnicity and class background. Often, a number of private and public universities and colleges in the same area were in competition for students. How these institutions distinguished themselves, communicated their special qualities and programs, and targeted particular groups of students as they carved up the local market was one of the main sources of diversity. At the same time, however, specializations proliferated in all of these institutions, and most offered a similar range of programs and certificates, although emphasis and quality varied.

The extent to which these institutions were research oriented was another important difference. It is not surprising that the older, major national universities were more research oriented. Some of these institutions sponsored national journals or research centers, perhaps under the direction of a senior researcher of national stature. Sometimes older faculty members at these institutions were granted exemptions from the expectation of doing research, in recognition of their special abilities and activities in teacher training.

The case studies did not reveal enormous pressure for research at most of the regional private universities. Most education faculty members in these institutions remain service and teaching oriented. There were signs, however, that this is changing. At Drake University and the National College of Education, expectations for research have increased recently; other institutions may follow suit.

Despite this geographical diversity and the variety of student clienteles, some striking similarities emerged in the histories of these nine institutions. Most were church affiliated in the beginning, sponsored religious education programs along with teacher training, and then became secular. Three—the University of Denver, Boston University, and Emory—were Methodist; Drake was begun by the Disciples of Christ; and Mercer Atlanta was founded by Baptists. Boston College retains its Jesuit affiliation and still enrolls a predominantly Catholic undergraduate student body. California Lutheran also maintains an association with the church that gave it its name, and a sizable proportion of its undergraduate students are Lutherans. Only Roosevelt University and the National College of Education had no specific denominational origin, although Roosevelt grew out of the Young Men's Christian Association, and the background of National College's founders was also pan-Protestant.

Another similarity was that most of these nine institutions began in urban areas, then moved to the suburbs or added suburban campuses. As with secularization, this exodus to the suburbs was one of the main characteristics of American middle-class life in the twentieth century. With the exception of Roosevelt University, all these institutions enroll a largely white, middle-class clientele, although some have targeted other student groups, and many serve older, nontraditional students, particularly "returning" women.

A final similarity was the emphasis on graduate and in-service education as opposed to preservice teacher education. At some of these institutions, graduate enrollments exceeded undergraduate enrollments, by a large number; at others, this was not the case. Undergraduate teacher education enrollments, which declined sharply beginning in the late 1970s and early 1980s, are rising again now but have not regained their earlier levels. Meanwhile, private universities have become one of the major, if not *the* major, suppliers of master's and doctor's degrees to current classroom practitioners, principals, and educational administrators.

In the next section, the history of teacher education in private universities generally is discussed briefly;[3] the following section provides descriptions of the evolution of teacher education at the major national universities and the regional universities. The universities in each group are discussed in the order of their founding. The case studies of the national universities are somewhat longer than those of the regional universities because the national universities are older and had more archival and secondary sources to draw upon.

History of Teacher Education in Private Universities

From the beginning, most teacher education programs in private universities had status and financial problems. In the 1890s, a few pedagogy courses began appearing in the catalogues of some private universities, but teacher educators often found it difficult to convince university administrators to expand education offerings. Frequently, it was not until Saturday classes for teachers or other external extension programs proved successful and lucrative, or women were admitted to the university, that departments, colleges, or schools of education were begun. After their establishment, such programs often remained marginal, suffering from lack of support and space.

Some liberal arts faculty members in older private universities expressed disparaging views of education's lack of substance and intellectual validity and disapproved of the vocationalism of undergraduate teacher preparation. As universities became more research oriented, these status problems were exacerbated. Education professors produced a more research-derived knowledge base for education but still found it difficult to convince other academic and professional faculties of the soundness of their methods or the uniqueness of education as a discipline.

Teacher education programs in most private universities experienced acute financial problems. Departments, colleges, and schools of education, for instance, could not count on the almost automatic support that a classics department received regardless of how few students it enrolled. As a result, some teacher education programs became actively entrepreneurial as a means of attracting students and expanding their activities, while others remained relatively small and increased or decreased in size in response to external cycles of teacher demand.

This entrepreneurialism coalesced with the service orientation of many educators, leading teacher educators in some private universities to seek closer contacts with schools and resulting in the proliferation of increasingly specialized graduate and in-service programs designed to attract and meet the needs of practicing teachers. Many teacher educators were genuinely interested in and committed to helping schools and to experimenting with pedagogical ideas in school settings. Many schools looked to private universities for help and solicited their services, although they were sometimes unsuccessful in their attempts to engage universities in teacher education as actively as they hoped.

In the early 1870s, for instance, the superintendent of the Boston public schools asked the newly established Boston University to begin a teacher education program when Harvard was discussing founding a pedagogical department. Because of its limited financial resources, however, Boston University could not respond. As President William Fairfield Warren later remarked, "In this case, as in some others, our lack of means lost to us a precious item of leadership."[4] Almost a century later, the Atlanta school superintendent asked Emory University to take the lead in "preparing great numbers of teachers," but, according to former vice-president for faculties Judson C. Ward, although "there was a dream Emory would develop into a major teacher training institution . . . it just didn't fit into our philosophy."[5]

In most of the institutions under study, however, there was a period of active expansion and work with schools during the boom years of the 1950s through the early 1970s, when large education enrollments and growing federal investment supported some ambitious educational initiatives and large-scale school-university projects. Education faculties in many private universities played leadership roles in school reform. These school-university collaborations were, however, strongest at the graduate level, where professional and in-service education meshed. The place of undergraduate, preservice teacher education in private universities became increasingly problematic.

The Evolution of Teacher Education in the Nine Universities

Among the major private national universities studied, three patterns emerged, with one place corresponding to each type. Teacher education programs in some private universities, such as Emory, adhered to a liberal arts model and, with the exception of a period of collaboration with schools under one department chair, did not attempt to become involved in teacher education on a large scale. Some places, such as Boston University, sought out relationships with schools early on and expanded, diversified, and reorganized rapidly; other institutions, such as Boston College, which enjoyed a special niche as a result of its religious identification, developed more to meet the professional needs of their particular student populations rather than to increase their share of the local education market.

Because the private regional universities in this study were generally less well established and well endowed than the major national universities, their teacher education programs were more sensitive to external economic forces and cycles of teacher supply and demand. Thus, although there were important differences in the history of teacher education at these six places, all were quite active in recruiting students and seeking "business" from schools, and none was as reluctant or secure in its niche as the national universities discussed. This is not to say that teacher education was central to the mission of all of these institutions, but at these six places there was less evidence of the prejudices against teacher education than was found in the major national universities, and in some of these places teacher education was accepted eagerly and wholeheartedly.

National Universities

Emory University. Chartered in 1838 as Emory College in Oxford, Georgia, by the Georgia Methodist Conference, Emory became a university almost overnight in the second decade of the twentieth century. Beginning in 1913, Emory received an influx of money and support when, after the Tennessee Supreme Court denied the Methodist Church complete control of Vanderbilt University, the church decided to look elsewhere to develop a major university in the Southeast. Within six years, Emory acquired a new campus on the outskirts of Atlanta, took over a medical college, merged with a school of theology, organized a law school, started a graduate school of arts and sciences and a school of business administration, and moved its undergraduate college to Atlanta.[6]

A Division of Teacher Education was founded at Emory in 1921, but it did not enjoy the same kind of instantaneous support and growth as did these other new professional programs. Nothing came of early plans to establish a teachers' college and model school. Many Emory graduates during this period became high school teachers, but they did so without taking any courses in the education division. The division ran an extension department for teachers in the Atlanta public schools for a while, which was discontinued in 1933. The division also housed, in the 1950s, a program for teachers of "speech correction," sponsored by Atlanta's Junior League.[7] In the 1940s, the university included education among the programs that offered graduate degrees. In general, however, until the 1950s, Emory remained a relatively small undergraduate teacher education program with a few courses in educational foundations and a large number of methods courses.

In the 1950s and 1960s, Emory's education programs expanded greatly and became involved with local schools. Enrollments burgeoned when women were admitted in 1953 and an education major was added, and Emory's education division enjoyed a period of postwar expansion similar to that of other institutions. But this was not the only reason for Emory's change in orientation. The division's new director, John Goodlad, was interested in working with schools, and, as at other institutions, the influence of a strong administrator was often a critical factor in energizing a program and making links between the university and the schools.

At Emory, this link took the form of the Atlanta Area Teacher Education Service (AATES), a consortium of colleges and school districts in which Emory played a major role for some twenty years. AATES sponsored laboratory-like courses and workshops for graduate students and teachers and fostered a spirit of action and school reform. Despite this period of activity and the solicitations of the superintendent of the Atlanta public schools, it became clear that Emory was not going to take a much larger role in teacher education. It was "not part of Emory's perceived role to provide massive numbers of people for anything," recalled former vice-president for faculties Judson Ward.[8]

Another factor contributing to Emory's period of expansion in the 1950s and 1960s was the award of a Ford Foundation grant for a master of arts in teaching (M.A.T.) program. Beginning in 1952, the foundation became very involved in trying to improve the quality of American high school teachers and supported a group of colleges and universities to expand their programs in secondary education. Most of the places selected for these programs were, like Emory, prestigious northern and eastern colleges and universities with strong liberal arts traditions but, also like Emory, not institutions that generally did large-scale teacher training.[9]

At Emory, the M.A.T. program resulted in a move away from the school-oriented activities of AATES. Consonant with the foundation's philosophy, a number of joint appointments were made in arts and sciences departments. Despite this new academic orientation, the education division still suffered from a lack of status within the university. As its head noted, it was, until 1971, a division of the College of Arts and Sciences, but not a department in the college.[10] When the foundation money ran out, most of the joint appointments ended as well.

In the 1970s, Emory's teacher education program moved toward a liberal arts model of teacher education and research. It was renamed the Division of Educational Studies and began a major in "the study of education as a social institution."[11] The division also shrank. The joint education and psychology doctorate moved to the psychology department; the speech faculty joined the allied health programs. Undergraduate enrollments in education fell toward their current level of only

one-third of the division's operations. In 1963, there were
twenty-two faculty members, and by 1988 there were ten; in
1967, there were ninety seniors in the teacher education program, and by 1984 there were eleven. At the same time, Emory
strengthened its focus on training school principals and developed a new research- and instruction-based doctorate oriented
toward knowledge of curricular content and instructional leadership rather than management and bureaucratic organization. Education faculty members today feel that the division's
turn to research was the right approach for Emory and that it
has finally won them the respect of other arts and sciences faculty members.[12]

   Boston University. In 1839, a year after Emory College
was founded, three Methodist lay people began a small training program and theology school for ministers in Boston.
Chartered in 1869, Boston University in 1872 added a School
of Law and a College of Music; and in 1873, it added a School
of Medicine and a College of Liberal Arts. Unlike Emory and
most other older private universities, Boston University was coeducational. In fact, it was the first university to award a Ph.D.
degree to a woman.[13]

   But, even though there were women at Boston University, in the beginning there was no department or college of
education. As at Emory, teacher education was slow to get going.
The first pedagogy course, offered in the 1890s, consisted of a
series of lectures by prominent area educators. Although concerned that the lecture series and accompanying classroom visitations did not "meet the standard of college instruction . . .
raised by enthusiastic advocates of this somewhat professional
line of study," Dean William E. Huntington was convinced of
the need for a department of education at Boston University.[14]
Meanwhile, the university sponsored a variety of external education programs, including a Saturday lecture course that
evolved into a series of courses for teachers in subjects such as
Latin, Greek, German, and English. These courses were profitable for the university and added to faculty salaries, which
were frozen in 1887 and remained so for thirty years.

Although the extension courses for teachers and graduates continued to flourish, a Department of Education was not begun until 1914, after the university's mission was redefined to emphasize its urban nature and professional training programs, and declining enrollments led to fears of loss of female students as well. The new department became the School of Education in 1918 and began offering a two-year degree program carefully designed to complement, but not conflict with, programs in the university's College of Liberal Arts. The new School of Education also began a variety of specialized professional programs in fields such as high school commercial science, recreational leadership, and art. Despite these new programs, the school suffered from persistent financial difficulties. As its first dean, Arthur Wilde, wrote in his 1920 annual report, "we anxiously canvass from year to year the comparative results of offering a more economical program or expanding our service in the hope that it will be so attractive as to finance itself." [15]

It was growing rapidly, but the preponderance of liberal arts courses taken by School of Education students exacerbated the new school's financial problems. In 1923, for instance, 30 percent of the school's income was paid out to other schools within Boston University. The School of Education was also severely limited in physical space. As Dean Wilde described, students in the school had "no building [they could] call their own, no rooms convenient for study, no halls for assembling formally or informally," and when in 1928 the school finally did acquire some space of its own, it was "noisy and dirty." [16]

In the 1930s, competition from state normal schools contributed to a push for a four-year program in education. Despite objections from liberal arts faculty members—who Wilde felt had "little or no confidence" in the work being done at the School of Education, and said so "more or less publicly"—the new program went through, and the school continued to grow. [17] By 1928, there were 2,767 students, 320 of whom were full-time; by 1935, when Wilde retired, the school had a full-time faculty of 25. [18] The most interesting aspect of the school's evolution in the 1930s was its involvement with public schools. Very early on, the faculty at the Boston University School of Education realized that for the school to thrive, it needed to take a leadership role in the schools.

This leadership role began with specialized programs on the Boston University campus that provided service to schools, such as the Education Clinic run by Donald Durrell and Helen Blair Sullivan, which evaluated thousands of school children; and the Division of Teaching Aids under the direction of Abraham Krasker, which provided audiovisual services to teachers. This school-oriented service and concomitant growth increased even more in the 1940s and 1950s under Durrell's deanship, despite a predictable slump during the war years. Durrell and other faculty members spent time in classrooms testing their ideas about teaching and learning and gave hundreds of public lectures and addresses to teachers. In his 1947 report, Durrell estimated that "approximately one-half of the 50,000 teachers and school officers in New England [had] at some time been enrolled in part-time or extension courses offered by the School" and that "conferences on school or personal professional problems" were "constant by letter, telephone, or in person."[19]

Following Durrell's deanship, the School of Education, under a succession of new deans, added more specialized programs, including institutes on exceptional children, guidance and personnel, economic education, and the principalship. In 1953, the school assumed publication of the *Journal of Education;* in 1958, Alice Crossley and Donald Durrell, who was still a professor at the school, began a research project known as the "Dedham Study" on "teaching to individual differences"; and in 1957, a Department of Foundations of Education was organized.[20]

In the 1960s and 1970s, the faculty and students at the School of Education became involved in the open education, special education, and urban education movements that engaged the energies of so many educators throughout the country. A large special education program developed in which students visited local mental health facilities and became involved with the deinstitutionalization movement and reform of Massachusetts special education laws, which became the model for Public Law 94–142, the Education for All Handicapped Children Act. The school also took an active role in Boston's traumatic school desegregation case when Dean Robert Dentler was named a special court-appointed master by U.S. District Court judge Arthur W. Garrity, Jr., and helped develop the city's desegregation plan.

After a peak of about 7,000 students in the mid 1970s, enrollments in the School of Education plummeted, as they did in other teacher education programs nationally. Although the former foundations program, now called humanistic education, was cut, and five tenured faculty members were let go in a move that attracted much publicity, Boston University president John Silber reconfirmed his commitment to public education and is reported to have reminded the university faculty that the school had once helped to finance other divisions and thus deserved continued support during lean times in education.[21]

In the 1950s, Boston University began actively recruiting students from Long Island, New Jersey, and other parts of the Atlantic seaboard, and it now enrolls large numbers of foreign students as well. Although Boston University is not a "hometown" school, recent surveys indicate that almost a quarter of School of Education graduates found jobs in Boston.[22] Education enrollments are rising again, particularly at the undergraduate level, in fields such as early childhood and elementary education in which there is a demand for teachers. President John Silber's plan to run the Chelsea schools has placed Boston University in the spotlight again in urban education. It remains to be seen, however, in what ways the School of Education will be involved in this new venture. Impetus for the plan came from outside the school, and the faculty was not initially consulted about its design. It is unclear whether and how the Chelsea plan will affect undergraduate teacher education.

Boston College. The history of teacher education at Boston College was shaped by the strong ethnic and religious forces so characteristic of Boston as a city, as well as by the traditions

of the Catholic church. In the mid nineteenth century, Jesuits
purchased land in predominantly Protestant Charlestown on
which to start a college. But prejudice against Catholics forced
them to move to Boston's South End, where Boston College
opened in 1864 as a small liberal arts college for men. By the
turn of the century, the city's rapidly expanding population of
Irish and other Catholic immigrants had outgrown the college's limited facilities, and in 1907, the Jesuits acquired land
in Chestnut Hill, an area of Yankee-owned farms and estates
adjacent to Boston. This prized suburban site became Boston
College's main campus, the location of the male, undergraduate liberal arts college, while evening classes for women and
other less prestigious programs remained downtown.[23]

Although beset by economic difficulties, Boston College
continued to grow in its new suburban setting and began adding professional schools. The Law School was opened in 1929,
the Graduate School of Social Work in 1936, and the College
of Business Administration in 1938. New Jesuits assigned to
the faculty in the 1940s had Ph.D. degrees, presaging the college's advancement to university status. After World War II,
the college began building dormitories and accepting residential students from outside the Boston area; however, the new
campus and undergraduate school remained a male preserve.
The first women to attend classes on the suburban campus were
students of the nursing school, which was founded in 1947 in
downtown Boston, but it did not have facilities for science classes.
They were not well received, and it was in this charged atmosphere that plans for a coeducational School of Education, to
be located on the Chestnut Hill campus, were announced in
1951.[24]

Pedagogy courses had been offered in the all-male undergraduate College of Liberal Arts since the 1890s, and they
gradually expanded into a small education department, with
course offerings primarily in the history of education, notably
the history of scholasticism, and other educational movements
related to Catholicism. In fact, a School of Education had opened
at Boston College in 1919, when the shortage of male secondary school teachers in Boston caused the city to enter into an

agreement with Boston College and Boston University to provide a one-year master's degree program, for which the city initially paid the tuition. This special program ended in 1926 because of competition from Boston's public normal school, which by then could offer comparable degrees and training for free. The School of Education became involved in offering extension courses for teaching sisters in diocesan schools and sought unsuccessfully to change Jesuit regulations so that female students might take courses on campus. In 1926, the School of Education was reorganized into a general graduate school, open to men and women but located off campus.

In the 1930s and 1940s, there were various education programs at Boston College, but none that enrolled women on the main campus during the regular academic term or hours. The Intown Evening Division offered late-afternoon and Saturday education courses to men and women and, for a period, operated a two- and then three-year normal course leading to elementary teacher certification, as well as B.A. or B.S. degree programs in education. The graduate school also offered numerous education courses in the late afternoons and on weekends to men and women in master's and doctoral programs. There was a Summer School of Arts and Sciences located on the main suburban campus, which offered graduate and undergraduate education courses to both men and women.

The decision to open a coeducational undergraduate program offering elementary as well as secondary certification at Boston College in the early 1950s came primarily as a response to changes in Massachusetts teacher certification regulations, which began requiring student teaching. Charles Donovan, the chair of the education department in the College of Arts and Sciences, informed the rector about the new state regulations and was instructed to immediately begin recruiting students for the new School of Education, which was to include women.[25]

The Jesuit order offered no resistance to the idea of female education students on the Boston College campus in 1952, but male undergraduates initially did. A male student was quoted as saying, "These mantraps all over campus are just not becoming for BC's tradition. We'll become just another university."[26] Some of Boston College's liberal arts faculty members also voiced disapproval of the new School of Education, although not as much as Donovan had expected. One philosophy professor, for instance, was overheard to remark upon observing construction of part of the School of Education building that "that was where they were going to store the sandboxes."[27]

Neither, apparently, was the new School of Education accorded high status in the pecking order of Boston College's other professional schools and programs, or by the archdiocese of Boston. One female student, who transferred out of the School of Education as soon as women were admitted to the College of Arts and Sciences in 1969, recalled that students ranked the School of Education at the bottom in prestige, even lower than the School of Nursing. Men who were enrolled in the School of Education were looked on with particular disdain on campus, as were the school's many commuter students, who rarely associated with the few residential students. The School of Education also did not receive the direct patronage of Boston's powerful Cardinal Cushing, who took a special interest in the School of Nursing—even ensuring that its building was air-conditioned, while the new School of Education building was not.[28]

The eventual acceptance and status of the new School of Education within the Boston College community was greatly enhanced, however, by the background and educational philosophy of its founder. A Boston College graduate and holder of a doctorate from Yale in philosophy of education, Donovan was a strong supporter of the liberal arts and firmly believed in the value of undergraduate teacher education. In a 1967 speech to the American Association of Colleges for Teacher Education, he praised the "humble," "plain origins of teacher education" and the "precious byproducts" of these origins: "simplicity and realism, practicality, the common touch, closeness to the people, commitment to service, and absence of pretentiousness and snobbery." He rejected the "dogma" that an "undiluted" undergraduate liberal arts education followed by professional education was the necessarily preferable way of training teachers and argued that there were "educational ways—formal and informal, curricular and extracurricular— by which the likelihood of teaching success and, in a broader sense, of school success" could be promoted beginning at the undergraduate level.[29]

Despite initial economic difficulties, the new School of Education thrived. There were 176 undergraduates in the first class, of whom about 60 percent were female. In the beginning, almost half of the students were in secondary education, but the elementary program, which enrolled most of the women, grew rapidly. Donovan was given great autonomy in selecting the faculty and designing curricula. He was able to pick which of the existing faculty members would teach liberal arts courses to School of Education students and brought in new lay faculty members. By the mid 1960s, when he left the deanship to become academic vice-president, the number of students in the School of Education had more than tripled to about 650, and by 1971 there were 1,284.[30]

The School of Education continued to expand under a succession of new deans. A program in early childhood education was begun in the early 1970s, and new programs in special education, including a campus school, grew rapidly with state grants, as Massachusetts instituted new regulations in special education. Testing and measurement became additional focuses. In the early 1980s, enrollments at the school began to decline, reaching a low in 1984–85 of 628—about half the number of students formerly in attendance.[31] Over the past year or so, as elsewhere, enrollments have started to rise again.

Records of Boston College's School of Education are not filled with the same references to marketing opportunities and school service as are those of Boston University. Instead, Boston College's School of Education saw itself as meeting the educational and professional needs of Boston's Catholic community. The school's curriculum was secular—its purpose, as Donovan described it, was not to supply teachers for Catholic schools but to educate public school teachers in a Catholic setting—but its Catholic identity gave it a special position in the crowded Boston educational marketplace, as well as a special relationship to Boston's public schools.

The tendency of Boston College graduates historically to teach in the Boston public schools was so well established that it was as if the college were a private Catholic normal school for the city. Numerous principals and headmasters in Boston were Boston College School of Education graduates, as were four of the city's superintendents in the first two-thirds of the twentieth century. Because of the separation of church and state, however, the relationship between Boston College and the public schools was not a direct one. Graduates formed a close community within the public schools—such as a gentlemen's club of like-minded, like-educated professionals—but Jesuit professors from Boston College were not involved in public education activities in the same way that professors from other private universities were.[32]

Recent surveys, however, reveal a marked change in where School of Education graduates obtain teaching positions. From the late 1970s onward, the majority have got jobs in suburban schools around Boston, New England, and even further afield. There is anecdotal evidence that this may not be a new pattern for women, since female graduates of the Intown, Summer, and Graduate School programs in the past may also have taught primarily in suburban school systems, in part because Boston's public normal school traditionally trained most of the female teaching force for the Boston public schools. Although Boston College has been very active in the school-university pairings that grew out of the Boston school desegregation case, and the School of Education requires some urban teaching experience, large numbers of student teachers are placed in suburban school systems. It is in these and similar systems that most graduates now find work.[33]

Regional Universities

The University of Denver. The University of Denver began as Colorado Seminary in 1864, the first institution of higher education in the territory of Colorado. Methodist in affiliation, the seminary's organization was much aided by Governor John Evans, a founder of Northwestern University, another Methodist institution. Despite Evans's support, the seminary closed in 1867 because of financial difficulties. It reopened in 1880 in the same building with a new name—the University of Denver—and with new aspirations. In the next decade, colleges of medicine, dental surgery, pharmacy, commerce, theology, and manual arts were added, and the university began moving out of its downtown location to a new campus in southeast Denver.[34]

Cycles of boom and bust in Colorado's struggling economy affected the new university acutely. Some programs closed during the panic of 1893, when the university found itself on the brink of financial collapse. Despite these economic difficulties that were to plague the university throughout its existence, a successful new Saturday school for teachers was begun in the 1890s; in 1905, it enrolled one in six of Denver teachers, and it eventually became the University's City College.[35] In 1903, a popular summer school primarily for teachers was begun, advertisements for which extolled the benefits of Colorado's climate and pictured scenes from Rocky Mountain National Park.[36]

In 1899, under new chancellor Henry A. Buchtel, who served for twenty-one years, the university began to enjoy a period of growth and relative prosperity. Economic factors, however, continued to be a problem. Like Boston University, the University of Denver saw its fortunes as tied to those of the city, and it began positioning and marketing itself as an urban university. During the war years, enrollments dropped precipitously, as they did at other universities, while female enrollment increased, and the university became involved with government-contracted training for the air force. Following World War II, again like so many other private universities, the University of Denver expanded rapidly. In 1982, it acquired nearby Colorado Women's College, thus incurring a sizable debt. Facing financial difficulties again, it was recently reorganized and is still going through a period of restructuring and transition.

Teacher preparation was a part of the university's operations since the beginning in the 1880s. There was a normal course, an education department, and then a school of education. Course offerings in education increased from 9 in 1900 to 15 in 1920 to more than 120 at present, with the largest increases coming in the 1950s.[37] But, despite the existence of a formal teacher education program, it is still possible to complete course work required for certification without enrolling in the School of Education.

Changes in the educational philosophy and curriculum of education programs at the University of Denver reflected national trends in teacher education. Originally Herbartian, the university gave students, who read Herbert Spencer's *Education*, increasingly more vocational training. Psychology and measurement were emphasized in the early 1900s, and guidance courses were begun. There were courses in school supervision and administration, but also one on rural education and by the late 1920s a course in playground management. Statistics became more important, but students could also take a course comparing education in Russia, Germany, Italy, and Mexico.[38]

This combination of liberal arts and education studies with practical training continued. In the 1930s, a division of education and psychology was established, and psychology became a mandatory part of teacher preparation. In the 1950s, special education became a major focus. The School of Education also became more research oriented, as is evidenced by the fact that in the mid 1970s the M.A. and Ph.D. degrees replaced the master's in education and doctor of education degrees.

Like many other regional universities, the University of Denver had close ties with the local public school system very early in its history. Former state superintendent of public instruction Joseph G. Shattuck administered the normal course for a period, and D. E. Phillips, who started the Saturday School for Teachers in 1897, was a member of the Denver school board.[39] This ongoing relationship with the Denver schools was critical to the university. Students came from the Denver schools to be taught there and then returned to teach in the schools, forming links for the university with other teachers and future students. Gradually, however, as the University of Denver, like Boston University, broadened its recruiting to students from out of state and fewer students chose education as a career, these ties weakened. Education courses are not the magnet they used to be to draw students to the university to then enroll in other courses as well.

Although the University of Denver was involved in teacher preparation from very early in its history, as at some other older private universities, teacher education does not seem to have been central to its mission as a liberal arts college and fledgling university. Education programs appear to have changed primarily in response to state certification regulations and external economic and demographic factors, rather than to have been determined by the university's internal aspirations. While no questioning of the legitimacy of teacher education appears in its records, the university seems to have offered teacher education to students who wanted it and to have used it when possible as a way of bolstering enrollments, rather than actively embracing it.[40]

Drake University. Organized by the Disciples of Christ, Drake University originated as Oskaloosa College, which was founded in 1857. Because of financial problems, the president and several faculty members left Oskaloosa for Des Moines, where Drake University was chartered in 1881. The university originally consisted of three schools—a Department of Literature and Art on its main uptown campus and the downtown medical school and law school. The liberal arts college offered bachelor's degrees in arts, philosophy, and science, as well as a nondegree "ladies' " course, which produced only one graduate.[41] It also offered a two-year normal course and short courses in other vocational subjects. In 1896, the university's programs were reorganized into bachelor's degree programs in ancient languages, modern languages, philosophy, scientific subjects, and civil engineering. Women were offered a course in *belles lettres* leading to a B.B.L. degree.

Teacher education at Drake was expanded when the university acquired Callanan College, a private normal school for women in downtown Des Moines, in 1888. Drake advertised the new normal course that it planned to offer at Callanan and emphasized the model school that would provide opportunities for practice teaching. Callanan College of Drake University offered a variety of two- and four-year courses as well as a one-year course for graduates of colleges and universities. Graduates received the bachelor of elementary didactics or bachelor of scientific didactics degree; graduates with college degrees who completed the one-year course received a master of scientific didactics degree.[42]

In the 1890s, Drake became independent from the Christian church, which could no longer support the university financially. Under new president Hill McClelland Bell, who had been a teacher, Callanan—called the Normal College—expanded and attracted new people to the faculty. In 1904, an elementary school was opened on campus as a site for practice teaching, and students also began practice teaching in public kindergartens in the Des Moines schools. In 1906, the Normal College became the School of Education, and—after more name changes—it became the College of Education, which it remained for seventy-two years. The College of Education offered undergraduate majors in elementary and secondary teaching and in health and physical education. Practice teaching was done in the Des Moines public schools, and graduates received a B.S. degree. Master's degrees were offered in 1928.

As elsewhere, the College of Education enjoyed a period of great expansion after World War II. It provided professional training for teachers, counselors, administrators, and specialists in adult, physical, and special education and offered work at the master's and doctoral levels. As undergraduate teacher education enrollments declined in the 1970s, graduate work became the main focus—so much so that the College of Education was closed in 1986 and its faculty transferred to the Department of Teacher Education in the College of Arts and Sciences. A new Graduate School of Education and Human Services was formed, which continued to increase its graduate offerings. In fact, education is the largest field of graduate study at Drake.

Meanwhile, the undergraduate teacher preparation program has shrunk and been relegated to a backwater, where it receives little attention or support. The graduate school even handles teacher certification for undergraduates. Drake's practitioner-oriented graduate programs receive a great deal of the university's resources and administrative support, but these programs do not generally train new teachers. Along with this demotion of undergraduate teacher preparation, Drake as a whole is becoming more research oriented, making the outlook for a renewed emphasis on the preparation of future teachers even less likely.

The National College of Education. The National College of Education has a very different history from those of the other private universities in this sample. It began in 1886 as a private kindergarten training school, and it claims to be the oldest private college in the country devoted to the training of educators. The college was founded by Elizabeth Harrison, a leader in the second generation of the American kindergarten movement, who was known especially for teaching classes of mothers. An urban progressive in the Chicago settlement house tradition, Harrison was determined to reach immigrant and indigent mothers and provide them with information about the importance of educating their young children.[43]

With the financial support of Mrs. John N. Crouse, Harrison's classes for mothers evolved into a formal training curriculum—the Chicago Kindergarten College. This "unique school for motherhood," as kindergarten leader Susan Blow described it, enrolled as many as 5,000 women in its first decade of operation.[44] Housed in the private Loring School, where Harrison taught kindergarten, the program began enrolling affluent young ladies interested in becoming kindergarten teachers, and it became one of the centers of the movement to establish public kindergartens in America. Harrison traveled widely, promoting the kindergarten cause, and her work helped lead to the founding of the National Congress of Mothers, a network of Mothers' Clubs, which in 1924 became the Parent Teacher Association.

In 1912, Harrison's training school became formally associated with the National Kindergarten Association and changed its name to the National Kindergarten College. In 1917, the college expanded to become the National Kindergarten and Elementary College, evidencing the incorporation of the kindergarten into public education and Harrison's belief in the continuity of the early childhood years. Harrison retired in 1920. She was followed by her colleague Edna Dean Baker, a graduate of Teachers College, who focused attention on the professionalization of teaching and on building the college into a larger, more comprehensive teacher education institution. Baker accepted Northwestern University's invitation for the college to move to the North Shore to become Northwestern's School of Education, but the formal merger never took place. Leaving its urban origins behind, the college built a new campus across the street from Northwestern and became a suburban teacher education school; in 1930, it changed its name to the National College of Education.

The college soon expanded its programs to offer four-year degrees in nursery, kindergarten, and elementary education. The college's Children's School, under the direction of the president's sister, Clara Belle Baker, became an important part of its training programs. Finally, the college was accredited in 1942 by the American Association of Colleges for Teacher Education and in 1946 by the North Central Association of Colleges of Teacher Education.

In 1949, the first male president, K. Richard Johnson, began building the college into a fully developed teacher education institution. The college became coeducational, launched a fund drive, and doubled the number of its buildings. In 1971, a graduate division was established and a master's degree offered through both on- and off-campus courses, ending the college's role as a wholly preservice training institution and beginning the ascension of graduate education as the college's major operation. The college received federal and state grants to run various training programs and regained an urban campus when, also in 1971, it acquired the Pestalozzi/Froebel College.

As a single-purpose teacher education institution, the National College of Education was particularly hard hit by the decline in teacher education enrollments nationally in the late 1970s and early 1980s. The college attempted to maintain its unitary mission by expanding its graduate and in-service programs. It also established more suburban centers. These measures did not offset the decline in undergraduate teacher education enrollments, however, and, facing possible closing, the college underwent a major reorganization. It diversified and targeted new markets—particularly adult learners and immigrants, thus returning to Elizabeth Harrison's original clientele.[45] In 1982, it divided into two schools—the School of Education and the School of Arts and Sciences. Although the School of Education maintained offices in most of the new branch locations and established a doctoral program, teacher education lost ground as the National College of Education became a multipurpose institution.

Over the years, the teacher education program at National College evolved from a progressive kindergarten training center to a diffuse, pragmatic collection of professional programs with no guiding philosophy. Consonant with this change, teacher education became certificate responsive rather than internally driven. Vestiges of the college's older philosophy remained in its active involvement with the Head Start program. In spite of being closely tied to the professional needs of schools, the college lost much of its reformist zeal and unique vision of what schools should be.

The student body at the college changed, too. Predominantly white, middle-class women remained in the majority, but in 1983 the college categorized 27 percent of its students as coming from minority backgrounds.[46] At the same time, undergraduate teacher education enrollments dropped to only 16 percent of the college's total student full-time equivalent.[47] Thus, although the college is serving an increasingly urban population, fewer of its students are interested in becoming teachers.

The faculty changed as well. Originally, it was entirely female, and most of its members held master's degrees. Teaching and service, not research, were the main emphases. The faculty's principal intellectual concern was bridging theory and practice, and all had school experience and maintained close contacts with schools. In an interesting holdover from the college's progressive origins, faculty members were tenured but not ranked, as a means of encouraging collegiality. Recently, however, research has become a more important criterion for tenure, and young, new faculty members with doctorates have been added. In the future, the college plans to introduce faculty ranks.[48]

Because of its unique origins as a private normal school, teacher education at the National College of Education does not have the second-class status it has had at so many other private universities. But as a result of economic pressures, National College is now a multipurpose institution, and preservice undergraduate teacher education has become a less important part of its operations. It appears that National College is moving even further away from its roots in education. It plans to open more colleges, establish doctoral degrees in other fields, and eventually change its name.[49] The School of Education will remain the National College of Education within the new university—rather like the Little House in the children's book that became dwarfed as the city grew around it.

Roosevelt University. Even more than the National College of Education, Roosevelt University's unique identity and history have been tied to that of the city of Chicago, where it is located. Relatively young compared to most of the other institutions in this sample, Roosevelt has always defined its mission as an urban university committed to the education of students of different ethnic and racial backgrounds, genders, ages, and economic backgrounds. Teacher education has always been part of Roosevelt's tradition, although it did not begin as a single-purpose teacher training institution as did the National College of Education.[50]

Roosevelt University grew out of the Central Young Men's Christian Association (YMCA), which sponsored elementary, secondary, and then postsecondary courses beginning in the early 1900s. By 1905, the Chicago association offered some college-level courses, which in 1919 were organized into two junior college programs: the Central YMCA School of Commerce and the School of Liberal Arts. In 1933, the two schools merged to form the four-year Central YMCA College, which was accredited three years later. The college, with its low tuition and flexible hours, met the needs of urban students, and it grew rapidly to become one of the nine largest four-year liberal arts colleges in the country.[51]

During the late 1930s and early 1940s, serious disagreements erupted between the college's administration and faculty and the YMCA organization. Administration and faculty, who held outspokenly liberal political and social views, bridled at the conservatism and racially discriminatory policies of the YMCA, which prevented the increasing numbers of black students from using some of the college's facilities. In 1945, President Edward Sparling resigned in protest and successfully sought the support of leading Chicago liberals to found a new college. About half of the staff and a third of the student body left with Sparling to form Roosevelt College, named in honor of recently deceased Franklin Roosevelt, whose liberalism embodied the values of the new institution. The college was accredited within a year, and a graduate division was established in 1951; in 1955, Roosevelt became a university, consisting of five colleges—arts and sciences, business administration, music, continuing education, and education. By 1987–88, the university had a student body of about 5,700, a third of whom were graduate students.[52]

Roosevelt's special urban character was symbolized by its location in the heart of Chicago's downtown area in the famous Auditorium Building, which the university remodeled to preserve its integrity and meet expanding needs. Roosevelt also consciously responded to the needs of its urban student body, of which, in 1985, 42 percent were classified as disadvantaged—the highest percentage among major universities in Illinois. In 1976, Roosevelt opened a new campus in suburban Chicago, and it now runs undergraduate and graduate programs in other locations as well.[53]

Teacher education has always been integral to Roose-

velt's urban mission. The university recently reported that it
placed over 60 percent of its graduates in the Chicago public
schools, and it claims to have been one of the largest suppliers
of teachers and administrators to the city's schools and to have
prepared more Chicago teachers than any other private college or university in the area.[54]

The teacher education program at Roosevelt, which began as part of the College of Arts and Sciences, was made into
a separate college in 1973, partly because of its large enrollments and also because its faculty thought that it was unfairly
supporting the rest of the liberal arts college. The fact that the
education faculty viewed the situation this way and acted on it,
rather than accepting any inequity as part of the liberal arts
mission of the university, says much about the status of teacher
education at Roosevelt. The education faculty had also negotiated a $1 million grant from Chicago's Spencer Foundation to
support the new arrangement. The liberal arts faculty protested the reorganization, leveling the usual charges of medi-
ocrity, grade inflation, and lack of substance in teacher education. The dispute, which the education faculty won, created
considerable dissension, even among education faculty members, some of whom felt that the new College of Education
would become too research oriented.[55]

In general, the evolution from a department to a college
of education enhanced the status of education at Roosevelt. It
gave education increased representation in the university's
governance, brought new visibility, and resulted in a rise in
enrollment. When the Spencer grant was withdrawn, a new
Research and Development Center and early childhood education programs were created. The initial research focus did
not permeate the new college, however, in part because of lack
of funding support and in part because those on the faculty
with interests in research and those with interests in teaching
failed to find a common ground.

The philosophy of teacher educators at Roosevelt was
progressive in origin. The faculty's emphasis on a child-centered approach was evidenced by the education program's links
to the television show, "Ding Dong School." This association

highlighted the department's early childhood education focus, but the liberal arts faculty was not impressed; animosity developed over use of funds from the show, and department chair Frances Horowitz—the show's creator—left Roosevelt. In the 1970s, the department became a major participant in the Teacher Corps and created its own Teacher Corps Center.

Recently, the child-centeredness of the department's early years has waned. Many of Roosevelt's programs seem more tuition and certificate responsive than internally driven. Commitment to urban education and to service and teaching remains strong, but no particular professional training model prevails or imbues the teacher education program with a united sense of purpose. At Roosevelt, as elsewhere, there has been a trend toward increased graduate enrollments and a decline in undergraduate preservice education, with graduate students now making up more than two-thirds of College of Education students. Undergraduate numbers are, however, on the rise again.[56]

California Lutheran University. The brief history of California Lutheran University contains little evidence of the prejudices against teacher education common at the major private universities and older regional universities. In fact, at California Lutheran, which is only thirty years old, teacher education has been accepted and welcomed, even openly solicited, as a major source of enrollments and revenue.[57]

Chartered in 1959, California Lutheran College was founded by the California Lutheran Educational Foundation, which was seeking to establish a liberal arts college in the Los Angeles area. The Lutheran foundation was given land in the Conejo Valley to locate the new college. Thirty faculty members were appointed immediately, and the college was granted accreditation by the Western Association of Schools and Colleges within its first year, largely on the basis of the strength of its academic appointments. The college changed its name to California Lutheran University in 1986.[58]

The undergraduate curriculum at California Lutheran was designed as an innovative "multiple-minor" system consisting of six divisions: social studies, science, mathematics, religion and philosophy, creative arts, and professional studies. Students completed five minors and developed one minor into a major. As the state of California had eliminated the elementary education major for teacher certification in 1961, no undergraduate education major was planned. Students were not allowed to minor or major in professional studies, which included education, and were thus to gain some of the breadth and depth provided by traditional liberal arts distribution and concentration requirements.

In the early 1960s, California Lutheran suffered from serious financial and administrative instability. The first president resigned in his first year, and the new president left after six months because of a cerebral hemorrhage. The dean of the School of Education served as chair of the administrative committee of the college until a new president was appointed. Administrative stability was regained, but financial problems continued. The campus became known during this period as a training site for the Dallas Cowboys football team. A new campus preschool was established—one of the college's proudest accomplishments.

In the 1970s, graduate enrollments grew rapidly to more than 1,000 students, a large number for a college with fewer than half that many undergraduate students. California Lutheran became essentially two institutions: a small residential liberal arts college with a heavily Lutheran enrollment and a large off-campus service operation providing in-service programs and master's degrees in business and education to a diverse graduate student body. During this period, a scandal developed over recruitment and course brokering practices, in which a number of teachers, among others, were given credit for courses that they paid for but did not take. The ensuing investigation resulted in much bad publicity, and California Lutheran was placed on probation by the Western Association of Schools and Colleges.

Economically, California Lutheran's booming graduate enrollments, most of which were in education, supported the undergraduate liberal arts college. Off-campus programs, generally located on Lutheran church property and designed to serve adults enrolled in part-time course work, proliferated in Santa Barbara, Los Angeles, North Hollywood, and other communities and throughout Ventura County. This predominance of graduate education did not develop immediately at California Lutheran, however. Initially, students were urged to complete elsewhere half of the thirty credit hours of the fifth year required for California teacher certification. But soon California Lutheran initiated internship programs and began keeping these teacher education students, and it also expanded its other graduate programs.[59]

As at many of the other institutions in this sample, teacher education at California Lutheran was greatly influenced by a strong administrator. Allen Leland, who has been with the program since its inception, recruited the faculty and developed a model for teacher education at California Lutheran, which he calls the "Four S's," or "Strategy Model." The model consists of four components: survival, or establishing authority as a teacher; skills; strategy; and synergy, a "holistic learning" concept that Leland attributes to John Dewey.[60]

The extent to which this model has permeated California Lutheran's teacher education program is problematic, however, as so many courses are taught in off-campus locations by part-time faculty members. The overall full-time to part-time graduate faculty ratio at California Lutheran is 3:7. Although the university still plans to be a major service provider to Ventura County public school systems, its long-range plan calls for hiring more full-time faculty members, for slowing growth in graduate enrollment, and for increasing undergraduate enrollment.[61]

The undergraduate teacher education program at California Lutheran has not grown substantially since the college's opening. The permanent faculty consists only of Leland, one other full professor, three associate professors, two instructors, seven part-time faculty members, and one "senior mentor."[62] Despite this slow growth, the university plans to open a school of education. Undergraduate teacher education enrollment is going up again now after the lows of the early 1980s, but it has not returned to the level of the 1960s.

Since California Lutheran's admissions standards are already rather unselective, it may not be feasible to substantially increase undergraduate enrollment. The university's records indicate that the teacher education program is also not very selective. Although the grade point average required for teacher certification candidates was raised in 1979 to 2.5, most students receive very high grades in education.[63] It is likely that the off-campus graduate degree programs, which do not necessarily add to the supply of new teachers, will continue to provide many of California Lutheran's education enrollments.

Mercer University, Atlanta. Teacher education at Mercer University, Atlanta—the most recently founded of the nine places in this sample—has also been an accepted part of the institution's mission. There is little or no evidence of the status problems that have plagued teacher training at older private universities. Opened in 1964 as Atlanta Baptist College, Mercer Atlanta was founded by a group of conservative Baptists who thought that Mercer University in Macon, also Baptist, had become too liberal and permissive. Atlanta Baptist College offered programs in pastoral music, religion, and liberal arts and had a small elementary education program. By the late 1960s, the college was failing financially, the faculty was down to twelve, and the future looked grim. In 1972, Mercer University in Macon bought out Atlanta Baptist and the Southern College of Pharmacy, and the new institution became Mercer University, Atlanta.[64]

The origins of teacher education at Mercer Atlanta date to before the Mercer takeover. The dean of Atlanta Baptist, who had worked in the DeKalb County schools, brought in Virginia Nelms, a reading and language arts teacher, to direct the teacher education program. Despite the college's financial difficulties, this small early program had a collegial atmosphere and sense of purpose. According to Nelms, it was liberal arts in orientation and was accepted as "equal" in status to other programs at the college.[65]

Happily, the philosophy of the new dean, Jean Hendricks, who came from Mercer Macon in 1973, was compatible

with that of Nelms, and the department's collegiality continued. Both Nelms and Hendricks espoused liberal language arts–
oriented views toward education. Nelms was an early advocate
of the "whole language" and "language experience" approaches to reading instruction and English teaching. Hendricks, a psychologist and former chair of the psychology department in Macon, had directed an experimental freshman
program that used journal writing as an educational method.[66]

After the Mercer merger, the education program changed
quickly. Atlanta Baptist had not been accredited, nor had its
students been eligible for Georgia teacher certification. Mercer
Atlanta was accredited in 1973, and its enrollments almost
doubled in one year. In 1974, the college won a two-year grant
from the Fund for the Improvement of Postsecondary Education (FIPSE) to strengthen college teaching, using an integrated arts approach, and to serve "nontraditional students"—
the bulk of Mercer Atlanta's older clientele of mostly white
suburban women returning to college after having children.
The college also began a prison-based degree program and a
continuing education program. In 1975, a teacher center was
begun, which was opened to the educational community.

In the 1970s and 1980s, Mercer Atlanta's education programs became more specialized. Certification was initially offered in elementary education and music education, as well as
in secondary-level English, behavioral sciences, and history.
Then, in response to changes in Georgia certification regulations, elementary education was divided into "early childhood
K–4" and "middle grades 4–8." In the 1980s, a specialist's certificate in health and physical education was added, along with
a choice of dual certification in classroom teaching and learning disabilities and master's degree programs in early childhood education and middle grades.

Despite the faculty's stated "liberal arts" orientation, most
of the department's offerings were methods courses. Only two
"foundations" and few of the education studies courses found
in many private universities with liberal arts traditions were listed
in early catalogues.[67] Undergraduate elementary education
majors, who make up somewhat fewer than half of all educa-

tion enrollments at Mercer Atlanta, take about half of their course work in general education and liberal arts and half in the professional education sequence, as is the common pattern. It appears that in this youngest of the teacher education programs under study, prospective teachers may take more practical professional education courses, such as those in the former teachers' colleges, than liberal arts–oriented education courses, as at most of the other private universities.

The philosophy of Mercer Atlanta's teacher education program continues to include courses advocating a language-experience approach to reading and hands-on methods of teaching. Both Nelms and Hendricks still teach in the department, although Hendricks is no longer chair, and other members of the faculty have similar interests in creative arts, experiential learning, and discovery approaches to science and other subjects. As at other younger private universities—such as California Lutheran and to a large extent Roosevelt—the Mercer Atlanta faculty is oriented primarily toward teaching and service rather than research. Although graduate enrollments exceed undergraduate enrollments somewhat, undergraduate teacher preparation at Mercer Atlanta does not seem to have receded into the background.[68]

Conclusions

As these historical case studies document, the evolution of teacher preparation in these nine private universities has not been toward training large numbers of new classroom teachers; instead, the trend has been to provide large numbers of current teachers with graduate degrees that would enable them to leave the classroom (whether they do or not is another matter) and to provide teacher certification to diminishing numbers of undergraduates.

Of course, there are a number of external reasons why graduate and in-service programs at private universities have grown while undergraduate, preservice programs have shrunk. The demand for new teachers has fallen precipitously in recent years and only now is beginning to rebound. Historically, however, most of these private universities have not been as enthusiastically involved in teacher education as they might have been because of the anomalous position of education within liberal arts– and research-oriented institutions. If teacher education had been viewed as more central to the mission of these institutions, it would have been supported more strongly internally. Instead, the education faculty was aware of the cautionary, even overtly negative views that many liberal arts faculty members held on the "peculiar dangers" of undergraduate teacher education.

This awareness seems to have had two effects. Some teacher educators—usually those in the older major research universities with strong liberal arts traditions—became more research oriented. They developed education studies programs based on the liberal arts disciplines of history, philosophy, and sociology or educational psychology programs, some of which eventually migrated to psychology departments. In the process of trying to achieve the respect accorded the liberal arts, these education faculties focused their energies increasingly on research, while their undergraduate teacher education programs remained static. This trend may not actually have resulted in the preparation of fewer new teachers, however, as many teachers receive certification through nonprogrammatic routes by combining course work from different institutions, and some graduate teacher education provides entry-level certification.

At the same time that undergraduate teacher education enrollments were shrinking, graduate education in education grew. This was in part because it was acceptable for graduate work to be unabashedly professional, as it was not competing with the liberal arts courses that well-educated undergraduates were supposed to take. It was also because graduate programs provided a source of revenue that, with the addition of new specializations and in-service programs in schools, could be expanded to meet increasing costs. As these private universities were tuition dependent, this kind of educational marketing became an increasingly important source of support.

This trend to graduate education may also have been spurred by the interests and values of the education faculty. Some education professors in private universities may not have actively pushed undergraduate teacher education because they preferred working with graduate students. Others may have felt, along with their colleagues in the Holmes Group (which is named for Arthur Wyman Holmes, the first dean of the Harvard Graduate School of Education), that some of their teacher certification candidates—particularly at the secondary level— were immature or inadequately prepared and would benefit from a year of additional graduate work.[69]

The trend toward graduate education also led education programs in some private universities to become more involved with schools. Schools were a source of candidates for degree programs and a market for in-service programs and consulting. This is not to imply, however, that these school-linked activities were entirely tuition driven, or that such entrepreneurialism was necessarily "bad." As Harry Judge points out in his study of American graduate schools of education, American universities have benefited from a measure of "healthy opportunism."[70]

Much of this involvement with schools was motivated by altruistic and research concerns, often spearheaded by a dean or group of faculty members with a strong commitment to school reform or interest in understanding and improving classroom learning or how a particular subject was taught. In some cases, this led to collaborations with teachers and school administrators through which education faculty members received the kind of support and validation that they often found difficult to find in academia. These periods of close involvement with schools were generally in the late 1950s, 1960s, and 1970s, when teacher education enrollments were high and federal money was available to support special projects; after that, the involvement waned. Although there is renewed interest in school-university partnerships today, it is not clear to what extent these new partnerships involve undergraduate teacher education or the regular education faculty.[71]

There has also been in private universities a trend away from urban teacher education. Many of these institutions began in cities and had strong links with urban school systems. They placed their student teachers and graduates in city schools, and their alumni moved up through the ranks of urban school systems to become principals and superintendents. As private universities began moving out to new suburban campuses or started satellite programs in the suburbs, however, their city connections weakened, and their teacher education students began student teaching and working in suburban schools. There were notable exceptions—particularly Roosevelt University, which still prides itself on its urban identity, and the National College of Education, where minority enrollments are rising— and there are other such institutions not in this sample. Boston University's new plan for running the Chelsea public schools also bears watching, but it appears to focus more on gover- nance and the provision of services than on making the Chel- sea schools into laboratories for urban teacher training.

These trends toward graduate education and away from urban education may have contributed to and in part been ex- plained by another trend—a decrease in the status of teacher education in private universities. Troubled since its inception, teacher education in private universities may have declined further in status since the early 1900s. This trend was difficult to track, however, in part because "status" is such a nebulous concept, but also because real and perceived indexes of status do not always coincide. Although comments such as those of Boston University's Dean William E. Huntington in the early 1900s about the low standards and preprofessionalism of some types of teacher education were probably echoed by other deans and liberal arts faculty members—particularly at major univer- sities with strong traditions in the liberal arts—some teacher educators may also have projected their own insecurities about status onto academic deans and other departments and been more "uncertain," to use Arthur Powell's term, than they needed to be.[72]

This is not to say that the record does not include evi- dence of real prejudice against teacher education and edu- cators, but it does not reveal as much as might be expected considering the quantity, quality, and persistence of teacher educators' concerns about status. One possible cause of this prejudice (and one to which teacher educators may themselves have contributed) was the fact that teacher educators were supposed to, and sometimes did, work with teachers and school administrators, some of whom may have been from lower social-class backgrounds than their own or from other liberal arts faculty members. These interactions with people whom teacher educators and other faculty members in private universities may not have thought of as colleagues or social equals may have exacerbated the real or perceived lack of prestige of teacher education within the university. It also may help explain why some teacher educators had as little contact as they did with school personnel, particularly urban teachers. More fine-grained research on the social history of teacher education and on the comparative social-class backgrounds of teacher educators, teachers, and other faculty members is needed to explore the extent to which such prejudice existed and whether it was imagined or real. Illusory or not, perceptions of the low status of teacher education relative to other fields have been powerful forces in education, both within academia and within schools.[73]

Finally, the fact that teacher educators in private universities had to comply with, or at least cope with, state teacher certification regulations and regulators may also have contributed to their real or perceived lack of status in academia. Few other faculty members had to ostensibly teach what the state told them to. As Robert Levin argues in Chapter Two, this loss of curricular autonomy rankled many teacher educators, particularly, I would argue, those in private universities, where state intervention is often perceived as antithetical to academic freedom and the professorial autonomy so prized in private university culture.[74]

On the other hand, the state's role in teacher certification may also have served to improve the status of some teacher education programs in private universities. At the same time that they complain about state intervention, teacher education faculties in private universities have not been above using the threat of removal of state approval as a means of maintaining or increasing faculty size internally—a main measure of departmental status in academia.

Exemplary of this potential of state intervention for both upgrading and downgrading the status and quality (which are not necessarily identical) of teacher education in private universities is the trend nationally to require an undergraduate liberal arts major and even a fifth year of professional teacher education. Although clearly intended as a means of improving the quality of teacher education by stressing the importance of liberal education—a goal that most teacher educators in most private universities wholeheartedly support—this new regulation may also have the effect of weakening undergraduate teaching by paring away some of the professional education courses and requirements. While some paring may be warranted, undergraduate teacher education programs in some private universities are already rather spare; shorn of the professional requirements instituted by state certification regulations, preservice programs in private universities may find themselves with an even less meaningful role to play within the university and with no new sources of support.

The concomitant requirement of additional graduate study in education to qualify for a permanent teaching credential will undoubtedly be a boon to private universities, however, which already provide so much of the graduate education in education. Thus, although the new certification regulations are meant to upgrade the profession, to make teaching "a major profession," like medicine or law—as a recent Massachusetts report on teacher certification is titled—diminishing undergraduate professional education could have negative consequences for teacher preparation generally, at a time when studies project a teacher shortage of major proportions in many parts of the country.[75]

This examination of the evolution of teacher education in private universities suggests that while basing undergraduate teacher preparation on a liberal arts model may provide teachers with a stronger academic background and knowledge of subject matter, as currently conducted it might also exacerbate other problems. Although some of the major graduate schools of education not in this sample are now taking a more active leadership role in undergraduate teacher education, most of their faculty members are still research oriented. Of course, being research oriented in and of itself is not problematic, although doing research can take time away from teaching—particularly from the kind of clinical teaching and supervision of student teachers in schools that teacher education professors do. In fact, a recent study of teacher education professors recommends that they produce more research. It is the type of research produced that is at issue. "Action-oriented," school-based research, relevant and responsive to the needs and concerns of teachers, may not be as acceptable to tenure committees or colleagues in academia as more traditional academic research. While teacher educators in other private universities may follow the lead of the major private universities and begin producing more of all sorts of research, it is not likely that other types of research or service or work in schools will be counted as much as academic research in determining tenure decisions or respect on campus. Thus, teacher educators in private universities will likely continue to be caught between their personal need to publish and the profession's need for them to spend more time with their colleagues in the schools.[76]

In spite of these negative aspects, there are some positive signs that the state and status of teacher education in private universities may be improving. Undergraduate enrollments were up in all of the nine places studied, and some faculty members and administrators spoke hopefully about increased interest in teaching on the part of students. Some of this revival may be due not to an increase in intrinsic interest in teaching, however, but to a resurgence of social activism, as a new generation of young Americans and some older Americans discover or rediscover the social issues and personal commitment that fired the reform movements of the 1960s. While this concern for social justice may translate into larger teacher education enrollments and renewed interest in urban teaching, these new teachers may not stay in the classroom much longer than did many of their predecessors (some of whom are now studying or educating educators), unless schools and schools of education change for the better, together.

Notes

1. W. M. Warren, "Report of the Dean of the College of Liberal Arts" (Jan. 8, 1906), as cited in A. S. Kahn, "An Historical Perspective on Teacher Education at Boston University's School of Education, 1918–1962" (unpublished doctoral dissertation, Boston University School of Education, 1962), p. 129.

2. H. Judge, *American Graduate Schools of Education: A View from Abroad* (New York: Ford Foundation, 1982); G. J. Clifford and J. W. Guthrie, *Ed School: A Brief for Professional Education* (Chicago: University of Chicago Press, 1988). The leading private graduate schools of education discussed in these studies but not included here are at Harvard, Stanford, the University of Chicago, and Teachers College at Columbia. For separate histories of Teachers College and the Harvard Graduate School of Education, see L. A. Cremin, D. A. Shannon, and M. E. Townsend, *A History of Teachers College, Columbia University* (New York: Columbia University Press, 1954); and A. G. Powell, *The Uncertain Profession: Harvard and the Search for Educational Authority* (Cambridge, Mass.: Harvard University Press, 1980).

3. This chapter does not deal with the larger history of private universities generally. For sources on this topic see, in particular, R. Hofstadter and W. Smith, *American Higher Education: A Documentary History* (Chicago: University of Chicago Press, 1961); F. Rudolph, *The American College and University* (New York: Knopf, 1962); L. R. Veysey, *The Emergence of the American University* (Chicago: University of Chicago Press, 1965); and B. M. Solomon, *In the Company of Educated Women: A History of Women and Higher Education in America* (New Haven, Conn.: Yale University Press, 1985).

4. W. F. Warren, as cited in W. O. Ault, *Boston University, the College of Liberal Arts, 1873–1973* (Boston: Trustees of Boston University, 1973), p. 53.

5. J. Ward, personal interview with R. A. Levin, as cited in

R. A. Levin, *Historical Case Study: Emory University* (Seattle: Center for Educational Renewal, College of Education, University of Washington, 1988), pp. 3, 5.

6. I am indebted to the collegial group of historians who
prepared the case studies on the institutions discussed in
this chapter. I have relied heavily on their work throughout, paraphrased their ideas loosely in places, and included direct quotations with citations when appropriate.
I hope I have done justice to their efforts, but I must
bear responsibility for the ways in which I have inter-
preted and used their work. Numerous archivists, institutional historians, faculty members, and administrators
also deserve recognition and thanks for their contributions to this research. General information on Emory is
from Levin, *Historical Case Study: Emory University.*

7. For a detailed discussion of the Junior League's speech
correction program, see B. Franklin, "The 'Best Ladies'
of Atlanta, Private Philanthropy, and Educational Reform: The Establishment of Special Classes for Learning
Disabled Children at the Junior League School for Speech
Correction, 1938–1959" (paper presented at the annual meeting of the History of Education Society, Oct.
1989).

8. J. C. Ward, personal interview with R. Levin, as cited in
Levin, *Historical Case Study: Emory University,* p. 17.

9. For descriptions of Ford's involvement in secondary education, see Clifford and Guthrie, *Ed School,* pp. 177–
182; and P. Woodring, *New Directions in Teacher Education*
(New York: Fund for the Advancement of Education,
1957).

10. J. Miller, as cited in Levin, *Historical Case Study: Emory
University,* p. 16.

11. Levin, *Historical Case Study: Emory University,* p. 17.

12. Levin, *Historical Case Study: Emory University,* p. 21.

13. For a general history of Boston University, and in particular its College of Liberal Arts, see Ault, *Boston University.*

14. W. E. Huntington, quoted in typescript, "The Training

of Teachers at Boston University" (undated typescript, Archives, Boston University), p. 5.

15. A. Wilde, "Report of the Director of the School of Education," in "Annual Reports of the President and Treasurer of the University for the Year 1919–20," *Boston University Bulletin*, November, 1920, 9 (25), 78.

16. A. Wilde, "School of Education, Annual Report," in "Annual Reports of the President and Treasurer of the University for the Year 1925–26," *Boston University Bulletin*, 1926, *15* (34), 66.

17. Wilde, President Marsh's file, Apr. 14, 1942, as cited in Ault, *Boston University*, p. 111.

18. Kahn, "An Historical Perspective," pp. 180–184.

19. D. Durrell, "School of Education, Annual Report 1946–47," in "Annual Reports of the President and Treasurer of the University for the Year 1946–47," *Boston University Bulletin*, 1947, *36* (16), 74.

20. Kahn, "An Historical Perspective," pp. 228–231; D. Durrell and others, "Adapting Instruction to the Learning Needs of Children in the Intermediate Grades," *Journal of Education*, 1959, *142* (Dec.), 2–78.

21. Interview with Burleigh Shibles, July 1988.

22. According to a survey of 1978 graduates, 23.7 percent found jobs in Boston. C. F. Shettle, *A Statistical Summary of Boston University's Survey of 1978 Graduates* (Boston: Office of Analytical Studies and Planning, Boston University, Mar. 1980), p. 16. Interestingly, these figures had not changed much; an analysis by the author of a listing of 133 graduates of the classes of 1919 to 1923 found that 26 percent of them had jobs in Boston. Boston University, *Alumni Directory of Boston University* (Boston: Alumni Bureau, 1924), pp. 199–201.

23. On Jesuit colleges and the history of Boston College, see P. A. Fitzgerald, *The Governance of Jesuit Colleges in the United States, 1920–1970* (Notre Dame, Ind.: University of Notre Dame Press, 1984); D. R. Dunigan, *A History of Boston College* (Milwaukee: Bruce, 1947); and B. Doyle,

"Points of Departure," *Boston College Magazine*, 1988, *47* (1), 25–31.

24. Doyle, "Points of Departure," p. 29. On women at Boston College, see L. Higgins, "The Development of Coeducation at Boston College," unpublished master's thesis, Boston College, 1973.

25. C. Donovan, "A Cheerful Reminiscence," *Boston College Magazine*, 1979, *41* (3), 9–16; and personal communication, May 4, 1988.

26. Doyle, "Points of Departure," p. 29.

27. Interview with Charles Donovan, May 4, 1988.

28. Interview with Kathleen Sullivan Connolly, Boston College, class of 1971, on Apr. 16, 1989; interview with Charles Donovan on May 4, 1988.

29. C. Donovan, "Tradition and Innovation in Teacher Education" (the eighth Charles W. Hunt Lecture of the American Association of Colleges for Teacher Education, Feb. 15, 1967, in Boston College Archives, School of Education Collection, RG16, Box 23, Folder 2), pp. 10, 12.

30. Donovan, "A Cheerful Reminiscence," p. 13; Donovan, personal communication; *Boston College Fact Book, 1971* (Boston: Boston College, 1971), p. 56.

31. *Boston College Fact Book, 1986–87* (Boston: Boston College, 1987), p. 26.

32. On the role of Boston College graduates in the Boston Public Schools, see, in particular, J. W. Sanders, "Catholics and the School Question in Boston: The Cardinal O'Connell Years," in R. E. Sullivan and J. M. O'Toole (eds.), *Catholic Boston: Studies in Religion and Community, 1870–1970* (Boston: Roman Catholic Archbishop of Boston, 1985), pp. 232–270.

33. Interview with Charles Donovan, May 1988; and telephone conversation with Joann Jones, director of field placements, July 1988.

34. K. Underwood, *Historical Case Study: University of Denver* (Seattle: Center for Educational Renewal, College of Education, University of Washington, 1988), pp. 2–3.

35. M. McGiffert, as cited in Underwood, *Historical Case Study: University of Denver*, p. 5.

36. *University of Denver Bulletin* (Mar. 1920), as cited in Underwood, *Historical Case Study: University of Denver*, p. 8.

37. Underwood, *Historical Case Study: University of Denver*, p. 17.

38. *Catalog of the University of Denver, 1900–01*, and *University of Denver Bulletin*, 1917, 1920, 1928, and 1933, as cited in Underwood, *Historical Case Study: University of Denver*, p. 19.

39. D. E. Angel, as cited in Underwood, *Historical Case Study: University of Denver*, p. 22; D. B. Connor, as cited in Underwood, p. 23; and Underwood, pp. 2–3.

40. In his 1967 quadrennial assessment, N. H. Evers, director of the School of Education, argued, concerning teacher education, that at "no time . . . had there been any serious questioning of the legitimacy of this aspect of the University's mission." Typescript, University of Denver Special Collections, as cited in Underwood, *Historical Case Study: University of Denver*, p. 18.

41. C. J. Ritchey, as cited in J. Herbst, *Historical Case Study: Drake University* (Seattle: Center for Educational Renewal, College of Education, University of Washington, 1988), p. 5.

42. Herbst, *Historical Case Study: Drake University*, pp. 7–8.

43. R. J. Altenbaugh, *Historical Case Study: National College of Education* (Seattle: Center for Educational Renewal, College of Education, University of Washington, 1988). Elizabeth Harrison's extremely popular book, *A Study of Child Nature from the Kindergarten Standpoint* (Chicago: Chicago Kindergarten College, 1895), went into fifty editions and was translated into eight foreign languages. On Harrison and her work and the Chicago Kindergarten College, see S. M. Rothman's *Woman's Proper Place* (New York: Basic Books, 1978), pp. 103–104; and E. D. Ross, *The Kindergarten Crusade* (Athens: Ohio University Press, 1976), pp. 55–56.

44. Ross, *The Kindergarten Crusade*, p. 56.

45. Altenbaugh, *Historical Case Study: National College of Education*, p. 7.

46. National College of Education, self-study report (1986), as cited in Altenbaugh, *Historical Case Study: National College of Education*, p. 12.

47. Altenbaugh, *Historical Case Study: National College of Education*, p. 11.

48. Altenbaugh, *Historical Case Study: National College of Education*, pp. 12–14, 19.

49. Altenbaugh, *Historical Case Study: National College of Education*, p. 19.

50. R. J. Altenbaugh, *Historical Case Study: Roosevelt University* (Seattle: Center for Educational Renewal, College of Education, University of Washington, 1988).

51. T. C. Lelon, as cited in Altenbaugh, *Historical Case Study: Roosevelt University*, p. 2.

52. Roosevelt University, *Report to the National Council for Accreditation of Teacher Education* (Chicago: Roosevelt University, 1986); Graduate Catalogue, Roosevelt University, as cited in Altenbaugh, *Historical Case Study: Roosevelt University*, p. 5.

53. Altenbaugh, *Historical Case Study: Roosevelt University*, p. 6.

54. Roosevelt University, *Five-Year Accreditation Report to the Illinois State Board of Education* (Chicago: Roosevelt University, 1985); faculty interviews, as cited in Altenbaugh, *Historical Case Study: Roosevelt University*, p. 7.

55. Illinois State Board of Education report (1985) and faculty interviews, as cited in Altenbaugh, *Historical Case Study: Roosevelt University*, p. 8.

56. Altenbaugh, *Historical Case Study: Roosevelt University*, pp. 10–12. Enrollment figures compiled by Altenbaugh (p. 13) from annual reports of the College of Education, Roosevelt University archives.

57. I. G. Hendrick, *Historical Case Study: California Lutheran University* (Seattle: Center for Educational Renewal, College of Education, University of Washington, 1988).

58. Mary Hekhuis, as cited in Hendrick, *Historical Case Study: California Lutheran University*, p. 2.

59. Hendrick, *Historical Case Study: California Lutheran University*, pp. 4–6.

60. Hendrick, *Historical Case Study: California Lutheran University*, p. 6.

61. "Long Range Plan," as cited in Hendrick, *Historical Case Study: California Lutheran University*, p. 8.

62. *Undergraduate Catalogue*, as cited in Hendrick, *Historical Case Study: California Lutheran University*, p. 11.

63. Hendrick, *Historical Case Study: California Lutheran University*, p. 9; *Academic Data Report, 1979–80, 1986–87*, as cited in Hendrick, *Historical Case Study: California Lutheran University*, p. 10.

64. R. A. Levin, *Historical Case Study: Mercer University Atlanta* (Seattle: Center for Educational Renewal, University of Washington, College of Education, 1988).

65. Virginia Nelms, as cited in Levin, *Historical Case Study: Mercer University Atlanta*, p. 3.

66. Virginia Nelms and Jean Hendricks, as cited in Levin, *Historical Case Study: Mercer University Atlanta*, p. 3.

67. Levin, *Historical Case Study: Mercer University Atlanta*, p. 6.

68. According to Virginia Nelms (as cited in Levin, *Historical Case Study: Mercer University Atlanta*, p. 6), in 1987–88 there were about 200 master's degree students registered, with about 90–125 on campus, and about 140 undeclared undergraduate majors (10 percent of undergraduates at Mercer Atlanta).

69. Nancy Zimpher and Kenneth Howey make the point that teacher education faculty members and their critics are divided on the issue of whether undergraduate teacher preparation is sufficient in length, while many, but not all, seem to agree that there are problems with the nature and quality of preservice teacher education. For a more detailed discussion and case studies of six midwestern preservice teacher preparation programs not included in the sample, see N. L. Zimpher and K. R. Howey, *Profiles*

of Preservice Teacher Education (Albany: State University of New York Press, 1989).

70. Judge, *American Graduate Schools of Education,* p. 53.

71. On the problems and promise of school-university partnerships, see K. A. Sirotnik and J. I. Goodlad (eds.), *School-University Partnerships in Action: Concepts, Cases, and Concerns* (New York: Teachers College Press, 1988).

72. Powell, *The Uncertain Profession.*

73. For a detailed study of the social class background of American teachers, see J. L. Rury, "Who Became Teachers? The Social Characteristics of Teachers in American History," in D. Warren (ed.), *American Teachers: Histories of a Profession at Work* (New York: Macmillan, 1989), pp. 9–48. On the ethnic and social class backgrounds of urban teachers in particular, see J. Perlmann, *Ethnic Differences: Schooling and Social Structures Among the Irish, Italians, Jews, and Blacks in an American City* (New York: Cambridge University Press, 1988).

74. An example of an objection to state intervention and loss of autonomy by a teacher educator in one of the private universities in this study is the recent response of Diana Pullin, dean of Boston College's School of Education, to proposed revisions in Massachusetts certification regulations. Pullin invokes both autonomy and academic freedom in her objections to specific aspects of the new regulations. Letter from Diana Pullin to Susan Zelman, associate commissioner, Division of Educational Personnel, Massachusetts Department of Education, Oct. 12, 1989, attached to agenda for November meeting of Massachusetts Advisory Council on Educational Personnel, with minutes of October meeting.

75. Joint Task Force on Teacher Preparation, *Making Teaching a Major Profession* (Quincy, Mass.: Bureau of Teacher Preparation of the Commonwealth of Massachusetts, 1989). For projections of teacher supply and demand, see National School Boards Association, *Good Teachers: An Unblinking Look at Supply and Preparedness* (Arlington, Va.: National School Boards Association, 1987).

76. See, in particular, R. Wisniewski and E. R. Ducharme, "Why Study the Education Professoriate?," M. Schwebel, "The New Priorities and the Education Faculty," and R. Wisniewski, "The Ideal Professor of Education," in R. Wisniewski and E. R. Ducharme (eds.), *The Professors of Teaching* (Albany: State University of New York, 1989).

6

Teacher Education
and Leadership
in Major Universities

Irving G. Hendrick

In 1984, about a year after assuming his post as dean of the Graduate School of Education at the University of California, Berkeley, Bernard R. Gifford stated well the lament of education in major research-oriented universities. Gifford wrote:

> Close scrutiny has rarely resulted in findings favorable to schools of education. More often than not, these reviews have found schools of education to be confused about their goals and objectives and unclear in their mission: driven too much by practical considerations and concerns, thus insensitive to the scholarly mission of the university; driven too much by scholarly considerations and concerns, thus insensitive to the problems that plague practitioners; too detached from the problems of schooling and too narrow in their intellectual pursuits to be relevant; too close to the problems of

Note: In addition to the author, those responsible for collecting information used in this chapter include Richard J. Altenbaugh, Kathleen Cruikshank, Linda Eisenmann, and Robert A. Levin.

schooling and too diffuse in their intellectual outlook to be scholarly.[1]

The seven institutions discussed here under the rubric of major universities have much in common, including a sharing of the lament articulated by Dean Gifford, albeit they are vulnerable to differing segments of it in differing proportions. The institutions are the University of California, Berkeley; the University of Illinois, Urbana-Champaign; Oklahoma State University; Pennsylvania State University; Temple University; the University of Georgia; and Georgia State University. All are large, with enrollments in excess of 20,000 undergraduate and graduate students. All derive a major share of funding from their host states. All are authorized to grant doctoral degrees. All have identified research as a significant part of their institutional mission. All have a history of exercising some leadership in matters affecting common school education in their states. All, except for the University of California, Berkeley, still prepare a substantial number of teachers; most, except Temple and Georgia State, have roots as land-grant institutions dating from the Morrill Act of 1862.

Four of the institutions—Berkeley, Illinois, Penn State, and the University of Georgia—meet R1 (Research 1) criteria of the Carnegie Classification of Institutions of Higher Education, meaning that they awarded a minimum of fifty Ph.D. degrees in 1983–84 and averaged at least $34.5 million in federal support for fiscal years 1983 through 1985. Temple and Oklahoma State—R2 (Research 2) institutions in 1987—trailed the first group in federal funding, while Georgia State—a Carnegie Class DG1 (Doctoral Granting 1) university—did not have sufficient federal funding in 1987 to be categorized as an R1 or R2 research university.[2]

Most important, *none* of the institutions has ever had teacher education as its primary, much less its exclusive mission. That said, one is also struck by the diversity of these institutions. Indeed, in some important ways, their diversity is more striking than their similarities. One finds, for example, that virtually every listing of "premier" universities since 1910

has included Berkeley and Illinois.[3] Rarely have the other five
institutions been so characterized. Yet even Illinois and Berkeley differ in fundamentally important ways as far as their approach to teacher education is concerned. Although both were
founded as land-grant institutions within a year of one another, in 1867 and 1868, respectively, the College of Education
at Illinois still helps prepare some 1,600 teachers annually, enrolls approximately 800 undergraduates as education majors,
is accredited by the National Council for Accreditation of
Teacher Education (NCATE), and has a professorial faculty in
excess of 100.[4] By contrast, while Berkeley demonstrated considerable involvement with teacher education through the mid
1960s, it now enrolls fewer than 100 teaching credential students, has no undergraduates in any of its teacher preparation
programs, and has fewer than 50 professorial faculty members.[5]

Of the seven institutions considered in this chapter, only
Berkeley is not affiliated with either NCATE or the American
Association of Colleges for Teacher Education (AACTE). The
other six universities are affiliated with both. Thus, it is on other
grounds, not teacher education, that Illinois and Berkeley look
much alike. Each has a substantial reputation for research and
graduate education, for extramural funding in support of research, and for having a high proportion of research-active
faculty members.

Founding Missions

Major public universities have had a substantial influence on the course of teacher education in their respective states.
Historically, they have had certain important advantages over
liberal arts colleges and teachers' colleges. Their comparatively
larger size, more generous budgets, more visible faculties, and
greater funding for research have given most of them a kind
of flagship status, even if only in their own states.

The Morrill Act of 1862 combined a policy for disposing
of public lands with a federal commitment to develop expertise
among the citizenry in agriculture and the mechanical arts. Each

state accepting Morrill Act land for the support of higher education was obligated to endow, support, and maintain at least one college that would, without excluding other scientific and classical studies, teach military tactics and "such branches of learning as are related to agriculture and the mechanic arts." The mandate was flexible enough to permit funds to be used by an established state university, as was done in fifteen states, or to be set aside for the establishment of an entirely new agricultural and mechanical college, as was done in twenty-eight states.

A lack of explicit language in the legislation permitted some interpreters to believe that a more general support of higher education was being encouraged, albeit one that would pay some heed to agricultural and mechanical studies. Other interpreters took the legislation as a clear call for "practical" studies. In some places, the struggle between contending forces as to whether the new university should stress literary or practical studies was heated, even bitter. Clearly, the Morrill Act did not settle the classical debate over the extent to which a land-grant university should stress thought over action. What it did do quite successfully was turn higher education into a kind of public property, thereby requiring that attention be given to the public's interests.

While considerable passion was expressed in some places over how much attention should be given to classical studies, there was never serious doubt that the act was intended to help farmers and the "industrial classes." Although liberal education could be promoted, there is little serious question that the legislation was intended to support practical and utilitarian studies. That notwithstanding, never in any of the debates concerning the Morrill Act was any mention made of preparing teachers. It must be assumed that during this Civil War period the Congress had military tactics and agricultural and mechanical education on its collective mind. If teacher preparation was thought about at all by Congress, it was likely seen as the responsibility of normal schools.

If the private liberal arts colleges were attending to classical and literary studies and the public normal schools were tending to the education of future elementary teachers, the new public land-grant universities were left with a giant niche in the scheme of things: everything that they wanted to take on. Certainly they were free to undertake most practical studies in the interest of providing higher learning for the working classes. By implication, that included the preparation of teachers for the emerging high schools and normal schools and eventually a panoply of professional schools. Nearly a century after passage of the Morrill Act, Clark Kerr referred to the institutional colossus that had become the modern-day manifestation of this development as the "multiversity."[6]

Because the founding of state normal schools sometimes predated the establishment of larger, more comprehensive collegiate-level institutions, it was perhaps inevitable that rivalry would emerge between the two types of institutions. This was especially true in Illinois, where the normal school had been given a significant early foothold. There, between 1857 and 1867, such funds as were appropriated from state sources for the support of higher education were directed to Illinois State Normal University for the preparation of teachers.

The major early movement, which was to lead eventually to the founding of the University of Illinois and other state universities of similar purpose, began at a meeting held at Granville, Putnam County, Illinois, on November 18, 1851. By invitation of an agricultural society known as the Buel Institute, various prominent citizens and farmers gathered to promote agricultural education. However, not until fifteen years later, on February 28, 1867, was an act approved incorporating the Illinois Industrial University.[7]

The first curriculum at Illinois included five departments, pedagogy not among them: agriculture; polytechnic (including mechanical science and art, civil engineering, mining and metallurgy, and architecture and fine arts); military; chemistry and natural science; and general science and literature, which included the curriculum of the classical colleges of the day.[8] The breadth of the curriculum, particularly the fact that literature and classical studies were included, caused early controversy at the Illinois Industrial University, as indeed it did at Berkeley and elsewhere.

For a time, early in University of Illinois history, the presidents were content to leave teacher preparation to the older normal schools. In 1882, the institution's name was changed to its present identity, albeit no commitment to the schools was immediately evident. Attempts to hire faculty members for the Department of Education in the College of Literature and Arts and the College of Science were halfhearted. Nevertheless, a kind of specialized niche was already emerging for education at Illinois. Preparing teachers for the growing number of public high schools as well as leaders in education—principals and superintendents—was becoming that niche.

Although the university would not, in the words of professor of pedagogy Arnold Tompkins, prepare work for "the great army of teachers," it would offer work on a "higher philosophic plane" for students with greater maturity, scholarship, and experience than those who would be attending normal schools.[9] Whatever the level of the students, with but one faculty member assigned to pedagogy for most of the period between 1891 and 1905, Illinois clearly would not be serving a large enrollment of aspiring teachers.

Richard Altenbaugh has characterized teacher education at Illinois as a "stepchild" program, early and late in the history of the institution.[10] Johnson and Johanningmeier, who authored the major scholarly study of education at Illinois, observed that the university could not "make up its mind" how to view the preparation of teachers.[11] Clearly, the first of several periodic upswings at Illinois occurred in 1904 with the appointment of Edmund Janes James as president. Having served as a village high school principal and as principal of the model high school at Normal, James not only was knowledgeable about public schools but was determined to advance their cause with help, even leadership, from the university.[12]

By the early 1900s, it was becoming evident to people at Illinois State Normal that James was committed to expanding the university's reach into all aspects of educational life in Illinois. Charles A. Harper, who served in 1935 as an associate professor of history at Illinois State Normal University, asserted that James had an "overwhelming and ruthless ambition to make of the University of Illinois an educational Colossus."[13] According to Harper, James believed in a great expansion of the work of the university in the field of teacher preparation and believed that the limit to that expansion was to be determined only by the amount of funding that could be secured from the state. James did not aim to put the normal schools and private colleges out of business, but he did aim to displace them with the University of Illinois at the head of the public school system. He also aimed to use the university's prestige and influence to secure greater state appropriations to be used in competition with the normal schools.

At issue in the emerging rivalry between the university and the state normal system was the proper role to be assumed by the latter institutions in the preparation of secondary teachers. The university under President James had for a time before 1910 successfully resisted the aspiration of the state normal university to train high school teachers. Even after that, the university reportedly used its power in accrediting high schools to dissuade school boards from employing any other than university-trained teachers and principals. Equally annoying to the normals was the university's practice of not recognizing bachelor's degrees from Illinois state normal schools for admission to the university's graduate school.[14] Both the University of Illinois and Illinois State Normal University recognized the long-running rivalry, even as they differed concerning which institution held the righteous ground. An intra-university letter from university provost A. J. Harno to President Arthur C. Willard in 1937 captures the rivalry's essence in raw terms: "Of this much I am clear. It should be the policy of the University to dominate the educational situation in the State. I believe we are called upon to do that by virtue of our position." Harno, as understood by Johnson and Johanningmeier, was persuaded that the teachers' colleges were "supposed to produce elementary teachers, and nothing more."[15]

The early experience with teacher education at the new University of California was similar in some respects to that which was unfolding at Illinois, albeit the feelings of institutional rivalry were less intense in California. Taking advantage of a Morrill Act grant of 150,000 acres, the California legislature established in 1866 an Agricultural, Mining and Mechanical Arts College. While the new college had funds but no campus, the private College of California had an adequate site in Oakland and additional property four miles to the north in Berkeley but inadequate funds to develop the institution. A year later, the college offered its buildings and its lands to the state on condition that a "complete university" be established to teach the humanities, as well as agriculture, mining, and mechanics. With state acceptance, the act of 1866 was repealed, and on March 23, 1868, a new act created the University of California. True to its charter, the university attempted to include in its curriculum a broad range of literary, agricultural, and scientific departments.

As was the case in Illinois, the early years at the University of California witnessed a controversy over the appropriate mix of liberal and technical studies in the curriculum and the funds that should be devoted to each. The issue was intense enough to provide substantial headaches for the early presidents. The most impressive of these leaders, Daniel Coit Gilman, could endure the pressure only for two years (1872–1874) before leaving to accept the presidency of the new Johns Hopkins University.[16]

Although most of the early presidents were able to define a course of action for the university that steered a delicate passage between literary and practical studies, none identified teacher preparation as an early or appropriate concern. As was similar to the situation in Illinois, California had earlier established a normal school in San Francisco (which was later moved to San Jose) for the preparation of elementary teachers. While it was assumed that the small proportion of the population preparing to teach in higher schools would acquire their preparation at the university, not until 1892 was there enough incentive to initiate a chair in pedagogy.

High schools in California were not state funded in 1892, and those that existed had small enrollments. Concern about the low enrollment levels in high schools, coupled with worries about the preparation level of students who entered Berkeley as freshmen, stimulated interest in teacher education. High school visitations had made some professors of literary subjects sensitive to the need for better-trained high school teachers, but, for the most part, their attention remained focused squarely on their subjects, not on the development of professional skill.[17]

As is typical in the case of vocational, technical, and professional studies, pressure for teacher education at Berkeley came from outside the university. Regents became aware of the need for high school teachers who would be better trained in academic subject and professional skills. They had been influenced by teachers and by the state superintendent of public instruction. By May 1889, public interest in teacher education was sufficient for the regents to authorize the academic senate to "announce the intention of this board to establish a course of instruction in the science and art of teaching as soon as the same can be properly organized."[18] After some additional prodding by the state superintendent, the academic senate agreed to approve the first program in teacher education, providing that the person chosen to head it be strong academically, including holding a Ph.D. degree.

Of the major universities, neither Berkeley nor Illinois was among the earliest in directing attention to pedagogics. The University of Iowa had converted its normal school into a Department of Pedagogy in 1873. Six years later, the University of Michigan established a full-time chair in education. In all, thirty-one institutions reported chairs of pedagogy by 1892, the year that one was finally established in the "science and art of teaching" at the University of California. A year earlier, both Illinois and Stanford University had initiated such chairs. The Stanford appointment was the first in a California university.[19] Perhaps not always coincidentally, the fate of education at Berkeley over most of the next century would be influenced by its fate at Stanford. Although a public university, Berkeley would take its cues over the next century at least as much from leading private universities as from public ones.

The other public agricultural and mechanical colleges

considered in this chapter held a more literal, more applied, and more populist interpretation of their Morrill Act mandate than did either Berkeley or Illinois. That is to say, Pennsylvania State, Oklahoma State, and the University of Georgia tended to follow rather faithfully the populist sentiment in favor of practical studies.

It was this popular view of the land-grant mission that shaped the course of teacher education at Penn State.[20] Prior to the widespread establishment of public high schools, the Penn State experience was not all that different from what was being experienced at Illinois and Berkeley. No education courses were offered during the institution's first thirty years, probably because the preparation of secondary teachers appeared unnecessary in the absence of a secondary school constituency. Although a chair in pedagogics was established in 1882, nineteenth-century enthusiasm for preparing teachers at Penn State was as restrained as it was at other major universities. According to Linda Eisenmann, once the need and the constituency became evident early in the twentieth century, Penn State seized teacher education as its firm mission and delivered it wherever it was needed, including eventually to a large group of "Commonwealth Campuses."[21]

If the popular sentiment at Penn State appeared a bit more "practical" or "applied" than it was at Illinois or Berkeley, at the new Oklahoma Agricultural and Mechanical College it was downright populist. There, both the state and the university got a later start. Not until April 22, 1889, was central Oklahoma opened to homesteaders in an area that earlier had been set aside by the federal government as Indian territory. Quickly the infant communities vied for institutional prizes. Guthrie laid claim to the territorial capital (which it later lost to Oklahoma City), Kingfisher fought successfully at first to be selected as the site for the state penitentiary (but later lost out to McAlester), Norman won the university, and Edmond won the territorial normal school. After a spirited community debate, the citizens of Stillwater and Payne County decided wisely to forgo contesting for the state capital and opted instead for the agricultural and mechanical college. In each case, the initial community victory was contingent on the community's ability to produce land and raise some funds locally. In the case of Stillwater, the legislature required eighty acres and $10,000 before it would finalize placing the A & M college in the community. As an institution heavily dependent on popular political support, Oklahoma A & M hardly could afford to become elitist. Indeed, it is unlikely that such a tendency was even considered. Only an institution that would prove itself useful to the sons and daughters of Oklahoma by remaining faithful to its agrarian and applied origins would stand a chance to succeed.

Thus, while agriculture, engineering, and veterinary medicine became prominent in the curriculum, consistent with the agricultural and mechanical tradition of the college, practically from the beginning the education of teachers became important to the campus as well. Considering the extremely modest educational level of the early settlers, the initial enrollment at Oklahoma A & M was tiny, partly because higher education was an option exercised by a very small percentage of the population, partly because the population base in Oklahoma was very small, and partly because there was no significant secondary school system to serve as a feeder institution for the college. Its potential constituency was not delimited by grade point averages or even by graduation from high school. Rather, it offered "technical and scientific education to white persons 14 years of age and over" almost without regard to their previous educational attainment beyond literacy. In effect, the opening wedge for what would one day become a school of education was the A & M college's preparatory department.

For many years, the preparatory department enrolled more students than were enrolled in the collegiate program, making it unlikely that the college could have survived its early years without the foundation provided by having secondary students. Although no courses in pedagogy were offered initially, Oklahoma A & M students used the preparatory department not only to prepare for collegiate education but also as a means to prepare for a teaching career.[22] By 1914, the campus had discipline clubs in agriculture, chemistry, and engineering, as well as a teachers' club. The latter, formed by John Bowers, the first professor of education, was described by the institution's historian as attracting "surprisingly strong" interest from students.[23]

Although Oklahoma State was a racially segregated institution during its first half century, it experienced a development pattern that was quite typical of land-grant universities in midwestern and western states. The University of Georgia, on the other hand, suffered the full effects of the Civil War and the Reconstruction period that followed. Black students were not admitted to the university until 1961, and its educational leaders on the whole attended little to the needs of black children. Even though a College of Agriculture was established at Athens with Morrill Act funds early in the 1870s, the traditional conservative aversion to public taxation restrained progress almost to the point of institutional stagnation. Thus, not only was teacher education admitted to the university as a way of serving the state, it was taken on practically as a matter of survival for the university itself. According to Kathleen Cruikshank, when teacher education first became a part of the university in 1903, it was part of a massive effort to redefine and finally establish the university as a permanent and integral part of Georgia's economic and social fabric.[24]

Since 1891, Georgia's state normal school had been designated as a "branch of the University," but ultimately the key to the survival of the university rested with the expansion of high schools. By 1905 and 1906, it was evident that the practical inclinations of the state's General Education Board would carry the Morrill Act spirit even to the emerging high schools. In 1906, the legislature approved a bill sponsored by the governor to establish a system of district agricultural and mechanical arts schools. While the curriculum of those schools at first emphasized traditional secondary school subjects, it is plain that vocational education and high schools got a boost from the legislation. The university's new Peabody School of Education was dedicated in the summer of 1913. According to Cruikshank, the Peabody School proved central to the future of teacher education in Georgia.[25]

In a sense, Georgia State University and Temple University in Pennsylvania had early missions not dissimilar in some respects to those at Oklahoma State and Georgia. Their roots, however, did not reside in the Morrill Act, or in rural America. Indeed, in the case of Temple, the roots were not even as a public university. Georgia State is a younger institution than the other major universities discussed in this chapter, having been founded in 1913 as a satellite engineering program of Georgia Tech. Later, it grew through the 1950s as the Georgia State College of Business Administration. Not until 1958 did the university form a Department of Education. Presently, the study of education shares center stage at the heart of Georgia State's reason for being. Issues of student and program quality have aroused some attention from the faculty of the College of Education, but the worry over "stepchild" status for teacher education, a frequent complaint at Berkeley and Illinois, does not seem to be a complaint there. With a powerful enrollment presence on the campus, and with a politically powerful group of school superintendents supporting the College of Education from the outside, Georgia State stands as a "profession-oriented" and "market-driven" institution.[26]

In some ways, Temple University has a mission that is not dissimilar to that of Georgia State. Both are urban-oriented universities. Temple serves primarily educators in Philadelphia; Georgia State serves educators in Atlanta. Neither place is likely to be accused of placing an undue emphasis on elegance or elitism. Both are practice-sensitive places. Although it was started as a private university, Temple was created as a modest and simple place to serve working-class interests in Philadelphia, albeit not necessarily by offering practical studies. Its founding and initial mission was unique by any standard. As told by former Temple president Robert L. Johnson, the first class came about almost by accident when one Sunday night in 1884 a young printer stopped by after worship services and advised his pastor, and the university's founder, Russell H. Conwell, that he wanted to enter the ministry but could not pay for an education. Johnson's story continued:

Dr. Conwell assured him that much could be achieved by evening study and offered to teach him one night a week. The youth asked whether he might bring a friend. Dr. Conwell told him to bring as many as he liked. When he appeared for the first appointment, he brought six friends. That was the first class, and Dr. Conwell began by teaching them Latin. Forty persons appeared for the third meeting of the group, and at this point Dr. Conwell, literally, had to hire a hall. They did not all aspire to the ministry, but, like the impoverished printer, they hungered for learning, and they had no other means of satisfying it.[27]

Over time, Temple became more traditional in its orientation, but its dedication to working urban students has been maintained.

Constituencies Served

More than in universities springing from the teachers' college tradition, education faculties at major state universities have been forced to take their behavioral cues from scholars in several related social science disciplines. This is especially so at the more research-oriented universities, such as Berkeley and Illinois. While it is less the case at the more service-oriented institutions, such as Temple and Georgia State, the priorities and values in all universities are to a substantial extent set by the most respected institutions. As has been the case since early in the century, education schools have had difficulty doing two jobs well. Thus, probably more definitively than in other professional schools, education faculty members have been encouraged to choose between a field-oriented, service-to-the-profession approach and a research approach, anchored in academic disciplines such as psychology and sociology.

Prior to the last two decades, Berkeley's School of Education had much in common with other schools and colleges of education in this group. While it was accelerating its efforts in teacher education, it was already engaged in graduate instruction.[28] By the 1920s, it was offering a full range of credential, master's, Ed.D., and Ph.D. programs for working teachers and administrators. Furthermore, it was already basing its selection of faculty members in education largely on the competence of the candidates to do research.[29]

A tabulation of all degree and credential holders in education made in 1939 in preparation for the university's display at the New York World's Fair of 1940 disclosed that Berkeley's education alumni were employed throughout the state as teachers, supervisors, principals, superintendents, and other administrative officers. In the sixteen years between 1923 and 1939, the school had granted 559 M.A. degrees, 83 Ed.D. degrees, and 42 Ph.D. degrees, including some to leading educators in the nation.[30] It is interesting that only in the last twenty years has Berkeley's orientation in favor of graduate degree programs and research completely overwhelmed its concern for preparing teachers.

On the other hand, the quality of the small surviving teacher preparation programs has been very high. Indeed, former dean of education Bernard Gifford observed that teacher education students, although they numbered fewer than a hundred, have become among the best students in the School of Education and compare favorably in academic qualifications with graduate students across the campus. Clearly, there is very limited pressure from the external community or from the campus community to educate teachers. Yet there is some support from the graduate division and from the central administration to maintain a small, selective, and exemplary program of teacher education.

Thanks to the approval of the Master Plan for Higher Education in 1960, the California State University System is able to offer large, full-service campuses at San Francisco, Hayward, and San Jose. Included are respected teacher education programs for Bay Area residents. Within the University of California, Berkeley ranks seventh among the eight general campuses in the number of teachers it produces, even though the campus enrollment is second in size only to that of UCLA.[31] Thus, with the basic supply of teachers being furnished by other state institutions, Berkeley has been able to concentrate on small, high-quality experimental programs, such as its Developmental Teacher Education Program.

Although teacher education at Berkeley is not without a history of attending to the state's need for teachers, especially before 1960, its programs of late have been much less market driven than those in any of the other six institutions. Because of rivalry with the normal schools, until the late 1930s the dean of education at Illinois felt obligated to deny that the College of Education had an undergraduate elementary teacher preparation program. True, some secondary students took their practice teaching in elementary schools and took jobs at that level, and some normal school graduates teaching at the elementary level came to Urbana for Saturday classes and summer sessions, but until 1941 the College of Education did not feel comfortable declaring overtly that it was serving elementary teachers.[32] Teacher education programs at most of the other institutions served primarily students who were the first generation in their families to attend college.

Perhaps Temple is the most vivid example of an institution designed to serve working-class evening students, but its service-oriented teacher education history is far from unique. Penn State experienced broad-based success offering summer courses to teachers early in the century and continued them through the 1920s, its emphasis on in-service teacher education with large summer and extension enrollments. Others, including Berkeley and Illinois, did this as well. The demand from teachers for summer work and "in-service" staff development work kept pressure on the universities to sustain and even expand their programs in education. During the first year of Professor Brown's services to the University of California before the turn of the century, he devoted considerable time aiding teachers at their institutes and associations, thereby providing early evidence of the university's helpfulness to the public school community. In the early years, some courses in education were scheduled for Saturday mornings to make them accessible to teachers, principals, and interested members of the public. In the summer session of 1922, Berkeley enrolled 2,695 teachers among its 5,212 summer session students.[33] By the late 1920s, the summer session was used as a means of relieving class loads during the regular year.

The in-service emphasis at Penn State experienced a bitter reversal during the 1950s, as the School of Education was unsuccessful in winning facilities and budget adequate to meet the heavy demand that was being placed on it by the public.[34] A decade later, prosperity returned under the presidency of Eric Walker. Education students, like the rest of the campus students, benefited from the growth wave.[35]

Almost anything that can be said about the service orientation of Penn State applies equally well to Oklahoma State, Georgia, and Georgia State. Programs useful to the people, including programs in teacher education, were at the center of what those institutions stood for. Although no direct comparisons of student qualifications are available, anecdotal information suggests that rarely, if ever, were teacher education students among the most capable or highest achievers on the campus. Frequently, however, they did not look very different from the average undergraduates on those campuses. Until recent years, the pressure was on enrollment, not on quality. Thus, the challenge became how to prepare large numbers of teachers to serve the growing school systems of the several states. Almost inevitably, the companion challenge was to prepare them rapidly and cheaply. Out of practical necessity, all teacher education programs, even the most selective ones, have tended to serve residents of their universities' local communities. Matters of cost, distance, shortness of programs, absence of lucrative scholarships, and state certification requirements have provided ample incentives for teacher candidates to limit their selection of institution to universities located in their home states, often near their own homes.

If the faculty in the liberal arts complained about education course content lacking in substance and rigor, it was a criticism that the campus administrations were prepared to endure. At least, they would endure it as long as enrollments were maintained at a high level and the public constituencies were pleased with the university's service to the schools.

Programmatic Development

The mid nineteenth century witnessed a general turning away from what Lawrence Cremin referred to as "shop culture," toward what he characterized as "school culture."[36] This general development was evident in most of what would become the "professions" of the twentieth century. Learning pharmacy, dentistry, veterinary medicine, or even the law by observing and working alongside an accomplished practitioner was slowly giving way to a pattern of planned instruction in schools and colleges. The practice of learning how to teach by presenting oneself before a class of children was slowly being replaced by the expectation that teachers would spend some time preparing for their work in normal schools. People—invariably women—who planned to teach in nineteenth-century elementary schools either did it without any advanced training at all or did it after some normal school preparation.

With the development of public high schools, universities became engaged in attending to the quality of those new schools by inspecting and accrediting them and by preparing their teachers. Over time, it became evident that some attention to pedagogy would be necessary to enhance the effectiveness of people who were assuming roles as high school teachers. To be sure, university faculty members in the liberal arts frequently did not jump at this new opportunity, but neither did they resist it with much passion. When the leadership was provided by a state school superintendent, by a university president, or by almost any visible and respected leader, almost inevitably a faculty position in pedagogy was created.

Because the few and scattered high schools were organized into departments or quasi departments, not unlike the structure at universities, it is not surprising that early secondary teacher education was undertaken by faculty members in

the university's subject matter departments. The appointment
of a professor of pedagogy, the creation of a department with
the same name, and eventually the establishment of schools
and colleges of education marked a departure from that practice and eventually led to greater professionalization of teaching and to competition between subject field and education
faculty members.

The case of Illinois was not unusual. There, in 1890, the
university appointed one faculty member—Charles De-
Garmo—from the Illinois State Normal University and, by so
doing, also formed the Department of Education within the
College of Literature and Arts and the College of Science.
DeGarmo, unfortunately, had bolder ambitions than the University of Illinois was prepared to nurture. He was determined
to organize a model school and attend to the practical matters
of teacher induction. University officials, on the other hand,
were content to have a person lecture on the theory and history of education.[37] DeGarmo stayed at Illinois only one year
before returning to the more hospitable—if not more prosperous—surroundings of Illinois State Normal University.

Over the next decade, a succession of professors occupied the "pedagogy" chair. However, while the university was
willing to offer lectures at teacher institutes and work with high
school teachers during summer months, it was not willing to
thrust itself wholeheartedly into the professional preparation
arena. It was willing to share insight from subject matter faculty members into determining how high school teachers might
best present their subjects to students; but, through the acting
presidency of Thomas J. Burrill, the university's leaders were
unwilling to risk offering work "below 'university grade.'"[38]
By early in the new century, the reluctance was softening, and
for a time it was even swept aside by a desire to establish firm
hegemony over public education in Illinois.

In 1901, professor of pedagogy Edwin G. Dexter offered nine undergraduate courses and one seminar, including
"principles of education," "psychology applied to the art of
teaching," several special methods courses, and one general
methods course featuring the Herbartian method as inter-

preted by Charles DeGarmo. Under Dexter, the special methods courses included English composition and rhetoric, English classics required for admission to the university, use of laboratory manuals, discussion and illustration of methods in algebra and geometry, and purchasing of apparatus.[39]

A pivotal advance in the university's teacher preparing commitment was realized in 1904 when the university senate adopted a position offered by its Council Committee on the University Preparation of Teachers for the Secondary Schools. The senate agreed that the university could do much more than it hitherto had done in the preparation of teachers for the secondary schools. A programmatic unit known as the "faculty of the school of education" was formed at Illinois in 1905 by organizing instructors from the several subject matter departments who taught courses to teachers. The school's mission was to prepare subject-based teachers for the high schools, as well as principals and superintendents. Although faculty members in the new school were to maintain their departmental affiliations, there was agreement that the faculty would need an administrative officer. The obvious choice, Edwin Dexter, was appointed as director of the School of Education for the 1905–06 academic year. Happily for Dexter, at least initially, he was supplied with all that he requested for operating the new school.[40]

Students preparing for secondary teaching followed what was characterized as a "general and flexible system of requirements" in order to meet the diverse needs of Illinois high schools.[41] In effect, students could decide whether they wanted to take a three- or four-year course in Latin, a one- or two-year course in chemistry, a half-year or a whole-year course in Latin, a one- or two-year course in botany. Choosing from lists of approved courses supplied by the subject departments, students would complete sixteen to twenty units of course work in at least one subject in order to qualify for a certificate of competency. After that, they could earn additional certificates in other areas by completing eight to ten semester units of work. These could be obtained either before or after graduation.

By 1909, under the leadership of Professor William

Chandler Bagley, the university even committed itself to the establishment of a practice school. Previously there had existed an academy, a preparatory school that was discontinued in 1912. Completion of the practice school was delayed because of numerous budget shortfalls and a weak commitment over the years. Finally, by 1921, the school was ready for use. Thus, for nine years, no practice teaching was offered to students. While its primary purpose was to train teachers, the practice school became what its predecessor, the academy, had been—a preparatory school for the university.[42] In creating training schools, major universities followed the normal schools, which had already been employing the approach in the preparation of elementary teachers. It was assumed that the training schools would showcase exemplary teaching practice, thereby fulfilling that part of teacher preparation for which apprenticeship was still considered important. At first, no provision was made for research or experimentation in the schools.

Like instruction in the rest of the university, the remainder of teacher preparation was carried out in university courses. Prior to the serious scientific study of education in the twentieth century, historical perspective was considered important because it represented the accumulated wisdom of humankind on the subject. At Illinois, as elsewhere, undergraduate students at the junior and senior levels enrolled in a standard sequence of educational history, theory, and methods courses. By the late 1920s, a student could either enroll in the College of Education and complete its curriculum or pursue a specialization outside the college with sufficient education courses to cover state certification requirements.[43] During the next decade, the University High School faculty began to play a more pronounced role in the undergraduate teacher preparation program—this by virtue of taking responsibility for various sections of the general methods course. Two consequences were a closer integration between practice teaching and methods instruction and a reduced dependency on specialized methods courses offered in the academic departments.[44]

The early teacher preparation curriculum at Berkeley was similar to that offered at Illinois. The first recorded course that was at all related to the professional preparation of teachers was offered by Professor George H. Howison in the Department of Philosophy, under the title "Teacher's Course, the Philosophy of Education."[45] As the nineteenth century was ending, Berkeley offered seven courses in pedagogy, all elective and all reserved for the third and fourth undergraduate years. As at Illinois, the offerings were heavily oriented toward a historical perspective. They included "The Art of Teaching," "School Supervision," "The History of Education (Earlier Periods)," "The History of Education (Later Periods)," "The Theory of Education," "The Origin and Development of School Systems," and "Seminar for the Comparative Study of Schools and School Systems." Students who completed the full teacher's course, made up of five of the seven courses, qualified for a certificate from the university. Requirements were:

1. Special knowledge: Ten hours per week for one year in the subject or group of closely allied subjects that the candidate expected to teach. Determination of student proficiency in those fields rested with heads of departments concerned.
2. Special knowledge: The completion of work in pedagogy, which might include the course on philosophy of education, amounted to six hours per week for one year.
3. General knowledge: This included four groups of courses from the following list: natural science, mathematics, English, foreign languages, history, and philosophy.

Of the seven original courses listed in 1892–93, Associate Professor Elmer Ellsworth Brown, an early Ph.D. from the University of Michigan, taught four of them. Alexis F. Lange of the English department taught a fifth, "The History of Education: the Latest Period." Beginning in 1904, "General Psychology" was made a prerequisite of all undergraduate courses in the Department of Education. In the initial year, the total enrollment in the five courses was fifty-five. There were nineteen students registered in "Theory of Education." Of the ten students enrolled in the seminar, one was listed as a candidate for the master's degree and two as candidates for the doctor's degree. The following year, additional students enrolled to obtain higher degrees.[46]

From the very beginning, teacher education at Berkeley was oriented toward making high school teachers proficient in the subjects that they expected to teach, but with the recognition that people other than Berkeley undergraduates could profit from the courses in education. Indeed, three constituencies were to be served: (1) students enrolled in education courses as electives contributing to "truly liberal culture," (2) students preparing to teach in high schools, and (3) graduates from the state normal schools of California. Enrollment of the third type of student indicated a conviction by university officials that their program could improve the competence of elementary teachers who previously had been trained in the normal schools. It is interesting that Berkeley had already conferred its first Ph.D. degree in education by 1897 and its first M.A. degree in 1898, well before 1905, when an undergraduate major was initiated in education.[47] By 1906, the Department of Education enrolled the largest number of graduate students in the university.[48]

Slowly over the next decade, faculty members were added, as were student assistants and temporary instructors. The Oakland and Berkeley school boards provided opportunities for students to do observation and some actual teaching under regular supervision and criticism.[49] In 1900, the title of the Department of Pedagogy was changed to the Department of Education. Among the staff appointments made over the next decade was that of examiner of schools in 1903, to spend half time examining high schools and the other half teaching in the department.[50]

Two years before the state prescription of "actual practice teaching" became mandatory in July 1906, the university mandated that only "students who have given evidence of superior attainments in the practice of teaching" would be given "a higher recommendation for the Teachers Certificate."

As early as 1904, President Wheeler advised the board of regents and the governor to consider the need for establishing and financing a high school to be used for practice teaching. Nothing was actually accomplished in that regard until a decade later, when University High School in Oakland was designated for teacher preparation. Even then, the university was not initially required to contribute to the school's support.[51] In 1919, the regents and the Oakland school board signed a new agreement, and construction was begun on a new building. The resulting new plant was completed in 1923 and was considered a superior facility for its day.

Courses required to meet the state board of education requirement beginning with the 1906–07 term included twelve units in the Department of Education:

1. Either "History of Education Later Periods" (three units) or "Historical Introduction to the Study of Education" (three units)
2. Either "Studies in Secondary Education" (three units) or "The High School" (three units)
3. Either "Studies in Educational Method" (two units) or "The Art of Class Teaching" (two units)
4. "The Practice of Teaching" (four units)

In 1913, Lange, then chair of the education department, which he had joined in 1906 after serving as professor of English and Scandinavian philology and dean of the College of Letters, recommended to President Wheeler the establishment of a School of Education comparable to the other emerging professional schools in the university. The academic senate concurred with the recommendation, and the school was established. Although Lange had served almost twenty years in the departments of English at the University of Michigan and at Berkeley, he was well prepared by training, experience, and— most important—interest to lead the education department. Further, there is no evidence that he looked on his reassignment as representing a serious loss of status or prestige.[52]

Early in the twentieth century, it became plain that the university was establishing itself at the head of the state's public school system and making itself useful to the lower schools. It is interesting that the university's leadership and autonomy over teacher credentialing came almost by default and was never greater than it was in the 1890s. Within a year after it adopted a set of requirements for students intending to teach in high school, the legislature amended the political code by empowering the state board of education to formulate conditions under which county boards of education could grant certificates without examination. The revised law established as the state's standard the university's diploma of graduation—a document that had been issued to students who had completed the required education program.[53]

In 1907, the Department of Education revised the list of groups that would be targeted for its services. Provisions were to be made for the training of teachers who (1) were preparing to work in the high school or in other schools of secondary grade, (2) were preparing to engage in school administration by becoming superintendents or principals, and (3) were graduates of normal schools but who were making further preparation for elementary teaching. The designated functions of the faculty included (1) furthering liberal culture by interpreting the significance of educational thought and institutions, (2) advancing the art and science of education through research, (3) providing professional preparation to future high school teachers and administrators, and (4) leading or assisting in the advancement of educational thought and practice.[54]

Considering his own standing in the humanities, Lange had no difficulty relating to the larger purposes of a liberal education, nor was he reluctant to consider courses in philosophy and other departments as prerequisites to education as a major subject leading to the bachelor's degree.[55] Apparently, the program and commitment of the faculty were appreciated by students who organized the Men's Education Club. Early in the 1910s, Lange selected a group of outstanding upper-division and graduate students to become charter members in Phi Delta Kappa, the professional education fraternity. Both organizations provided a means for the faculty to meet informally with selected groups of students and to influence the young men committed to careers in education.[56]

The broadening reputation of Berkeley among state educators led shortly to the appointment of Cyrus D. Mead as assistant professor of elementary education. Students in Mead's courses included people with teaching experience who were interested in advancing their levels of preparation. Although Berkeley was hardly hospitable to the training of elementary teachers, the move was not opposed by President Wheeler. In 1921—Wheeler's last year as president—the preservice training of elementary teachers was initiated. Even though elementary teaching was still considered to be the responsibility of normal schools, expediency dictated that the university begin at least a modest program. For many years, graduates of the university with no professional training had been obtaining teaching certificates by passing the county and city examinations. According to George C. Kyte, who soon became supervising principal of the University Elementary School and later a professor of education at Berkeley, the lack of professional training for aspiring elementary teachers had become a source of embarrassment to the university. Criticisms were heard that Berkeley graduates lacked teaching skill and thus did not compare favorably with normal school graduates.[57] Soon the university entered into an agreement with the Berkeley board of education to establish and jointly maintain an elementary school.

By the mid 1920s, there was a reorganization of the curriculum to revise and eliminate courses that had accumulated during the previous thirty years. Twenty-one courses were eliminated and six were reorganized in an effort to reduce duplication.[58] Slowly during the 1920s and 1930s, elementary education grew at Berkeley. To be sure, the focus was not exclusively on the preparation of teachers but included an evolving responsibility for the preparation of elementary school administrators, the construction of elementary curricula, and even some research in elementary education utilizing the University Elementary School facility. In 1939, a new facility was opened in cooperation with the Berkeley board of education, suggesting that the university was settling in rather well to its commitment and identity with preparing school personnel for the elementary schools.

It was clear through the 1950s and well into the 1960s that Berkeley was continuing to be actively engaged in the preparation of teachers. Increasing enrollments in both the elementary and secondary programs caused the adding of numerous sections of courses prerequisite to student teaching. One solution to the problem was to replace the general course in educational psychology and growth and development of children with specialized sections of "The School in American Society." A second solution was to provide systematic information about children in public schools through a course in "Learning and the Learner." In "The School in American Society," every section provided for observation of teaching and the consideration of other matters affecting schools and pupils.[59]

In an effort to be responsive to the shortage of elementary teachers, in 1962 a class of thirty-four postbaccalaureate students desiring to become elementary school teachers was organized. All of the students had obtained bachelor's degrees by pursuing majors other than education and without the usual sequence of education courses necessary for the teaching credential. For that experimental group, all of the necessary credential courses and student teaching were distributed over the two semesters of the fifth year.

Inside the Institutions

On questions concerning how university work on education and training teachers would proceed, the established organizational norms of the universities prevailed. Thus, departments, schools, and colleges were created. Teacher training never could be a primary mission of a major university. Thus, faculty members, such as Charles DeGarmo in the 1890s and William C. Bagley in the 1910s, who wished to work in an environment where teacher training was a paramount and respected mission appeared to be less than content with the major university environment. According to Johnson and Johanningmeier, Bagley "managed to advance both the education of teachers as a university function and the extension of pedagogy as a subject for full-scale, university-level inquiry."[60]

He had inaugurated graduate research in education and had also worked directly with educators in the field. Thus, while Bagley was proving successful by University of Illinois norms, he left Illinois in favor of joining the faculty of Teachers College, Columbia University—an institution whose mission was clearly and exclusively focused on the education of educators.

The classical conflicts between discipline-based methods faculties and education faculties not infrequently have been conflicts over turf. In many ways, they were not dissimilar to conflicts between letters and science faculties and business and engineering faculties over the extent of general education that should be required outside the major. In any case, evidence here suggests that intrauniversity conflict between liberal arts faculty and education faculties, while real, was not a continuing or particularly intense problem at major universities, nor was it unique to education. Not unlike what other professional accrediting bodies offered to business and engineering, state- and NCATE-mandated professional requirements in education served to undergird and protect the offerings of that field.

One must assume that the historically low status of teaching, as a female-dominated occupation, had much to do with the suspicion directed at the education faculty within major universities. That, coupled with sometimes lower admission standards in teacher education programs and a prevailing belief that teaching comes naturally, has left education schools in a disadvantaged position. Under Dean Thomas E. Benner, the College of Education at Illinois during the 1930s attempted to redefine its relationship both with the schools and with the letters and sciences faculty of the institution. His view was that high schools needed teachers who were educated in socially relevant content, undergirded by a broadly philosophical and social value orientation. Teachers, Benner reasoned, would need to be not merely pedagogically competent but especially well educated in content knowledge from the faculty in the College of Liberal Arts and Sciences.

At first blush, the approach appeared promising. Benner was even prepared to reduce the number of courses in education in order to accomplish his objective. The rub—one that would cause continuing conflict for Benner and eventually lead to his dismissal—concerned the fragmentation of liberal arts courses. The liberal arts departments had virtually no general education courses to give prospective teachers. Benner did not quarrel with the claim that the College of Liberal Arts and Sciences was really responsible for preparing secondary teachers. He did have a substantial quarrel with their neglect of that responsibility, especially as they allegedly neglected general undergraduate courses in favor of graduate-level scholarship.[61] Attempts beginning in 1936 to create a new University Committee on Teacher Education failed, while bitterness between Benner and his fellow deans grew. By 1940, the College of Liberal Arts and Sciences had almost come to developing its own college of education. For several years during the 1930s, courses in education carried no credit toward graduation, and central campus administrators contributed nothing constructive to resolving the disputes.[62]

Basic internal forces at the University of California, Berkeley, were no more hospitable toward preparing teachers than they were at Illinois. Berkeley did, however, enjoy one major advantage during the early years. Whereas Illinois educators from Chicago and much of the rest of the state looked at the University of Chicago for intellectual and professional leadership, Berkeley was California's university. The University of California's southern branch at Los Angeles, soon to be known as UCLA, was a rapidly growing but not yet mature university. Stanford was approaching but had not yet achieved its greatness; and while the University of Southern California (USC) enjoyed some regional prominence in certain professional fields, including education, it was not yet highly regarded by scholars in letters and sciences.

Chairperson Lange from the education department at Berkeley recommended to President Wheeler the establishment of a School of Education comparable to other professional schools in the university. Similarly, on March 10, 1913, the academic senate recommended that a school be established, with its intended constituency being undergraduates intending to become secondary or college teachers, students preparing to engage in school administration or teach in normal schools or university departments of education, and graduates of normal schools who wished to further their preparation for teaching in elementary schools. The faculty in the school would consist of members of the Department of Education, professors or instructors in other departments who taught professional courses approved as such by the president and the School of Education, and one member from each department representing a secondary school subject, but as yet offering no professional courses.[63]

The growing demand for teachers and expanded educational services following World War I stimulated the board of regents to become more sensitive to the educational needs of California. The state superintendent of public instruction, himself an ex officio member of the board, was a leader in this regard. Although the regents had been slow to act during the 1910s, in 1919 their finance committee included a recommendation regarding the School of Education that set forth clearly the committee's aspirations:

> That plans be immediately made for the establishment, not later than August 1, 1920 at the University of California, of a School of Education which at that time or soon as possible thereafter shall be adequately financed and equipped to train men and women for the teaching profession on lines comparable to opportunities offered in the Teachers College of Columbia University and the University of Chicago. That under the School of Education there be drawn together all those efforts now being made by the University of California in the training of teachers, and in addition there shall be created such further functions as shall be necessary to give new light and opportunity for perfection of teaching.[64]

The school was indeed founded and was supported well by President Wheeler. Clearly, however, preparing elementary

teachers was not a responsibility that the university entered into
without pause. True, it had done so in 1921, but only on a
modest scale. Wheeler's second successor, President William
Campbell, several regents, and more than several academic administrators and faculty members had never looked with favor
upon preparing teachers, especially elementary teachers. They
considered the activity to be below university level and considered the large and prominent Teachers College at the university's southern branch in Los Angeles to be a particularly
"illogical and unfortunate" development.[65]

It is likely that Berkeley's increasing ability to extend itself into elementary teacher preparation was reinforced by the
will of the public, as expressed through a majority of the regents and the state superintendent of public instruction. President Campbell and certain traditionally oriented letters and
sciences faculty members were powerful, but they were not all-
powerful. The showdown event was the university's decision to
move the southern branch from its location near downtown
Los Angeles to a large new campus on the west side of the city.
Although his predecessors and the regents had weakened in
allowing the university to acquire the normal school in Los Angeles, President Campbell reckoned that he had one final chance
to redress that mistake. His strategy was to vigorously oppose
allowing the Teachers College to accompany the College of
Letters and Sciences to Westwood when the branch was relo-
cated. On July 2, 1927, Campbell told southern branch provost
Ernest Carroll Moore that "the training of elementary teachers
does not belong in the University." As the conversation un-
folded, he acknowledged that "what I object to is that as President of the University of California I have to sign kindergarten credentials."[66] Eventually, Provost Moore, himself a strong
teachers' college supporter, and the regents, led by Edward A.
Dickson of Los Angeles, prevailed over the president's objection, and UCLA was permitted to move to its new Westwood
location with both a School of Education and a College of Letters and Sciences.

Not all presidents, of course, were as hostile to the university's participation in preparing elementary teachers as

Campbell had been. Clifford and Guthrie recall the inaugura-
tion speech of University of California president Robert Gor-
don Sproul in 1930, on which occasion he observed that the
university could not afford to be less than a great university if
it were still to "be worthy of the splendid public school system
of which it is a part."[67] Sproul defended the work of his education schools at Berkeley and Los Angeles but seemed to acknowledge a reluctance even then on the part of many education professors to be associated with teacher education, as well
as doubts by many in the academic community concerning the
appropriateness of maintaining departments and schools of
education.

Nevertheless, in spite of some hostility from within the
school and university, it seemed that during the half century
following establishment of the School of Education, the unit
was fulfilling its teacher preparation and educational leadership roles quite well. The school's deans, professors, and graduates filled influential positions in California education, and each
dean through 1962 maintained strong and active support for
teacher preparation programs. Professor of Education Emeri-
tus James C. Stone remembers that when he came to Berkeley
to direct the Division of Teacher Education in 1956, having
served immediately prior as chief of the Bureau of Teacher
Certification in the California State Department of Education,
the atmosphere on campus was positive toward teacher education. Stone recalled that Dean Herbert Brownell held teacher
education in high regard. True, research was growing in importance, but its growth did not appear to be coming at the
expense of teacher education. Stone's additional responsibility
involved intensive planning, developing, and directing of an
experimental interning path to secondary teaching. Berkeley,
like other major universities, proved itself responsive to the
serious teacher shortage of the 1950s. By the time of Brownell's retirement in 1962, enrollment in the elementary and
secondary credential programs hovered around its peak of 400.[68]

It is difficult to realize that as recently as thirty years
ago, Berkeley was the largest producer of credentials for school
service in California. Data from the state department of edu-

cation revealed that in 1957–58, 3,358 people with bachelor's degrees from Berkeley held some form of credential for school service in California. The university's sister campus, UCLA, ranked second, with 3,231. By contrast, the largest producer of credential holders among the state colleges was San Jose State, with 2,871, followed by San Francisco State, with 2,306. Among people awarded certificates in 1957–58, 2,991 had completed graduate units applicable to a credential at Berkeley, ranking it first among public institutions in the state.[69] Only the University of Southern California, a private institution, had produced more. In addition to producing a significant number of teachers, Berkeley also prepared a large number of people who held advanced degrees and credentials relevant to school service, particularly administrative service. In 1963, Berkeley employed forty professorial faculty members and forty supervisors of teacher education.[70] Twenty-five years later, the number of professorial faculty members remained at nearly forty, but the number of supervisors had declined to ten, and five of them were working in the school psychology and administrative services areas.

A development of some significance in the university was the establishment of this two-tier faculty. Although the policy permitted supervisors to remain active in preparing teachers without fear of termination for lack of producing published research, this was not why the policy was initiated. The discontinuance in 1946 of the University High School led the university and the Oakland board of education to adjust their complicated system of sharing expenses pertaining to the school's operation. The supervisory staff, which had been responsible for the clinical experiences of student teachers at University High School since the early 1920s, was moved to the campus. From that day to this, supervisors of teacher education, as full academic—but not professorial—employees of the university, have assumed increasing responsibility for the preparation of teachers. At first, their role was limited to supervising practice, but slowly during the post–World War II era, it was expanded to include methods instruction. For their part, professorial faculty members retreated from teacher education in favor of assuming increasing responsibility for graduate instruction. By 1950, the supervisory staff had grown slowly to twenty-one full- and part-time members; by 1959, it was thirty-five, with most of the increase at the secondary level.[71]

Even in the early post–World War II period, Berkeley's greatest days in teacher education were still ahead of it, and educating teachers was still prominent among its missions. A 1948 statement on the subject listed educating leaders in education, educating teachers (both preservice and in-service), research, and field service as the stated functions of the school.[72]

Concerns about quality have always been paramount at Berkeley. In 1934, the American Council on Education published its "Report of the Committee on Graduate Instruction." Fortunately, the School of Education did rather well, in relation both to other education schools and to other fields on the Berkeley campus. Of the sixty-one university divisions of education included in the study, Berkeley's department was one of the ten rated as "distinguished." It was also one of nineteen fields at Berkeley receiving this highest rating, while ten other units were rated as "adequate."[73]

The 1920s at Illinois were, according to historians Johnson and Johanningmeir, marked by a perception of stagnation or even decline in teacher education—this in spite of an enrollment growth in education from 87 in 1919–20 to 1,031 in 1929–30 and a growth in faculty from 22 to 74.[74] Most of the increase, however, was not in teacher education but in the athletic coaching program. By 1930, Illinois had lost most of the national leadership that it had been able to claim in education at the end of World War I. There was a continuing mix of signals on campus from outside the College of Education as to what leadership Illinois should be exercising. Unlike his predecessor during the 1920s, Dean Thomas Benner in the 1930s did know where he wanted to take the college. Yet, even as he was failing to persuade his fellow deans and the central administration that his view of teacher education was the proper one, the central administration did not couple its disdain for Benner with a more generalized desire to disengage from the preparation of teachers.[75]

Benner's forced departure in 1945 did have a salutary effect on internal harmony and, for the College of Education, ushered in an opportunity to pursue new teacher education ideas under new faculty and administration leadership. Although Benner's vision of a "University Committee on Teacher Education"—to be composed of representatives of all subject matter departments preparing teachers—was rebuffed, the idea was accepted after he left. To this day, a similar council has jurisdiction over teacher education programs. Under Dean Willard Spalding's less confrontational leadership, not only was this university-wide coordinating body initiated, but commitments to continuing programs were deepened.[76] From the mid 1950s through the early 1970s, teacher education prospered because the College of Education was prospering. The twin sustainers of academic programs—growing enrollment and increased funding—had a favorable impact on teacher education. Teacher education programs prospered even as inquiry and research were growing in importance within the College of Education and throughout the campus.[77]

Heavy enrollment declines beginning in the early 1970s led to an accelerated decline in the morale of faculty members participating in both the elementary education and secondary education programs at Illinois. If the teacher education and research-inquiry missions appeared to coexist nicely during prosperous times, they increasingly seemed at odds in the face of scarce resources and a sharp decline in the need for teachers. For a time at least through the 1960s, faculty members could be promoted and otherwise rewarded for teacher education work, albeit the rewards would be slower in coming and more modest than those that accrued to the nationally prominent researchers.[78] By the mid 1970s, the ticket to respect and recognition was placed increasingly on publications of high quality.

At Oklahoma State, life was pretty pleasant for education dean Napoleon Conger during the 1930s and 1940s, thanks to Conger's leadership and to the fact that his policies were also favored by the university's president, Henry Bennett. Certainly it did not hurt that Conger and Bennett were close friends and that the president had recruited Conger. If teacher education was not pursued with great creativity, neither was it subject to much criticism at Oklahoma State.

At Penn State, Will Grant Chambers served as first dean of the School of Education. His fourteen-year deanship lasted from 1923 to 1937 and was enormously successful by prevailing standards of that day. According to Linda Eisenmann, the Chambers years were "a lively, fruitful, and activist time for teacher training at Penn State."[79] His success doubtless was the product not only of his own personal leadership qualities and knowledge of education but also of the fact that he was recruited to Penn State by its new president, John M. Thomas. The new president placed education at or near the center of his plans for higher enrollment at the institution and greater Penn State influence around the state. Second, Chambers was as well connected in state education circles as he was with the president. With President Thomas's support, Chambers was able to make several organizational and programmatic moves to enhance the size and influence of education at Penn State.

Certainly, schools and colleges of education changed a good deal in the decades after Will Chambers, Willard Spalding, and Napoleon Conger experienced their successes at and before mid century. Yet, for two decades after World War II, the teacher education faculties at Oklahoma State, Georgia, Georgia State, Temple, and to a lesser degree Penn State and Illinois were able to carry on their work much as that work had been conducted decades earlier. Perhaps what made teacher education particularly vulnerable as university attitudes favorable to research became dominant was that many faculty members who engaged in preparing teachers were ill prepared in research and inquiry. Not only did teacher educators become isolated from those who pursued research questions, but those who engaged in the research became substantially isolated from everyone except other researchers. At bottom, the problem became one of a confused mission in major universities.

External Forces

A basic conclusion that one derives from the study of teacher education at major research institutions is that, for the most part, the activity was initiated and sustained by outside influences. True, a few university presidents seemed to demonstrate a genuine interest and desire to advance the cause of teacher training. More often, especially at Berkeley and Illinois, they consented to it, not infrequently with a sense of skepticism. Relatively few of the external events were truly epochal in nature; the Civil War, which substantially delayed developments in Georgia and other southern states, was one that was. Some events were national in scope and influence—for example, the Great Depression of the 1930s, World War II and its impact, and the national criticisms of teacher education that appeared in the early 1960s.[80] Some were more regional in nature—market conditions affecting the placement of teachers; some were unique to developments and institutional responsibilities in a single state—the Master Plan for Higher Education in California. Others were generally prevailing but had more to do with the economic attractiveness of teaching as a career than with a particular state policy.

Every state has examples of external forces playing a role in shaping the nature and extent of teacher education in that state. For example, a resolution of support from the Eastern Illinois Teachers Association in 1910 was used by President James and Professor Bagley to counteract the efforts of Illinois State Normal's president Felmley to contain and minimize the university's work in teacher education.[81] The external reality of dramatic growth in high school enrollments provided a major stimulus to programmatic developments in all of the states. In the absence of other significant institutions for training high school teachers, the major universities could not ignore their obligations. But external forces, specifically the small size of high schools, the need of high schools for teachers who were generalists instead of specialists, and the fact that these realities were reflected in state certification requirements, also did much to direct and constrain the quality of secondary teacher preparation. Pressures and limitations considered, the new result was that by the 1930s high school teachers in California, Georgia, Illinois, Oklahoma, and Pennsylvania were looking to the major state universities for programs applicable to their professional needs.

One major external force that drove the teacher education curriculum throughout the century was state certification requirements. Not only did such requirements shape programs within universities; they took on a distinct life of their own, making it possible for students to enroll in classes at a diversity of institutions and apply directly to the state credentialing offices for their credentials. In California, when the state board of education was attempting to meet the teacher shortage of the early 1920s, it first approved direct application by candidates to the state for credentials. Consistent with the letter and spirit of the new policy, beginning in 1923 the University of California listed the state requirements and permitted students to proceed to the credential under those requirements. Since the state had assumed responsibility for establishing the teacher preparation curriculum, the university's minimal obligation was to offer the courses and provide students with responsible advice concerning requirements. The new policy was of particular service to out-of-state applicants, who could submit their transcripts to the university's credential counselor for a comparison with California requirements.[82] Except for an occasional experimental program, most of Berkeley's effort and responsibility in teacher education from that time forward was directed toward meeting state prescriptions. This does not imply that the faculty objected to the state requirements, although from the 1960s onward, that was increasingly the case.

The fertile climate in California for legislated solutions to what allegedly was ailing teacher education was manifest in reform laws approved by the legislature in 1961 and 1970. While the legislated elimination of the elementary education major through the Fisher Act of 1961 and a nine-semester-unit cap placed on professional courses required preliminary to student teaching through the Ryan Act of 1970 were aimed mainly at the regional state colleges, all colleges and universities were affected.[83]

Such legislation served to point out that doubts about the academic credibility of teacher preparation programs could be played out within the larger political process of the state, as well as through the institutional politics of a university. State teacher credentialing laws were proving to be a mixed blessing for teacher educators. As was previously noted in reference to Berkeley, the California legislature had enacted a law during its 1901 session authorizing the state board of education to determine what level of teacher preparation was equivalent to graduation from the University of California with a faculty-recommended certificate to teach. Although the university's standard for determining teaching competence became for a time the state standard, in the years that followed, the influence of major universities was reduced, as school officials, accrediting agencies, teacher organizations, citizen groups, and the state educational agencies grew in power and influence.[84] Yet, through the 1950s in California and to the present day in most other states, state requirements have not been viewed as an alien or antagonistic force by most teacher educators.

On the contrary, in most states, external state controls frequently continued to be compatible with the wishes of education deans and directors of teacher education. Recent reform legislation in Oklahoma was influenced heavily by education deans from Oklahoma State University, the University of Oklahoma, and the regional state universities.[85] There, in 1980, the state legislature passed Bill 1706, which raised admission standards for teacher preparation programs, required more clinical fieldwork in the preparation process, mandated competency examinations in subject areas before graduation, added an entry-year internship before certification, and included regular monitoring of first-year teachers by a committee composed of a principal, a consulting teacher, and a teacher educator. While this legislation was indeed an external force on teacher preparation programs in Oklahoma, it also was the product of an initiative from deans of education. A similar example can be cited from Georgia, where the education faculty from the University of Georgia contributed heavily to the state's competency-based teacher education initiative of the last decade. While the state department of education also took a leadership role in Georgia, the major ideas and testing of ideas came from the university.[86]

An inevitable conclusion to be drawn from these examples in California, Oklahoma, and Georgia is that schools of education in major universities frequently can be highly influential when they choose to be. However, unlike in former days, deference will not be accorded to them automatically by government agencies; nor, indeed, may it be assumed that education deans and faculties will even choose to enter the fray.

Within national teacher education circles, the National Council for Accreditation of Teacher Education is the major external force in guiding programmatic decisions. To university faculty members involved with teacher education, NCATE often appears as a nuisance—an external force that is as likely to limit programmatic creativity in teacher education as to enhance standards. Yet, except for Berkeley, all of the major universities represented in this sample are members of NCATE. For teacher education directors and deans in these institutions, NCATE is as likely to be seen as an ally as an intruder. Sometimes NCATE standards help education deans negotiate for faculty positions, budget, curriculum resources, and space. Indeed, many NCATE officers are or have been employed as faculty members and administrators at education schools of major universities. Most importantly, NCATE standards are those that have been agreed to by insiders within the profession. It is mainly when education deans and faculties set their sights beyond the teacher training school mission that serious alienation from NCATE is likely to set in.

An example of NCATE fraternity with a major university is evident in the recent history of Oklahoma State. There, the linkage between the School of Education and NCATE was positive and unmistakable. One of the institution's popular deans from the 1950s and early 1960s left the Stillwater campus to serve as associate director of NCATE. Even now, both the professional accrediting agency and the state department of education serve as bastions of reinforcement for the College of Education. The agency's requirements, written essentially by like-thinking persons, and often by education deans sitting in committee, typically help the dean of education achieve his or her objectives.

Parenthetically, it should be pointed out that external forces have helped shape the nature not only of preservice

teacher education but of in-service education as well. For example, beginning in 1923, public school systems in California,
including those in the San Francisco Bay area, joined the national movement to add salary increments to their salary
schedules on the basis of the additional training obtained.[87]
This policy influenced greatly the attractiveness of fifth-year
preservice programs for high school teachers, as well as master's degree programs and advanced credential programs in all
fields. Among other things, it encouraged teachers to accu-
mulate college units toward administrative or other advanced
credentials during summer and evening classes at Berkeley and
elsewhere.

Leadership

Several rather obvious observations are in order. First,
strong, effective leadership matters. Schools of education that
have prospered have done so when the dean of education and
the university president were able to maintain good communication and held compatible educational views. Second, state-
supported institutions are enrollment driven, meaning that
programs with stable and growing enrollments are likely to
survive relatively unscathed. Several illustrations from the case
histories would seem to support this view. Similarly, a consistent institutional commitment to the education of teachers frequently has proved to be too weak to transcend the loss of a
supportive and effective university president or dean of education. Thus, for example, without the vision and energy provided by President Edmund James and Professor William Bagley during the 1910s, teacher education languished in the
subsequent decade at Illinois during the presidency of David
Kinley and the deanship of Charles Chadsey.[88]

Notwithstanding the increasing research orientation at
many major universities, teacher education continues as a program on all seven campuses. Furthermore, whatever its problems with status, the place of teacher education seems secure
on all of the campuses, at least at current enrollment levels.
Although teacher education students invariably are drawn from

neighborhoods near their universities, the number of them present on a given campus inevitably says something about the niche that that campus has found for teacher education programs. It is probably fair to suggest that all seven of the campuses would lay claim to leadership in teacher education, albeit the basis for their claims would vary, ranging from a large number of graduates prepared to the development of model programs to influence on state policy.

Certainly not all leadership rests on research and model program development. Oklahoma State, sometimes Oklahoma's largest university, invariably maintains the largest teacher education program in Oklahoma. Since the mid 1930s, when Dean Conger first articulated his aspiration that the School of Education "no longer be known as one of the several schools of education in Oklahoma, but as *the* School of Education in Oklahoma," the school (later the College of Education) has never been far removed from the public education scene in Oklahoma.[89] Although it is not likely to be found on any list of the most prestigious—that is, research-oriented—education schools in the nation, Oklahoma State still can make a credible claim as having the leading school or college of education in Oklahoma. It has remained close to the profession over the years, while at the same time maintaining compatibility with values common to the culture of the campus.

Among the campuses studied here, only at Berkeley do Ph.D. and preservice teacher credential students compete for the same allotted student vacancies. There, the number of student applications for various programs greatly exceeds the number of graduate student spaces available. Since the campus is at its capacity, the several academic units operate with enrollment quotas. Thus, School of Education officials have the option of admitting students to teacher education programs, to various M.A. and advanced credential programs (such as administrative services), or to Ed.D. and Ph.D. programs. With that kind of constraint on enrollment, coupled with an opportunity for selectivity, it is little wonder that teacher education students at Berkeley are small in number but very good. Considering the culture of Berkeley and the high volume of teacher preparation being assumed by campuses of the California State University, it is also quite understandable that the small pre-service teacher education programs are experimental and innovative.

Perspective

The American common school filled a need primarily for public school teachers, but it also filled a need for principals, superintendents, and people to prepare teachers and provide leadership in aspects of curriculum development and pupil progress. Seventy years ago, William Chandler Bagley held a conception of mission for major universities that placed them at the top of the state's school system. The universities certainly would engage in preparing teachers, but just as certainly they would not insist on any exclusive jurisdiction in that regard. Unlike normal schools, their unique contribution to public schools, and to the teachers working in those schools, would be research of a social service sort.[90] If that leadership was a sometime affair, perhaps it is fair to suggest that such leadership as was in evidence tended to come from major public and private universities.

Among the institutions studied here, in no case did university presidents provide sustained psychic support for teacher education, much less provide generous financial support for the enterprise. Neither, of course, was their neglect complete and consistent. Generally, the schools and colleges of education were at least tolerated or indulged; often they were accepted as necessary to helping fulfill the institution's public mandate; rarely were they respected for the rigor of training that they offered students or for the depth of their scholarly inquiry. Over time, as the culture of universities became more committed to pure inquiry, the fate of teacher education became more problematic. If education school deans and faculties *sometimes* recognized that an orientation toward teachers, pupils, and schools was necessary to fulfilling the professional school mission of their units, that orientation was challenged by the dominant research and inquiry culture of the universities. The predictable result was that the most inquiry-oriented schools and colleges of education became confused as to their mission and direction. It is regrettable, if understandable, that a consistent professional school orientation involving the integration of high-level inquiry with a commitment to improving teaching practice in the schools has yet to be realized in any consistent way. The good news, of course, is that no type of institution is better equipped to achieve that virtue than major universities.

Notes

1. B. R. Gifford, "Prestige and Education: The Missing Link in School Reform," *Review of Education,* 1984, *10* (Summer), 186.
2. Carnegie Foundation for the Advancement of Teaching, *A Classification of Institutions of Higher Education* (Princeton, N.J.: Carnegie Foundation for the Advancement of Teaching, 1987).
3. G. J. Clifford and J. W. Guthrie, *Ed School: A Brief for Professional Education* (Chicago: University of Chicago Press, 1988), pp. 51–55, 127.
4. Association of Colleges and Schools of Education in State Universities and Land Grant Colleges and Affiliated Private Universities, *Directory, 1986–88* (Stillwater: College of Education, Oklahoma State University, 1986).
5. Office of Information Systems and Administrative Services, *Statistical Summary of Students and Staff, University of California, Fall, 1988* (Berkeley: Office of the President, University of California, 1988), p. 1; B. R. Gifford, *Graduate School of Education Faculty Recruitment Proposal for Target Years 1989–90 and 1990–91* (Berkeley: Graduate School of Education, University of California, 1988), p. 1.
6. C. Kerr, *The Uses of the University* (Cambridge, Mass.: Harvard University Press, 1963).
7. F. W. Scott, *The Semi-Centennial Alumni Record of the University of Illinois* (Urbana: University of Illinois, 1918), pp. vii–viii.
8. Scott, *The Semi-Centennial Alumni Record,* p. x.

9. H. C. Johnson, Jr., and E. V. Johanningmeier, *Teachers for the Prairie: The University of Illinois and the Schools, 1868–1945* (Urbana: University of Illinois Press, 1972), p. 105.
10. R. J. Altenbaugh, *Historical Case Study: University of Illinois* (Seattle: College of Education, University of Washington, 1989), p. 19.
11. Johnson and Johanningmeier, *Teachers for the Prairie*, p. 456.
12. Johnson and Johanningmeier, *Teachers for the Prairie*, pp. 135–137.
13. C. A. Harper, *Development of the Teachers College in the United States* (Bloomington, Ill.: McKnight & McKnight, 1935), p. 325.
14. Harper, *Development of the Teachers College*, p. 334.
15. Johnson and Johanningmeier, *Teachers for the Prairie*, p. 368.
16. V. A. Stadtman (ed.), *The Centennial Record of the University of California* (Berkeley: University of California Press, 1967), pp. 1–2.
17. G. C. Kyte, "Education in the University of California at Berkeley, 1892–1965" (unpublished manuscript, Education Library, University of California, Berkeley, 1965), p. 1.
18. Kyte, "Education in the University of California," p. 4.
19. I. G. Hendrick, "Academic Revolution in California, Part I," *Southern California Quarterly*, 1967, *49* (June), 133, 161.
20. L. Eisenmann, *Historical Case Study: Pennsylvania State University* (Seattle: Center for Educational Renewal, College of Education, University of Washington, 1988).
21. Eisenmann, *Historical Case Study: Pennsylvania State University*, p. 2.
22. T. A. Karman, "History of the College of Education at Oklahoma State University" (unpublished manuscript, College of Education, Oklahoma State University, Mar. 1988), p. 5.
23. P. R. Rulon, *Oklahoma State University Since 1890* (Stillwater: Oklahoma State University Press, 1975), p. 132.
24. K. Cruikshank, *Historical Case Study: University of Georgia*

(Seattle: Center for Educational Renewal, College of Education, University of Washington, 1988), p. 3.

25. Cruikshank, *Historical Case Study: University of Georgia*, p. 49.

26. R. A. Levin, *Historical Case Study: Georgia State University College of Education* (Seattle: Center for Educational Renewal, College of Education, University of Washington, 1988), p. 2.

27. R. L. Johnson, *The Case for Temple University* (New York: Newcomen Society in North America, 1954), p. 9.

28. Kyte, "Education in the University of California," pp. 17–18.

29. Kyte, "Education in the University of California," p. 47.

30. Kyte, "Education in the University of California," p. 93. Included among the alumni of that period was Helen Heffernan, director of elementary education for the California State Department of Education, who served for forty years to implement John Dewey's philosophy of education in a state system of education. See R. W. Morpeth, "Dynamic Leadership: Helen Heffernan and Progressive Education in California" (unpublished doctoral dissertation, University of California, Riverside, 1989).

31. University of California, *Teacher Preparation Programs in the University of California*, report submitted to the California Postsecondary Education Commission (Berkeley: Office of the President, Academic Affairs, University of California, Mar. 1989), table 2.

32. Johnson and Johanningmeier, *Teachers for the Prairie*, p. 379.

33. Kyte, "Education in the University of California," p. 81.

34. L. Eisenmann, *Historical Case Study: Pennsylvania State University* (Seattle: Center for Educational Renewal, College of Education, University of Washington, 1989), p. 27.

35. Eisenmann, *Historical Case Study: Pennsylvania State University*, p. 36.

36. L. A. Cremin, *American Education: The National Experience, 1783–1876* (New York: Harper & Row, 1980), p. 365.

37. Altenbaugh, *Historical Case Study: University of Illinois*, p. 4; Johnson and Johanningmeier, *Teachers for the Prairie*, pp. 70–73.
38. Johnson and Johanningmeier, *Teachers for the Prairie*, p. 121.
39. Johnson and Johanningmeier, *Teachers for the Prairie*, p. 119.
40. Johnson and Johanningmeier, *Teachers for the Prairie*, pp. 149–150.
41. Johnson and Johanningmeier, *Teachers for the Prairie*, p. 140.
42. Johnson and Johanningmeier, *Teachers for the Prairie*, pp. 171–174.
43. Altenbaugh, *Historical Case Study: University of Illinois*, p. 13.
44. Johnson and Johanningmeier, *Teachers for the Prairie*, p. 301.
45. Kyte, "Education in the University of California," p. 3.
46. Kyte, "Education in the University of California," p. 9.
47. Kyte, "Education in the University of California," p. 22.
48. Stadtman, *Centennial Record*, p. 72.
49. Kyte, "Education in the University of California", p. 11.
50. Stadtman, *Centennial Record*, p. 72.
51. Kyte, "Education in the University of California," p. 30.
52. Kyte, "Education in the University of California," pp. 20–21. While a student at Michigan, Lange had studied education under Professor William H. Payne, completing the course work that earned him the university's "Teacher's Diploma."
53. The certificate granted was known as a "University Document" and was the forerunner of the "Certificate of Completion"; Kyte, "Education in the University of California," pp. 7–8.
54. Kyte, "Education in the University of California," pp. 22–23.
55. Kyte, "Education in the University of California," p. 3.
56. Kyte, "Education in the University of California," p. 26.
57. Kyte, "Education in the University of California," p. 33.

58. Kyte, "Education in the University of California," p. 53.

59. Kyte, "Education in the University of California," pp. 139–140.

60. Johnson and Johanningmeier, *Teachers for the Prairie*, p. 220.

61. Johnson and Johanningmeier, *Teachers for the Prairie*, p. 296.

62. Johnson and Johanningmeier, *Teachers for the Prairie*, pp. 304–305.

63. Kyte, "Education in the University of California," pp. 34–35.

64. Kyte, "Education in the University of California," p. 36.

65. A. Hamilton and J. B. Jackson, *UCLA on the Move* (Los Angeles: Ward Ritchie Press, 1969), p. 47.

66. Hamilton and Jackson, *UCLA on the Move*, pp. 49–50.

67. Clifford and Guthrie, *Ed School*, p. 259.

68. James C. Stone, personal interview with the author, Apr. 16, 1988; Kyte, "Education in the University of California," p. 126.

69. C. A. Larson, "Certification in California Public Schools, July 1, 1957 to June 30, 1958," *California Schools*, 1959, *30* (Jan.) 34–35.

70. Kyte, "Education in the University of California," p. 181.

71. Kyte, "Education in the University of California," p. 130.

72. Kyte, "Education in the University of California," p. 120.

73. Kyte, "Education in the University of California," p. 92; R. M. Hughes, "Report of the Committee on Graduate Instruction," *Educational Record*, 1934, *15* (Apr.), 192–234.

74. Johnson and Johanningmeier, *Teachers for the Prairie*, p. 259.

75. Johnson and Johanningmeier, *Teachers for the Prairie*, pp. 368–369.

76. Johnson and Johanningmeier, *Teachers for the Prairie*, pp. 389–446; Altenbaugh, *Historical Case Study: University of Illinois*, p. 9.

77. In addition to the written report of Richard Altenbaugh, the author's impressions of teacher education developments at the University of Illinois have been assisted by

conversations on Nov. 5–7, 1989, with James Raths, Colleen Blakenship, and Theodore Manolakes, all of whom directed, for a period, teacher education at Illinois during the 1970s and 1980s.

78. James Raths, personal interview with the author, Nov. 5, 1989.

79. Eisenmann, *Case Study: Pennsylvania State University*, pp. 11–13.

80. See in particular J. D. Koerner, *The Miseducation of American Teachers* (Baltimore: Penguin Books, 1963); and J. B. Conant, *The Education of American Teachers* (New York: McGraw-Hill, 1963).

81. Johnson and Johanningmeier, *Teachers for the Prairie*, pp. 175–176.

82. Kyte, "Education in the University of California," pp. 81–82.

83. See Hendrick, "Academic Revolution in California, Part I."

84. Hendrick, "Academic Revolution in California, Part I," p. 134.

85. L. Coppedge, D. Robinson, and F. Wood, "Teacher Education Programs for Oklahoma, 1992–2002" (photocopied report, Sept. 1987).

86. Cruikshank, *Historical Case Study: University of Georgia*, pp. 109–112.

87. Kyte, "Education in the University of California," p. 57.

88. Johnson and Johanningmeier, *Teachers for the Prairie*, p. 219.

89. Karman, "History of the College of Education," p. 73.

90. Johnson and Johanningmeier, *Teachers for the Prairie*, p. 181.

PART THREE

Evolution of Teacher Education: State Perspectives

7

The Influence of
Bureaucracy and Markets:
Teacher Education
in Pennsylvania

Linda Eisenmann

In this chapter, we change the lens through which we view the history of teacher training institutions. Thus far, we have used a wide-angle focus, looking nationally for similarities among institutions of the same type, be they converted normal schools or flagship research universities. But now we shift to a narrower focus—one that encourages us to examine an array of institutions that share a single characteristic: they all developed in the same state. In making this shift, we are, in some ways, bucking a trend in the history of higher education that finds institutions over time looking beyond their local borders to seek identification with national types. As Laurence Veysey, Christopher Jencks, and David Riesman have long noted, even small colleges emulate the research ideal in the age of the university.[1] Thus, even the schools in our study that began with the clearest intent to train teachers—the normal schools—find themselves today in a race to become "little Harvards."[2]

But refocusing our attention through a geographical perspective reminds us of another important fact in higher educational history: Colleges were local creations, founded by various groups for various reasons, but nurtured through the continuing support of local communities. In addition, few aspects of any college's mission have been more locally tied than the training of teachers. No matter how each of the colleges in our study had revamped its mission by the late 1980s, each has trained teachers for local schools throughout most of its history. Thus, each school's fortunes and plans have been linked to the local situation, sometimes more than that school might wish.

The use of a state perspective in the historical examination of teacher training shows that the facts of geographical proximity have affected collegiate development in two ways. The first is a direct effect: the influence of a governmental bureaucracy that controls who may become a teacher in that state. The second is indirect: the influence of market forces as various types of institutions compete to serve the same needs. This chapter will consider examples of each in Pennsylvania.

In no other aspect of higher education does a state agency exercise the widespread control that it does over the certification of teachers. An important question for the history of teacher training, then, is the extent to which state regulation has influenced colleges and universities. As the case of Pennsylvania illustrates, this influence can stem from either direct action by the state bureaucracy or its inaction and laissez-faire approach.

Direct action by the state in Pennsylvania's early normal school legislation, for example, allowed an unusually strong degree of private management in those public-service institutions, a situation that affected the schools' development for many decades. A second example of state action was a fervent Progressive reform movement in the 1920s, which produced big changes in the direction of teacher training in the state. Examples of the state's inaction abound as well. One was Pennsylvania's inconsistent support of its normal schools, which kept them as the poor cousins of mighty Penn State University and the powerful private school lobby. A second example was the absence of a collegiate master plan that allowed schools such as Penn State and the University of Pittsburgh in the early 1960s to establish statewide branch campuses at the expense of a burgeoning community college movement.

The second influence that appears when one adopts the lens of a state perspective is the importance of market forces. No matter how different Penn State, West Chester, and Bucknell universities may have been in origin and size, each trained teachers for the schools of Pennsylvania. What a history focusing on market issues shows is that the unspoken (and sometimes spoken) agreements about which schools train for which markets depend less on any state bureaucratic intervention than they do on the economic prospects facing the colléges. In flush times, the markets are free enough for all to pursue their shares; in those eras, the strongest institutions work to expand their markets, and the weaker schools try to hold their own. In tight times, an "every school for itself" rule holds, as do efforts to force each institution into a narrow market niche. This chapter explores how those market forces played out in Pennsylvania—in curricular matters concerning the provision of in-service, secondary school, and graduate training and in student population issues of gender and class.[3]

Pennsylvania's history of teacher education is not atypical, although that history does reflect the state's affinities with eastern states on its one border and the Midwest on its other. Like the eastern locales of Horace Mann and Henry Barnard, Pennsylvania assigned a relatively low status to its early normal schools, feeling that the private institutions were well enough established to serve advanced collegiate needs. In this eastern mode, as Jurgen Herbst reminds us, the normals were kept within a clearly defined role of elementary teacher training.[4] To some extent, Pennsylvania also resembled the midwestern states, where, without a long tradition of private higher education, the teacher training institutions served as flexible "people's colleges" in areas where other advanced education was unavailable. However, unlike states such as Illinois and Wisconsin, which then built a wider public educational structure around their normal schools, Pennsylvania left its early normals alone to compete with the fledgling high schools, throwing full support behind neither movement. Except for some periods of active involvement and special purpose, the Pennsylvania department of education was a relatively "hands-off" bureaucracy.

Direct state action on behalf of the normal school movement was slow to appear in Pennsylvania. Unlike most states, where the normal schools were planned, built, or administered by the state government, Pennsylvania allowed all of its normal schools to develop independently and did not move toward state ownership of these private institutions until the 1910s. Many critics maintained that this long tradition of private ownership adversely affected not only the growth of normal institutions in Pennsylvania but the standards of teacher training as well.[5]

Before the state's Normal School Act of 1857, most Pennsylvania schoolteachers were not formally trained for their work. Some students, especially in the rural areas, merely finished their studies in the common schools (established with the Free School Act of 1834) and then moved to the head of the classroom. Others attended colleges such as Bucknell or academies such as the one in West Chester, twenty-five miles outside of Philadelphia. Still others prepared for their jobs at the few county or city normal schools that served students in their immediate areas, such as the Normal School at Philadelphia, founded in 1818. Black teachers, needed especially for the segregated urban schools, received their most formal training at the Institute for Colored Youth in Philadelphia, which moved to its suburban location in Cheyney in 1903.[6] A few of these meagerly prepared teachers attended summer or short-term teacher institutes around the state to brush up on their skills. Teachers were examined and certified by the county superintendent, rather than by any statewide agency. The training of Pennsylvania's teachers was actively pursued by private institutions; no provisions for state-aided teacher education existed before the Normal School Act of 1857.

Even this significant legislation, however, did not greatly affect the state's role in the education of teachers. Instead, the act was "merely permissive in character," providing guidelines under which privately owned institutions could qualify for "normal school status" and the authority to grant teacher certification—all without the benefit of state funding.[7]

Rather than create a new public system of normal schools, the law divided the state into normal school districts and put up for grabs the opportunity for any institution to be designated as that district's teacher training site. Twelve districts were defined, each to have a normal school "erected and controlled by private corporations." The act did establish minimum standards for the physical plant and curriculum of the aspiring normal schools: Each must possess ten acres of land, buildings to accommodate 300 students, a model school with at least 100 students, a library, and a faculty of at least six professors.[8]

Pennsylvania legislators apparently saw no need to create new teacher training institutions or to provide state funding for schools when so many institutions around the state were already preparing students for teaching and were happy to vie for the normal school designation of their district. They would simply wait for existing schools to upgrade their financial and physical status in order to meet state standards. Apparently, the lawmakers believed that the prestige and increased enrollments accruing to each school that qualified for the normal school designation would provide all the incentive necessary for the provision of adequate teacher training throughout the state. They were wrong.

In fact, for the next several decades, Pennsylvania's institutions would never train a sufficient number of teachers for its schools. This undersupply contributed over time to substandard training, disproportionate numbers of provisional and emergency teaching certificates, competition for students, overextended curricula in the normal schools, and rivalry between colleges and normals. In addition, the long reliance on private ownership set up patterns in the development of the normals that likely hampered their ultimate success in meeting the needs of Pennsylvania teachers. For instance, the schools were very dependent on enrollments for their success, often leading trustees to accept any and all comers, regardless of preparation or real intent to teach. The regional origins of the schools also kept their focus on local rather than state needs for a long while, thereby hindering development of a strong state plan for teacher preparation in Pennsylvania. Also, the trustees were business people whose interest in or commitment to education frequently was overshadowed by their need to turn a profit on their investment. The private beginnings of the normals also encouraged a good deal of graft and patronage in the schools—a characteristic that apparently did not disappear even after state ownership arrived later. So influential was the private origin of these schools that their harshest critic blamed the private management for "most of the other existing evils" in the teacher training system in Pennsylvania.[9]

The plan to avoid any public contributions to the normal school system did not last very long. When the Normal School Act was passed in 1857, only the Lancaster County Normal School (later Millersville State) was anywhere near the standards required for acceptance as a state normal school. Even that sturdy enterprise required another $20,000 to meet requirements. Millersville citizens contributed handsomely to the task and saw their institution accepted in 1859 as the first of the state normal schools. Edinboro followed in 1861.[10]

Within a mere four years, the state realized that the budding system of normal schools could never flower without some direct financial help from the state. In 1861, $5,000 was given to Millersville and to Edinboro. By 1871, when the West Chester Academy qualified for state approval, Pennsylvania had eased its earlier policy of no financial support; in fact, West Chester received $15,000 in state funds for the necessary purchase of land and the erection of new buildings. But neither state control nor state authority accompanied this provision of public support. Except for the limited standards written into the act, the state exercised no other authority over which schools were approved. Thus, a rural institution with few opportunities for practice teaching could be approved as easily as a well-situated school.

In the last quarter of the nineteenth century, the curricula of the normal schools were set by the principals, and other matters of policy were determined by the boards of trustees.

The initial course of study was divided into four departments: the preparatory, for those with little background; the elementary, a two-year course covering subjects taught in the common schools; and the scientific and the classical, each a two-year course following the elementary and each leading to a teaching certificate. Both students and trustees found it advantageous for students to shift into the teacher training curriculum as early as possible. The state provided 50 cents per week to all students training to be teachers (provided they stayed in school for twelve weeks) and would add a $50 bonus upon graduation to all students who agreed to teach in Pennsylvania for two years. This provision, probably more than most other factors, encouraged students with little real aptitude or interest in teaching to pursue pedagogical training and encouraged the schools to promote and certify an inconsistent group of trainees.

The normal school courses did change between 1880 and 1910. An advanced normal course of five years was differentiated from a regular normal course of three years in 1894, and other curricular shifts appeared in 1900. But at the same time, no real entrance requirements were in effect at the schools. Any student with a rudimentary command of common school material could present himself or herself at the school during any point in the term, and the professors would have to carve out time to place that student in a program. The preparatory aspect of the normals also was not diminished in this era, heightening the normal schools' direct competition with the high schools.

In fact, the normals actually discouraged high school attendance through their practice of "passing off" required course work through examination (a version of today's advanced placement exams). For instance, a student with two years of high school training who came to the normal school would ordinarily be expected to spend three years in the regular normal course to earn a teaching certificate. Yet, by "passing off" some courses, he or she could usually reduce normal school attendance to two years. In addition, the entering student with two years of high school work was given the same introductory placement as the student with no high school background. Little incentive existed, then, to encourage a student to spend an extra two years at a secondary school.[11]

The years around the turn of the century witnessed numerous instances of financial and political corruption in the various Pennsylvania normal schools. The school at East Stroudsburg, for example, received wide publicity in 1904 for charges that its trustees had paid themselves from school funds for nonexistent bills. Two years earlier, Clarion Normal School had been discovered giving a 10 percent kickback to a legislator who helped with its state appropriation. Even more damaging to the reputation of the normal schools was the reaction of Clarion's registrar to the charges: "The Clarion Normal School is no better nor no worse than twelve other normal schools in this state. They have all paid to get appropriations and I suppose they will all do it again."[12]

As the perception of financial, managerial, and curricular problems at the normal schools worsened, one solution was suggested more frequently: Put the system of normal institutions directly under state ownership and control. There was widespread support for this move, including the highly critical study of Pennsylvania's normal schools by Ernest O. Holland of Teachers College, Columbia, in 1912.

Holland systematically criticized every aspect of the normal school system in Pennsylvania, especially practices that hindered the professionalization of the teaching force. Certainly the nonexistent entrance requirements and the pecuniary draw of any student to the pedagogy course prohibited any possibility of selectivity. In nearby Massachusetts and New York, with their more fully developed secondary systems, Holland explained, such students would never qualify for normal school entrance. On other standards the Pennsylvania students fared just as poorly. Compared to others around the eastern part of the nation, Pennsylvanians entered with less high school preparation and less teaching experience. Nor did the Pennsylvania curriculum encourage a professional viewpoint. As Holland discovered, only 23 percent of the normal student's time was devoted to professional teacher preparation; the remainder was spent in courses that duplicated the high school curriculum.[13]

Holland summarized the problems and their negative effects on the Pennsylvania situation:

> The result is that instead of raising the teaching profession to a level with the other professions, thereby enabling it to fulfill its obligations to society, these institutions actually retard the educational advancement of some localities because, to have successful schools, the principals are obliged to lower the standards, admit all applicants, and finally to send forth into the teaching profession many young men and women poorly equipped for their important duties.[14]

This critic and many others around the state believed that the answer for Pennsylvania was the establishment of state control of the normal schools. In fact, Pennsylvania had resisted much longer than most states the push toward state ownership. After considerable advocacy, a provision was made in the 1911 Pennsylvania School Code for the state to begin purchase of the thirteen normal schools. An annual appropriation of $200,000 would be provided until the state had purchased all the institutions. As might be expected, the smaller and less stable schools generally were purchased first, their trustees frequently glad to be freed from the large financial obligations of their institutions. The larger, more viable institutions could afford to hold out longer for better terms from the state.[15]

The resistance to state absorption by these more stable schools might also have signified a belief—or even a foreshadowing—that statewide control was not the solution for everyone's problems. In fact, the shift to state ownership did not immediately rectify management and curricular problems within the normal schools. The two traditions of minimal state intervention and maximum local control were too strong. Instead, the schools drifted for another half decade. Historian Janet Baker suggests that the decade of the 1910s, when state ownership gradually prevailed, was actually a difficult era for the normals when no one party assumed a leadership role. The trustees no longer had a strong interest in the schools, but the state had not yet stepped in with a firm sense of control. Baker notes that "Trustee decisions, in spite of state ownership, met with little interference from the state's Department of Public Instruction." Neither did the principals step in to take control; they suffered from historically weak authority, fostered by the tradition of strong private boards of trustees.[16] The new tradition of state control would face a long uphill fight in the effort to improve teacher training.

A second example of how direct action by the state bureaucracy in Pennsylvania influenced the development of teacher training appears toward the end of the Progressive Era, as the state department assumed a leadership role. The influence of a new reformist state superintendent resulted in an unusually active period for the state normal schools, leading them to challenge the teacher training strength of other institutions around the state.

Pennsylvania's Department of Public Instruction took its step into the Progressive Era with the governor's 1919 appointment of Thomas Finegan to the state superintendency. Finegan had worked for twenty-seven years in New York's state department of education and brought with him a reputation as a "dynamic, successful proponent of legislative reform in education."[17] The first superintendent to bring expertise from outside Pennsylvania, Finegan was also the first to represent the new breed of "administrative progressives" in education.

Finegan's reforms, which were sanctioned by Governor William Sproul, who had hired him, affected all levels of education in Pennsylvania. Centralization and professionalization of the department were his first moves. He reorganized his own department, created positions for deputy superintendents, and searched nationally for well-trained and experienced educational experts.

Finegan also had a plan for the upgrading of the normal schools. His first action was to gain passage of legislation giving his office the power to appoint and dismiss normal school trustees. This was an initial step toward shifting real control to the state—an intention long promised but seldom empowered.

Finegan also acted to strengthen the normal principals as a group and worked toward enhancing their power in relation to their boards and to his office. He assembled them for a meeting in 1920 and charged two committees to create new systems badly needed by the normal schools—one committee would rework the curriculum, the other would tackle fiscal management.

Demonstrating his dedication to progressive educational ideas, Finegan appointed a strong three-person advisory group to help the curriculum committee with its work. Pennsylvania's movement toward Progressivism was led by William C. Bagley from Teachers College, a scholar already well known for his management studies; Frank Graves, a progressive educator then dean of education at the University of Pennsylvania; and Will Grant Chambers from the University of Pittsburgh, a man dedicated to the professionalization of teaching, who would later lead the Penn State School of Education to prominence in the state. Both a national influence and the strength of Pennsylvania's private school lobby can be seen in Finegan's choices.

Each of these men believed in the current push for professionalization in teaching, and their reforms indeed strengthened teacher education in Pennsylvania over the next several years. For the first time, high school graduation would be required for normal school entrance, and a uniform curriculum would exist among the thirteen normals. Further, the system dedicated itself to the "professional point of view" in its courses, thereby staking a claim that normal schools were different from either high schools or colleges in serving as professional teacher training institutions where each course would emphasize the needs of future teachers. No longer would these schools try to be all things to all comers; the purely academic side of the curriculum would give way to the professional training of teachers.

At the same time, however—again following a national trend—Finegan also envisioned a shift to college status for the normals. He and the principals worked toward a four-year course in the normals that would offer bachelor's level training to high school graduates. But this training would clearly be that of a "teachers' college," not a high school liberal arts institution.

At least that was the idea behind the changes. In practice, the curricular shifts were not so dramatic. The normal school principals, after some initial tentativeness, did ally themselves with Finegan, but they retained some reservations about complete state control. The tradition of local interpretation was still strong, and principals managed to implement the new curriculum while still maintaining some unique features on their campuses to respond to local pressures and needs.[18]

One area where Finegan's reforms were undeniably successful was in the passage of the 1921 Edmonds Act, a piece of legislation that had unprecedented influence on teacher training throughout Pennsylvania. Cognizant of the need to upgrade and professionalize the status of teaching in the state, Finegan worked to consolidate many of his reforms into the Edmonds Act. The law provided for the first time a guaranteed salary scale for all properly certified teachers, and it also required two years of course work beyond high school for any teacher to qualify for the new minimum salary. Current teachers were granted six years to meet this requirement, a provision that allowed them to retain their jobs while attending evening or summer school.

The Edmonds Act proved its success in two ways. First, the teaching profession in Pennsylvania was considerably improved, at least insofar as standardization signified improvement. One study found that just prior to the Edmonds Act, in 1919, only one-half of all Pennsylvania teachers had received any professional training before they took their jobs.[19] In 1922, as the act went into effect, one-third of the teaching force enrolled in additional term-time work at the normal schools and private colleges; fully one-half of the force engaged in summer work.[20]

Furthermore, the Edmonds Act was generally regarded as successful and significant. A 1924 analysis of the reforms found that faculty training had improved, turnover in the teaching force had dropped, salaries had increased, and the proportion of in-service teachers pursuing further professional training had increased significantly. The analyst called the act "the greatest stimulus to professional education so far given to Pennsylvania's teachers" and added that the whole situation in Pennsylvania displayed "a marked improvement since Holland's 1910 study."[21]

A second measure of success was the stimulus given to the colleges and universities around the state that engaged in teacher preparation. Although the normal schools quickly mobilized to add summer and extension programs to meet teachers' needs, the larger colleges were the clear financial beneficiaries of the new requirements. The private colleges at Penn State, Temple, and the Universities of Pittsburgh and Pennsylvania[22] had been in the teacher education business as long as the normal schools, most forming colleges of education in the early 1900s.[23] Since they already envisioned themselves as offering advanced training compared to the noncollegiate normal schools, these colleges seized a greater share of the in-service teacher training market. In fact, one study estimated that Penn State University alone provided one-third of the new in-service training.[24]

The requirements of the Edmonds Act were a boon to these colleges, each of which accepted the impact of this advanced work, even when those efforts overwhelmed the preservice teacher training programs. At Temple, for example, the numbers of evening students (in-service teachers) far outran the daytime students, a situation that continued for decades.

Temple managed the situation by viewing its daytime program as the core of its effort; there was found a tight departmental control and strict monitoring of courses. In the evening division, on the other hand, a curricular anarchy reigned at times. Courses were not organized by department, and many topics not offered in the daytime program could be found there. Generally, whenever some group expressed a need for a course, Temple would give it a trial run, adding that course to the evening curriculum if it proved its worth and its drawing power. Although this approach added a huge enrollment to the college, many daytime professors scoffed at the

evening division. College historian Joseph Butterweck, himself
the longtime head of secondary education at Temple, assessed
the situation negatively. These courses "served the needs of the
Department of Public Instruction of Pennsylvania. They served
little else to Teachers College."[25] In his preference for the tighter
control of the daytime division, Butterweck conveniently ignored the financial benefits that Temple accrued through the
evening students.

At Penn State, the boost was equally dramatic. The land-
grant college's involvement in teacher education had been mild
before 1910, and its early efforts to provide in-service work
had failed. But in 1910—encouraged by the support of both
the state superintendent and the teachers' own Pennsylvania
State Educational Association—Penn State entered the extension market in earnest. Knowing Penn State's dedication to the
flexibility of its land-grant mission, the superintendent noted
that "surely it is a waste of our resources to let an equipment
of a quarter million dollars lie idle during the three vacation
months of every year." What better use of these facilities than
in-service teacher training? The superintendent's solution was
that "teachers of skill and experience be induced to go to the
state college for a period of six weeks in order to fit themselves
for this work."[26]

With this encouragement, the summer sessions took hold
at Penn State, attracting a large number of students as well as
providing a base of operations for faculty members with a professional interest in education. S. E. Weber arrived as the dean
of the new School of Liberal Arts in 1911. His academic background was in education, and while dean he served as professor of education at Penn State, as well as the director of the
summer session. His role established a model for Will Grant
Chambers, who was drawn away from the University of Pittsburgh to set the stage for an expanded teacher training mission at Penn State—an effort that would result in a consolidated School of Education in 1923.

Chambers presided over a burgeoning in-service enterprise, fueled not only by its own success but by federal money
from the Smith-Hughes legislation as well. When the Edmonds

Act created the need for more extension service, Penn State
was ready and able. Although Temple and the University of
Pittsburgh could attract teachers from their urban areas, Penn
State, with its lovely surroundings and its semipublic status,
nonetheless managed to outdraw those two institutions.[27]
Chambers, never a modest fellow in his ambitions, proudly declared in 1928 that Penn State offered "the largest extension
service for teachers in any higher institution of the state as well
as the largest summer session in the commonwealth." Penn
State's focus was clear: The dean cited the enrollment of 627
students in the on-campus teacher education curriculum, compared to 8,252 extension students and 3,000 summer session
students, "seven-eighths of whom are teachers in service."
Chambers indicated the increasing articulation between Penn
State and the normal schools by noting that more than 1,100
normal school graduates were among those summer students,
"practically all of whom are working for a Penn State degree."[28]

Superintendent Finegan's efforts and the Edmonds Act
are good examples of how direct state action affected the development of teacher education in Pennsylvania, both for the
public institutions and for the private colleges. Yet these actions also set the stage for examples of less direct influence by
the state, for, although Finegan's era was characterized by strong
support and clear leadership for the normal schools, it stands
in contrast to the state's overall inconsistent commitment to those
public institutions.

For all of the supposed support for Finegan and his reforms, the superintendent lasted in his job only until 1923. Farm
and grange organizations did not favor Finegan, and historian
Baker suggests that the governor bowed to their wishes in dis-
missing him.[29] Much of Finegan's program was already in place,
however, and with the support of the newly empowered normal school principals and the revitalized state department, many
of the reforms were carried forward. Most notable was the push
during the 1920s to upgrade all the normal schools into state
teacher's colleges.

One principal, John Keith of the Indiana Normal School,

assumed leadership of this push for four-year college status and degree-granting authority. In 1925, the state approved such rights for normal schools that could upgrade their curricula. West Chester was one of the first to do so, gaining approval for the bachelor of science in education degree in 1926 and acquiring the new name of West Chester State Teachers College. The change was not so easy for many of the other normals, however, and as the decade waned, so did the state's focused support for the normal schools.[30] The economic challenges of the Depression era would fragment state and educational support for the new teachers' colleges, leaving them once again to fend for themselves in the face of the greater strength of the state-related and private colleges.

The unreliable support offered to Pennsylvania's normal schools stems from a lack of commitment to their unique mission as teacher training institutions. Other places, with stronger political connections, can and do carry out the work of teacher education. In fact, politics have plagued teachers' colleges throughout their history and have seldom worked to their advantage. West Chester's historian Sturzebecker cites numerous examples of party influence and pressure on the public employees of the teachers' colleges. In one instance, highlighting the wisdom of those workers' holding the proper political affiliation, Sturzebecker notes that "It was not uncommon after their party suffered a reversal in a state election, to see a line of employees patiently waiting in the Court House to change their registrations."[31]

From the 1930s to the 1960s, there were periodic and politically motivated calls to close the normal schools for their supposed inefficiencies; sometimes those calls came from the state superintendent himself. In 1942, for example, Superintendent Francis Haas discussed publicly a proposition to change six or eight of the teachers' colleges into vocational schools—a proposal that he had not yet discussed with the college presidents.[32] In 1945, the teachers' colleges were praised highly for their flexibility in taking on huge numbers of veterans returning from World War II. It is, however, interesting that this praise came only one year after the Association of College

Presidents (from fifty-six of the state's liberal arts colleges) had recommended that the governor close eight of the teachers' colleges because of their low enrollments. Those presidents had "magnanimously" offered to provide scholarships to 6,000 students who would now be free to attend liberal arts schools.[33]

The challenges continued, usually accompanied by threats to severely reduce teachers' college appropriations or to eliminate them entirely, letting other institutions take on their jobs. In 1952, the governor appointed a commission that recommended the closing of one-half of the teachers' colleges. The commission's charge was that too few of the graduates actually went into teaching in Pennsylvania, thereby wasting the taxpayers' money. Sturzebecker recalls that many observers felt this report "was inspired by those sympathetic to the private colleges' stand."[34] The teachers' colleges weathered that attack, only to have those same ideas reactivated in 1954.[35]

By the 1960s, when college enrollments were booming, at least one teachers' college president decided to confront directly the state's tepid support. Earl Sykes of West Chester launched a publicity effort to show that Pennsylvania had not supported its state colleges sufficiently. His work garnered support from several other presidents and eventually won over Governor William Scranton as well. But the state college appropriations continued to be mired in politics. In the especially difficult year of 1965, the $1.5 million earmarked by the legislature for the teachers' colleges was held out of their reach, while at the same time the legislature awarded huge emergency funds to bail out the financially devastated University of Pittsburgh. Sykes tried to push the state to respond to its own colleges, noting pointedly that over a fifteen-year period (1950–1965), enrollment in private (state-aided) colleges had risen only 19 percent, while enrollments in the state schools (teachers' colleges) had increased 182 percent. Only moderately successful in his effort, Sykes concluded that the teachers' colleges were "the poor country cousins" of other Pennsylvania institutions.[36]

In the eyes of faculty members who worked at the teachers' colleges, the state's move to transform them into "multipurpose institutions" in the 1960s represented the expiration of support for their unique mission. Of course, Pennsylvania was hardly alone in changing its teachers' colleges into state universities; the national trend was clearly in this direction. In fact, the teachers' college faculty agreed that this was a "natural" move, done in the best interests of the college.[37]

However, faculty members who served in the 1950s and 1960s lamented the loss of focus on the teacher training mission. At West Chester, for example, the faculty felt that knowing that all students were heading into teaching was a strong asset in their planning and delivery of courses. They felt that it was "wonderful" working with these students, especially in an atmosphere that was "ingrained with teaching."

After the shift to university status, the faculty at West Chester noticed a huge loss of power and purpose in the education programs. Teacher education programs were shifted from one department to another. Eventually, even the deans were renamed "coordinators," symbolizing the shift to a more centralized authority. At times, the teacher education programs were given a reduced share of voting members on important committees, ensuring a minimized role for their approach. When asked why this shift was so acrimonious at their college, professors suggested that some people in the liberal arts faculty had felt undervalued when the school's emphasis was so strongly on teacher training. Then, with the 1960s shift in mood and focus, these programs could come to the fore. One professor felt that the result was a wish to create a "little Harvard" at this former normal school, playing down the historical attention to teacher training in return for an enhanced research impetus.[38]

Although the state took a strong hand in the mid 1960s in reorienting the teachers' colleges and protecting some of the private schools with a "state-related" status, Pennsylvania had, in fact, lacked a master plan for higher education prior to that era. In the absence of such state control, the strongest colleges were allowed to use their political savoir faire to their own advantage. The history of Penn State University exemplifies that of a strong institution that deftly used its advantages to acquire and enhance a great deal of influence in Pennsylvania, and it serves as a second example of the effects of a laissez-faire bureaucracy.

Because of its status as the land-grant institution of Pennsylvania, Penn State always maintained a special and favored relationship with the people and the legislators of the commonwealth. The land-grant designation proved especially flexible in Penn State's hands, constantly providing justification for any new programs of interest. When the university would venture into a new arena, it could always cite its mission to "provide selected educational programs in the professions essential to the continued well-being of the Commonwealth and the nation."[39]

Nonetheless, Penn State did, over time, acquire an image as an "octopus," reaching its arms into higher education programs at all levels and in all corners of the state. The origin of the image may have begun with the efforts of education school dean Will Grant Chambers, who conceived new ways for Penn State to expand in the 1920s and 1930s.

Building on the tremendous success of the extension programs in teacher education, Chambers envisioned Penn State extending its physical presence around the state. As early as 1924, he recommended the establishment of branch campuses (he unhesitatingly called them "junior colleges") around the state as market potential dictated. Some locales not only were interested in the in-service teacher training courses but expressed a desire for wider collegiate opportunities as well. Chambers had heard that the people of Erie, for example, were seeking some sort of college in their area. The first college to respond to Erie's offer was the University of Pittsburgh, a school that had proved very successful in drawing students and in responding to new markets. Yet, when Penn State expressed to the city of Erie its own interest in meeting their needs, the Erie board of education gave the nod to the state college—an interesting demonstration of Penn State's appeal and influence. Chambers attributed this approval to "the friendly attitude of the school officers toward the Pennsylvania State College."[40]

Chambers's idea for the branch campuses was not acted upon in the 1920s; however, when the dean recast the idea in

1933 as a way to bolster sagging Depression era enrollments, it was implemented successfully. In fact, many parties around the state had encouraged Penn State and other four-year institutions to open branch campuses to lessen living expenses for Depression era students. Penn State's president Ralph D. Hetzel (1926–1947) had wavered, however, worrying that strong moves into the branch campuses would thwart the growth of the junior college movement, which was slowly moving toward Pennsylvania. By 1934, however, Hetzel had already decided to implement Chambers's idea in order to forestall further enrollment difficulties at Penn State.

Chambers framed the plan as a clear solution to a supply-and-demand problem. Too many trained teachers were jobless because of the Depression, while too many potential college students could not afford to leave home and travel to the well-established institutions. Why not bring the two together in "undergraduate centers" where freshman- and sophomore-level courses would be offered? President Hetzel agreed, and four centers were established, at Sayre-Towanda, Uniontown, Hazleton, and Pottsville. All but Sayre-Towanda flourished, and it was replaced by a center at DuBois two years later.[41] In a state that did not exercise a strong hand in the planning of higher education, Penn State had both identified and met a need on its own.

Not only did the undergraduate centers boost Depression enrollments and enhance Penn State's visibility throughout the state, but they also laid the foundation for the next stage in Penn State's statewide expansion—the commonwealth campuses. New leadership for both the university and the School of Education in the 1950s and 1960s pushed Penn State toward further expansion. President Eric Walker (1956–1970) brought to his job close ties to both government and corporate leaders in Pennsylvania, as well as a good vision of the growth about to hit higher education. He fully expected Penn State to enjoy its share in that expansion. In complete agreement with Walker's view of an expanded, research-oriented Penn State was the new dean of the College of Education, John Ralph Rackley.

Walker took his plans, and with them the requisite fiscal

demands, to the state, hoping for quick approval. Acceptance of his vision did not come easily, however. A new fiscally conservative governor was wary of Penn State's interests. Walker shrewdly argued the land-grant background of the university, realizing the wisdom of emphasizing what Penn State could do for the commonwealth rather than what the commonwealth could do for Penn State. At one point, relying on the mixed public-private nature of his institution, Walker sounded out the governor on a plan to cede some control of Penn State to Pennsylvania in return for a larger share of appropriations. In effect, Penn State would become "more public" in return for more money. Although the governor did consider the plan, President Walker withdrew it when he decided that the promised fiscal increase was not worth the long-term concession.[42]

Through continued lobbying, Walker eventually won a steady enough level of appropriations to allow him to proceed with his own master plan for growth. The 1960s were a heady time for higher education generally; Penn State alone grew from an enrollment of 19,300 in 1964 to 34,900 by the end of the decade.[43] But that growth also brought to Pennsylvania the challenge of managing expansion. Because the state had been lax in creating a master plan for higher educational development, much of that challenge centered around who would be the initiators and recipients of the boom in money and in students.

Penn State had been remarkably successful in its own expansion efforts; growth at the branch campuses was "spectacular" in the 1960s.[44] In 1959, the branches had been redefined as the "commonwealth campuses" to indicate their relationship as satellites to the main university Park complex. At the same time, these campuses became an integral part of the whole university, being freed from the demand that they be self-sustaining enterprises. Students could begin their studies on the extension campuses, come to University Park for the two senior years, and graduate with a Penn State degree that never indicated where their course work was taken. The growth of these campuses faced a stern challenge within the state, however, when Pennsylvania passed the Community College

Act of 1963, and the state department issued a report critical of Penn State's continued movement into a curricular area that might properly be the province of two-year community colleges.

With the Community College Act, the state took a more proactive role than it ordinarily assumed in higher education matters—a symbol of changes to come. Under the legislation, which was designed to bring low-cost education to the citizens of the commonwealth, Pennsylvania would pay one-half of the construction costs and one-third of the operating costs of new community colleges. Because they would need fewer research and laboratory facilities, and because they would be tied to local communities, these colleges were assumed to have lower costs than Penn State's commonwealth campuses.

Although some of the criticism of the lower-division campuses was aimed at the University of Pittsburgh (with several undergraduate branches of its own around the state), most of the fire was directed at Penn State for the "octopus" image it was acquiring. President Walker tried a nonconfrontational approach, arguing that enough room and resources existed in Pennsylvania for both the community colleges and the commonwealth campuses. A state-sponsored study in 1965 concluded otherwise, and the state Council of Higher Education created a master plan in 1966 that would push Penn State out of the competition for public money in favor of the community colleges.

Penn State continued to argue its past and future service to the commonwealth, and over time, the strength of citizen support for the Penn State campuses helped the university win its argument. While state planners might see the unique and strong role that locally based community colleges could fill, citizens and legislators were apparently swayed by the long tradition of service and academic strength offered by Penn State. With such public support, Penn State did pursue its plan for building and strengthening the commonwealth campuses. Community colleges were established around the state as well, but the Penn State programs continued to attract huge numbers of beginning students.

In summarizing the role of Penn State during this period of growth in Pennsylvania's higher education, its historian judged:

> There can be little question that the Commonwealth Campuses at least partially duplicated services that community colleges could have offered, or that the Commonwealth Campuses retarded the growth of a community college system. However, the state government was slow to commit itself to that system. Consequently, Penn State . . . had no alternative but to establish more branch campuses if Pennsylvania's educational needs were to be met.[45]

In other words, in an open market with little regulation, competition would be the order of the day.

In fact, competition at all levels had always been present in Pennsylvania. Although some of the particulars of the Pennsylvania situation might differ from that in other states, the overall competitive pressure of market decisions resembles that found in other locales. The use of a state perspective on this history can clarify ways in which local, regional, and statewide market forces have affected both institutions' curricular planning and their claims on student populations.

Pennsylvania's normal schools undeniably engendered competition. This history has already shown how those institutions, carefully apportioned around the state, challenged and even inhibited the growth of secondary schools in Pennsylvania. But in their early years, those schools were also the scene of considerable statewide competition of their own. When the normals still operated as private ventures, enrollments were the driving force, and the institutions competed for students all around the state. Many of the teacher training institutions, for example—especially in the central and western parts of the state—advertised in local newspapers and hired field agents to recruit students.[46]

Although such direct competition eased in the 1910s when the state designated one normal school per district, not until the 1920s leadership of Thomas Finegan were the normals sufficiently inspired to work together as a group. During that era, the normals saw the advantage (albeit limited in success) of making a united case to the legislature on matters of finance and policy.[47] At the same time, the Board of Normal School Principals found new success as a group, working with the superintendent on curriculum matters, including, for example, the division of program responsibilities among the campuses.[48]

Competition also surfaced on a regional basis in Pennsylvania, with the whole constellation of normal schools, private colleges, state-aided institutions, and others in an area vying for their share of the student market. Philadelphia provides a good case study of such ongoing competition.

At least four institutions competed for the training of teachers in turn-of-the-century Philadelphia.[49] The Philadelphia Normal School was a municipal normal that more or less filled the role played by the state-designated normals in the rural areas. Founded in 1818, that school provided low-cost training to urban Philadelphians and, like most normals, focused on the preparation of elementary school teachers. Since Philadelphia had a segregated school system, a separate institution developed for the preparation of black teachers. The Institute for Colored Youth, which moved to suburban Cheyney in 1903, trained teachers for black schools far beyond the Philadelphia area.

Most of the remaining market for local teachers was claimed by Temple University and the University of Pennsylvania (Penn)—institutions that approached teacher training from different viewpoints. Although engaged in the preparation of secondary school teachers, Penn did not view itself initially as providing professional preparation in that area. Like most other private colleges and universities, Penn expected that a solid liberal arts background would fit the interested student as he (or in some cases she) moved to the front of a high school classroom. In turn-of-the-century colleges, little need was seen for professional pedagogy in the training of high school teachers.

Temple, on the other hand, had organized much of its early undergraduate curriculum around normal courses—at least with a "normal" label, if not the pedagogy. When Baptist minister Russell Conwell founded Temple in 1888 as an institution to provide "an education intended primarily for the benefit of working men," he had not provided a clear curricular plan for the delivery of such education. The curricular organization was conceived and administered by Conwell's long-time assistant, Laura Carnell, who took a job as coordinator of teacher training in 1893; by the time of her retirement in 1919, she had moved up to become dean of Temple College and finally associate president to Conwell's successor, Charles Beury.[50]

Carnell tried in the early years to give a purpose and a direction to the unwieldy enterprise at Temple, which, as historian Richard Angelo points out, was not properly "postsecondary" and only "nominally" a college.[51] Although some of the areas of the college—notably the School of Business—resisted her influence, Carnell tried to subsume many areas of the curriculum under her egis as coordinator of teacher training. Thus, she instituted normal programs in the music, physical culture, and household arts departments, allowing the promise of a teaching certificate to serve as a lure for potential students. However, most Temple students in these early years were not interested in degrees; many came for only a short period of time or for a diploma, frustrating educators such as Carnell who tried to instill order into the curriculum.[52]

Astutely assessing the market, Carnell found most of her success in an unusual program that she created for the preparation of kindergarten teachers. Philadelphia itself was a pioneer in seeing the value of an educational program designed for young children. In 1887, the city's school department had assumed responsibility for thirty public kindergartens.[53] Although Carnell had little experience in this work, she saw its potential. Over the years, she built a unique program at Temple for the education of young children. That program sometimes drew criticism from Carnell's colleagues within the university, but the program at Temple drew national attention over time.[54]

The situations at Temple and at Penn differed in another respect: the character of their student bodies. Although

it is facile to suggest that the long-established Ivy League school
at Penn naturally attracted a more elite student body than the
"working-class-oriented" Temple, historian Angelo has provided some support for that notion—at least in the early years
of the institutions—and thus can clarify some of the market
issues at work within the city.

Temple was created for the working class, those "bur-
dened and circumscribed manual laborers" who would use the
opportunities at the college to "reach the fields of profitable
and influential professional life."[55] Angelo notes, however, that
such laborers apparently "failed to appear in any significant
numbers" within the first twenty years. In his search of alumni
backgrounds, Angelo found that only 10 percent of the alumni
who could be traced came from a clearly blue-collar situation.
Although more than 40 percent were working in white-collar
settings after their graduation, the origins of many of these
students were unknown.[56] In a more focused look at the ma-
triculants of one year (1894–95) at Temple, Angelo found that
5 percent of students who graduated came from professional
families, whereas 14.5 percent came from blue-collar situations.[57]

The University of Pennsylvania, on the other hand, served
a larger percentage of the sons of professional families. Angelo's study of the Penn alumni body of 1898 found that "their
ranks were top-heavy with the sons of doctors, lawyers, and
ministers," although "sons of farmers and craftsmen were just
as numerous as those of small merchants and clerks, and together they almost equaled the number of young men whose
fathers were professionals or more prominent businessmen."[58]
The closer comparison is revealed in a look at the Philadelphia
addresses of the Temple and Penn students. Angelo found that
both schools drew heavily from the Philadelphia area but that
Temple had a much greater representation from the less wealthy
parts of the city, notably from the South and Northeast wards.
Students from the more desirable West Philadelphia and Center locations were more numerous at Penn than at Temple.[59]

The normal schools generally attracted a larger percentage of students from farm and laboring families than did either

of the universities at Temple and at Penn. Studies of the Pennsylvania normal students in 1920 and again in 1940 suggest that about 50 percent of the students came from these types of families—a figure similar to the national average for normals.[60] But, as this study has shown, the normals frequently served as the only advanced education for rural students, and many of those young people came to the normal with little firm intention to enter teaching. The same situation was true at both Temple and the University of Pittsburgh, where nominally normal programs attracted students who were more interested in the technical education provided in those program areas than in the pedagogical focus.[61]

Another category of students who were undeniably more drawn to teacher training programs—especially at the normal schools—was women. Considering the overwhelming preponderance of women as students at these institutions, the lack of attention to them in the histories of the normal schools is staggering. The situation for female faculty members is little better.[62]

In the early years when the normal schools represented the rare chance for advanced education, either men predominated in the student body or the numbers of men and women were roughly equal. A study of West Chester conducted at the time of that school's twenty-fifth anniversary found that from 1871 to 1883, neither men nor women overwhelmed the student body. After the school's first dozen years, however, women students always outnumbered the men.[63]

A 1921 alumni catalogue provides good information not only about the numbers in each class but about their subsequent career histories as well. These data suggest that many more women students pursued the normal course than did men, but also that women stayed with their teaching careers for a good many years after graduation.[64] In the class of 1910, for example, 187 women and only 26 men graduated from the "regular normal course," which represented the established curriculum of that era. Yet the men more often than the women moved into fields other than teaching with their normal school backgrounds. By 1921, 11 of the 26 men who listed their occupations cited a nonteaching field; these included several in business, an engineer, a physician, a chemist, a navy surgeon, and two attorneys. Nonetheless, one-half of the men in the class did commit themselves to teaching. Ten of the 26 graduates had taught for five years or more by 1921.[65]

Eleven women also listed other occupations, including bank teller, stenographer, bookkeeper, laboratory technician, accountant, and supervisor of household accounts—but, at least insofar as these figures are accurate, a large number of these women graduates remained as teachers, most in the Pennsylvania area. Sixty-four of the 187 women graduates (34 percent) were listed as teaching for the full eleven years since their graduation from West Chester. Another 21 percent had entered teaching but stayed for less than five years. These figures suggest that the normal school training was, in fact, a true career opportunity for these Pennsylvania women. One-third of those who stayed through the course at West Chester were still working as teachers more than a decade after they finished the program.[66]

The figures are much the same for the class of 1915, which graduated 253 women and 24 men. Six years after their graduation, more than half of the women (163 of 253) had taught school continuously. Fifty-one of the graduates had married by 1921, and although a very few of those women continued to teach after their marriage, most of those marriages accounted for the graduates who taught for three or four years and then left the teaching force.[67] These figures strongly support the notion that women used these "people's colleges" for job-related reasons, and that these jobs were important to their independent futures.

The rare opportunity to speak with one of those graduates provides some insight into the life of a normal school student of the era, as well as the importance of a normal school certificate. Ada G. Kessler, a graduate of the West Chester class of 1915, was one of the few students who came to the normal school with only an eighth-grade education in 1913. After her graduation, she taught for thirty years in the schools around Chester County.[68]

Now in her late eighties, Kessler remembers the "overwhelming" feeling of coming to West Chester as Ada Stanford, a fourteen-year-old girl with much less experience and schooling than the majority of her classmates. Ada's mother had been a teacher in her native England, and the daughter had "always planned" to follow in her mother's footsteps. Ada, the oldest of eight Stanford children, lived in nearby Glenloch and traveled to school in West Chester via the railroad, which employed her father and later some of her brothers. One other sister would eventually also become a teacher.

Seventy years later, some of the memories of life at West Chester are still keen, especially the young woman's pride in her normal school work and the sense of community life on the campus. Some of this communal living was foreign for commuter students such as Ada Stanford, but she also recalls being a part of the campus culture. She was a student at the time of a furious fight between Principal George Philips and the board of trustees, and she remembers that the students were prohibited from reading about the "scandal" in the local newspapers. Control of student life was strong in the 1910s, as it would remain over several decades.

Interviews with two other former students from different eras confirm both the closeness of life at the normal school and the significance of these degrees for many women students. Johanna Havlick, a 1928 graduate who is now a trustee of West Chester University, had also "always wanted to be a teacher." Although she lived in the county, her acquaintance with West Chester came through one of her teachers who was a graduate. Johanna was the only child in a family of five to attend college. She views her education at West Chester as the starting point for her career, providing her the basics upon which to build her skills through experience. She taught for forty-two years after her graduation, working as a teacher and a principal.[69]

Anna Highley graduated from West Chester in 1947, accelerating her program into three years because of the pressures of World War II. She describes her rural family life and remembers how the faculty firmly influenced the students, especially those young women from the country who needed advice about how to dress and act as they entered the teaching profession. Anna feels that values were instilled in the students not only through direct teaching but through the indirect influences of a "gracious life-style" as well. When this woman, who also taught for more than thirty years, reflects on the opportunities provided by West Chester, she emphasizes that without the availability of low-cost public education at the normal school, she would never have been able to enter the profession.[70]

Normal schools provided the best opportunity for advanced training for women. The same could not be said of the quasi-public school at Penn State. At the turn of the century, the state college had a student body of 3,000, only 10 percent of whom were women; of that 10 percent, three-fourths of the women pursued a home economics curriculum within the School of Education.[71]

Housing opportunities for the women who needed to travel to College Park were scant, and they did not improve until an on-campus housing program boomed during World War II. Without housing provisions, the number of women could not expand significantly. In the 1930s, the women's share of enrollment grew to only 14 percent; by 1940, women made up one-fifth of the student body. Much as in the earlier era, three-fourths of the student body at the School of Education were female.[72]

Yet the intended drawing power of schools such as West Chester and Penn State differed. At least for the first part of the twentieth century, West Chester and other teachers' colleges expected to train elementary teachers, most of whom were women, and to offer only smatterings of other specialized programs. Penn State, on the other hand, built its education programs on its advanced work, including in-service, graduate, and specialized training. Although some of that differentiation occurred through the natural operation of market forces, much of it resulted from conscious compromises and negotiations among the various players in Pennsylvania's teacher education programs.

Since the liberal arts institutions had always provided

teachers, whether or not they specifically trained them, those colleges took the lead in training teachers for the secondary schools. The normal schools, which were busy finding their own professional niche through the 1920s and 1930s, focused on elementary training. As the secondary market expanded in the 1920s—at the same time as the normals moved toward baccalaureate status—the lucrative high school teacher market threatened to upset the balance among teacher training institutions.

The first battle occurred between Penn State and the normal schools—two parties that could benefit from a negotiated compromise. At the initiation of the state superintendent, but with the support of the schools, the three parties—state bureaucracy, state institutions, and quasi-public university—held a series of meetings in 1929 and 1930 to clarify their relationship. The result was a sort of "gentlemen's agreement" that would assign the beginning levels of training to the normals and advanced work to Penn State.[73] The state college would now accept at full value the credits offered by normal school graduates who wished to finish a baccalaureate degree or pursue a graduate program at Penn State. Earlier, the state college had not offered full transfers to normal graduates. In return, the normal schools, deep in their fight for acceptance as teachers' colleges, agreed to leave the development of graduate work solely in Penn State's eager hands.

Dean Chambers of Penn State cited this agreement as "a milestone in the expansion of our graduate work."[74] His school had already offered the M.A., M.S., and Ph.D. degrees in education, although graduate enrollments had never been large and only one Ph.D. degree had been awarded. As part of this agreement "to work out closer relations in the educational work of the State," Pennsylvania's state department authorized Penn State to create the M.Ed. and D.Ed. degrees, both of which "could be better adapted to the conditions of State Teachers College graduates." Both of these new degrees were extremely successful, and their appeal to the teachers' college graduates helped cement Penn State's future as a huge provider of graduate training.[75]

Penn State's reliance on its public nature helped secure

this agreement with the state bureaucracy and the state schools. In fact, the pamphlets that announced the new articulation with teachers' colleges emphasized Penn State's responsibilities as "part of the State's public school system . . . maintained at the expense of the State."[76] The private liberal arts colleges were not a part of this 1929–30 agreement, and tensions between those institutions and the normal schools continued to escalate.

The economic challenge brought by the Depression quickened the arrival of confrontation. As finances and enrollments threatened the security of all institutions, the strongest schools took action to define teacher training market shares.[77] One point was clear: Teachers, especially new teachers, were oversupplied in the state. All the parties looked for someone to blame; naturally, someone had to be cut out of the teacher production business.

Many of the private colleges, through their Pennsylvania Association of Liberal Arts Colleges for the Advancement of Teacher Education, protested the influence that the state teachers' colleges were gaining in the market, and they laid the blame for the oversupply on these upstart schools.[78] The private institutions, which were not without influence in the state department and in the legislature, petitioned to have some of the normals closed down.

Both Penn State and the superintendent rose to the defense of the public side of the system, saying that, in fact, the liberal arts colleges contributed to the worst of the oversupply by dumping too many teachers into the crowded urban markets and by allowing their otherwise unemployable graduates to shift into teaching jobs. In contrast, the normal schools were carefully apportioned around the state, one school for each district, thereby creating a more measured flow of new teachers into each region. In fact, they argued, it was the liberal arts colleges that should be discouraged from producing new teachers, and boards of education should be less willing to hire those cheaper but poorly prepared liberal arts graduates.[79]

Although Penn State took up the cudgel for the normal schools in this debate, it had its own interests to protect as well. After its spirited defense of the normal schools (which provided the bulk of Penn State's graduate enrollment), the state college then proceeded to criticize those schools for their encroachment on a territory that Penn State perceived as its own:

> Again the State Teachers Colleges cannot escape responsibility for a large part of the over supply because of their having undertaken to train secondary school teachers in addition to their original task of training elementary teachers only. There are many acknowledged leaders in the field of education who believe that this broadening of the scope of our State Teachers Colleges was a serious mistake from several points of view.[80]

With the Depression in full swing, market shares could not be ceded so easily. In fact, Penn State went on to emphasize its unique strengths in this time of tight competition, strengths that should provide it with a greater share of scarce resources—industrial education, home economics, nature education, and agricultural education. The college was also finding more persuasive an old argument that secondary school teachers actually needed five years of training. Since that extra year was seldom available at other institutions, it was obvious where advanced work should be centered.

Penn State proceeded to develop its own plan for advanced teacher training and extension work in those areas, as well as in administration, in special education, and in its new field of educational research. The state college had its own markets to define, and it was not bashful in staking its claim against both the normal schools and the private colleges:

> Work in an institution devoted solely to teacher training [the normals] could have neither the breadth nor the depth of that given under our unusual conditions. It would seem, therefore, that any necessary curtailment of the work in teacher training in the state should not apply to this institution but to those which have neither the equip-

ment nor the sincere interest in the work which
are necessary to make the work effective [the liberal arts colleges].[81]

Clearly, with the stakes so high, the battle could be nasty.

In a state with a stronger or more intrusive central bureaucracy, perhaps the fighting could have been less acrimonious; but in Pennsylvania, both Penn State and the private
school lobby were strong. Unfortunately, support for the normal schools never matched the influence of those other institutions. As the Depression continued, a reasonably strong superintendent, Lester Ade, tried to reconcile the various interests,
but his constant calls for cooperation and conciliation suggest
that this fight was not to be refereed by the state government.[82]

Availability of resources has a way of changing matters,
however, as the experience of the 1960s in Pennsylvania shows.
When financial troubles hit both Pitt and Temple, those private institutions entered into a new relationship with the state,
ceding much of their control as they became "state-related" institutions, with many of the same ties to the government as
Penn State. Yet the 1960s also showed Penn State some challenges. As the budget problems of 1965 and the push for the
Community College Act of 1963 have shown, the university's
ability to determine its future could not remain entirely its own.

In the end, Pennsylvania's history does offer some unusual examples, especially with its unique provisions to the state-
related institutions. Yet its story of mixed state support for the
normal institutions, along with the tendency of the private college lobby to flex its muscles, is not singular in the history of
teacher training. What a history—which concentrates on all the
players within a market—contributes, however, is a comparison of interests and reactions by all parties. Like the notion
that "all politics is local," perhaps a focus on the training of
teachers reveals the inevitability of local, regional, and statewide compromises.

Notes

1. L. Veysey, *The Emergence of the American University* (Chicago: University of Chicago Press, 1965); C. Jencks and

D. Riesman, *The Academic Revolution* (Chicago: University of Chicago Press, 1968).

2. This phrase was used to describe the current effort at West Chester University by a retired faculty member who had seen the school weather a difficult shift from state teachers' college to "multipurpose university." Interview with Ruth Reed, West Chester, Pa., June 10, 1988.

3. Nonetheless, this chapter does not purport to offer a complete history of teacher training institutions in Pennsylvania. It has been most influenced by the four institutions that were selected by our project for case studies: West Chester University, Bucknell University, Temple University, and Pennsylvania State University.

4. For a discussion of the differences in normal school development by region and state, see J. Herbst, "Nineteenth-Century Normal Schools in the United States: A Fresh Look," *History of Education*, 1980, *9*, 219–227, and his later refinements in *And Sadly Teach: Teacher Education and Professionalization in American Culture* (Madison: University of Wisconsin Press, 1989).

5. The strongest critic in the early years was Ernest O. Holland, in *The Pennsylvania State Normal Schools and Public School System*, Contributions to Education no. 55 (New York: Teachers College, Columbia University, 1912). His specific criticisms will be discussed later in this chapter. For a more favorable but still critical review, see W. S. Taylor, *The Development of the Professional Education of Teachers in Pennsylvania* (Philadelphia: Lippincott, 1924).

6. For a discussion of the Institute for Colored Youth, see L. N. Perkins, *Fannie Jackson Coppin and the Institute for Colored Youth 1865–1902* (New York: Garland, 1987). Vincent P. Franklin provides a brief discussion of Cheyney State Teachers College in his *The Education of Black Philadelphia* (Philadelphia: University of Pennsylvania, 1979), pp. 70–71. In his otherwise excellent study of schooling for black Philadelphians, however, Franklin does not give much attention to the preparation of black teachers.

7. Taylor, *The Development of Professional Education*, de-

scribed the Normal School Act as "merely permissive" (p. 103).

8. See Taylor, *The Development of Professional Education*, pp. 105–106; and Holland, *The Pennsylvania State Normal Schools*, pp. 7–8.

9. Holland, *The Pennsylvania State Normal Schools*, p. 93.

10. The original law provided for twelve districts, but a thirteenth was added later because of growth in population, and a fourteenth school, Cheyney, was established solely for the training of black teachers. The fourteen state normal schools, in order of their recognition by the state, are Millersville (1859), Edinboro (1861), Mansfield (1862), Kutztown (1866), Bloomsburg (1869), West Chester (1871), Shippensburg (1873), California (1874), Indiana (1875), Lock Haven (1877), Clarion (1887), Slippery Rock (1889), East Stroudsburg (1893), and Cheyney (1921).

11. Several historians have asserted that these policies inhibited the development of high schools around Pennsylvania, especially in the rural areas. See Holland, *The Pennsylvania State Normal Schools*, chap. 9; J. Baker, "An Organizational Analysis of Pennsylvania's Normal School Transition to Teachers College Status" (unpublished doctoral dissertation, Harvard University, 1987), p. 37; and R. L. Sturzebecker, *Centennial History of West Chester State College* (West Chester, Pa.: Tinicum Press, 1971), p. 78.

12. Cited in Holland, *The Pennsylvania State Normal Schools*, p. 29. References to the financial problems of the various normal schools are widespread; see, for example, Baker, "An Organizational Analysis"; Holland, *The Pennsylvania State Normal Schools;* Taylor, *The Development of Professional Education;* and Sturzebecker, *Centennial History of West Chester.*

13. See Holland, *The Pennsylvania State Normal Schools*, chap. 5, for his discussion of the curriculum.

14. Holland, *The Pennsylvania State Normal Schools*, p. 73.

15. The first of the schools purchased was West Chester in 1913 (although it was financially quite stable); the last was Mansfield in 1920.

16. See Baker, "An Organizational Analysis," pp. 39–42, for a discussion of this transition era.

17. Baker, "An Organizational Analysis," p. 44.

18. Baker notes some evidence of new "mutual negotiation" between Finegan and the principals that allowed the schools to keep some of their old programs while they instituted his new ones. She also explains that this cooperation had never existed between the normals and the state, or among the normal principals (p. 93).

19. Taylor, *The Development of Professional Education*, p. 252.

20. Taylor, *The Development of Professional Education*, pp. 264, 280.

21. Taylor, *The Development of Professional Education*, pp. 257, 274.

22. Although Penn State is the land-grant college of Pennsylvania, it is not a fully public institution and is not state controlled. Throughout its history, it has been considered a "state-aided" or "state-related" institution, clearly favored by the legislature for its public functions but not entirely under state control. Since 1965, as a result of financial exigencies, both Temple University and the University of Pittsburgh have joined Penn State as "state-related" institutions. In some ways, this unusual mix of private and public status relates to Pennsylvania's long reliance on private institutions.

23. Separate schools of education were founded at Pittsburgh and Temple in the 1910s; Penn State consolidated its education programs into a school in 1923.

24. W. A. Yeager, "State Certification as a Factor in the Training of Elementary Teachers-in-Service" (unpublished doctoral dissertation, University of Pennsylvania, 1929). Yeager's study is somewhat useful in assessing the success of the Edmonds Act, but his focus is on the need for a separate type of training for elementary teachers. His strongest conclusion is that the private colleges are not equipped for this role.

25. J. S. Butterweck, *The Story of Teacher Education at Temple University* (Philadelphia: Temple University, 1977), p. 122.

26. These statements from the superintendent's annual report are quoted in an unsigned report titled "The Summer Session," [1930 ?], p. 3, in the Penn State Collection, Penn State Room, Pattee Library of Pennsylvania State University.

27. Many of Penn State's early publications repeatedly stress its "splendid location, fine climate, and healthful surroundings." See, for example, *College Degrees for Normal School Graduates: A Dozen Pertinent Questions on a Vital Professional Matter,* pamphlet in the Penn State Collection, Penn State Room, Pattee Library of Pennsylvania State University (University Park: Pennsylvania State University, 1927).

28. Figures and quotations from Will Grant Chambers, "The School of Education" (document in the Penn State Collection, 1928), p. 4.

29. Baker, "An Organizational Analysis," p. 98.

30. Indiana Normal School president Keith became superintendent in 1927. Although Keith also had a strong vision for the normals, Baker suggests that he was not fully supported by the other normal principals, thus limiting the success of his work. See Baker, "An Organizational Analysis," chap. 5.

31. Sturzebecker, *Centennial History of West Chester,* p. 261.

32. Sturzebecker, *Centennial History of West Chester,* p. 172. Although it is likely that the pressures of World War II prompted the superintendent to suggest this move as a way to meet the state's training needs, it is offered here as an example of the continuing shaky support for the teachers' colleges and their missions.

33. Sturzebecker, *Centennial History of West Chester,* pp. 175–176. The term in quotation marks is Sturzebecker's.

34. Sturzebecker, *Centennial History of West Chester,* p. 187.

35. Sturzebecker, *Centennial History of West Chester,* also mentions in passing a 1958 proposal by the Veterans of Foreign Wars to have the fourteen teachers' colleges made a permanent part of Penn State University (see p. 193).

36. Sturzebecker, *Centennial History of West Chester,* p. 228, does

not say what the actual appropriations were in that same era, although he and Sykes imply a disproportionate share to the private schools.

37. This impression was conveyed in interviews with seven current and retired faculty members of West Chester University, conducted June 9–10, 1988.

38. All of the professors interviewed at West Chester expressed this sentiment, including active and retired faculty members from across the disciplines. The reference to "a little Harvard" comes from retired professor of health education Ruth Reed.

39. This language, repeated frequently over time in various school of education documents, can be found, for example, in *A Perspective on the 80s: Agenda for Action for The Pennsylvania State University,* Penn State Collection, Pattee Library of the Pennsylvania State University, January 1980.

40. Will Grant Chambers relates the incident only briefly. See his letter to Penn State president John M. Thomas, Nov. 1, 1923, in the Penn State Collection.

41. Michael Bezilla provides information on this development in his *Penn State: An Illustrated History* (University Park: Penn State University Press, 1985), pp. 153–154.

42. Bezilla, *Penn State,* p. 268.

43. Bezilla, *Penn State,* pp. 309–311.

44. Bezilla, *Penn State,* p. 323.

45. Bezilla, *Penn State,* p. 337. Bezilla provides the story of the Penn State–community college struggle on pp. 325–337.

46. Baker, "An Organizational Analysis," p. 37.

47. See Baker, "An Organizational Analysis," chap. 4 (especially pp. 93–100), on the "task environment" of the normal schools for a good discussion of how they responded as a group to the challenges before them.

48. In this division, two or three programs were singled out for specialization on each campus. West Chester, for example, was "awarded" a focus on physical education and music education; Edinboro, the program in art education; and Indiana, commercial education. See Taylor, *The*

Development of Professional Education, p. 271. With such a clear market niche, then, these special programs flourished on the separate campuses.

49. Certainly, other institutions were also involved in the Philadelphia market. Central High School, for example, had a training course for teachers around the turn of the century (see Taylor, *The Development of Professional Education,* p. 171). However, the project on the Education of Educators studied only certain cases and does not purport to provide a complete history of the city or the state. For an interesting recent discussion of market forces at work in the secondary market in Philadelphia, see D. F. Labaree, *The Making of an American High School: The Credentials Market and the Central High School of Philadelphia, 1838–1939* (New Haven, Conn.: Yale University Press, 1988).

50. For a discussion of these early years and Carnell's influence, see the history of Temple provided by Butterweck, *The Story of Teacher Education at Temple University,* especially chap. 2.

51. See discussion of the Philadelphia situation in R. M. Angelo, "Unassigned Frequencies: Four Essays on the Historiography of American Education" (unpublished doctoral dissertation, Temple University, 1979), and his later revision, "The Students at the University of Pennsylvania and the Temple College of Philadelphia, 1873–1906: Some Notes on Schooling, Class, and Social Mobility in the Late Nineteenth Century," *History of Education Quarterly,* 1979, *19* (Summer), 179–205. His later article emphasizes the wide range of acceptable "higher education" at the turn of the century.

52. Angelo, "Unassigned Frequencies," explains that "degrees represent only a part of the instructional story [at Temple,] for . . . the overwhelming majority of graduates until 1909—most until 1927—were the recipients of diplomas and certificates, not degrees" (p. 59).

53. S. K. Stevens, *Pennsylvania: Birthplace of a Nation* (New York: Random House, 1964), p. 242.

54. Butterweck, *The Story of Teacher Education at Temple University*, describes some of the criticisms, both subtle and open, of Carnell's work with children (see pp. 172–173 and, generally, chap. 3).

55. Such phrases, easy to find in descriptions of the early college, come from the 1888 and 1893 *Bulletins* of Temple College.

56. Angelo, "The Students at the University," p. 188 and table 1.

57. Angelo, "The Students at the University," pp. 191–192.

58. Angelo, "The Students at the University," p. 184.

59. Angelo, "The Students at the University," p. 192.

60. These Pennsylvania figures are provided in Baker, "An Organizational Analysis," pp. 57–59, which also cites the national studies by William S. Learned and William C. Bagley.

61. Butterweck says of Temple, for example, that many of the students registered in the School of Education only because they felt that its requirements were easier than those of the liberal arts (p. 61). Historian Robert Alberts of Pitt indicates the widespread net of teacher education programs at that university. When the School of Education was "downscaled" in the early 1920s, for example, several of its programs were sent to other curricular areas, including a whole host of technical programs that were shifted over to the Carnegie Institute of Technology. See R. Alberts, *Pitt: The Story of the University of Pittsburgh, 1787–1987* (Pittsburgh: University of Pittsburgh Press, 1986), p. 88.

62. At West Chester, for example, there is no particular focus in the extant histories on the school's service to women over time. Although catalogues reveal that a large percentage of the teaching staff was female, there is no particular attention to their contributions. Some of the longtime women faculty members at the institution discussed the inequities they saw between men and women, including the fact that women coaches seldom received the plum summer teaching opportunities, and women athletes never

received the desired dining hall jobs that were "reserved" for male athletes (discussions with female faculty and staff at West Chester University, June 9–10, 1988).

63. A. T. Smith (professor of pedagogy), "Quarto-Centennial History" (document in West Chester University Archives, 1896).

64. These figures are gathered from the published lists of alumni in the *Fiftieth Annual Catalogue of the Pennsylvania State Normal School* for the first district, West Chester, Pennsylvania (West Chester: Horace F. Temple, 1921). There is no record of methods used to gather the information; accuracy cannot, therefore, be assessed.

65. See *Fiftieth Annual Catalogue*, pp. 48a–52a.

66. *Fiftieth Annual Catalogue*, pp. 48a–52a.

67. *Fiftieth Annual Catalogue*, pp. 70a–74a.

68. Information from an interview with Ada G. Kessler conducted in West Chester, June 10, 1988.

69. Interview with Havlick conducted in West Chester, June 10, 1988.

70. Interview with Anna Highley, conducted in West Chester, June 10, 1988.

71. Bezilla, *Penn State*, pp. 122–123. Bezilla, unlike many institutional historians, is very conscientious about providing information on enrollment over time, including percentages of men and women students and a bit of data on their social backgrounds.

72. Bezilla, *Penn State*, pp. 156–157.

73. The description of the arrangement as a "gentlemen's agreement" was provided by retired Penn State professor Paul Bixby in an interview June 14, 1988.

74. Dean Chambers, cited in Bezilla, *Penn State*, p. 160.

75. The quotations are from W. G. Chambers, "A Brief Sketch of the Origin and Development of the School of Education," 1937 (document in the Penn State Room at the Pattee Library of Penn State), p. 7. The sketch includes a description of the 1929–30 meetings and the agreement. The history of the agreement is also provided in Baker,

"An Organizational Analysis," chap. 5; Baker stresses the role of the normal schools.

76. See "College Degrees for Normal School Graduates," p. 2. This bulletin is an excellent example of the way Penn State perceived its relationship to the normal schools and its students.

77. It should be remembered that in Pennsylvania, considerable state funding always went to private as well as public institutions, so the level of state contribution was an issue for the private colleges, too.

78. Butterweck cites this group briefly in his *History*, p. 111.

79. The arguments are presented succinctly in "A Brief on the Function of the Pennsylvania State College in the State Program of Teacher Training in Light of the Alleged Over Supply of Teachers" (unsigned and undated document [c. 1933] in the Penn State Collection).

80. "A Brief on the Function," p. 2.

81. "A Brief on the Function," p. 9.

82. See, for example, *Institutions of Higher Learning in Relation to a State Program of Teacher Education* (Harrisburg: Department of Public Instruction, 1939), which emphasizes the state's role in balancing demand for teacher training.

8

Centralization, Competition, and Racism: Teacher Education in Georgia

Kathleen Cruikshank

The dominant source of higher education in Georgia today is the University System of Georgia, a network of two- and four-year colleges spread over the state. Although the system emerged, in 1932, as a result of state fiscal crisis, its mandate lies in the 1785 charter of the University of Georgia, which establishes university stewardship of all publicly funded education in the state.[1] How and to what degree that stewardship has been asserted—and particularly why and in what context—provide a main thread in the history of teacher education in Georgia.

Another thread is the wide variety of institutions that became involved in teacher education.[2] Schools were established that distinguished themselves, often vehemently, along denominational lines—the Baptists and Methodists' becoming most vigorous in founding schools to educate white preachers and teachers following the revivals of the early nineteenth century and, after the Civil War, in a kind of domestic missionary crusade to train blacks in basic Christian beliefs and service to their race in perpetuating those beliefs. The firm sense of purpose behind these schools challenged what was seen as the lax morality of nondenominational schools, such as Franklin College—the small liberal arts school that constituted the University of Georgia for its first hundred years—or Atlanta University, launched by the American Missionary Society. In addition, there were state schools that were intended to be normal schools to a greater or lesser degree, such as the Georgia Normal and Industrial School for Women, established in 1889 at Milledgeville as a female equivalent of the newly founded Georgia School of Technology in Atlanta—at its founding apparently only nominally a normal school; or the State Normal School founded in Athens in 1892, which was the state's one full-fledged commitment, albeit hesitant, to teacher education. There were also private schools directed to specific populations for specific educational purposes, such as the Berry Schools, designed to uplift the white mountain people of northwest Georgia, or the forerunners of Fort Valley State College and Albany State College, serving the poverty-ridden blacks of the Georgia "black belt."

Georgia thus presents a wide array of schools involved in teacher education, but there is a common backdrop for all of them. In a state that until well into the twentieth century remained in many senses a frontier state with a mobile population and rural poverty among the challenges to be faced, public education, let alone public teacher education, had little public support. Permeating Georgia's history is the emphatic maintenance by Georgia's white citizens of two different worlds, and thus of two different systems of education, along the lines of race. The history of teacher education in the University System of Georgia is almost exclusively the history of white teacher education. Georgia's black population, with substantial help from the North, built a separate and dynamic history of teacher education, which intersected with the university system's history only when it became prudent, economically or politically, for the university to have it so. The integration of black education into that system is still very much in process and problematic. The governing dynamic, as in other states, is that of centralization, of the management and administration of a cohesive whole built on common standards; but this works itself out against the backdrop of institutional competition and of a pervasive racism allowed to run rampant for nearly eighty years, and of the residue that lingers on.

Pervasive as well is a stark distinction between rural and urban worlds. This distinction may well be as sharp today, with the explosion of Atlanta's growth as a corporate headquarters contrasting with the persistent poverty of middle and southwest Georgia, much as the textile centers of Augusta and Columbus contrasted with the resuscitated plantations of middle Georgia at the turn of the century. One has then a society fractured first along racial lines, then along urban-rural lines that to some extent—though not by any means completely—correspond to economic class distinctions.

Moreover, the Georgia economy has, for virtually the full period covered by a history of teacher education, been struggling to find a footing. After Reconstruction, the economy returned to antebellum economic relations, which, however, were undermined both by a slow but steady growth of black self-confidence (despite, or perhaps in part because of, brutal disenfranchisement throughout the South) and by the national economic disasters brought on by depression in the 1890s and then again in the 1930s and the ravages of the boll weevil in between. It was only toward the end of the 1930s that the state budget began to offer more than nominal support for public white education; black education received attention twenty years later, as desegregation began to appear an increasingly likely alternative to schools that were very much separate and blatantly unequal. There are then, for a great part of Georgia's history, two histories of education and thus of teacher education, which intersect in particular ways.

The Beginnings of White Teacher Education

The history of teacher education in Georgia begins with the white population of the state and the peculiarly white Georgian culture it embodied. A passionate loyalty to tradition tied Georgia to a colonial past shared with the Northeast, which at the same time opened it to influences that threatened the sharply stratified and decentralized sociopolitical world created by a plantation economy. The struggle to build and maintain a southern reality that culminated in the Civil War included a constant battle against growth in the power of state government over social life, making organization for popular political action virtually impossible. The repeated attempts throughout the antebellum and Reconstruction periods to establish a state-wide educational system are eloquent testimony to the internal conflict between social needs and the aversion to collective response through government. It was only from a position of economic prostration that Georgians were compelled to organize themselves through legislation in order to claim the benefits offered by northern philanthropy and the federal government, which seemed their only hope of rebuilding their world in any form.

When teacher education first became a part of the University of Georgia in 1903, it was part of a massive effort to redefine and finally establish the university as a permanent and integral part of Georgia's economic and social fabric. Although originally chartered in 1785 with a state grant of 40,000 acres, the university had struggled almost continuously during its first hundred years for survival in the face of impending financial collapse, accusations of elitism, political and religious factionalism and the accompanying growth of denominational colleges, and—perhaps most significantly—an uncertainty as to its relationship to its sponsoring society.[3] Strong opposition to state support of higher education forced early sale of lands that should have ensured the university's future support.

At the same time, recognition of the value of education as cultural capital has been consistent among the elite from colonial days. Thus, the sons of gentlemen were sent to the North or to Europe for higher education, but anything beyond the rudiments of learning was considered "improper to their station" for the "children of the plain people."[4] As the state developed after the Revolution, however, local pride and a measure of democratic sentiment began to suggest that more of Georgia's children should be educated, and in the course of the nineteenth century, some 583 academies were opened. Many of these were denominational, tracing their roots to similar academies in the Northeast; many of the early directors came from northeastern states, responding to advertisements in northern papers.

The small but persistent group of progressive educators whose names reappear throughout the antebellum period were caught in a complex web of social, political, and economic forces through which there was no clear path to establishing the comprehensive educational system envisioned in the 1785 mandate. For one thing, Georgia had in 1837 a white population (and education was at this point considered strictly a matter for whites) of 300,000 scattered over its 58,000 square miles of largely agricultural land, or five people per square mile. The agricultural economy, based increasingly on a single crop, determined what little taxation was allowed to such a degree that attempts to establish free schools evaporated with the fall of cotton prices.[5] Further, the definition of wealth in terms of land and slaves to work the land kept resources on which the state could draw to a minimum in the best of times.

Beyond these ubiquitous forces, there were such obstacles as the possibility from 1828 to 1838 of an independent Cherokee nation being established within Georgia's borders, which deflected attention from the first major efforts to establish a common school system. In similar fashion, promising efforts in the early 1850s had to battle for attention with the growing conflict with the North and the possibility of secession. When the common school law was finally passed in 1859 and a plausible county organization implemented, it was on the eve of a war that would shatter not only the economy but the entire social fabric of Georgia, and with it the self-respect and confidence of the state.

The development of state-supported teacher education must be seen within this larger context. While its formal emergence came much later in the century, there were men who drafted public school legislation, wrote in newspapers, and attempted to organize teachers; some of them were concerned about the education of teachers. Just before its demise in 1854, the all-male State Teachers' Association took up the cry for the creation of normal schools, and in 1857 Joseph E. Brown, newly elected as governor in a break with the old aristocratic domination of state politics, laid out a plan for common schools, including a provision for the education of teachers. Also interested was President Alonzo Church of the University of Georgia, but for him it was part of a much broader educational vision, which would eventually affect teacher education dramatically. Under his leadership (1830–1859), a more scientific orientation began to develop at the university, which had hitherto consisted of Franklin College, a classical liberal arts school for the sons of the wealthy.

A report to the board of trustees in 1855 proposed a massive reorganization that included not only schools of agriculture and applied science but "the expansion of the institution's role in teacher training."[6] The report was overshadowed by internal faculty-president discord, however; and when the plan resurfaced and was approved in the fall of 1859, teacher training had been left aside in favor of creating the four new schools of agriculture, civil engineering and applied mathematics, law, and commerce. Despite lack of legislative support, the University of Georgia emerged at the brink of the Civil War with the rudiments of a modern university in place, but teacher education was not a part of it.

With the end of Reconstruction in the early 1870s, conservative forces reasserted themselves in the General Assembly and eventually within the university as well, making the vision of a modern, public-service-oriented university seem premature.[7] At the same time, popular interest in the university increased, albeit in a critical vein, as agriculturalists demanded more effective agricultural education than that offered by giving Franklin College's liberal arts faculty joint teaching assignments in the State College of Agriculture. The university found that, because of virtually nonexistent secondary education and very uneven elementary preparation, admission standards for agriculture students had to be waived in order to keep sufficient numbers to comply with Morrill Act requirements.[8] Such inequities resulted in a variety of social discrimination and organizational demands, which led to a return to a fixed curriculum that put all students on the same footing and reasserted the university's identity as a traditional classical liberal arts college—an identity that lasted twenty years despite a shattered southern economy and calls from the "New South" spokesmen for improved agricultural, engineering, and teacher education.

In spite of the inequities, the first moves toward expansion, popular sentiment, and, perhaps more significantly, a drop in Franklin College's enrollment to 116 in 1878[9] had given birth to a tendency that was to play a major role in the university's growth and particularly in the history of teacher education—namely, competition among state-supported institutions.[10] In the face of consistent lack of support from the state, the control of education lay in the hands of the institutions that could command funds, a factor, no doubt, in the university's incorporation in 1872 of North Georgia Agricultural College in Dahlonega[11]—a privately founded school that had developed strong support in the northwest mountain regions by offering "education at whatever level individual students needed with low expense."[12] What the university gave to the Dahlonega school was access to Morrill Act funds; what it acquired was a strong branch college and, incidentally, the first normal department founded in a state college.

Thus began, nominally at least, formal teacher education at the University of Georgia, although it was another twenty-five years before the Athens campus undertook to educate teachers, and then to some extent as a survival tactic in the face of legislative favor to the rapidly expanding State Normal School, which had grown up on its back doorstep out of a coalescence of efforts around support from the Peabody Education Fund. The fund, established in 1867 to support education for young children in the devastated areas of the South and Southwest, consisted of the annually disbursed interest from $2 million worth of investments, with the possibility of disbursal of 40 percent of the principal after two years and the power to close the trust after thirty, on the condition that two-thirds of the fund be distributed in the southern states.[13]

The means chosen by the Peabody board to achieve their

ends were, among other things, support throughout the region for state normal schools "on account of their superior excellence over Normal Departments in Colleges and Academies, which will be overshadowed by literary and scientific departments, and fail to win the regard and excite the enthusiasm of students or the interest of the general public," for "training of female teachers for Primary Schools, rather than . . . young men in Colleges, who will be likely to teach in the higher schools for the benefit of the few," and for attendance of "colored" teachers at regular normal schools "and, only in exceptional cases, at other schools which attempt to give·normal instruction."[14]

The Peabody trustees began agitation for teacher education in Georgia immediately upon the fund's establishment with an address by general agent Barnas Sears to the 1867 meeting of the newly formed Georgia Teachers Association. The state constitution passed in 1868 included clear provision for a state-supported normal school, but its association with the discredited Bullock government—which fled in 1871, leaving the first state school commissioner $300,000 in debt to teachers and county boards—guaranteed it little credence; the commissioner was forced to leave as well, abandoning the 1,573 schools he had urged into existence.[15]

It was within the setting of the predictable conservative backlash that Gustavus J. Orr, as second state commissioner of education (1872–1887), tackled the problems of public schooling, local taxation, and the preparation of teachers. While his role in the development of Georgia's public schools can to some extent be measured by increased enrollments, teachers, and funding, his public assertions of the federal responsibility for aid to southern education immeasurably affected attitudes in both South and North toward the southern situation and helped bring into focus what Rockefeller was to acknowledge in 1902 in establishing the General Education Fund—namely, that there would be no hope for southern educational improvement without increasing the wealth of the South.

The economic problem was severe. An agricultural depression from 1873 to 1898, coming on the heels of virtual bankruptcy by a corrupt Reconstruction government, provided the backdrop to the development of a tenant farming system, which left rural residents with virtually nothing to tax. Orr estimated in 1881 that, with the population one-third black and half of the whites impoverished, more than half of Georgia's population essentially paid no taxes. With property values on what was taxed at three-fifths their value before the war, the state was trying to do the impossible. Movement to the cities exacerbated the problems of rural districts, although increased wealth and Peabody support encouraged local initiatives in cities and towns, which eventually provided the state with some model school systems.

When Orr's efforts failed to persuade the 1881 legislature to turn Middle Georgia College at Milledgeville into a normal school and to give funds to support a normal department for blacks at Atlanta University, the only teacher education available was through teacher institutes, which, with Peabody support, were offered around the state from 1882 to 1885. The Peabody trustees made further support contingent on legislation. Eleven hundred teachers—767 whites, 333 blacks—and 105 county commissioners participated in the segregated sessions.[16] The success of these institutes built pressure for a normal school, but the legislature's response was the creation in 1889 of Georgia Normal and Industrial College at Milledgeville as another branch of the university, this one clearly the female equivalent of the Georgia School of Technology established in Atlanta in 1887.

Although the optional nature of normal instruction at the Georgia Normal and Industrial College made it seem a normal school in name only, it was the first state institution offering education above the elementary level to women—a definite breakthrough. Teacher education and female education were often linked, since supporters of the latter, often opposed to common schools as posing competing claims for scarce resources, frequently buttressed their appeals by pointing to the potential for teacher education.[17] Economic considerations being what they were, the idea of educating women to teach had gained ground, albeit slowly. In 1853, Alonzo Church, president of the University of Georgia, who had voiced a plea for the establishment of normal schools during the second annual meeting of the State Teachers' Society in 1832, outlined a detailed plan for organizing the common schools. The plan included employing women in one-half of the teaching positions to take advantage of their cheaper services.[18]

At last in 1891, J.L.M. Curry, the powerful general agent for the Peabody Fund and, not insignificantly, a native Georgian, apparently provided sufficient incentive in a speech to the general assembly to incite action on teacher education.[19] His suggestion that two or three normal schools be established around the state with Peabody support was met by an offer from the University of Georgia Board of Trustees of the old University High School land, plus interest from the $15,000 Gilmer Trust Fund, a bequest from 1884 to support elementary teacher education. The State Normal School was to be established at Athens and to be overseen by the university chancellor, the state school commissioner, and "three citizens of Georgia, experienced in teaching, to be appointed by the governor." Tuition was to be free to all white male residents of Georgia.

True to form, the legislature failed to appropriate operating funds, leaving the commission to launch course work with the annual interest of $1,050 from the Gilmer fund. Nevertheless, a seven-week course was offered in summer 1892, attended by 112 students representing thirty-two counties. Total enrollment in the 1894 summer session was 175 students from fifty-one counties, apparently a substantial enough increase to move the legislature, since an annual appropriation of $10,000 was established and the State Normal School was put on a firm, if modest, footing.

The first ten years of its existence saw phenomenal growth. As word spread of the work of the school and its cooperative approach to expenses—which held students' monthly costs to six to eight dollars—enrollment increased dramatically. The 178 students in 1895 filled the available accommodations, and the legislature was prevailed upon to provide $7,000 for building purposes. The new space was likewise quickly filled, and the demand for housing was still unmet, leading the president in the summer of 1896 to enlist the grand jury of Clarke County to create tents to help house the more than 300 students enrolled.

After its first year, the normal school offered four terms of ten weeks from March to December, and a full curriculum was in place. Instruction was offered in the theory and practice of teaching, which included attention to "the nature and development of the child mind" as well as to school organization and discipline; English, which included grammar and American English literature; a course of lectures in U.S. history; geography, including map drawing and astronomy and consideration of "the geology, chemistry, physics, botany, zoology, and mineralogy of the earth"; mathematics, including both content and methods of teaching; primary methods; a presentation of the German kindergarten and its methods; vocal music; drawing; and psychology—this last to be taught by Chancellor Boggs of the University of Georgia. The certificate course included "all subjects known as the legal branches" and resulted in a one-, two-, or three-year license to teach in the common schools, depending on proficiency. The elective course consisted of at least two studies and yielded no certificate.[20] In 1897, the curriculum was expanded to include Latin, more science, penmanship, manual arts, and a model elementary school of which the normal school was apparently justifiably proud, taught by a former student of Colonel Francis Parker at the Cook County Normal School.[21]

Despite the normal school's phenomenal growth, support was far from ensured. The irregularity of payment, even when money had been appropriated, forced the president to occasionally pledge his personal credit in order to pay faculty salaries.[22] It is possible that tenacious local loyalties may have played a role as well, as then governor W. Y. Atkinson (1894–1898), a staunch advocate of education for women, had authored the 1889 bill establishing the Georgia Normal and Industrial College at Milledgeville and continued to favor it over the originally all-male State Normal School.[23]

The Beginnings of Black Teacher Education

For the whites of Georgia, the coming of teacher education may have been slow—they had, after all, a fairly steady supply of young white men trained in the North to meet the modest needs of the few institutions that remained active after the war. For blacks after the Civil War, it became an immediate priority as northerners poured in during Reconstruction to respond to the desires of freedmen for education. As a historian of Atlanta University describes it:

> One of the major problems facing the freedman in Georgia was to train and supply teachers for the children of approximately one-half million illiterates. The existence of two separate worlds, the Negro and the white, compounded the problem. Negroes were not admitted to the University of Georgia; few southern whites were trained as teachers, and those who were would not teach in Negro schools; and the North was unable to supply teachers in the needed numbers. Therefore, if the freedmen were to be educated to become useful citizens, their teachers had to come from their own race and had to be trained in their own schools.[24]

For blacks, the drive for education was both more individual and more collective. With freedom came a rush for the learning that seemed to be the key to achieving full citizenship, resulting in a flood of students, young and old, into whatever space could be found, to be taught by anyone who knew more then they. The northern schoolmarms who came fresh from the best normal schools of the North may not only have launched schools but have given blacks a sense of what education and teaching could be, because black standards, despite the obstacles to meeting them, were high. Like the Georgia whites who supported Franklin College, the visionaries in black education set a strong liberal arts school at the top of their educational hierarchy, to train the teachers and leaders who would help to uplift the race.

By 1870, the American Baptist Home Mission Society had founded the Augusta Institute for the training of black teachers and preachers, amid considerable hostility from white citizens;[25] the Albany Normal School in middle Georgia had been founded by six northern women under the aegis of the American Missionary Association;[26] and Atlanta University had been launched with a twenty-year charter, establishing a "normal department" even before it had permanent buildings. It became "the first educational institution of higher learning in Georgia to open its doors to all people, regardless of race, color or creed,"[27] and its primary mission was to train teachers. The normal department, established in 1869, was followed by the preparatory department in 1871 and the college and lower normal departments in 1872, the latter "to meet the growing demand for primary teachers and in order to prepare students for the preparatory and normal courses."[28]

This pattern of development was shared by other schools, both black and white. The divisions of primary or elementary school, grammar school, high school, and normal courses are neither clear nor consistent across institutions, although they seem to have become focused as time went on. The difficulty that all early colleges faced, including the University of Georgia, was that the students who came to them were not necessarily prepared to undertake what the colleges felt that they should offer as collegiate-level work. All colleges therefore had what they generally called a "preparatory department," which students attended in order to reach the level of the collegiate work proper. Depending on the knowledge levels of entering students, they might also have a grammar school and even elementary work. In fact, enrollment in these lower levels frequently exceeded that of the college itself. Atlanta University enrolled an average of 61 percent of its students in its grammar school from its founding in 1869 until the discontinuation of the grammar school in 1894, with grammar school enrollment being a minority only six times in that period.

By 1882, the various levels at Atlanta University had sorted themselves out into a five-year grammar school, a three-year preparatory department, and a four-year collegiate department. The grammar school curriculum included reading, spelling, grammar, geography with map drawing, U.S. history, elementary geometry, botany and physiology, writing, inventive and freehand drawing, and vocal music and gymnastics, with attention also to moral and Christian instruction, including Bible study, temperance, and hygiene. Entrance to the preparatory department required passing tests in most of those subjects. It offered a curriculum that followed New England models: higher arithmetic, algebra, geometry, ancient history, ancient geography, Latin (lessons, prose composition, Caesar, Cicero and Virgil), and Greek (lessons, prose composition, Anabasis, and Testament). Successful testing in these subjects was the condition of admission to the college department, which, again, followed the New England colleges as its model.

The "higher normal course" was a four-year course covering essentially the same subjects as the preparatory course and was modeled on normal schools in the North. Several terms of both grammar school work and high school subjects were followed by work in methods of teaching and practice teaching, as well as household sciences, including plain sewing, cookery, and nursing the sick, for the girls, and woodworking and metalworking for the boys.

Atlanta University's reputation for high standards was established quickly. An annual appropriation of $8,000 from the legislature brought with it annual examination of students by the Board of Visitors of the University of Georgia. Realizing the importance of those examinations in establishing not only Atlanta University's standards but the capabilities of blacks as a whole, President Edmund Ware requested that the governor appoint a majority of the board from the old slaveholding class to avoid any danger of charitable views toward blacks. The board's report to the governor, calling the state appropriation to Atlanta University a wise investment that should receive "kindly sympathy and approval of the people in whose midst it is located," concluded its assessment of the students with the statement that "Many of the pupils exhibited a degree of mental culture which, considering the length of time their minds have been in training, would do credit to the members of any race."[29]

The success of these first examinations established Atlanta University unequivocally as a first-class institution and allayed some of the fears of southern whites that it might have been involved in fostering racial hatred. It did not, however, create unanimous support, as the battle in 1874–1887 for the Morrill Act appropriation demonstrated.

When the University of Georgia hastily pulled together the College of Agriculture in 1871 to enable the legislature to claim the state's allotted portion of Morrill Act land scrip, Atlanta University president Ware had written to President Brown of the University of Georgia to ask if the college's claim to all the funds indicated that blacks would be admitted and, if so, under what conditions. Brown's response was indirect, but in 1874 the $8,000 appropriation to Atlanta University was specifically designated by the legislature as being "in lieu of any claim of the colored population of the State upon the proceeds of the Agricultural Land Scrip, donated by the Congress of the United States." Further, the money would not be paid until a committee of three University of Georgia faculty members had approved the plan of the trustees of Atlanta University, and Atlanta University would agree to educate gratis one student nominated by every member of the House of Representatives.[30] The appropriation itself was opposed by many for different reasons, among them the "sectarian" nature of the institution and the fact that black students and white faculty ate together.

Legislative battles defeated a bill withdrawing public funds from any school sponsoring coeducation of the races and disqualifying pupils of such a school from ever teaching in Georgia, but the passage of resolutions making Atlanta University's appropriation contingent on evidence of no coeducation led two newly established black schools—Morris Brown College and the Spelman Seminary for girls—to seek the funds as well. With the passage of the 1890 Morrill Act and the imminent threat to Georgia's share of funds because of the absence of vocational and agricultural education for blacks, the State College of Industry for Colored Youth in Savannah was established to receive the one-third intended to support such education. The other two-thirds went to the College of Agriculture in Athens.

Despite the growing racism foreshadowed by these legislative battles, Atlanta University emerged with a stronger sense of its role than before. As president-to-be Bumstead (1888–1907) described the black university in 1882, it had to represent "in the most perfect form, all the successive grades of education from the lowest to the highest, and should train all ages rather than extraordinary persons of mature age only."[31]

In 1873, the short-lived Scientific Preparatory Department offered a parallel but alternative to the normal department, but it was discontinued within two years. Atlanta University, like the white schools Mercer and Emory some fifteen to twenty years later, was to find that a solid classical education would provide its most reliable foundation. While Emory's Department of Toolcraft and Design would eventually evolve into the Georgia School of Technology as a branch of the University of Georgia, Mercer's attempt to build a Department of Practical Arts, growing out of the manual labor ideal that it shared with Emory, lasted only two years before it was dropped to concentrate fully on maintaining a high-quality liberal arts curriculum, determining to some extent its future as an educator of secondary teachers in the classical tradition.

Yet for other schools, a component of manual labor or industrial education was a mainstay. The debate over industrial education deserves attention, because it was a crucial issue in curriculum for most black schools and thus for the training of teachers.[32] The industrial education model of Booker T. Washington's Tuskegee Institute and the northern support it received were to exert a powerful influence on schools for blacks. Schools that undertook extensive industrial education programs found themselves the recipients of the attentions and the funding of the Peabody and Slater funds and then of the General Education Board, which supplemented and then superseded them.

It would be a mistake to ignore the fact that the manual training school movement that had sprung up in the 1870s in the United States, following the patterns of Pestalozzi and Fellenberg, among others, was an influence on white education as well and, in some cases, on white elite education. The education of hand and heart as well as mind was a goal for educators of very different stripes, although they had varying success. There was significant pressure for industrial and agricultural education for whites in Georgia, and, as usual, it was for white children that the first innovations were made. The fact that both blacks and whites were to receive it may indicate that this was first and foremost a class issue rather than solely an educational prescription based on race.

The development of teacher education, black and white, was driven by changing coalitions of interests. Public school supporters influenced by the so-called common school revival in the northeast and southerners who were beginning to focus on the vision of a New South were among the most vocal. Although the New South would be some time in coming, there were those who saw education of the masses as essential to the economic health of Georgia, in some cases extending that vision to include the blacks who composed around 50 percent of those masses.

There had been blacks and whites on both sides of the issues during the 1874–1891 legislative battles, particularly when the possibility of establishing a normal school as well as supporting Atlanta University came under consideration. However, division in their ranks was soon to become a democratic luxury that they could ill afford. As disenfranchisement of blacks gained ground in the beginning of the twentieth century, it became increasingly clear that white Georgians of means were on the whole not willing to take the responsibility for black education, unwilling as they were to support any publicly funded education. In fact, it may well have been the strength of privately funded black education that in a backhand way brought about legislation supplementing state support with local taxation for schools in general, since church and philanthropic efforts had provided better-quality educational facilities for blacks than for whites in some of the cities and towns at least.

The hope that blacks may have allowed themselves for their future clearly had to undergo drastic modification in the face of a hostile political environment, virtual absence of public funds for schooling, and the vicious circle of low educational standards. Yet it is clear from the histories of such schools as those at Forsyth and Fort Valley that a few relentlessly tenacious individuals were able to marshal the bare minimum of support to provide opportunities for a few black young people and thus to keep alive the hope for an "uplifting of our race."

The foundation on which they built was almost nonexistent. There were some 350,000 black children to be educated, but with no means of training teachers except through the very schools in which they would teach, unless they could afford to go out of state or to one of the private black universities. Those who could afford higher education could hardly be expected to return to teach in dilapidated one-room schoolhouses for one and a half to three months of the year to earn a monthly salary of $45.53 for men or $25.83 for women,[33] payment to be delayed in most cases, since the state habitually was unable to meet its obligations.

Three schools arose out of this need between 1895 and 1905, all of them led virtually from their inception by men totally committed to the betterment of their people. Building on the base of the Albany Normal School, which with its primary, grammar, and normal departments had operated since Reconstruction, in 1904 Joseph Holley opened what he called the Albany Bible and Manual Training Institute, officially the Albany Manual Training and Agricultural Institute, which he was to head for forty years. His model was Tuskegee Institute, and the title of his autobiography may well capture his guiding principle: *You Can't Build a Chimney from the Top.* Inspired by DuBois's description of Dougherty County in *The Souls of Black Folk*,[34] Holley developed over the next thirteen years an excellent relationship with his community and an enrollment of 160. He pursued funds through annual trips to the North, with a zeal appropriate to what he considered a "missionary effort."[35] Taken over by the state in 1917, the Albany school was given a mandate to conduct farmers' institutes and teach the elementary branches of English education, agriculture, domestic science, mechanical arts, and all that was "suitable for the training of colored teachers for the schools of Georgia."[36] As the other two schools founded in these years were also to learn, takeover by the state did not necessarily mean better financial status, and the Hazard family of Rhode Island remained the school's chief benefactor until formation of the university system in 1932, as it had been since its founding.

Although southern white expectations of black education were that it would provide needed black labor in agricultural or domestic service roles, the Albany school of the late 1920s was to blacks the source of an education that might enable them one day to own a farm or business. With its junior college, grammar school, and vocational studies leading to postal work or a job in the Railway Mail Service and a two-year normal course for home economics teachers with an elementary and practice school and strong ties to Tuskegee, it was among the best black high school units in the state.[37]

The Forsyth Normal and Industrial School under William Hubbard, also influenced by Booker T. Washington, was another. Like both the Albany and the Fort Valley schools, Forsyth began with course work in the lower grades, gradually adding on as its students progressed until in 1917 it was accredited for high school work through the state department of education. It also was designated a "county training school," for the purposes of financial support from the Slater Fund, and became the first vocational agricultural school for blacks in Georgia under the Smith-Hughes Act. As a Slater-funded school, it was (1) to offer all common school studies as well as advanced work for at least an eight-month term, (2) to emphasize industrial training related to home and farm with an eye to preparing students for rural self-sufficiency, (3) to prepare young men and women to become rural and elementary school teachers by enabling them to meet legal requirements by giving them "close acquaintance and sympathy with rural activities" and giving them elementary training in teaching.[38] This last was outlined as work in the general aims and principles of elementary teaching, rural and elementary school management, reviews and special objectives in common school branches, and practice teaching and special methods.

The Slater trustees' intention, like that of most philanthropic groups, was to develop the school to the point where it would become an integral part of the public system. To that end, county training schools became in part secondary schools, in part specialized schools, and to a great extent community centers offering continuing agricultural and home economics education to those beyond school age.

Like Holley and Hubbard, Principal Henry Hunt of the Fort Valley High and Industrial School devoted his life to his school. It was founded on the initiative of the town's black citizens, and it quickly came to the attention of George Foster Peabody, at whose behest Hunt sought the principalship. Peabody, along with the Slater, Jeanes, and Rosenwald funds, was to be crucial to Fort Valley's survival. Like Hubbard at Forsyth, Hunt recognized that, despite his immediate attempt to implement an academic curriculum and a continuing emphasis on it, the first priority would have to be improving the quality of rural life for as many of the 500,000 blacks within a 100-mile radius as he could reach.

By 1905–06, he had an enrollment of 446—half of them in the primary classes, the rest in the grammar school and normal department—plus over forty in the night school for working students. Like Hubbard at Forsyth, and facing the same constant fiscal crisis, he began to implement extended agricultural production programs in order to cut back the need for cash outlay. His emphasis on teacher training in 1911, extending practice teaching to both senior and junior years, may well have been a way of dealing with the ever-increasing elementary enrollments. That year, he had thirteen teachers to deal with 27 secondary, 191 grammar, and 134 elementary students. Teacher education was, however, a main emphasis, and it was to remain so. The four-week summer school for teachers in 1913, offering a wide variety of subjects and activities in addition to teaching methods, attracted 52 students from several counties.

In 1919, the school was saved from fiscal disaster by the American Church Institute, which eliminated its financial worries until the school's takeover by the university system in 1939. In those twenty years, a massive building program was undertaken, and involvement with the community was expanded to include a full range of agricultural and homemaking outreach work as well as an infirmary and programs to help black citizens obtain low-interest loans for home purchase, the whole of which was considered extraordinary by at least one observer.[39]

Community involvement was not characteristic just of rural teacher education, although it was clearly its mainstay. With the addition of W.E.B. DuBois to its sociology department in 1897, Atlanta University undertook a series of conferences and publications on the city world of black Americans. Its effects on teacher education included the introduction of the model home and an expanded domestic science program in 1899 and the opening of the Oglethorpe Practice School in 1904. By 1905, fifty of the Atlanta school system's sixty-two teachers were Atlanta University graduates, which was significant in view of the unpopularity of the institution because of its refusal to abandon social equality for blacks and whites.[40]

Atlanta University was not producing an elite corps of city teachers, however. Early graduates went out into the rural areas, where the need was greatest and life difficult at best. An 1894 graduate who moved to a small poverty-stricken community near Athens managed to set up a school with General Education Board assistance on land given by the county, finally putting together "a modern two-room Model and Training School." However, "This school was envied by the whites in the community, who expressed their jealousy by throwing a dead dog on the front porch of the school and by placing wagons across the road to make the approach to the building impossible."[41] Undeterred, she went on to gain the goodwill of her neighbors and the community's leading citizens and to contribute to improved farm methods and housing, as well as to the children's education.

The city of Atlanta was also the site of perhaps the largest teacher education effort in the state—the Spelman Seminary for girls, founded in 1881 in the basement of Friendship Baptist Church by two northern women dedicated to helping black women and girls. The shakiness of Spelman's early years may be attributed to the veritable flood of young women and girls who wanted to learn in order to teach others. By December 1883, it had an elementary normal course in place and over 400 students, 90 of them boarders who were already returning to their rural homes to teach between seminary sessions.

Teachers for the New South

The turn of the century saw a major effort by northern philanthropists and southern educational leaders to join forces to improve southern education. With the formation in 1901 of the Southern Education Board to tackle regional problems and the General Education Board in 1902 by Rockefeller and other northern philanthropists, an era of intense concentration on the rural South commenced. A massive survey project undertaken for a 1902 conference of Georgia county superintendents revealed clearly that while Georgia wanted public schools, it could not support them. With 85 percent of the South's rural average annual earnings as low as $150, compared to Iowa's average annual farm earnings of $1,000, the key to improved education was clearly economic development, which meant agriculture, which, in turn, meant agricultural and industrial education.

Little had changed in the last thirty years, with tenant farmers, who changed location on the average of once every two years, accounting for two-thirds of Georgia's farms. Improvements in public schools had to be made against this backdrop of constant mobile poverty. Illiteracy had kept pace with population growth during the postwar years, and in 1900 Georgia ranked forty-fifth among the fifty states and territories in literacy of those ten years and older. Although many in power were fond of pointing to the high number of blacks (nearly 50 percent of the population) as being a drain on Georgia's resources, the literacy ranking increased to only forty-first place when only whites were considered.

For the University of Georgia, this would be a turning point. As a result of the decline of private academies following the 1868 establishment of common schools, the problem of all colleges was now not "inducing some hundreds out of some thousand qualified men to enter one of the state or church colleges" but increasing the number of prepared men so that there might be any material for colleges at all.[42] The key linkage of agricultural development and secondary education pointed to teacher education, and a visionary president opened the way to putting the University of Georgia at the forefront of white educational development in Georgia. Reasserting the dominance of the university over the other state colleges, Walter B. Hill (1899–1905) drew outside funding into the creation of a university that would, among other things, undertake improvement of the state's secondary school system through accreditation standards to guide entrance to the university, prepare numbers of qualified secondary teachers, and establish a new College of Agriculture in direct service to the state.

The ramifications for teacher education were enormous. First moves in 1899 toward adding courses in pedagogy so that "as many teachers as possible may be associated in feeling and interest with the University"[43] were eclipsed by the establishment of a "School of Pedagogy" in 1901–02, which offered three courses as a program of professional education for teachers: history of education, the art of teaching, and school organization and management. Winning increased state funding, Hill was able in 1903 to hire Thomas Woofter and Joseph Stewart away from branch institutions to build a college of education and a statewide system of accredited secondary education over the next thirty years.

Woofter and Stewart's first project was a university summer school for teachers, which had been mandated earlier to provide "Graduate work, and courses closely related thereto including Psychology and the History and Philosophy of Education for the special benefit of white teachers of the State, without regard to sex or age,"[44] but it was a mandate without funding. With General Education Board and local support, the university offered summer sessions in 1903 and 1904, which incorporated the summer terms of the State Normal School, the cumulative enrollment of which was 700, some 500 of them Georgia teachers.

Both the university summer school and the State Normal School expanded rapidly, although the normal school still attracted twice the summer enrollment and between three and four times the academic-year enrollment of Franklin College. The two institutions were able to exist side by side until 1932, possibly because the university was rapidly creating for itself the vision of a truly "professional" kind of teacher education. Woofter's arguments to persuade Governor Hoke Smith, a member of both the Peabody and university boards of trustees, that the entire allotment of Peabody funds for Georgia should go to the university for a school of education rather than being divided among the university Department of Philosophy and Education, the State Normal School, and the Georgia Normal and Industrial College at Milledgeville rested on asserting the need for a school to prepare high school teachers.

If there was any implication here that the university was stepping in because the State Normal School was unable to prepare secondary teachers, the next twenty years would prove the contrary. The normal school had already in 1907–08 added a postgraduate course "in answer to the call on us for extended scholarship and riper experience in teaching, with salaries much beyond the pay received by the average teachers."[45] Before it was absorbed into the University of Georgia College of Education in the 1932 creation of the University System of Georgia, the State Normal School would offer to its consistent annual enrollment of 600 normal students not only practice teaching in a model rural school to contrast with its Deweyan Muscogee Elementary School but a full range of courses and degree offerings that were very similar to those offered by the Peabody School of Education.

The foundation on which the development of both institutions rested was the secondary school system, for which Jo-

seph Stewart was largely responsible. Starting in 1903 with seven
four-year high schools in the state, Stewart traveled constantly,
publishing rules for accreditation and handbooks for accredited high schools, which detailed recommended curricula
and the entrance requirements for university B.A. and B.S.
programs. Arguments for the establishment of high schools included the teacher preparation that they would provide for
common school teachers.

In 1912, state legislation was passed allowing tax support
of high schools. It followed on the heels of a reform bill in
1911 that set up a whole new system of certification, reconsti-
tuted the state board of education, increased the staff of the
state department of education, made each county a school district, and required normal instruction and a system of certification for teachers. From this point on, teacher education programs would respond more and more to state certification
requirements. With the passage of the Smith-Lever Act in 1914
and the Smith-Hughes Act in 1917, federal funding began to
influence the teacher education curriculum, as well as that of
secondary schools. One-third of the Peabody School of Education's budget was to come from federal funds for agriculture; the State Normal School also offered extensive course
work in agriculture and industrial arts. When it became Georgia State Teachers College in 1928, its curriculum was barely
distinguishable from that of the Peabody School of Education.

The new certification system was followed in 1921 by a
report on the state of teacher education in Georgia.[46] Through
a questionnaire sent out to the state superintendent and to
presidents of the institutions of higher learning, J. O. Martin
ascertained that of the 10,969 teachers in the public school system, 45 percent had normal, college, or summer school training. Only one-eighth of graduates from those schools could be
expected to enter teaching, and one-third of those who did
enter quit the profession annually, leaving a deficit of trained
teachers.

Martin's report confirmed phenomena in Georgia that
were taking place in the rest of the country as well—namely,
that programs intended to prepare teachers were instead being

used as higher education in the absence of a system of secondary education, and that teachers were leaving teaching at a high
rate. The apparent market for teacher education that resulted
drew institutional responses, Emory establishing a teacher education program in 1921 and an extension department in
1925,[47] the University of Georgia setting up a Division of Extension Teaching in 1922, and Atlanta University's board of
trustees even considering renaming the institution Atlanta
University and Teacher Training College.[48]

J. O. Martin's second report on the status of the teaching
profession, issued in 1926, served to fuel these movements.[49]
Collecting data over a full school term in all 161 Georgia counties, he concluded that over 56 percent of Georgia teachers
had less than the minimum standard of teacher training—
namely, high school graduation and two or more years of professional training. Only one-third had either a normal diploma
or a bachelor's degree. As in 1921, Martin chided the teacher
education institutions for their inability to prepare a sufficient
number of teachers. Assuming an annual turnover of 2,162, or
17.6 percent, of the state's teachers, the projected 1,018 graduates in 1924 would leave a shortage of 1,144.

Yet this was not the whole picture. The profession that
those graduates entered was hardly ideal. The average number
of students per teacher for the state was 33, but there were
681 one-teacher schools in which the ratio ran from 35 to 69,
and another 9 in which it ran from 69 to 124. Calculating 33
students per teacher, the state in 1925 needed 18,104 teachers,
but they would receive an average annual salary of $567, with
fully 75 percent of teachers receiving less than $684 a year.

That the graduates of the Peabody School of Education
were not serving in the most needy rural areas was evident
from a 1931 study undertaken by John Denton, director of the
school's Department of Administration, which had by then
emerged.[50] The average salary for the 2,156 teachers in 215
independent (not county-controlled) school districts was $938
per year. The teacher placement services initiated in the School
of Education in 1927–28 placed 62 of the 165 teachers enrolled in positions with an average annual salary of $1,318.15.

Denton's study did not even include rural districts, and 87 percent of the teachers he studied were making below the average
received by those placed by the university—an indication that
the Peabody School's graduates were definitely not going into
the countryside.

Building a State Educational System

The state government reorganization in 1932 created a
single board of trustees to oversee the University of Georgia
and all the branch colleges, with responsibilities assigned to avoid
overlap. Although the State Normal School and the Forsyth
Agricultural and Mechanical School had blossomed into thriv-
ing teacher preparation programs for the rural schools, they
were to become part of a larger plan, driven by different dynamics than dedication to the preparation of country teachers.
The Peabody School of Education would become the College
of Education in the flagship institution of the system, training
educational leadership and the teachers of teachers. All programs, including that for elementary education, would become
four-year programs, and the College of Education would concentrate on the preparation of high school teachers in all areas,
including agriculture and home economics—the major responsibility for which had previously been outside its domain.

Graduate work for all types of teachers, principals, supervisors, and superintendents would be developed exclusively
at the University of Georgia, as would preparation for physical
education teachers. Extension work would be under a separate
Division of General Extension outside the College of Education. Secondary teacher preparation would be shared with the
Georgia State College for Women at Milledgeville, presumably
largely along gender lines. Women—although now allowed in
certain programs on the university campus—were to spend their
first two years at the Co-ordinate College, which was housed
on the campus formerly occupied by the State Normal School.
Elementary education would be undertaken by both the Athens and Milledgeville campuses, with the assistance of the four-

year institutions at Statesboro, Americus, and Valdosta covering the rural southern half of the state. The immediate goal would be the preparation of 800–1,000 elementary teachers annually with two years of college work, 200–400 elementary teachers with four years of preparation, and 150–200 high school teachers with four years of preparation, which was supposed to have covered immediate demand.

This, of course, did not take into account the 50 percent of the state's population that was black. Relying heavily on privately funded education to take care of black needs, the state had, however, taken over the Albany School in 1917 to make it the Albany Agricultural, Industrial and Normal School for Colored. Under Holley's continuing strong leadership, by the late 1920s it became one of the best black schools in Georgia. His leadership was to be called into question, however, as the reorganization demanded direct accountability to the board of regents and tighter central control throughout the system. Strapped by their desire not to lose the still substantial financial support of the Hazard family of Rhode Island, the regents grappled with what they saw as an exercise of arbitrary power and what Holley saw as discrimination and a failure of genuine support for the black colleges. Holley's unfortunate alliance with Eugene Talmadge during his attacks against the University of Georgia led to his dismissal in 1943.[51] The state then granted to the school what it had denied Holley ten years earlier—four-year degree-granting status. The new Albany State College would concentrate on a four-year program to prepare elementary teachers.

The Forsyth State Agricultural and Mechanical School had not fared so well. Expanding steadily in the late 1920s, by 1932 it had added a teacher training course, including practice teaching, to the high school curriculum and established a correspondence course for in-service teachers to provide the necessary documentation of their studies. Study groups of teachers were set up in every county during the summer school session of 1937 under the motto "Better Teachers, Better Schools and Better People," and Hubbard sought the endorsement of county superintendents for the efforts "to stimulate [and] encourage the Educational uplift for Negroes in rural Georgia."[52]

It was a difficult task. In 1927, there were still only twelve accredited black high schools, of which Forsyth and Albany were the only ones with state support. By 1930, the number was up to twenty-nine, with graduates totaling 1,078; seventeen of these were public. Although progress was being made, the establishment of secondary education when there had been no state efforts to build up elementary education was slow at best. The extensive report published in 1930–1932 by J. C. Dixon, supervisor of Negro education for the state Department of Education, stated that, according to the 1928 census, out of 341,963 black children, 182,072 were attending school.[53] They were taught by 4,970 elementary teachers and 286 high school teachers, who had an average of 47.55 pupils and 30.49 pupils, respectively. They went to school an average of 136 days a year. By all measures, black children were much more poorly served than their white peers. County superintendents' reports indicated that while 77,401 white students were transported to consolidated schools by some 1,970 teams and trucks, only 361 black children could be transported by the 13 teams and trucks available to them.

With black students composing 40 percent of the school-age population, it was not hard to see the inequities. In fact, Dixon stated, perhaps for the first time, that state policy, the Equalization Fund, and all the best state-level attempts at equal opportunity would be doomed as long as the "minor political subdivisions" did not follow the same principles as the state in distributing funds. Under current conditions, those counties with large black populations were able to serve their white students better, since they received money by total number of students and then distributed it as county government saw fit. As a result of years of subtle and not-so-subtle disenfranchisement of blacks, power rested fairly consistently in white, and often racist, hands. The problem has not disappeared entirely even in the 1990s.

Dixon's plan was to establish a one-teacher experimental

school in an average community with money offered by thé Jeanes Fund, as a model for teacher preparation.[54] Four such demonstration schools had been financed by the General Education Board at black schools during the 1932 summer school term, among them Forsyth and Fort Valley. Coordinating the money available from the Jeanes, Slater, and Rosenwald funds and from the General Education Board,[55] Dixon and his new assistant, R. L. Cousins, saw the possibility of at last bringing about significant change in Georgia's treatment of its black children.

Their first goal was to establish at least one two-year or four-year accredited high school in every county that had a sufficient concentration of black children to warrant it, building on the network of forty-one county training schools supported by Slater funds. These schools were essential to teacher training, since the minimum requirement for a state license was graduation from an accredited high school plus thirty semester hours at the college level, including six hours in education. Dixon and Cousins also initiated meetings among the various funding agency officials and county superintendents, as well as with the university system officials, to develop the institutional network to support a statewide effort.

In white education, there appears to have been a major shift in the last years of the 1920s in which most of the characteristics of the modern University of Georgia College of Education emerged in skeletal form. The market pressures on higher education were being felt. Given the nearly explosive growth pattern in its first years, it appeared that a saturation point would soon be reached and that clientele for course work in education must be sought or stimulated elsewhere. The number of illiterate school-age white children had dropped to under 10,000—a near miracle considering the 1872 figure of 125,000 whites over the age of ten. The increase in the number of accredited high schools (367 in 1930–31) meant that an increasing number of teachers were college graduates. While the abolition in 1928 of Latin and Greek as entrance requirements had doubled University of Georgia enrollments almost overnight, and a good 67 percent of the 1,831 extension students could be expected to take subsequent study on campus, the momentum toward its becoming a true university demanded growth.

The College of Education emerged from the reorganization with essentially the same programs, differently organized and with few additions. What the reorganization was less clear on was how all high school– and junior college–level work could be eliminated from system institutions and left to local support, given the needs of the state and the state of local finances. In particular, the relationship of both to the preparation of teachers would be debated for years to come. For example, the twelve district agricultural and mechanical schools that had been authorized in 1906—although almost immediately obsolete because agricultural and industrial education were soon incorporated into the rapidly growing public secondary system—did retain their usefulness in teacher preparation. As it became clear, however, that by the 1930s, certification standards would require four years of college work, the district schools were faced with either closing or transforming themselves into junior colleges. A university system council with representation from all system schools scrutinized these issues as well as the content of and responsibility for teacher education among the member institutions. By 1938, council committees had studied virtually every aspect of teacher education programs.

During this period, the College of Education began what would become a continual process of self-evaluation and study. With substantial help from the General Education Board and the Rosenwald Fund—which seemed determined in this period of fiscal crisis to preserve what progress had been made in Georgia—the Athens campus became involved with in-service work in the state, through both its revitalized Bureau of Research and Field Services and participation with the state department of education in a massive overhaul of the public school curriculum that became known as the Georgia Program for Improvement of Instruction. Its main concern, however, was the expansion of graduate programs, the need for which it established by reference to requests from the Georgia Association of Superintendents and the Georgia Education Association, among others. As the regents put it in 1936, "without graduate and research schools we only have a college and not a university system."[56]

As more "professional" programs developed, the standards for teachers rose as well, and the system council recommended in 1937 that a master's degree for elementary teachers be required in the not too distant future. At the same time, the reality was that as recently as 1933 there had been, out of a total of 14,311 white teachers employed, 905 who held no type of teaching certificate and 4,229 who had less than one year of college training. By 1937, the number holding a one-year license or less had shrunk to fewer than 2,000, but that number was still high enough to merit continuing both two-year and four-year certification programs. These teachers were predominantly in rural areas, many in unaccredited schools, although pressure through incentive legislation to consolidate had also followed the state government reorganization. Although a significant drop from the 1932 figure of 3,030, there were in 1936 2,724 white schools not accredited, 534 of them one-teacher schools, and most of these could not be reached by consolidation. The solution seemed to lie in increased attention and support for small schools and preparation of teachers for actual settings in which they would teach.

The University System of Georgia and Black Teacher Education

Solutions to these problems were particularly complex for the black institutions of the university system.[57] Their focus was to be teacher training, agriculture, trades, home economics, and commerce and business education.[58] Three institutions were considered sufficient—one of them a four-year college and two of them junior colleges.

From 1932 to 1939, the Forsyth campus strove to meet its assignment of preparing quality elementary teachers and supervisors for the rural schools. It became clear in 1939, however, that the system plans had been to eliminate Forsyth, as

the Rosenwald Fund made possible the purchase of the Fort
Valley campus from the American Church Institute. Now a
ninety-acre campus valued at $500,000, the Fort Valley Nor-
mal and Industrial School had eighteen buildings, among them
an infirmary and model hospital unit, fully modernized girls'
dormitories, a trades building with power machinery, barns, a
dairy, and extensive athletic facilities. It was officially an accredited high school and junior college, with teacher training
exclusively at the junior college level for both high school and
elementary teachers. All teachers received training in funda-
mentals of agriculture, general shop work, and home economics in addition to extensive course work in English, social studies, science, and education and a smattering of music and
handicrafts.

What the Fort Valley school was to become was a land-
grant college offering four years of college work in agriculture, home economics, trades, teacher training, and liberal arts,
but with emphasis on the first two. The college would be responsible for preparing high school teachers and have in addition 200–300 elementary teachers in training per year. The
last two years of high school work would be continued, but
only temporarily. Teaching training would have to take place
during the last high school year for a time, but—as the standard for teaching in the elementary schools should be raised
to at least one year beyond high school as soon as possible—
the high school courses would eventually be eliminated.

The education of blacks emerged as a major university
system concern with the comprehensive study of black education in Georgia funded by the General Education Board and
the Rosenwald Fund and directed by the dean of the University of Georgia College of Education, Walter Cocking, at the
request of the regents. Cocking's report asserted that in spite
of nearly 75 percent of the 2,414 black college students being
in private schools, the state would have to take greater responsibility for black education. Its role was to train teachers, which
is what 110 of the 117 state college graduates in 1937 became.
Improvement of teacher quality was seen as the key to holding

students in school; of those who enrolled in first grade, only 2.3 percent graduated from high school.

The private black schools had been making a substantial contribution; Spelman Seminary in particular had been training 75–100 normal students a year. But those students, like students in the state schools, did not always finish the course, returning instead to their homes to teach on the basis of what they had already learned. In addition, Spelman, like Atlanta University and Morehouse, had become a regional school, with over half of its students coming from outside Georgia.

The role that the new Fort Valley State College was to play as a university system school was major but not well defined, perhaps because the state's role in black education generally was not defined. Significant underwriting by the state did not really begin until nearly the 1950s, when it became clear that the only chance for racial separation rested on achieving an appearance of educational equality. Another difficulty was that Fort Valley had been prosperous enough to develop a sense of itself. The leadership that launched it as a system college was also strong—not necessarily in the ways hoped for by the regents. The six-year presidency of Horace Mann Bond is a study in cross-purposes. Bond attempted to build upon a sense of community and spiritual strength that had been integral to the Fort Valley campus, at the same time aspiring to make it a campus of 1,500 that would provide the same education for black students that the University of Georgia provided for whites.

In 1942, Fort Valley was among twenty-five black colleges surveyed in a U.S. Office of Education study, receiving high marks for the clarity and extent of its aims and for "unique and particularly noteworthy types of pioneer efforts" as well as the adjustment of instructional procedures and curriculum to individual differences. Administrative concern for instruction was also rated high, as was integration of knowledge in courses and the organization and content of the curriculum. These were not, however, the criteria by which its performance as a university system institution would be judged. The indications are that the goals of the Rosenwald trustees who sought Bond for the presidency and those of the system board of regents were based on quite different premises, perhaps both of them different from Bond's own vision. The result was a kind of identity crisis for Fort Valley State College.

The crisis was resolved somewhat when in 1943–44 the regents authorized the addition of business education courses and foreign languages and expanded the areas in which bachelor's degrees could be earned. The bachelor of science degree was offered in education, home economics, business education, public school music, chemistry, and zoology. Although the farm had been enlarged, the agriculture program—formerly a mainstay of the school—became a standard two-year course preparing students for either employment or transfer to another institution. On the other hand, summer workshops in special subject areas such as biological and botanical sciences were being developed for teachers. Student teaching field experiences were expanded, with the former high school serving as a laboratory school.

By September 1944, programs had been expanded and modified again, adding B.S. degrees in mathematics and in agriculture, with majors in agronomy, general agriculture, or animal husbandry. Home economics offerings were likewise increased, with a concentration possible in either home economics education or the arts. Further expansion of agricultural and home economics programs continued throughout the 1940s, leading up to Fort Valley's official designation as a land-grant college in 1949.

That year also marked the publication of a major report on a survey of the University System of Georgia to be used for charting future directions.[59] Fort Valley State College was to concentrate on the preparation of elementary teachers for grades one through eight at the bachelor's level and to upgrade its facilities to prepare teachers minoring in physical education and in the fine arts. Most importantly, the programs for preparing vocational agriculture and home economics teachers for the state were to be placed at Fort Valley, where the current agricultural and home economics programs were to be upgraded with an eye to eventually offering a master's degree in those areas. Training for agricultural extension and home demonstration agents would also be limited to Fort Valley. The report also recommended that the bachelor's programs emphasize the biological sciences as part of the general agricultural emphasis. Finally, acceptable observation and practice facilities were to be developed before professional teacher education work leading to the bachelor's degree in secondary school academic fields could be offered.

Along with other system institutions, Fort Valley was being nudged toward serving the whole state of Georgia in particular program areas, overlapping only in nonteaching agricultural and home economics programs with the black colleges at Albany and Savannah. Agricultural extension and terminal and short courses in agriculture, plus general extension work, were to be part of its mission too, much as they had been in its earlier days. It was, in a sense, being asked to be, if not all things to all people, at least a great number of things to a wide variety of people. It appears, in addition, that its faculty may have begun in the late 1940s to envision a broader mission—one not restricted to either black students or the state of Georgia.

The quality of education at Fort Valley State College appeared to be on the rise, but the problems of rural black education were still acute. While leaders with vision could see that the economic prosperity of the state as a whole depended on improved education for blacks, a faltering economy led many whites to view their livelihoods as threatened by competition from blacks who received that education. The working out of economic and racist fears at the local level limited available funds for upgrading schools and hiring teachers in many counties.

Things had not changed substantially by the end of the war, but it had apparently become clear to an increasing number of state leaders that Georgia's fate would depend on raising the quality of life and the productivity of its black population. Black school supervision was made part of the responsibilities of state school supervisors, and extensive work was undertaken to train local supervisors and to lengthen the school term and encourage transportation for black children.

Jeanes Fund supervisors were serving eighty-eight counties in 1947–48, working out of a central training program at Atlanta University. All of them held teaching certificates based on four years of college work or more, and seventy-three held the professional supervisor's certificate based on an additional year of graduate study.

The Rise of the State Department of Education

The state department of education emerged from the 1932 state reorganization as a significant force in teacher education, through both continually upgraded certification requirements and involvement in the teacher education curriculum. Certification standards eliminated the eligibility of high school work in the early 1930s, and by 1937 they were based on years of college course work. The recommendation was also made that county teachers' examinations and county licenses be abolished, these being the main gateway into the system for teachers not meeting certification standards. However, for many small rural schools, these provided the only possibility of having a teacher at all, so they continued a legal part of the system until 1944, despite new certification standards.

Teacher education was in the forefront of attention during the 1940s. The advisory group for the Georgia Program for Improvement of Instruction of the 1930s had evolved into the Georgia Council on Teacher Education, a permanent advisory group. The National Commission on Teacher Education in 1940 approved Georgia as the third state targeted for program improvement. A 1942–43 College of Education self-evaluation yielded the recommendation that teacher education become an all-university responsibility. From 1946 to 1950, the deanship of O. C. Aderhold was emphatic in its emphasis on both self-evaluation and outreach to the state as the college moved toward its fiftieth anniversary.

The nationwide teacher shortage generated by World War II was instrumental in focusing attention on teacher education. By October 1944, Georgia had lost 2,250 teachers to duty in the armed forces and another 2,500 to industrial work. Fully

25 percent of the state's 24,000 teachers either left teaching or left the state during 1942–43. More than half of Georgia's teachers had less than the four years of collegiate work required for state certification. At the same time, as of April 1946, 2,500 teaching positions could not be filled because of lack of applicants. Salary still was not commensurate with that in other occupations requiring similar education, running at least $500 less than the average earnings in industry and even $400 below the range for clerical workers in the Georgia civil service.

The immediate problem was twofold: upgrading the quality of current teachers and providing a sufficient future supply. Considering that in 1940, fewer than 1,000 white teachers were graduated, the drop in 1945 to a combined white and black total of fewer than 300 indicated a crisis. By 1950, the annual need would be 700 for kindergarten, 780 for new high school services (vocational education, health and physical education, social studies, and fine arts), 950 for primary grades, and 200 for upper elementary grades. An estimated 4,300 white teachers would have to be provided annually to bring the full teaching force up to the minimum of four years of college preparation by 1958.

According to the 1947 General Assembly report,[60] the College of Education's role was to provide increased in-service training in cooperation with the state Department of Education and to drastically increase the capacity of the system's teacher education programs. A further recommendation was that the gap between the state Department of Education as the employer of teachers and the university system as the educator of teachers be more effectively bridged, in part through delegating leadership to the state department in formulating guiding principles for teacher training and certification and in developing the standards to be used as the basis for certification of institutional programs.

This last was essentially in place since the change to program certification had been acted on in the legislature in February 1948, but more importantly, it was the beginning of an expansion of responsibility that essentially shifted the initiative in teacher education away from the University of Georgia. The new teacher certification law went into effect in 1950, not only establishing program certification rather than individual processing of applications by the state department but also eliminating licenses for less than one year of collegiate work.

The outside survey of the university system published in 1949 in response to the 1947 report attempted to establish the distribution of responsibilities for the state's teachers, confirming to a large degree the position of the Athens campus as "the one great center for graduate and professional education and for research."[61] High priority was given to elementary education as both more difficult and more important than any other public school service, thus posing more problems to those seeking to formulate an adequate four-year program. In secondary education, the problem of compartmentalization as obstructing a more comprehensive view of the curriculum was cited as a central concern.

Results of the studies notwithstanding, the College of Education continued to put its energies into expansion in order to maximize the availability of outside money. Programs in educational administration, the Cooperative Program in Elementary Education with five Athens Schools, and a National Science Foundation grant awarded jointly with Emory University for exploring television instruction in the sciences were among the additions, as well as the new Division for the Education of Exceptional Children.

The 1950s and 1960s were characterized by a flurry of studies of education, but the real dynamics appear to have been a shifting of power between the University of Georgia and the state Department of Education. With the switch to program approval, the department became directly involved in the curriculum for teacher education, which was precisely the area that the College of Education did not seem inclined to examine. The 1953 report of the Joint House and Senate Committee on Education specifically reminded the department that in its requested reorganization, it should not forget that its chief function was the improvement of curriculum and instruction. The report, undertaken chiefly to look for waste in the administration of the state's public school system as the Minimum

Foundations Program was being implemented, pointed out that while state grants to local schools had increased from $13 million in 1937–38 to $94.6 million in 1953–54—a jump of 626 percent—it was hardly likely that the instructional program had improved proportionately.

The Minimum Foundations Program that the 1953 report set out to examine had been authorized in 1937 and funded in 1951. It was a comprehensive program setting standards for all aspects of public school life. Supported by the sales tax, the program guaranteed every person attending the public schools a competent teacher, a decent classroom, safe transportation, adequate textbooks and learning aids, and a minimum school year of 180 days. It was to be administered by the state board of education and thus dominated the activities of the state Department of Education for the next thirty years.

The College of Education, on the other hand, seemed little interested in the specifics of the public school curriculum or of the teachers who would carry it out. In the 1956–57 self-study that grew out of the 1946 planning conference reports, its thrust was clear: more time for research, more travel money for national exposure, more support staff, and more administrative time for program planning and promotion.

The self-study points out several strengths: the existence of planned programs worked out in cooperation with the state Department of Education and other system institutions, a constant self-study process in place, the professional laboratories experience, the off-campus activities built into the graduate programs, and the student counseling service. Weaknesses cited were the low level of participation with other schools and colleges on campus and, thus, lack of cooperative planning of teacher education programs, lack of adequately controlled admission policies, and lack of provision for superior students to test out of certain requirements and devote their time to higher-level work. To remedy the first, a cross-campus advisory committee was recommended to facilitate program planning for education students; for the second and third, additional staff time was provided for guidance.

The College of Education thus perceived its problems as

not so much a matter of quality as of quantity. The consideration of curriculum was not a university-wide priority either,
and the College of Education was very much in the mainstream of university development. Looking to other major universities in the country, as it had since the turn of the century,
the University of Georgia saw the path to greatness as the development of research. The 1958 Brumbaugh study of the
university, described as the most thorough study of a university ever undertaken, recommended expansion of research with
outside money, larger classes with discussion sections and graduate assistants to make smaller departments function more
economically, and upgrading of graduate degree programs to
include fewer classes also taken by undergraduates.

The curriculum of teacher education does not seem to
have been a concern of the state Department of Education
either, preoccupied as it was with the Minimum Foundations
Program, the teacher shortage, and the constant push for
higher-level certificates issues. Foreseeing the postwar baby boom
and its accompanying 30,000 new pupils to be added annually
through 1963, it hired two staff members to work with teacher
recruitment, establishing Future Teachers organizations in the
high schools, portraying the profession positively, and launching a Teacher of the Year Program with the Georgia Chamber
of Commerce. It was in fact doing the hard work of recruiting
undergraduates in teacher education, a task that not so many
years before had been a key to survival for the University of
Georgia.

A 1960 report of the Joint Committee on Teacher Education of the General Assembly recommended examination of
the teacher education curriculum for excessive requirements
in professional education, attention to content area study, and
adoption of a teacher test for entrance to the profession. The
state Department of Education responded, and the National
Teacher Test was made available for teachers who wished to
take it—a requirement in any event for jobs in several of the
larger independent school districts, for obtaining grants-in-aid
for graduate study, and (by 1970) for adding a teaching field

to a current certificate and obtaining a new six-year certificate of any type.

Credentials and programs proliferated in a kind of see-saw between the raising of standards by the Department of Education and the refinement of specializations and research areas at the Athens campus. With national recognition of its competency-based elementary education model, the College of Education began to work toward implementing that approach in all teacher education programs. In turn, the Department of Education undertook a series of joint projects with the college toward conversion to performance-based teacher certification, resulting in the development of the Teacher Proficiency Assessment Instrument (TPAI) and the Teacher Certification Test (TCT) of subject matter knowledge as the basis for standard certification. Since May 1980, all initial teaching certificates are classified as nonrenewable, the issuance of a renewable professional certificate being contingent on the demonstration within three years of the eight competencies defined by the TPAI.

Conclusions: Commitment, Markets, and Systems

Despite the long-standing assumption that the problems of improving rural education in predominantly black areas would be tackled by the black colleges, with Fort Valley responsible for secondary teacher education and all three producing elementary teachers, Fort Valley in particular was being urged toward ever greater diversity of offerings, including graduate work in certain areas. All three black colleges were expected to follow the system's lead toward higher entrance requirements and generally higher standards. There is a certain irony in the tensions that developed out of what appear from the perspective of white education to be a thoroughly positive progression toward better schools and better teachers.

By the end of the 1940s, Fort Valley State College, which had only a few years earlier gained praise for the community involvement aspect of its teacher education program, was being faulted by its students for failing to keep them in touch with the real world that they would enter as teachers. The earlier program had sent second-quarter sophomores out into rural communities as participant observers, then brought them back for a full quarter of formulating both the rural school problems as they saw them and their projects for their own self-improvement in order to teach in the rural setting. It had been discontinued for lack of faculty resources and replaced by an integrative education course still strong in fieldwork, which was gradually phased out as the teacher education programs were brought into line with system standards.

With the implementation of the Minimum Foundations Program in the early 1950s, conditions for black teachers improved substantially, but with a negative by-product. As schools were consolidated to improve conditions—an option for which legislation had provided financial incentives—the least qualified teachers tended to lose positions, with the result that by 1956 there was a surplus of qualified black teachers in many fields. Yet, as a result of local politics, the benefits of the program often did not reach the rural black schools, and in 1960 the state Department of Education was still deploring the overcrowded black classroom, lack of textbooks, and substandard maintenance caused by improper expenditure at the local level of funds designated for support of black schools.

As the threat of desegregation grew in the 1950s, Fort Valley State College was authorized to begin a program of graduate studies, and in the 1960s its scope was broadened to include degrees in zoology, botany, secretarial skills, business administration, sociology, social welfare, history and political science, and economics, in addition to new specializations within home economics, mathematics, and counseling and guidance. Course work was added to Spanish, German, and Russian. Fort Valley State College saw an increase in enrollment over the 1962–1967 period from 928 to 1,807 but with teacher education majors decreasing from 80 percent to 61.5 percent. It was moving in the direction of a multipurpose institution.

In the 1960s, pressure began to grow for tougher entrance standards. Serving the area of middle Georgia, where support for elementary and secondary public education for blacks was extremely recent, if indeed it existed at all, Fort Valley was being asked to raise its standards to a point that would cut out members of the community it had traditionally served. In addition, the scholarships that the university system board of regents offered to black students who wished to pursue studies not available to them in Georgia's state institutions resulted in a substantial number of the more capable students being channeled away from the black state colleges altogether.

In addition, over the last seventeen years, Fort Valley State College has been the object of two lawsuits charging that the college had failed to desegregate and had failed to maintain academic standards. Some observers suggest that the litigation may be the outgrowth of a movement to transfer Fort Valley's programs into a traditionally white school nearby; others see it as a way of forcing black schools to bear the burden of desegregation. Whatever the motives, the lawsuits bring into sharp relief the tensions that a traditionally black college groomed to serve a black population faces when its survival depends on climbing the ladder of increasingly higher standards.

Fort Valley's situation is a reminder that institutions of education are very specifically situated and that, regardless of the pressure to centralize and to standardize, their relationship to their constituency must be respected. For Georgia's black colleges, this is a complicated problem, as their mission has changed not only with the needs of their communities but through fluctuating definitions by the central system administration of the community that they are to serve and fluctuating definitions of the mission itself.

Yet the strength of the black colleges, particularly in their early years, when they were driven forward on minimal resources and the unwavering commitment of those who built them, suggests that commitment may well be the crucial element of teacher education. Regardless of the test results and the national norms, the success of an educational institution is not in the caliber of the students it admits but in how far it is able to bring those students once they are there. Even a superficial look at the history of black education in the South provides clear evidence of the distance that can be traveled in the company of committed teachers. Whether that commitment can survive the pressures of being part of the university system remains to be seen.

Commitment seems to be a characteristic of private schools in Georgia. For private schools, mission and funding were the major considerations, the latter being sought on the basis of a firm commitment to the former. Schools needed to have either strong organizational backing, such as from the various Baptist conventions, or a rich patron or group of dependable patrons, in order to avoid annual prolonged fund-raising drives in the North. With patronage or philanthropy, of course, came influence—as the industrially oriented curriculum of Slater-supported schools or the crisp new schoolhouses of Rosenwald recipients would show—and teacher education was clearly affected.

While several of the black schools show evidence of this influence, Paine College being notable as an exception,[62] white private schools were somewhat less radically influenced. The Berry Schools—perhaps the only white schools that could match the intensity of the black schools' community involvement— began in 1902 with virtually no resources except Martha Berry and her private funds.[63] Arduous trips north were an annual event until the schools received Carnegie and, eventually, Ford funding. Like the black colleges, Berry encompassed the full range of subjects and trades to improve the homes, work opportunities, and quality of life of white mountain children. Like the schools of the "black belt," the Berry Schools were primarily preparing students who would teach their people, and, like black students, many of Berry's students did not graduate but returned home to teach others what they had learned.

Also like the black schools, Berry had to struggle for collegiate recognition, shedding to a certain extent its community school image as well as eliminating lower school work in order to obtain accreditation, finally granted to Berry College in 1957. After Martha Berry died in 1942, the college's development took a direction more in line with that of other small independent colleges, although teaching continued to be held in high esteem. Approximately half of every graduating class through

1980 became teachers, consistently receiving high marks from district school personnel in northwest Georgia.

In other private schools, teacher education has not enjoyed the center stage it had at Berry College. For Emory University, plans in 1919 for a professional Teachers' College to join its Medical School, School of Theology, and School of Business Administration got no further than the building of a model school as the first unit, although an M.A.T. degree was offered just after World War II. However, Emory spearheaded the Atlanta Area Teacher Education Service (AATES), a collaborative effort with the University of Georgia College of Education. The need for graduate work in education, which grew out of AATES, is no doubt responsible in part for Emory's emphasis on graduate work.

The private schools, once teacher certification standards were set, were faced with the choice of either building a certifiable program or abandoning teacher education. The decision is a market decision: whether there are enough students to support the program. The answer clearly depends on the part of the state one is considering. Atlanta, since the 1960s, has provided a sufficient market not only for the Atlanta University Center and the schools affiliated loosely with Emory University but also for the relatively new Georgia State University School of Education, growing from an education department in 1958 to a school of education in 1970, the program of which is overwhelmingly geared to the granting of advanced degrees. The Atlanta campus of Mercer University,[64] founded in 1964 as a more conservative Baptist campus than the parent school in Macon, was bought by the Macon institution in 1972, two years after the launching of its teacher education program. It, too, has clearly found a market, as its programs have expanded steadily, reaching the master's level in elementary education areas in the early 1980s.

The presence of the University System of Georgia, although dominant, should not overshadow other dynamics within teacher education in the state. In contrast to the accretion mode of developing a system controlled from the top, so to speak, there is another mode, a drawing together of complementary parts for mutual support, that shows up among some of Georgia's private schools. Relatively early, the church-related colleges were feeling the need to establish clear ties with particular precollegiate schools in order to ensure enrollments when conflict among congregations and associations erupted. In 1902, the Mercer System was organized, only to die out over the next ten years. A few years later, Atlanta Baptist College became Morehouse College, at the top of a hierarchy of other Baptist schools. In 1912, Morehouse College, with Spelman Seminary, Atlanta University, Clark College, Morris Brown College, and Gammon Theological Seminary, formed the Atlanta Federation of Schools for the Improvement of Negro Country Life, an initial stage in what was to become the Atlanta University Center.

In 1929, with assistance from the General Education Board, Spelman, Morehouse, and Atlanta University affiliated, with Atlanta University becoming solely a graduate institution, fed in part by strong undergraduate education programs at Spelman and Morehouse. The university opened a School of Education in 1944, and in 1953 it launched a cooperative program with black undergraduate colleges to improve teacher training through teacher leadership. Like other schools, Atlanta University raised admission standards, requiring the National Teachers' Examination in 1961. As of 1969, the School of Education was Atlanta University's largest unit, responsible for a third of all graduate degrees granted. Interestingly, the success of the Atlanta University Center was not repeated at Emory University and the other white schools of the Atlanta area, despite strong support from the General Education Board throughout the 1930s.

In the last analysis, teacher education in Georgia is very similar to teacher education in other states. The tensions between general and professional education, between theory and practice, are there, as are the increased attention to field experience and a fairly consistent concern in schools and departments of education about balancing teacher preparation with research. The tendency to move from a strong teacher education focus toward a multipurpose curriculum is also evident in several of Georgia's institutions, but the important dynamic is the tacit partnership between the state agency and the "cutting-edge" research university in the state. It is this relationship that drives the intricate and complex machinery of bringing together the teachers and students supported by the state. It is through this relationship that the comprehensive reforms of the 1985 Quality Basic Education Act have been undertaken, affecting not only school curricula and financing but teachers' salaries and a career ladder. With these and its program of teacher testing now in place, Georgia may well be a state to watch.

Notes

1. The terms *system* and *university system* refer to the entity formally organized in 1932. The term *university* may refer to either the University of Georgia, Athens, or Atlanta University—the context will clarify which. *College of education* refers to that entity on the Athens campus.

2. This chapter, while attempting to sketch the basic dynamics of the development of teacher education in Georgia, is by no means a complete history. The institutions that were covered by the historical portion of the education of educators project include the University of Georgia, Athens, Fort Valley State College, Berry College, and—to a somewhat lesser extent—Emory University, Georgia State University, and the Mercer Atlanta campus. Most of the material for analysis is thus drawn from them.

3. T. G. Dyer, *The University of Georgia: A Bicentennial History, 1785–1985* (Athens: University of Georgia Press, 1985), p. 27.

4. D. Orr, *A History of Education in Georgia* (Chapel Hill: University of North Carolina Press, 1950), p. 16.

5. Orr, *A History of Education in Georgia*, pp. 97–98.

6. Dyer, *The University of Georgia*, p. 84.

7. Dyer, *The University of Georgia*, p. 121.

8. Dyer, *The University of Georgia*, p. 128.

9. R. P. Brooks, *The University of Georgia Under Sixteen Administrations, 1785–1955* (Athens: University of Georgia Press, 1956), p. 233.

10. Dyer, *The University of Georgia,* p. 135.

11. Until formal creation of the University System of Georgia in 1932, institutions retained a large degree of autonomy through having their own boards of trustees who negotiated directly with the state legislature for funds.

12. C. J. Dismukes, "North Georgia College Under the Trustees," *Georgia Historical Quarterly,* 1972, *56* (1), 96.

13. J.L.M. Curry, *A Brief Sketch of George Peabody and a History of the Peabody Education Fund Through Thirty Years* (New York: Negro Universities Press, [originally published 1898]), pp. 20–21.

14. Curry, "A Brief Sketch," p. 39.

15. Orr, *A History of Education in Georgia,* p. 200.

16. Orr, *A History of Education in Georgia,* p. 244.

17. Orr, *A History of Education in Georgia,* p. 150.

18. Orr, *A History of Education in Georgia,* p. 163.

19. Dyer, *The University of Georgia,* p. 141.

20. E. S. Sell, *History of the State Normal School, Athens, Georgia* (Athens: Georgia State Teachers College, 1923), pp. 43–44.

21. J. D. Bradwell, "An Address of J. D. Bradwell to the Alumni Association of the State Normal School, May 22, 1926 [on] 'The Early History of the Normal School' " (typescript in the Georgia Room of the University of Georgia Main Library), pp. 13–14.

22. Bradwell, "An Address of J. D. Bradwell," p. 16.

23. Bradwell, "An Address of J. D. Bradwell," p. 15.

24. C. A. Bacote, *The Story of Atlanta University: A Century of Service 1865–1965* (Atlanta: Atlanta University, 1969), p. 29.

25. B. Brawley, *History of Morehouse College* (College Park, Md.: McGrath, 1970), p. 19.

26. B. C. Ramsey, "The Black Public College in Georgia: A History of Albany State College, 1903–1965" (unpub-

lished doctoral dissertation, Florida State University, 1973), p. 9.

27. Bacote, *The Story of Atlanta University*, p. 24.

28. Bacote, *The Story of Atlanta University*, p. 29.

29. "Report of the Board of Visitors," June 28, 1871, as cited in Bacote, *The Story of Atlanta University*, pp. 181–185.

30. *Acts and Resolutions of the General Assembly of the State of Georgia Passed at the Regular Session—January 1874*, as cited in Bacote, *The Story of Atlanta University*, pp. 32–33.

31. "The Kind of University Most Needed in the South" [1882], as cited in Bacote, *The Story of Atlanta University*, p. 164.

32. See J. D. Anderson, *The Education of Blacks in the South, 1860–1935* (Chapel Hill: University of North Carolina Press, 1988), for a sophisticated treatment of this and other aspects of southern black education.

33. *The Thirty-Eighth Annual Report of the Department of Education to the General Assembly of the State of Georgia*, 1909, p. 10.

34. W. E. B. DuBois, *The Souls of Black Folk* (Millwood, N.Y.: Kraus-Thomson, 1973); see especially chap. 7 and 8.

35. Ramsey, *The Black Public College in Georgia*, p. 46.

36. Ramsey, *The Black Public College in Georgia*, p. 58.

37. Ramsey, *The Black Public College in Georgia*, p. 71.

38. L. M. Favrot, "A Study of County Training Schools for Negroes in the South," Occasional Paper no. 23 (Charlottesville, Va.: Trustees of the John F. Slater Fund, 1923), p. 10.

39. See in particular pp. 19–21 of the report of New York University assistant dean E. George Payne to the American Church Institute, *An Estimate of Our Negro Schools* (New York: American Church Institute, [1930?]).

40. Bacote, *The Story of Atlanta University*, p. 146.

41. Bacote, *The Story of Atlanta University*, p. 416.

42. "Chancellor's Report," University of Georgia *Bulletin*, 1904, *4* (3), 10.

43. "Chancellor's Report" [June 15, 1899], as cited in J. B.

Burks, "The College of Education, University of Georgia, and the Development of Teacher Education 1908–1958" (unpublished doctoral dissertation, University of Georgia, 1958), p. 19.

44. "Chancellor's Report, 1899," as cited in Burks, "The College of Education," p. 32.

45. University of Georgia *Bulletin*, 1907, *8* (1), 11.

46. J. O. Martin, *Some Facts and Figures Pertaining to Teacher Training in Georgia* (Covington, Ga.: State Superintendent of Schools, 1921).

47. With regard to Emory, see T. H. English, *Emory University 1915–1965: A Semicentennial History* (Atlanta, Ga.: Emory University, 1966).

48. Bacote, *The Story of Atlanta University*, p. 158.

49. J. O. Martin, *Varying Types of Service Rendered Georgia by Teachers, with Recommendations for Their Training in Service* (Atlanta: State Department of Education, Aug. 1926).

50. J. N. Denton, *Teacher-Salary Practice in Georgia* (Atlanta: Research Council of Georgia Association of Superintendents of Georgia Education Association, 1931).

51. See B. C. Ramsey, "The University System Controversy Reexamined: The Talmadge-Holley Connection," *Georgia Historical Quarterly*, 1980, *64* (2), 190–204.

52. State Teachers and Agricultural College *Bulletin*, 1937–38, *5* (1), 18.

53. Georgia State Superintendent of Schools, *Biennial Report, 1930–32* (Atlanta: Georgia State Superintendent of Schools, 1932), pp. 27–58.

54. For an account of the Negro Rural School Fund of the Anna T. Jeanes Foundation, or Jeanes Fund, see A. D. Wright, *The Negro Rural Education Fund, Inc.* (Washington, D.C.: Anna T. Jeanes Foundation, 1933); B. G. Brawley, *Doctor Dillard of the Jeanes Fund* (New York: Revell, 1930).

55. For the Slater Fund, see E. E. Redcay, *County Training Schools and Public Secondary Education for Negroes in the South* (Washington, D.C.: John Slater Fund, 1935); for the Rosenwald Fund, which focused on the building of rural

schools, see E. R. Embree, *Julius Rosenwald Fund: Review of Two Decades, 1917–1936* (Chicago: Julius Rosenwald Fund, 1936); for the General Education Board, see R. B. Fosdick, *Adventure in Giving: The Story of the General Education Board* (New York: Harper & Row, 1962).

56. "Annual Report of the Board of Regents of the University System of Georgia 1936," p. 101.

57. As Fort Valley State College was the only one of Georgia's black institutions studied for the project, it provides the main source for observations on black teacher education.

58. For a full account of the recommendations, see L. D. Coffman and others, "Report to the Board of Regents of the University System of Georgia," Athens, 1932.

59. G. E. Strayer, "A Report of a Survey of the University System of Georgia, Regents of the University System," Atlanta, 1949.

60. "A Survey of Public Education of Less than College Grade in Georgia" (report to the General Assembly of the Special Committee on Education, 1947), p. 127.

61. Strayer, "A Report of a Survey," p. 41.

62. For a history of Paine College, see A. C. Johnson, "The Growth of Paine College: A Successful Interracial Venture, 1903–1946" (unpublished doctoral dissertation, University of Georgia, 1970).

63. An admiring and very readable account is given in H. T. Kane, *Miracle in the Mountains* (New York: Doubleday, 1956).

64. For a history of the main campus of Mercer University, Macon, see S. Dowell, *A History of Mercer University 1933–1953* (Macon, Ga.: Mercer University, 1958).

PART FOUR

Perspective on
the Future

9

Beyond Reinventing
the Past:
The Politics of
Teacher Education

Roger Soder
Kenneth A. Sirotnik

In responding to Marx's dictum "the philosophers have only described the world in various ways; the point, however, is to change it," another philosopher tells us that "the world endures, that what changes are the modes of explanation."[1] Both positions have merit and fit well our gleanings and reflections on the eight chapters preceding. For us, what our colleagues have identified are enduring themes of the world of teacher preparation and of the places that house that enterprise—schools, colleges, and departments of education. At the same time, we place much weight on the need to change this world. That the world of teacher education endures does not mean that it does not need changing or should not be changed.

We think that it must. As educators committed to the concept of a professional school of education and the centrality of educating educators, we become less concerned with enduring themes and more concerned with this question: Can we afford to endure them much longer? And if not, what must be

385

changed? What endurance does suggest, of course, is that making the needed changes will be difficult, much like the progress of Sisyphus up the mount. The alternative, however, is to continue in a reactive and regressive mode until the historical weight of recurrent themes renders schools of education immovable and useless as units within institutions of higher education.

We prefer a proactive stance. In what follows, we address first what we believe to be four enduring themes of teacher education that emerge with particular salience from the work of our colleagues. We then turn to a discussion of these themes as they bear on the circumstances and prospects for needed change.

The Enduring Themes

In any consideration of enduring themes in teacher education, it must be said at the outset what Goodlad does, indeed, say in Chapter One: For all the apparent similarities in schools of education and teacher education across the nation, there are differences in background, style, context, demography, and numerous other variables. What we glean as commonalities we also recognize as common on some levels only; we shall attempt to note where, for us, differences make a difference.

Differences notwithstanding, therefore, four themes appear to be common across institutional and state contexts: (1) loss of identity accompanying the shift to a research orientation; (2) search for prestige; (3) intrusion of external forces; and (4) market competition. As will be seen, each of these themes, although treated separately, is related to the other three.

Research Orientation and Loss of Identity. As William Johnson notes, "the history of twentieth-century teacher training can be seen as a series of institutional displacements, with normal schools becoming state teachers colleges, then multipurpose liberal arts colleges, and now, in many instances, regional state universities."[2] The displacement, for all types of institutions with teacher training programs, has been in the direction of research and away from traditional teaching and service activities.

For those institutions already influenced by the research university ideal, the displacement was, of course, moderate.[3] For others, the displacement was of greater consequence. Normal schools, Altenbaugh and Underwood tell us in Chapter Four, turned to the university model at some cost: The university schools of education "have consciously distanced themselves from training and serving classroom instructors" and the "university research agenda has produced little useful knowledge for the practitioner or scholarship respected by members of traditional academic disciplines." Moreover, as research comes to the fore, a sense of mission is lost, there is competition for "prestige, power, and pay" between the "teaching faculty" and the "research faculty," and morale is lowered.

The increased emphasis on research is noted by other chapter authors as well. Cruikshank points out in Chapter Eight that in recent years, the University of Georgia College of Education "seemed little interested in the specifics of the public school curriculum or of the teachers who would carry it." As of the mid 1950s, the emphasis was on "more time for research, more travel money for national exposure, more support staff, and more administrative time for program planning and promotion." Burgess notes in Chapter Three that the liberal arts colleges are not immune to the incursion of the research university ideal: "Pressures to publish have invaded all of these institutions. Grounds for promotion and tenure are beginning to read more like those at the flagship university than at a liberal arts college 'teaching place.' " Similar notions are expressed by Beatty (Chapter Five) on private institutions trying to become "little Harvards" and Hendrick (Chapter Six) on public universities.

What the historians note in their examinations of past events does not differ from what we found in our own examination of current conditions at the twenty-nine institutions in the study.[4] The shift from a teaching and service emphasis to a research emphasis continues. It is not a fait accompli. And it is not without costs. As Goodlad points out in Chapter One, faculty morale is lowered because of the changes in reward structure: That which was honored no longer is, leading to a sense of betrayal and resentment. Faculty feel resentful, too, because the addition of new tasks and responsibilities is not accompanied by reduction of demands in other areas. Finally—and perhaps most critically—faculty members share, along with others in the teacher preparing enterprise and the larger institution, a sense of loss of identity. It is difficult to define yourself in relationship to your job when the definition of your job appears to be in constant flux, subject to addenda and qualifying footnotes added by a bewildering array of politicians, education bureaucrats, and academic administrators. As we discuss in greater detail in a subsequent section, a major consequence of loss of identity (for individuals and for groups), in addition to low morale and resentment, is a sense of powerlessness, a sense of the futility of involvement in the enterprise. Among and within institutional types, of course, these sentiments vary in their intensity.

Search for Higher Status. The low status of teaching and teaching teachers has long been noted, as has the desire to seek a higher status.[5] The search for higher status and the rejection of one's lowly beginnings, we would argue, are often influential factors in determining institutional strategies. Thus, for example, the shift from teaching teachers to research and publication has often been accompanied by edifying talk of The Responsibility of Higher Education to Create Knowledge or some such, but the interlinkages of the high prestige of research, money, foundation support, endowments, and the like suggest that the search for higher status has been a factor—albeit not always acknowledged—in the shift.

The relationship between the push for higher status through emulation of the research ideal and the rejection of the older, lower status is noted by Goodlad in Chapter One: As the university's status goes up, the teacher education program's status tends to decline. Moreover, we should add, within the school of education, teacher education increasingly loses status to other divisions within the school that are busying themselves with emulating the arts and sciences.

Altenbaugh and Underwood (Chapter Four) draw our attention to status issues in normal schools, where "ambitious students saw normal schooling as a stepping-stone to an occupation other than teaching; and pretentious normal school pedagogues wanted the prestige of preparing educational professionals instead of training lowly elementary teachers." Beatty tells us in Chapter Five that most teacher education programs had status problems from the beginning, with liberal arts faculty members having dim views of education's substance and validity; her observations on status in the larger private institutions are echoed by those of Hendrick (Chapter Six) on the status of education in the larger public institutions.

The liberal arts colleges are the only exception here, as noted by Goodlad in Chapter One and Burgess in Chapter Three: Education in these institutions tends to be less plagued by status issues than is education in the other institutional types in our study. One such indication of relatively higher status is found at Bucknell, where education courses are given equal weight with other liberal arts courses in satisfying distribution requirements.

Intrusion of External Forces. Viewed in terms of organizational theory, schools of education and the programs within them are open systems interacting with other open systems.[6] Other organizations, each with its own set of values, priorities interests, and roles, intrude on teacher education. Individuals in other organizations intrude on individuals in teacher education. Intrusions come from within the university or college community as well as from outside the walls of academe.

What Burgess concludes in Chapter Three about the professional faculties at Berry and Coe might well apply to most teacher education enterprises: "They acknowledge a sense of vulnerability to those external forces. . . . Theirs is a rather fatalistic helplessness to resist the will of either the major universities in their state, their respective state departments of education, or national accrediting agencies." Two other colleges treated by Burgess—Mills and Bucknell—are said to have a relatively higher sense of independence. But here, too, we are talking of degree, for Mills and Bucknell are also subject to accreditation, certification, and other state intrusions.

Altenbaugh and Underwood talk in Chapter Four of external forces similar to those identified by Burgess in their consideration of normal schools: "the state, with its control over funds and its ability to determine certification standards [and] accreditation agencies," along with the "larger social forces, such as depression and war." In her discussion of teacher education in Georgia, Cruikshank (Chapter Eight) addresses the impact of teacher shortages following World War II, combined with acknowledged unacceptably low standards of preparation. It was at this time, Cruikshank tells us, that the emphasis shifted from the University of Georgia to "the state department in formulating guiding principles for teacher training and certification and in developing the standards to be used as the basis for certification of institutional programs." Eisenmann (Chapter Seven), scanning the Pennsylvania panorama, reminds us that a critical factor in that state—indeed, any state—is the influence of the government bureaucracy: "In no other aspect of higher education does a state agency exercise the widespread control that it does over the certification of teachers."

The concern is not that there *are* external forces. Each chapter in this volume can be viewed as focusing in large part on the impact of intrusion of external forces on the teacher education enterprise. Our concern, detailed subsequently, is with the strategies for dealing with external forces and the consequences of denying that external forces do or should exist.

Competition. Competition as an enduring theme in the teacher education enterprise can be viewed variously. There is competition within an institution for resources, faculty positions, space, and a decent place at high table. There is competition between specific institutions for students and other resources. There is competition between types of institutions within a state as to appropriate mission and jurisdiction. Finally, there is competition for higher status, among both institutions and individuals. Competition for resources can be exacerbated by other external forces. Several of the chapter authors speak, for example, of the Depression and the concomitant decline of funds.

Thus Altenbaugh and Underwood (Chapter Four) tell us that "State-supported colleges and universities vied for limited public funds, requiring strong advocates to prevent their programs from being dismantled and/or awarded to other schools." In reflecting on the private institutions, Beatty (Chapter Five) notes that many became actively entrepreneurial: Tuition-dependent institutions became increasingly involved in educational marketing. Much of Cruikshank's analysis of teacher education in Georgia deals with institutional competition; similarly, Eisenmann's analysis of the Pennsylvania situation focuses on competition for market shares and what happens when times are tight.

Hendrick (Chapter Six) relates to us the story of a normal school professor in Illinois who claimed that a University of Illinois president had an "overwhelming and ruthless ambition to make of the University of Illinois an educational Colossus." Hendrick also reminds us that NCATE standards are a useful weapon when engaging in competition; such standards can help education deans negotiate for faculty positions, resources, and space. Other weapons are available too, according to Hendrick: Georgia State became a strong, "market driven" institution with a "powerful enrollment presence on the campus, and with a politically powerful group of school superintendents supporting the College of Education from the outside."

The Enduring Themes: Discussion. There are four observations we would like to make in considering the themes identified here. First, and perhaps most obvious, there are other themes as well. As various chapter authors point out, such themes as instability of leadership, fragmentation of the curriculum, sexism, racism, inattention to urban education, and demand for local control can guide our thinking about the teacher education enterprise. While recognizing the usefulness of these other themes, we elected to focus on identity, status, external forces, and competition, both for the usual reason of space constraints and because these themes, while sometimes openly acknowledged, tend to be overlooked—at least in their implications.

Second, and perhaps as obvious as the first observation, the four themes can be regarded as truisms and hardly as new ways to give meaning to the enterprise. Quite clearly, no major claims are made here or, as we see it, in the preceding chapters for startling new findings or approaches. Again, our response is that labeling a particular theme or notion as obvious or as a truism does not advance a claim for abandonment in favor of the new or the *outré*. Nothing is as difficult to see as the obvious, Malinowski once commented, and we would only add that nothing is as difficult to attend to as the obvious.

With these comments in mind, we turn to a more general observation about the themes. The four themes are not unique to the teacher education enterprise. Other professional schools must deal in one fashion or another with the centrality of the research university ideal and loss of identity, the search for higher status, external forces, and competition.

The centrality of the research university ideal affects professional schools in several ways. First, the reward structure is tied to research and publication, rather than teaching or professional preparation. Thus, for example, critics of medical schools note that "The greatest impediment to improvement in teaching appears to be a lack of recognition and reward. Promotions and tenure depend almost exclusively on research."[7] Second, research and the generation of new knowledge come to be seen primarily—indeed, solely—as a university function rather than a joint function of the university and professional practitioners in the field. A dichotomy is established between theory and practice, between professor and practitioner.[8] The dichotomy contributes to the sense of two cultures and to the "problem" of how to bridge the theory-practice gap. Although this has led to identity crises of one form or another in many professional schools, the crisis for education is exacerbated by matters of lower status.

The search for higher status is common within professional schools.[9] Again, higher status and identification with the research ideal tend to be connected. The low status of teacher education within schools of education has parallels, for example, in law, where the clinical law professor may be viewed as a second-class citizen,[10] or in medicine, where, as noted above, medical student teaching is reported as having low priority.[11]

Intrusion of external forces is common across professional schools. In our interviews with faculty at the twenty-nine institutions, we sometimes heard the notion expressed that education was peculiarly inflicted with intrusion from the outside and that other professional schools were less likely to be tampered with because of their status and heft. As we note below, teacher education is indeed different in some respects in terms of intrusion. But even the higher-status professional schools are not immune.

For example, medicine as a profession may have high status—certainly higher than education—and academic medical centers may have higher status on campus than education, but this higher status does not shield medical schools from involvement in the cold political world of the economics of health care, health maintenance organizations, an aging population, and teaching hospitals unable to gain preferred provider status and thus becoming financial burdens on the rest of the university.[12] Nor does this high status shield medical schools in other respects. Medicine has become less likely to attract good students because of an increasingly regulatory climate, the disappearance of solo entrepreneurial practice, the ascendance of massive, bureaucratic, high-technology institutions, and the increase in patient litigation.[13]

Some medical school faculty members are not pleased with the intrusion of external forces, as reflected by these comments at the opening of a conference on clinical medicine:

> By our failure to guard militantly against all comers our precious responsibilities for the educational independence of institutions giving the MD degree, we gave away much of the store and sharply

restricted our opportunities to try innovative or risky experiments in admission and education. We did so by giving external bodies—examining groups and specialty boards—the final say in what the doctor should be. Thus today we have medical institutions comparing themselves or jockeying for position on the basis of the Medical College Admission Test averages of those they admit. Incredible! Further, to pretend that National Board scores—or even the percentage of a school's students passing National Board examinations—represent some kind of Good Housekeeping Seal of Approval demonstrating a school's educational excellence seems to be a declaration of educational bankruptcy! [14]

One wonders what the response of this speaker would be to legislative attempts to limit the number of professional preparation hours in medicine as the Texas legislature has limited to eighteen the number of preparation hours in teacher education. One also wonders what the response would be to a national standards board examination signifying high professional status to those who pass—whether or not they hold a state license or certificate of completing an accredited program of medical education. [15]

External forces intrude on professional schools generally. We have focused on medicine because of its historical high status: If high status cannot protect medicine, then other professions, too, will no doubt be affected by intrusion. What makes the external forces intruding on education more difficult to deal with is the low prestige of education, the low status of the clients, and the general disrespect accorded teaching in the nation's schools.

Finally, competition is a common theme found generally in professional schools. Within a given university, dentistry may compete with business, both may compete with law, the three may compete with medicine, and so forth, for resources and support. There are no givens here: Nowhere is it written that a given professional school will maintain its share of resources in perpetuity. The accession of a president or provost, the provision of large grants requiring matching funds, or a change in legislative priorities can occasion a shift in allocations of faculty positions, capital funding for new buildings, or the amount of buffering and protection provided by the university, and the competition for limited resources is often quite keen. There is also competition for students. For example, after enjoying several decades of steady or increasing numbers of applications, medical schools since 1985 have been experiencing declining numbers.[16] In addition, there is the competition between professional schools of a given type. Just as in education, where prospective candidates look for the best economic value in preparation programs, competition for students in business, law, the health professions, and other professional training programs can get quite lively, especially in metropolitan areas where four or five M.B.A. centers or law schools are within a diploma's throw of each other.

The four themes, then, are not unique to schools of education and the teacher education enterprise. But in some respects, neither are they unique to professional schools. Nor are they solely a function of the present or even the past 150 years treated in this volume. The themes, in one form or another, have been in evidence for quite some time.

We note an early suggestion of the inverse relationship between subject matter knowledge (research) and teaching in Plutarch's biography of Alcibiades. In the course of looking for a volume of Homer, Alcibiades finds a teacher who claims to have not only a copy but one that he had corrected himself. "What," Alcibiades exclaimed, "you are teaching boys to read when you know how to edit Homer? Why aren't you teaching young men?"[17] In later years, of course, the more one specialized, the older and fewer one's students, to the point where one would not be doing any teaching at all.

As for the comparatively low status of teaching, we can ask Juvenal about the situation in Rome: The Romans demand that the teacher

Shall mould these tender minds, like an artist who
shapes a face out of wax, with his thumb. He must,

they insist, Be a father to all his pupils, must stop
them getting up to Indecent tricks with each other
(although it's no sinecure to keep check over those
darting eyes—and fingers). "See to it," you're told,
"and when the school year's ended, You'll get as
much as a jockey makes from a single race."[18]

The susceptibility to external forces was noted by Machiavelli in commenting on Livy:

It is impossible for a state to remain forever in the
peaceful enjoyment of its liberties and its narrow
confines; for, though it may not molest other states,
it will be molested by them.[19]

Regarding competition in a rough-and-tumble world,
Hobbes is as good a guide as any:

As for the Passions of Hate, Lust, Ambition, and
Covetousnesse, what Crimes they are apt to produce, is so obvious to every mans [sic] experience
and understanding, as there needeth nothing to
be said of them, saving that they are infirmities, so
annexed to the nature, both of man, and all other
living creatures, as that their effects cannot be hindered, but by extraordinary use of Reason, or a
constant severity in punishing them.[20]

In short, the struggle for prestige and respect, the competition, the lack of stability, the uncertainty, and the accompanying bickering, attacking, defending,. conniving, promoting, and finding all available means of persuasion—all are with
us and have been with us for a long time in all aspects of human existence and surely in professional schools of education.

Moreover, the uncertainty over how we should proceed
in education is exacerbated by a lack of first principles, or at
least disagreement over what those first principles are. In
Chapter Five, Hendrick points out that there were disagree-

ments over interpretations of the legislative intent behind the Morrill Act. More largely—and perhaps more disturbingly—consultation with the ancients does not appear to provide us with anything more than choices about the most fundamental matters:

> That education should be regulated by law and should be an affair of the state is not to be denied, but what should be the character of this public education, and how young persons should be educated, are questions which remain to be considered. As things are, there is disagreement about the subjects. For mankind are by no means agreed about the things to be taught, whether we look to virtue or the best life. Neither is it clear whether education is more concerned with intellectual or moral virtue. The existing practice is perplexing; no one knows on what principle we should proceed—should the useful in life, or should virtue, or should the higher knowledge, be the aim of our training; all three opinions have been entertained. Again, about the means there is no agreement; for persons, starting with different ideas about the nature of virtue, naturally disagree about the practice of it.[21]

In terms of the four enduring themes of the teacher education enterprise we have selected, we are therefore talking about endurance over a longer period of time than might first have been suspected. We are dealing with the perennial: the perennial world of principles, interests, ambition, resources, exchange, status, force, persuasion, negotiation, and compromise. In a word, *politics*. In this world of the perennial, politics implies definition: We must deal with the politics of defining who we are as teacher educators, defining our audience, defining our interests, defining how our short-term and long-term interests might best be met, and defining our sense of justice in relation to our interests and the interests of others.[22] It is to the political situation of the teacher education enterprise, then, that we must turn if we are to understand the requirements and prospects for change.

The Politics of Change

It is our view, based on our own perceptions forged by hundreds of hours of interviews with faculty in the twenty-nine institutions studied, that a particularly pernicious reaction is precipitated by the thematic chemistry characterizing the history of places where teachers are taught. The loss of identity, the search for prestige, the intrusion of external forces, and the competitive context have combined in what would appear to be a crisis of passivity on the part of individuals and organizations that are responsible for preparing educators. In our travels, we encountered many good people, thoughtful educators, who had simply retreated to the false security of passive resistance, to periodic cycles of reactive behavior, and to a vigilant wait for the "new dean" or the "next dean" who would finally lead them to the promised land of professional and academic excellence. Somehow, the idea that we are our own best agents of change and the will to act have taken a second seat to quiescence.

To be sure, the crisis that we speak of is one of degree, affecting education faculty and their organizations variously. This was certainly the case for the twenty-nine institutions in our study. Yet we did not sense that there was a strong bond of shared identity in purpose and self-confidence sufficient to ward off intrusion and to develop political strategies for long-term survival and organizational renewal. Perhaps other professional schools in multiversities are similarly affected. But it seems to us that schools of education are particularly vulnerable to being pushed around by arts and sciences, by central administration, and by state lawmakers and certification boards.

Authentic involvement in politics, of course, is not easy, especially without strong, long-term coalitions. It is also difficult if one is forced into a game played by the wrong rules. We would argue, in fact, that the notion of politics as a game—that is, as a set of rules and techniques amenable to scientific test and refinement quite apart from ideology and human interests—is the wrong model. The more educators try to compete along these lines, the more ground they will lose. It is a sucker's game.

Educators must educate. They must return to old-style politics—political philosophy, really—which was intended to be at once knowledge-producing and transformative. Old-style politics, Aristotle's politics, was, in a word, educative. Habermas's analysis is most illuminating:

> The old politics has become alien to all of us, especially in three respects: (1) Politics was understood to be the doctrine of the good and just life; it was the continuation of ethics. . . . (2) The old doctrine of politics referred exclusively to *praxis* . . . this had nothing to do with *techne,* the skillful production of artifacts and the expert mastery of objectified tasks . . . politics was always directed toward the formation and cultivation of character; it proceeded pedagogically and not technically. . . . (3) Aristotle emphasizes that politics, and practical philosophy in general, cannot be compared in its claim to knowledge with a rigorous science. . . . For its subject matter, the Just and the Excellent, in its context of a variable and contingent praxis, lacks ontological consistency as well as logical necessity. The capacity of practical philosophy is *phronesis,* a prudent understanding of the situation.[23]

Following Habermas's argument, Bernstein notes that the very inability of modern society to even understand the idea of praxis and the difference between the *practical* and the *technical* suggests serious problems for social action: "When practical discourse is eliminated or suppressed, the public realm loses— in the classical sense of politics—its political function."[24] This is a serious problem for society generally, and one that could only be exacerbated for weakly organized units within society.

If, as some have argued, power and conflict are at the core of university life, organizational units within universities would be well advised to study and act on their own self-interests in a context of limited resources and competing ideologies.[25] Moreover, if we take seriously the idea of politics as political philosophy, then schools of education must take seriously the demands for critical inquiry and action.

But critical inquiry into what? Action about what? If we limit our analysis to only the four themes considered here—certainly enough to worry about for openers—answers to these queries begin to surface. The loss of identity and search for prestige suggest a critical inquiry into the raison d'être of professional schools of education. The intrusion of external forces and institutional competition suggest aggressive and strategic action. Schools of education must consider critically not only the reasons for their own existence but also the necessary strategic responses to their organizational environment. We can only briefly sketch some directions that such inquiry and action might take.

Paths for Change

We are arguing here that the reconstruction of schools of education is at least twofold: First, they must rediscover their mission as professional schools, built around the moral and ethical responsibilities of teaching and preparing to teach and all the scholarly and service activities that would be expected to support, nurture, and sustain this central purpose. (This may be the toughest of the two.) Second, they must learn well how to vie for power and resources, gain control of reward systems, form important coalition groups, and negotiate successfully in their own best interests (grounded, of course, in their mission). We consider briefly each of these efforts.

Mission. Education faculty members must critically inquire into the appropriate reasons, the normative foundations, for justifying something called a professional school of education. Obviously, for education schools to take strong political action that is educative and transformative in nature, they have to have a good idea as to the nature of their own mission.

The crucial task in this rediscovery of organizational self will be a reordering and redefinition of the "holy trinity"—research, teaching, and service. If there were no doctors or lawyers to prepare, would there be schools of medicine or law? If there were no teachers to prepare, what would be the justification for schools of education? We think that educators have sold themselves and their professional units short by denying the very essence of what their organizations should be about—teaching, preparing to teach, and a deliberate program of inquiry and action growing out of this central mission. To the extent that schools of education downplay their role in the preparation of teachers and overplay their image as behavioral science research centers, they run the risk of undermining their rightful claim to professional unit status within the multiversity community. This is no small threat, even for prestigious "ed schools" in major research universities.[26]

Teaching carries extraordinary burdens of responsible judgment, responsibilities that carry over in like kind to the teaching of teachers. The curriculum, as we have argued elsewhere, must derive from the moral and ethical dimensions of the enterprise—be it healing, building, litigating, or teaching.[27] For example, ethical roots pertaining to inquiry, knowledge, competence, caring, and social justice can be argued for any pedagogical enterprise, particularly the teaching of children and youth in compulsory public schools.[28]

Organizations—schools of education—conceived for the purpose of educating educators must see that purpose as central. Research and scholarly interests must grow out of and support organizational mission. In short, schools of education must demonstrate and celebrate the fact that pedagogy is not an empty concept and that much can be built around its centrality. For so long as conventional wisdom has it that anyone can be a teacher, schools of education are going to have a difficult time justifying their existence, no matter how far they stray from the central task of educating educators.

Although exceptional teaching and supervision of stu-

402

dents should be demanded by all units within the university community, nowhere should the demand be higher than in schools of education. Nowhere is it more incumbent upon educators to pursue excellence in education than in those places presuming to be disciplined in pedagogy itself. Schools of education should be places where faculty and students from all areas of the university can come to see and experience outstanding teaching and curriculum. Excellence in teaching and mentoring does not come easily or cheaply; much time and resources go into it. We have come to a point in many research universities where faculty members have to be released from nonteaching responsibilities in order to plan and deliver a high-quality curriculum. All faculty members in schools of education should teach, and they should be rewarded substantially for high-quality teaching.

Scholarly inquiry and excellence in teaching and the preparation of educators are interlinked. Scholarly inquiry is not necessarily the equivalent of "research and publication." Scholarly inquiry requires time and effort. It is long-term. It enriches the scholar's understanding through immersion in both historical and contemporary understanding and practices. It requires much reading and thoughtful reflection. It requires sustained discourse with colleagues who are similarly engaged. Scholarly inquiry is—or ought to be—a way of professional life for faculty in schools of education, the fruits of which must be deliberately brought to bear on teaching and learning. No course should ever be taught exactly the same way from quarter to quarter, semester to semester. Scholarly inquiry must enrich lives of both scholars and students. Nowhere should this be better modeled and more rewarded than in schools of education.

Teachers in schools of education prepare teachers, who, in turn, teach in our nation's schools. Educational practice must be as close to the professor in a school of education as the land is to the professor in a school of agriculture. Each must connect to the field in ways that simultaneously enrich both inquiry and practice. This, of course, is the concept of *praxis*. Praxis is reflexive and evaluative. It influences and shapes the bases of knowledge that, reciprocally, influence and shape human action. It is influenced by underlying beliefs, values, and human interests, and it must therefore make such normative content manifest and subject to critical inquiry and action. It is knowing in action—a dialectical process of reconstructing knowledge in the context of practice. This cannot be done in an armchair or in front of a personal computer. One must be with educators, experience their problems, work with them in knowledge-using and knowledge-generating activities. In short, "service" must be reconceptualized and reconstructed as *praxis* and rewarded highly in decisions regarding promotion and tenure.

Finally, teaching and the preparation of educators, scholarly inquiry, and praxis can and should come together in the generation and dissemination of new knowledge—research and publication can and ought to be a valued part of academic life. But these activities must be placed in proper perspective. Scholarship, for example, does not necessarily imply publication. Nor does the converse necessarily hold. It is nice, however, when both obtain and the products are amply rewarded. Securing extramural funds for these efforts is also to be rewarded. But when winning huge grants consumes the work life of faculty, the organization becomes a "RAND Corporation," not a professional school. Schools of education must find parity in their reward systems for all four valued features composing their educational mission: teaching and the preparation of educators, scholarly inquiry, praxis, and research and dissemination.

Strategic Action. No matter how clear schools of education become in their mission and place in higher education, they still need to hold their own in the university setting. They must lay claim to (and in many cases reclaim) their rightful share of the higher education pie. In large part, this can be seen as an application of critical pedagogy—that is, as a program for educating colleagues through a process of political transformation. Again, we can only suggest several features of the curriculum.

First, schools of education must counter the hegemony of the arts and sciences. The arts and sciences are worthy disciplines, but the rules that they have developed for academic advancement are not the stuff for emulation by professional schools. Schools of education must create their own rules, grounded in the multidisciplinary nature of education and the necessary field connections of professional preparation and development. These rules grow naturally out of the fourfold mission of schools of education: teaching and teacher education, scholarly inquiry, praxis, and the creation and dissemination of new knowledge. Dewey's admonition in 1904 must finally be taken seriously by educators in universities: Those in schools of education must see themselves as more closely akin to the professional school faculty than to the arts and sciences faculty, and they must gain control of their intellectual methods.[29]

Second, schools of education must take the lead in forming a coalition of professional schools within the university community. Schools of education are not alone; other professional schools—medicine, nursing, dentistry, business, engineering, fisheries, law, social work, public affairs—have similar problems within the academic establishment. The multiversity is here to stay. Professional schools are a permanent fixture in academic life, and they must have their own rules—rules that must be justified, to be sure—for academic tenure and advancement.

Third, schools of education should form another kind of a coalition: a university-school-community partnership of significant educational constituencies outside of the university—namely, school districts, community colleges, carefully selected private corporations, local private foundations, and state education agencies. A track record for collaborative work toward the improvement of educational programs in universities, colleges, and schools must be established in this coalition.

Fourth, with the help of these two coalitions, the central university office (president, provost, and so on) must be educated as to the mission and modus operandi of a professional school of education. A high level of commitment must be obtained from the central office, expressed not only in terms of resources but also in terms of rhetoric.

Fifth, lobbying and negotiating for appropriate reward systems for professional schools should accompany the education of central administration. Increased emphasis on teaching and field service and collaborative work with educators, enlightenment as to the distinction between scholarship and inquiry versus publish-perish research, and the appropriate role of research and dissemination must be part of a reconstructed reward system endorsed and supported by the coalitions and central administration.

Sixth, schools of education must demonstrate that there is, indeed, something to the idea of pedagogy through their development of exemplary programs in preparing teachers, administrators, and other educators. Such programs will have to do more than they do currently for the education of educators. For example, they will have to authentically involve a critical mass of university faculty members dedicated to teaching teachers and a critical mass of school-based educators with clinical status in the university. The program will have to model the praxis ideal—a knowledge-based/practice-based dialectic using exemplary schools as clinical training sites.

Seventh, the school of education must provide pedagogical training for university instructional staff (other professors and teaching assistants)—with results—to put to rest any lingering notions that all one has to know to teach is one's subject matter.

Eighth, the reality of teacher education being part of a graduate school of education cannot be ignored. The legitimacy and status of professional programs are inexorably tied to the legitimacy and status of academic programs. Standards of quality must apply to courses of study and the meaning of higher degrees. Schools of education need to be clear as to the differences (if any) among M.A.T., M.I.T., M.Ed., and M.A. degrees and between Ed.D. and Ph.D. degrees. Theses and dissertations, open to public scrutiny, should reflect these distinctions and standards of quality.

Ninth . . . we could go on with this enumeration, but such is not the main focus of this chapter or this book. Consider the above list as a beginning—not for tinkering around with the past, but for inventing the future.

The Prospects for Change

We have argued that those in schools of education must redefine their interests and must become actively involved in the political world around them. But specification of conditions for success (however defined) is not enough. One might say that to win a horse race, a horse must run faster than the other horses. But the question of particular interest to the wagering public is the chances that a given horse will indeed meet the conditions. For our purposes here, our question of interest becomes: What are the chances of education faculty members overcoming passivity in favor of political action?

An assessment of the chances must consider the sources of faculty passivity that we have observed. It may be that this passivity derives in part from a belief that the academic world should be inviolate to the greatest extent possible, that intellectual objectivity and a critical perspective are necessarily threatened by political involvement. This belief reflects a tension between the world of thought and the world of action, a tension having roots going back to fifth-century Athens.[30] From this perspective, an unwillingness to engage in political action stems from the deeply held belief that such engagement will make the university something other than a university, that such engagement is of the nature of "we had to destroy the village in order to save it." Passivity, then, derives at least in part from a particular definition of the university role in society.

Another source of the passivity is how faculty members define appropriate behavior for themselves and others in their occupational group. It may be that some faculty members feel that there is something distasteful about the hurly-burly world of politics and that anything beyond forced involvement in politics is in some vague sort of way a violation of occupational or cultural norms. Clearly, cultural ideals, or images of a "way of life," can have considerable potency for influencing behavior. Among many faculty members in higher education, there is a disdain for the gritty ethos of politics stemming from the attitude that "we just don't do that sort of thing." Passivity, in part, then, derives from a particular definition of faculty role within the university.

The beliefs of a university inviolate and a faculty that is above—or at least apart from—politics are to be found among faculty members in all branches and divisions of a given university or college. These beliefs, however, are more likely to reflect views of arts and sciences faculty than the views of professional school faculty. Those in professional schools such as medicine and law have traditionally maintained involvement with the external world. If, for example, the primary function of a law school is to prepare lawyers, then we would expect to find law school faculties and administrators comparatively at ease with their external involvement. Such involvement is part of the definition of a law school. But schools of education have tended to eschew the professional school model in favor of an arts and sciences model. In accepting the arts and sciences model, schools of education have accepted—to their disfavor— the notions of a university that is inviolate and disdains political involvement.

There are no doubt other sources of passivity, ranging from malaise, ennui, and burnout and lack of rewards and bureaucracy to live-and-let-live attitudes. In addition, we need to consider self-selection into the occupation. Those who wish to engage in active warfare can find plenty of outlets in law, business, the armed services, and ward politics, while those who are inclined away from such activities may find the image of the contemplative, semimonastic life of academe an appealing one. If we consider just the two sources of passivity we have adumbrated here, we can make some assessment of the chances of education faculty members overcoming passivity in favor of political action.

To address the first source of passivity means to deal with a fundamental definition of the university in relation to the state and society. There is no agreement—nor are we ourselves certain—as to the extent to which we wish to alter the function of a university as independent critical agent of society. Again, there is no one view of the proper function of the university, and those in professional schools might well hold views different from those typically found in arts and sciences. Our point is that many in schools of education do adhere to a fundamental definition of the university as inviolate, and to alter the definition of a school of education means far more than drawing up a new mission statement: The redefinition necessarily cuts to the fundamental meaning of the university itself.

To address the second source of passivity means to deal with deep-seated beliefs of many faculty members as to what is proper behavior. Even if we were to agree that disdain of politics is an attitude to be discouraged, there is little to suggest that occupational norms of this kind can be easily changed. Once again, such norms are found to varying extents in all parts of a university but are more likely to be found in arts and sciences and thus more likely to be found in schools of education: The decision to emulate arts and sciences as opposed to professional schools carries with it considerable costs.

There is, then, much to be done if we are to move beyond reinventing the past. Schools of education, and teacher education programs within them, need to change if we are to have suitable teachers for the kinds of schools we must have. These changes would be difficult to achieve under the most ideal circumstances of a closed organizational system. However, those in schools of education must deal with change in the context of the four enduring themes identified in this volume: the trend toward a research orientation, the search for status, external intrusion, and competition. Those in schools of education must ascribe new meanings to what they do and must persuade others to accept these new meanings. The task, then, becomes twofold: Make the changes needed in specific programs, and deal with the political context. But, as we have just noted, to deal with the political context will demand enormous shifts from inaction to action. The task, then, becomes threefold—make the changes needed in specific programs, deal with the political context, and devise ways to deal with the sources of passivity and unwillingness to contend. Herculean labors, indeed.

Notes

1.   J. A. Campbell, "A Rhetorical Interpretation of History," *Rhetorica*, 1984, 2 (Autumn), 227–266.
2.   W. R. Johnson, "Teachers and Teacher Training in the Twentieth Century," in D. Warren (ed.), *American Teachers: Histories of a Profession at Work* (New York: Macmillan, 1989), p. 243.
3.   G. J. Clifford and J. W. Guthrie, *Ed School: A Brief for Professional Education* (Chicago: University of Chicago Press, 1988).
4.   R. Soder, *Faculty Work in the Institutional Context*, Technical Report no. 3 (Seattle: Center for Educational Renewal, University of Washington, 1989).
5.   See, for example, W. S. Elsbree, *The American Teacher* (New York: American Book Company 1939); M. Lieberman, *Education as a Profession* (Englewood Cliffs, N.J.: Prentice-Hall, 1956); R. Soder, "The Rhetoric of Teacher Professionalization," in J. I. Goodlad, R. Soder, and K. A. Sirotnik (eds.), *The Moral Dimensions of Teaching* (San Francisco: Jossey-Bass, 1990).
6.   See D. Katz and R. L. Kahn, *The Social Psychology of Organizations* (New York: Wiley, 1966); W. R. Scott, *Organizations: Rational, Natural and Open Systems* (Englewood Cliffs, N.J.: Prentice-Hall, 1981).
7.   Panel on the General Professional Education of the Physician and College Preparation for Medicine, "Physicians for the Twenty-First Century," *Journal of Medical Education Part II*, Nov. 1984, p. 74.
8.   See Donald Schön's very useful volumes *The Reflective Practitioner* (New York: Basic Books, 1983) and *Educating the Reflective Practitioner: Toward a New Design for Teaching and Learning in the Professions* (San Francisco: Jossey-Bass, 1987).
9.   See, for example, R. Soder, *Status Matters*, Technical Re-

port no. 4 (Seattle: Center for Educational Renewal, University of Washington, 1989).

10. B. Thorne, "Professional Education in Law," in E. C. Hughes and others (eds.), *Education for the Professions of Medicine, Law, Theology, and Social Welfare* (New York: McGraw-Hill, 1973), pp. 101–168; see also K. Ludmerer, *Learning To Heal* (New York: McGraw-Hill, 1985).

11. See G. N. Gill, "The End of the Physician-Scientist?" *American Scholar*, 1984, *53* (Summer), 353–368.

12. R. H. Ebert, "Medical Education at the Peak of the Era of Experimental Medicine," *Daedalus*, 1986, *115* (Spring), 55–81.

13. B. Gastel and D. E. Rogers (eds.), *Clinical Education and the Doctor of Tomorrow* (New York: New York Academy of Medicine, 1989), p. 7.

14. Gastel and Rogers, *Clinical Education*, p. 8.

15. See the current guidelines proposed by the National Board for Professional Teaching Standards—which do *not* require completion of a preparation program. National Board for Professional Teaching Standards, *Toward High and Rigorous Standards for the Teaching Profession* (Detroit: National Board for Professional Teaching Standards, 1989), p. 49. For a reaction of one group to such a proposal, see A. Bradley, "AACTE Decides Not to Support Teaching Board," *Education Week*, 1989, *9* (3), 1, 21.

16. Telephone interview with August Swanson, director of academic affairs, Association of American Medical Colleges, Dec. 20, 1989.

17. Plutarch, "Alcibiades," in Plutarch, *The Rise and Fall of Athens: Nine Greek Lives* (I. Scott-Kilvert, trans.) (Harmondsworth, England: Penguin, 1960), p. 250.

18. Juvenal, "Satire No. 7," in Juvenal, *The Sixteen Satires* (P. Green, trans.) (Harmondsworth, England: Penguin, 1967), p. 17.

19. N. Machiavelli, *Discourses*, II, 19 (L. J. Walker, trans.) (Harmondsworth, England: Penguin Books, 1970), pp. 335–336.

20. T. Hobbes, *Leviathan*, II, 27 (C. B. Macpherson, ed.) (Harmondsworth, England: Penguin Books, 1968), p. 342.

21. Aristotle, "Politics," 1337a34, in R. P. McKeon (ed.), *The Basic Works of Aristotle* (B. Jowett, trans.) (New York: Random House, 1941), pp. 1305–1306.

22. See J. B. White, *When Words Lose Their Meaning: Constitutions and Reconstitutions of Language, Character, and Community* (Chicago: University of Chicago Press, 1984). Equally useful are White's *The Legal Imagination* (Chicago: University of Chicago Press, 1985) and *Heracles' Bow: Essays on the Rhetoric and Poetics of the Law* (Madison: University of Wisconsin Press, 1985).

23. J. Habermas, *Theory and Practice* (J. Viertel, trans.) (Boston: Beacon Press, 1973), p. 42.

24. R. J. Bernstein, *The Restructuring of Social and Political Theory* (Philadelphia: University of Pennsylvania Press, 1978), p. 188.

25. J. V. Baldridge, *Power and Conflict in the University* (New York: Wiley, 1971).

26. See Clifford and Guthrie, *Ed School.*

27. Goodlad, Soder, and Sirotnik, *The Moral Dimensions of Teaching.*

28. K. A. Sirotnik, "Society, Schooling, Teaching, and Preparing to Teach," in Goodlad, Soder and Sirotnik, *The Moral Dimensions of Teaching.*

29. J. Dewey, "The Relation of Theory to Practice in Education," in C. A. McMurry (ed.), *Third Yearbook of the National Society for the Scientific Study of Education* (Chicago: University of Chicago Press, 1904).

30. On this point, see particularly L. Strauss, *Thoughts on Machiavelli* (Chicago: University of Chicago Press, 1959) and *Socrates and Aristophanes* (Chicago: University of Chicago Press, 1966).

Index

A

Accreditation: of high schools, 242, 348, 354, 361; and liberal arts colleges, 90, 91, 93–94, 111, 127, 128; and normal schools, 159–161, 166, 171; and private institutions, 210, 213, 215, 216, 219; and research universities, 238, 263, 275

Ade, L., 320

Aderhold, O. C., 366

Adler, D., 188

Administrators: commitment by, 404–405; and stability, 18–19, 41–42, 49–50, 91–92, 112. *See also* Leadership

Agricultural, Mining and Mechanical Arts College, evolution of, 243. *See also* California at Berkeley, University of

Agriculture, College of, evolution of, 247. *See also* Georgia, University of

Albany Agricultural, Industrial and Normal School for Colored, evolution of, 357

Albany Bible and Manual Training Institute, evolution of, 347

Albany Manual Training and Agricultural Institute, evolution of, 347–348

Albany Normal School, evolution of, 342, 347

Albany School, evolution of, 357

Albany State College, evolution of, 331, 357, 365

Alberts, R., 327

Alcibiades, 395

Altenbaugh, R. J., 12, 65, 77, 81, 136, 231, 232, 236n, 241, 280, 282, 283, 387, 389, 390, 391

American Association for Higher Education, 39

American Association of Colleges, 91

American Association of Colleges for Teacher Education (AACTE), 202, 210, 238, 410

American Association of Teachers Colleges, 150

American Association of University Professors (AAUP), 166, 172

American Baptist Home Mission Society, 342

American Church Institute, 350, 362

American Council on Education, 101, 269

American Educational Research Association, 10, 69

American Missionary Association, 342

American Missionary Society, 331

American Normal School Association, 148, 167

Anderson, J. D., 77–78, 145, 183, 379

Anderson, R. H., 77, 78

Angel, D. E., 231
Angelo, R. M., 311, 312, 326, 327
Aristotle, 309, 411
Armstrong, F. R., 104–105, 132
Association for Supervision and Curriculum Development, 80
Association of American Medical Colleges, 410
Association of American Universities, 160
Association of American Universities and Colleges, 101
Association of College Presidents, 302–303
Atkins, M., 99–100
Atkinson, W. Y., 340
Atlanta Area Teacher Education Services (AATES), 64–65, 81, 194–195, 375
Atlanta Baptist College, evolution of, 218–219, 376
Atlanta Federation of Schools for the Improvement of Negro Country Life, 376
Atlanta University: and black teacher education, 341, 342–346, 350, 363, 366; evolution of, 331, 338, 355, 376; niche of, 375; School of Education of, 376; Scientific Preparatory Department of, 345
Atlanta University Center, 376
Augusta Institute, evolution of, 342
Ault, W. O., 227, 228

B

Bacote, C. A., 378, 379, 380
Bagley, W. C., 255–256, 262–263, 272, 276, 278, 297, 327
Baker, C. B., 210
Baker, E. D., 210
Baker, J., 295–296, 301, 322, 323, 324, 325, 327, 328–329
Baldridge, J. V., 411
Baltimore Colored Normal School, founding of, 144
Baptist tradition: and Bucknell University, 116, 117–119; and

Georgia institutions, 330, 342, 351, 374, 376; and Mercer Atlanta, 189, 218, 375; and Temple, 311
Barnard, H., 137, 138–139, 181, 289
Barnard, R. M., 182, 183
Barre, Massachusetts, normal school at, 139–140
Barth, R. S., 80, 81
Bates, G. E., Jr., 141–142, 182
Beatty, B., 12, 54, 58, 64, 67, 71–73, 77, 78, 79–80, 81, 82, 187, 387, 389, 391
Bell, H. M., 208
Benner, T. E., 263–264, 269–270
Bennett, H., 270
Berea College, impact of, 103
Bernstein, R. J., 399, 411
Berry, M., 73, 88–93, 97–98, 129–130, 374
Berry Academy, evolution of, 98
Berry College: and accreditation, 90, 91, 93–94, 127; administrative instability at, 91–92; attributes of, 88–98; austerity at, 96; charter changes at, 94–95; context of, 87, 374–375, 389; Early Childhood Education Center at, 98; faculty at, 92, 95, 96, 127–129; founding of, 88–91; Laboratory School at, 98, 128; modern trends at, 95–97; and populism issues, 73; research emphasis at, 96; in sample, 10, 377; student groups at, 93, 131; teacher education at, 97–98, 105; uncertainties at, 91–93; uniforms at, 89, 92, 93, 95, 129–130; work for students at, 89, 90, 92, 93, 95, 131
Berry Junior College, evolution of, 91, 130
Berry Schools: evolution of, 90, 92, 97, 98; in state system, 331, 374–375
Berry Women's Club, 130
Bertrand, J. R., 93–96, 130–131
Beury, C., 311
Bezilla, M., 325, 328

Bill 1706 (Oklahoma), 274

Bixby, P., 328

Black teachers: Georgia programs for, 341–351, 357–359, 361–366, 371–374; normal schools for, 144–147, 154; in Pennsylvania, 290, 310

Blakely, D., 108

Blakenship, C., 284

Bloomsburg Normal School, 322

Blow, S., 209

Blumer, I., 80

Board of Normal School Principals, 310

Boggs, Chancellor, 340

Bond, H. M., 363, 364

Borrowman, M. L., 181, 182, 183, 184

Boston: desegregation in, 199, 204; normal school in, 148–149, 201, 204

Boston College: evolution of, 199–204; Intown Evening Division of, 201, 204; pedagogy at, 200–201; religious affiliation of, 189–190, 193, 200, 201, 203–204; in sample, 11, 188; School of Education of, 67–68, 200–204; site of, 188–189, 200; Summer School of, 201; and urban education, 67–68

Boston State College, evolution of, 149

Boston State Teachers College, evolution of, 149

Boston University: and Chelsea schools, 199, 223; College of Business Administration at, 49; constituencies of, 199, 207; and Dedham study, 198; Department of Education at, 57, 187, 197; Department of Foundations of Education at, 198; Division of Teaching Aids at, 58, 64, 198; education dean at, 49, 197; Educational Clinic at, 58, 64, 198; evolution of, 196–199; extension services of, 196–197, 198; institutional context at, 16; journal from, 198; and knowledge-practice tension, 64; leadership of, 198, 199; mission of, 197; program proliferation at, 57–59, 79–80; religious affiliation of, 189, 196; in sample, 11, 188; and Sargent School of Physical Education, 58; and school involvement, 192, 193, 198–199, 201, 203; School of Education at, 49, 57, 58, 64, 69, 197–198, 199; School of Religious Education at, 57; status of, 50, 223; and urban education, 59, 197, 198–199, 205

Bowers, J., 247

Boys' Industrial School, evolution of, 89, 90, 98, 130. *See also* Berry College

Bradley, A., 410

Bradwell, J. D., 378

Brawley, B. G., 378, 380

Bridgewater, Massachusetts, normal school at, 139–140, 144, 178

Brooks, C., 139

Brooks, R. P., 378

Brown, E. E., 251, 257

Brown, J. E., 335

Brown, President, 344

Brown University: impact of, 118, 119; and networks, 66

Brownell, H., 267

Brumbaugh study, 370

Buchtel, H. A., 205

Bucknell, W., 119, 122–123

Bucknell Junior College, evolution of, 120–121, 125

Bucknell University: attributes of, 116–126; and Bucknell Conference on Education, 124; Bucknell Education Club at, 124; building, 119–122; context of, 87, 390; decentralization at, 121; Department of Education at, 120, 123, 125; faculty at, 126, 127–129; Female Institute at, 118, 119; founding of, 116–117; niche of, 289; professional departments at, 120, 123; in sample, 10, 321; and state regulation, 47, 123; summer session at, 124; teacher ed-

Bucknell University (*continued*)
    ucation at, 122–126, 290; teacher
    placement service of, 123
Buel Institute, 240
Bullock government, 377
Bumstead, President, 345
Bunkder, F. F., 173
Burgess, C., 12, 77, 82, 87, 387, 389,
    390
Burk, F. L., 74, 166, 173
Burks, J. B., 379–380
Burrill, T. J., 254
Butler, N. M., 147
Butterweck, J. S., 300, 323, 326,
    327, 329
Byers, T., 129, 130, 131

                    C

California: certification in, 216, 217,
    273–274; credentials in, 103–104,
    260; Department of Education of,
    267, 281; in-service education in,
    276; Master Plan for Higher Ed-
    ucation in, 175, 250, 272; nor-
    mal schools in, 42, 243; teacher
    education studied in, 5–6, 10, 11.
    See also California institutions;
    Mills College; San Francisco in-
    stitutions
California, College of, evolution of,
    243. *See also* California at Berke-
    ley, University of
California at Berkeley, University
    of: and certification, 273–274;
    constituencies for, 249, 250, 251–
    252, 258; credentials from, 260,
    273–274; Department of Educa-
    tion at, 258, 259, 260, 265; De-
    velopmental Teacher Education
    Program at, 251; Division of
    Teacher Education at, 267; ex-
    ternal forces on, 272, 273–274,
    275, 276; Greek Theater at, 74;
    impact of, 101, 105; internal
    forces at, 264–269; leadership of,
    243, 277–278; Men's Education
    Club at, 260; mission of, 242–
    244; niche of, 174, 175, 238;
    practice teaching at, 258–259;

program development at, 256–
    261; in sample, 11, 236, 237;
    School of Education at, 250–251,
    259, 264–265, 267, 269, 277; two-
    tier faculty at, 268–269
California at Los Angeles, Univer-
    sity of, teacher education at, 251,
    264, 266, 268
California Lutheran College, evo-
    lution of, 215
California Lutheran Educational
    Foundation, 215
California Lutheran University: ac-
    creditation for, 215, 216; and
    certification, 216, 217; evolution
    of, 215–218; football training at,
    216; leadership of, 216, 217; part-
    time faculty at, 217; religious af-
    filiation of, 190, 215; in sample,
    11, 188; School of Education at,
    216; service orientation of, 216–
    217, 220
California Normal School (Penn-
    sylvania), 322
California State University, Hay-
    ward, niche of, 250
California State University System,
    niche for, 250, 278
Callanan College, evolution of, 207–
    208. *See also* Drake University
Campbell, J. A., 409
Campbell, W., 266
Carnegie Corporation, 374
Carnegie Foundation for the Ad-
    vancement of Teaching, 3, 5, 37,
    237, 279
Carnegie Institute of Technology,
    evolution of, 327
Carnell, L., 311, 326, 327
Carson, L. C., 101
Carter, J., 137
Carver, R., 5, 38
Cather, W., 106–107, 133
Catholic tradition, and private uni-
    versity, 189–190, 200, 201, 203–
    204
Cedar Rapids Collegiate Institute,
    evolution of, 107, 108–109. *See
    also* Coe College

Center for Educational Renewal, 8, 39

Central High School, 326

Central State University: and institutional identity, 44; in sample, 10, 153

Central Young Men's Christian Association, 212–213

Central YMCA College, evolution of, 213. *See also* Roosevelt University

Certification: in Georgia, 33, 34, 219, 340, 354, 360, 361, 366, 367–368, 371, 375; impact of, 47–48; and knowledge-practice tension, 33–34; and normal schools, 146, 155, 158–159, 174; in Pennsylvania, 290, 291; and private institutions, 201, 207, 208, 211, 215, 216, 217, 219, 220, 224–225, 234; and research universities, 260, 272, 273–274

Chadsey, C., 276

Chambers, W. G., 271, 297, 300–301, 305–306, 317, 324, 325, 328

Change: and mission, 400–403; paths for, 400–406; politics of, 398–400; prospects for, 406–409; and strategic action, 403–406

Chase, L., 64

Cheyney Normal School, evolution of, 290, 322

Chicago, University of: impact of, 264, 265; lab school at, 54; status of, 227

Chicago Kindergarten College, evolution of, 209. *See also* National College of Education

Chicago State University: and accreditation, 160, 185; and black students, 66–67; constituencies of, 163; and Depression, 161; in sample, 10, 153

Church, A., 335, 337–339

Ciardi, J., 88, 129

Civil War: and Georgia institutions, 330, 332, 333, 334, 341; and research universities, 239, 247, 272

Clarion Normal School: and corruption, 294; evolution of, 322

Clark College, evolution of, 376

Clark University, impact of, 173

Class, and populism, 70–73

Clifford, G. J., 38, 179–180, 183, 184, 186, 188, 227, 228, 267, 279, 283, 409, 411

Cocking, W., 362

Cody, W. F., 107

Coe, D., 108, 109, 112

Coe College: academic agenda for, 110–113; Academic Policies Committee at, 114; accreditation of, 111; administrative instability at, 112; attributes of, 106–116; beginnings of, 108–110; Department of Education at, 110, 114; Department of Philosophy and Political Science at, 113; faculty at, 111–112, 127–129; founding of, 106–107; institutional context at, 16, 87, 389; and mission, 110, 111; in sample, 10; students at, 115; teacher education at, 113–116; Teacher Education Committee at, 114

Coe Collegiate Institute, evolution of, 107, 109–110

Coffman, L. D., 381

College Board, 113

Colorado: certification in, 159, 207; institutional niche in, 154; normal schools in, 183, 184; teacher education studied in, 5–6, 11. *See also* Colorado institutions; Denver, University of; Northern Colorado, University of

Colorado, University of, niche of, 172

Colorado A & M, niche of, 172

Colorado Commission on Higher Education, 172, 185

Colorado Seminary, evolution of, 204–205. *See also* Denver, University of

Colorado State College: evolution of, 168; pedagogy at, 156. *See also* Northern Colorado, University of

Colorado State College of Education: evolution of, 168, 170; extension program of, 170; and GI Bill, 162, 185. *See also* Northern Colorado, University of

Colorado State Normal School: constituencies of, 163, 164, 165; evolution of, 168–172; extension division of, 169–170; leadership at, 166; mission of, 168–169; niche of, 172; pedagogy at, 156, 169; program at, 156–157, 158, 169–170. *See also* Northern Colorado, University of

Colorado State Teachers College: and accreditation, 160; evolution of, 168, 169; and military training, 162, 185; niche of, 167. *See also* Northern Colorado, University of

Colorado Women's College, acquisition of, 205

Columbia University, impact of, 170. *See also* Teachers College

Commission on Teacher Credentialing, 174

Common school movement: in Georgia, 334, 335, 339, 346, 352, 354; and normal schools, 138, 140

Community College Act of 1963 (Pennsylvania), 307–308, 320

Competency-based programs, 47, 52, 274, 370–371, 376–377

Competition: antiquity of, 396; in Georgia, 336, 375–377; and professional schools, 394–395; and teacher education, 390–391

Comprehensive universities, in sample, 6

Conant, J. B., 4, 27, 38, 56, 284

Concord, Vermont, teacher training school in, 137

Condit, R. A., 109, 133

Conger, N., 270, 271, 277

Connolly, K. S., 230

Connor, D. B., 231

Consortia, in Atlanta area, 64–65, 81, 194–195, 375

Constituencies: of normal schools,

163–165, 170–171, 174–175, 177, 178–179; of private institutions, 190, 199, 207, 211, 213, 219; of research universities, 249–253, 258

Conwell, R. H., 249, 311

Cook County Normal School, impact of, 340

Cooperating teachers. *See* Student teaching

Coppedge, L., 284

Council of Higher Education, 308

Cousins, R. L., 359

Crane, I., 4

Cremin, L. A., 38, 227, 253, 281

Crossley, A., 198

Crouse, Mrs. J. N., 209

Crozier Theological Seminary, impact of, 118

Cruikshank, K., 13, 47–48, 70, 77, 82, 236n, 247–248, 280–281, 284, 330, 387, 390, 391

Cuban, L., 75, 82

Curriculum: fragmentation of, 27–29; in Georgia, 340, 343, 364–365, 372; issues of, 50–66; normative issues of, 51–56; in Pennsylvania, 292–293, 294, 297–298; proliferation of, 56–61; of research universities, 253–262

Curry, J.L.M., 339, 378

Cushing, R. J., 202

D

Daily Normal School for Females, mission of, 149

Dallas Cowboys, 216

Danforth Foundation, 115, 134

Davidson, P. E., 173

Davis, F. G., 124–126

Davis, J. B., 64

Day, S., 60, 65

DeGarmo, C., 254, 255, 262

Dentler, R., 69, 199

Denton, J. N., 355–356, 380

Denver, University of: City College of, 205; evolution of, 204–207; expansion of, 205; leadership of, 205; and military training, 205;

and normative issues, 53; religious affiliation of, 189, 204–205; in sample, 11, 188; Saturday School of, 206; school involvement by, 206–207; School of Education of, 206; summer school of, 205; and urban education, 205

Depression: and competition, 391; and Georgia institutions, 332; and normal schools, 161, 165; and Pennsylvania institutions, 302, 306, 318–320; and research universities, 272

Dewey, J., 51, 53, 54, 78, 156, 217, 281, 353, 404, 411

Dexter, E. G., 254–255

Dickeson, R. C., 171

Dickson, E. A., 266

Disciples of Christ, and private university, 189, 207

Discontinuities: aspects of, 29–32; issues of, 56–61

Dismukes, C. J., 378

Dixon, J. C., 358–359

Dodd, L., 65

Domestic Science Association of Colleges and Secondary Schools, 111

Donovan, C., 201–203, 230

Douma, G. H., 133

Dowell, S., 381

Doyle, B., 229–230

Drake University: Callanan College of, 207–208; College of Education of, 208; Department of Teacher Education at, 46, 208; evolution of, 207–209; Graduate School of Education and Human Services at, 46, 208; and institutional identity, 45–46; religious affiliation of, 189, 207; research emphasis of, 189; in sample, 11, 188; school involvement of, 208; School of Education of, 208

DuBois, W.E.B., 347, 350, 379

Ducharme, E. R., 235

Dumke, G. S., 43, 186

Dunham, E. A., 186

Dunigan, D. R., 229

Dunne, F. P., 116–117, 134

Durrell, D. D., 64, 198, 229

Dyer, T. G., 377, 378

E

East Stroudsburg Normal School: and corruption, 294; evolution of, 322

Eastern Illinois Teachers Association, 272

Ebert, R. H., 410

Edge, I. A., 131

Edgerly, J. G., 175

Edinboro Normal School, evolution of, 292, 322, 325

Edmonds Act of 1921 (Pennsylvania), 298–299, 300–301, 323

Education for All Handicapped Children Act (P.L. 94–142), 199

Ege, H. B., 101

Eisenmann, L., 13, 52–53, 77, 78, 79, 236n, 245, 271, 280, 281, 284, 287, 390, 391

Eliot, C. W., 119

Elsbree, W. S., 181, 182, 183, 184, 409

Embree, E. R., 381

Emerson, R. W., 88, 89

Emory College, evolution of, 193

Emory University: Division of Educational Studies at, 45, 195–196; Division of Teacher Education at, 65, 194; evolution of, 193–196, 345, 355; grant to, 368; and institutional identity, 45, 192, 193; and knowledge-practice tension, 64–65, 81; leadership of, 194–195; M.A.T. program at, 195, 375; niche of, 355; religious affiliation of, 189, 193–194; in sample, 11, 188, 277; school involvement by, 194–195, 375; and state regulation, 47

English, T. H., 380

Eriksson, E. M., 133, 134

Ethical dimensions, and mission, 401–402

Europe: sloyd courses from, 156, 170; teachers' seminaries in, 139

Evans, J., 205

Evers, N. H., 231

External forces: on normal schools, 158–162, 174, 390; on private institutions, 220–225; on research universities, 271–276; on teacher education, 389–390

F

Faculty: and collegial dialogue, 30–31; congeniality and collegiality for, 63, 80–81; issues of, 61–66; at liberal arts colleges, 92, 95, 96, 101, 102–103, 105–106, 111–112, 126, 127–129; maturing of, 43; morale of, 22, 26, 46; passivity of, 398, 406–409

Favrot, L. M., 379

Fayetteville, North Carolina, normal school at, 145

Fellenberg, and Pestalozzi, 346

Felmley, President, 272

Finegan, T., 296–298, 301, 310, 323

Fisher Act of 1961 (California), 273

Fitchburg Normal School, evolution of, 54, 71–72, 175

Fitchburg State College: constituencies of, 163, 177; evolution of, 175–178; institutional niche of, 154, 177–178; leadership at, 166, 176; and military training, 162; mission of, 176; and normative issues, 54; pedagogical ideals of, 156; and populism issues, 71–72; programmatic approach of, 156, 157, 176–177; in sample, 10, 153

Fitchburg State Teachers College, evolution of, 176

Fitzgerald, P. A., 229

Ford, H., 92

Ford Foundation, 195, 228, 374

Forsyth Normal and Industrial School, evolution of, 347, 348–349

Forsyth State Agricultural and Mechanical School, evolution of, 356, 357–358, 359, 361–362

Fort Valley High and Industrial School, evolution of, 349–350, 362

Fort Valley State College: and black students, 66, 154; constituencies of, 163; institutional niche of, 154, 166, 363–365, 371–373; mission of, 154–155, 347; programmatic approach of, 157, 348, 359, 364–365, 372; in sample 10, 11, 153, 377, 381; in state system, 331

Fosdick, R. B., 381

Foundation School, evolution of, 98. See also Berry College

Fox, M. L., 134, 135

Fragmentation: aspects of, 27–29; issues of, 50–66

Franklin, B., 228

Franklin, V. P., 321

Franklin College, evolution of, 331, 335–336, 353. See also Georgia, University of

Free School Act of 1834 (Pennsylvania), 290

Friendship Baptist Church, 351

Fund for the Improvement of Postsecondary Education, 219

G

Gage, H. M., 111–112

Gammon Theological Seminary, evolution of, 376

Garrity, A. W., Jr., 199

Gastel, B., 410

Geiger, C. H., 114, 134

Gender, aspects of, 73–75. See also Women

General Education Board (GEB), 145–146, 247, 345, 350, 351, 353, 359, 360, 362, 376, 381

General Education Fund, 337

George Peabody College for Teachers, status of, 44

Georgia: accreditation in, 93; aspects of teacher education in, 330–381; background on, 330–332; black teacher education in, 341–351, 357–359, 361–366, 371–374; certification in, 33, 34,

219, 340, 354, 360, 361, 366, 367–368, 371, 375; commitment in, 374–375; community involvement in, 350–351; community involvement in, 350–351; competency-based teacher education in, 274, 370–371, 376–377; competition in, 336, 375–377, 391; conclusions on, 371–377; curriculum in, 340, 343, 364–365, 372; Department of Education in, 91, 358, 366–371, 372; desegregation in, 372, 373; external forces on, 390; in New South, 351–356; normal schools in, 183, 331, 335, 337, 339–340; private schools in, 374–375; and racism, 70, 330–381; regulation in, 47–48; state system in, 356–361; summer sessions in, 339, 349–350, 352–353, 357–358, 359, 364; teacher education studied in, 5–6, 10, 11, 13; white teacher education in, 332–340, 359–361; women in, 331, 338–339, 340, 344, 351, 356. *See also* Berry College; Emory University; Fort Valley State College; Georgia institutions; Mercer University in Atlanta

Georgia, University of: and Berry College, 91; branches of, 345, 352; College of Education at, 353, 356, 359–361, 362, 366, 367–368, 369–370, 371, 375, 387; constituencies of, 252, 342; Cooperative Program in Elementary Education of, 368; Division for the Education of Exceptional Children at, 368; Division of Extension Teaching at, 355; Division of General Extension at, 356; external forces at, 272, 274, 390; impact of, 340, 343, 344; internal forces at, 271; and knowledge-practice tension, 64–65; mission of, 245, 247–248; in New South, 352–353; Peabody School of Education of, 247–248, 353,

354, 355, 356; in sample, 11, 237, 377; School of Pedagogy at, 352; and state regulation, 47; in state system, 330, 331, 333, 335–336, 339, 341

Georgia, University System of: and black teacher education, 361–366; evolution of, 330, 331, 353, 375–376

Georgia Association of Superintendents, 360–361

Georgia Council on Teacher Education, 366

Georgia Education Association, 361

Georgia Educational Models, 47

Georgia Institute of Technology, branch of, 248

Georgia Normal and Industrial College, evolution of, 338, 340, 353

Georgia Normal and Industrial School for Women, evolution of, 331

Georgia Program for Improvement of Instruction, 360, 366

Georgia School of Technology, evolution of, 331, 338, 345

Georgia State College for Women, evolution of, 356

Georgia State College of Business Administration, evolution of, 59, 248. *See also* Georgia State University

Georgia State Teachers College, evolution of, 354

Georgia State University: and black students, 67; College of Education at, 59, 60, 67, 391; constituencies for, 249, 252; external forces on, 272; internal forces on, 271; and knowledge-practice tension, 65; mission of, 248; program proliferation at, 57, 58, 59–61; in sample, 11, 237, 377; School of Education at, 59, 375; status of, 50

Georgia Teachers Association, 337

GI Bill, and normal schools, 162, 163, 171

Gifford, B. R., 236, 237, 250, 279
Gill, G. N., 410
Gilligan, C., 75, 82
Gilman, D. C., 243
Gilmer Trust Fund, 399
Girls' High and Normal School, evolution of, 148–149
Goldsboro, North Carolina, normal school at, 145
Goodlad, J. I., 3, 38, 40–44, 46, 49–53, 58–67, 69–70, 72–73, 75, 77, 78, 80, 81, 82, 132, 194, 234, 386, 388, 389, 411
Gordy, J. P., 181, 182, 183
Graduate education: at liberal arts colleges, 110; at normal schools, 147–148, 150, 156–157, 171, 175; at private institutions, 190, 191–192, 195, 196, 201, 206, 208–209, 210, 211, 213, 215, 216–217, 221–222; at research universities, 237, 250, 258, 263, 268, 277
Grant, C. A., 78
Graves, F., 297
Great Depression. See Depression
Guthrie, J. W., 38, 179–180, 183, 184, 186, 188, 227, 228, 267, 279, 283, 409, 411
Gutmann, A., 78

H

Haas, F., 302
Habermas, J., 399, 411
Hall, G. S., 169, 170, 173
Hall, S., 137
Hamilton, A., 283
Hamilton College, impact of, 117
Hampton Normal and Agricultural Institute: founding of, 144; as model, 145, 146
Harno, A. J., 242
Harper, C. A., 150, 182, 183, 184, 241–242, 280
Harris, J. H., 120, 122–123, 135
Harris, W. T., 136
Harrison, E., 155–156, 209–210, 211, 231

Harvard University: electives at, 119; Graduate School of Education at, 222, 227; impact of, 170, 192, 287, 304; and research emphasis, 152
Havlick, J., 315, 328
Hazard family, 348, 357
Head Start, 211
Hedley, G., 132
Heffernan, H., 281
Hekhuis, M., 233
Hendrick, I. G., 12, 42, 43, 76, 82, 185–186, 232, 233, 236, 280, 284, 387, 389, 391, 396
Hendricks, J., 218–219, 220, 233
Herbart, J., 53, 78, 140, 169, 206, 254
Herbst, J., 43–44, 46, 53, 69, 71, 76, 77, 78, 82, 138, 139–140, 141, 148, 150, 181, 182, 183, 184, 231, 289, 321
Hercules, 409
Hetzel, R. D., 306
Higgins, L., 230
Highley, A., 315–316, 328
Hill, D. J., 119
Hill, W. B., 352
Hobbes, T., 396, 411
Hodgson, N., 81
Hofstadter, R., 227
Holland, E. O., 294–295, 299, 321, 322
Holley, J., 347–348, 349, 357
Holmes, A. W., 222
Holmes Group, 222
Homer, 395
Hoover, H., 107
Horowitz, F., 215
House, E. R., 3, 37
Howard University, Normal and Preparatory Department of, 144
Howey, K., 233–234
Howison, G. H., 257
Hubbard, W., 348, 349, 357–358
Hughes, R. M., 283
Hunt, E. W., 120
Hunt, H., 349–350
Huntington, W. E., 196, 223, 228

I

Illinois: certification in, 211, 215; competency-based programs in, 47; normal schools in, 144, 183, 184, 240–242, 289; populism in, 71; teacher education studied in, 5–6, 10, 11. *See also* Chicago State University; Illinois institutions; National College of Education; Roosevelt University

Illinois, University of: accreditation of, 238; chair of pedagogy at, 244; College of Education at, 251, 263–264, 269–270; and competition, 391; constituencies for, 249, 251; Department of Education at, 241, 254; external forces on, 272; internal forces on, 263–264, 269–270, 271; leadership of, 241–242, 276; mission of, 240–242, 244; niche of, 238; practice school at, 256; program development at, 254–256; in sample, 11, 237; School of Education at, 255

Illinois Industrial University, evolution of, 240

Illinois Normal University: constituencies of, 163, 164; and Herbartianism, 53, 140; impact of, 254; mission of, 144, 154–155; niche of, 166, 240, 241–242, 272; pedagogical ideals of, 155; and populism, 70–71; program of, 149–150

Illinois State Board of Education, 232

Illinois State University: and normative issues, 53; and populism issues, 70–71; in sample, 10, 153

Indian reservations, and teacher training, 156

Indiana, private institution in, 137

Indiana Normal School (Pennsylvania): evolution of, 322, 325; impact of, 301, 324

Industrial education: in county training schools, 145–146; in Georgia, 345–346

Institute for Colored Youth, role of, 290, 310

Institutional identity: aspects of search for, 20–23; issues of, 41–50; loss of, and research emphasis, 386–388. *See also* Mission

Institutional niches. *See* Niches

Institutions: case histories on evolution of, 8, 9–10, 12–13; chairs of pedagogy at, 147; contexts of, 16–17; evolution of, 85–284. *See also* Liberal arts colleges; Normal schools; Private institutions; Public institutions; Research universities

International Reading Association, 65

Iowa: branch campuses for summer school in, 165; certification in, 209; farm earnings in, 351; institutional niche in, 154; normal schools in, 184; State Department of Public Instruction in, 133, 134; teacher education studied in, 5–6, 10, 11. *See also* Coe College; Drake University; Iowa institutions; Northern Iowa, University of

Iowa, University of: Department of Pedagogy at, 244; impact of, 103; and institutional niche, 167

Iowa State Normal School: constituencies of, 163, 164–165, 185; leadership at, 166; programmatic approach of, 43, 156, 157

Iowa State Teachers College: Malcolm Price Laboratory School at, 158; niche of, 167

Iowa State University, and institutional niche, 167

J

Jackson, J. B., 283

James, E. J., 241–242, 272, 276

James, E. O., 132

Jeanes Foundation, Anna T., Negro Rural School Fund of, 349, 359, 366

Jefferson, T., 88

Jencks, C., 287, 320–321

Johanningmeier, E. V., 241, 242, 262, 269, 280, 281, 282, 283, 284

John Swett Elementary School, 105, 132–133

Johns Hopkins University, impact of, 243

Johnson, A. C., 381

Johnson, H. C., Jr., 241, 242, 262, 269, 280, 281, 282, 283, 284

Johnson, K. R., 210

Johnson, R. L., 248–249, 281

Johnson, W. R., 14, 77, 149, 150, 151–152, 184, 386, 409

Joint Task Force on Teacher Preparation, 234

Jones, D. P., 173

Jones, J., 230

Jones, W., 108

Jordan, F., 81

Judge, H., 25, 39, 188, 222, 227, 234

Junior League, and Emory, 194, 228

Juvenal, 395–396, 410

K

Kaestle, C. F., 181

Kahn, A. S., 227, 229

Kahn, R. L., 409

Kane, H. T., 129, 381

Karman, T. A., 280, 284

Katz, D., 409

Keene State College: and normative issues, 55–56; and populism issues, 71

Keep, R. A., 131, 132

Keith, J., 301–302, 324

Kerr, C., 240, 279

Kessler, A. G., 314–315, 328

King, M., 80

Kinley, D., 276

Kirkpatrick, D., 78

Klein, F., 77, 78

Knowledge-practice tension: aspects of, 32–34; issues of, 61–66

Knox College, impact of, 108

Koerner, J. D., 284

Kohlberg, L., 75

Kraemer, Director, 104

Krasker, A., 198

Kutztown Normal School, 322

Kyte, G. C., 261, 280, 281, 282, 283, 284

L

Labaree, D. F., 326

Lagemann, E. C., 52, 78

Lambert, R. S., 93

Lancaster, J., 137, 155

Lancaster, Massachusetts, teacher training school in, 137

Lancaster County Normal School, evolution of, 292

Lange, A. F., 257, 259, 260, 264, 282

Larson, C. A., 283

Law schools: and knowledge-practice tension, 34; and public trust, 48; and socialization, 28; and status, 393

Leadership: at normal schools, 166, 169, 171, 173, 176; of private institutions, 194–195, 198, 199, 205, 213, 216, 217, 218–219; for research universities, 241–242, 243, 252, 276–278. *See also* Administrators

Leander Clark College, absorbed by Coe College, 110

Learned, W. S., 184, 327

Leland, A., 217

Lelon, T. C., 232

Leonard, J. P., 42–43

Lesson planning, and state certification, 33

Levin, R. A., 17, 40, 77, 79, 80, 81, 82, 224, 227, 228, 233, 236*n*, 281

Lewisburg, University at, evolution of, 117–119, 122. *See also* Bucknell University

Lexington Normal School: impact of, 177–178; mission of, 138, 139

Liberal arts colleges: and accreditation, 127, 128; attributes of, 87–135; background on, 87–88; conclusions on, 126–129; and external forces, 389–390; faculties at, 92, 95, 96, 101, 102–103, 105–106, 111–112, 126, 127–129; future of, 129; graduate education at, 110; and institutional identity, 20–21, 22; and research emphasis, 26, 387; in sample, 6, 7, 10, 12; and stability, 18; and status, 389. *See also* Berry College; Bucknell University; Coe College; Mills College
Lieberman, M., 409
Lilly Endowment, 98
Lindenwood College for Women, impact of, 112
Lindsay, J. A., 92–93, 95
Livy, 396
Lock Haven Normal School, 322
Loomis, J. R., 118–119
Loring School, and kindergarten teaching, 209
Ludmerer, K., 410
Lutheran tradition, and private university, 190, 215
Lyon, M., 99, 101

M

McCabe, J. E., 112–113, 115, 133, 134
McGiffert, M., 231
Machiavelli, N., 396, 410
Madison University, impact of, 117
Major universities. *See* Research universities
Malcom, H., 118
Malinowski, B., 392
Mann, H., 101, 138, 289
Manolakes, T., 284
Mansfield Normal School, 322
Manual training: in normal schools, 156, 170, 177; and normative issues, 54
Marquis, J. A., 110–111
Marshall, President, 110

Martha Berry School for Girls, evolution of, 89, 90, 93, 98. *See also* Berry College
Martin, J. O., 354, 355, 380
Marts, A. C., 121
Marx, K., 385
Maryland State Normal School, faculty at, 151–152
Massachusetts: Board of Education in, 175; certification in, 48–49, 201, 225, 234; normal schools in, 137, 138, 139–140, 141, 143, 150, 151, 182, 294; populism in, 71; special education in, 198–199, 203; teacher education studied in, 5–6, 10, 11. *See also* Boston institutions; Fitchburg State College
Master Plan for Higher Education, 175, 250, 272
Mattingly, P. H., 181
Mead, C. D., 261
Medical College Admission Test, 394
Medical Schools: and external forces, 393–394; and knowledge-practice tension, 34; and public trust, 48; and research emphasis, 392; and socialization, 28; and status, 393
Melder, K. E., 181
Mercer University in Atlanta: accreditation of, 219; and certification, 219; constituency of, 219; Department of Practical Arts at, 345; evolution of, 218–220, 376; expansion of, 218; leadership of, 218–219; niche of, 375; pedagogy in, 219–220; religious affiliation of, 189, 218, 375; in sample, 11, 188, 377; and urban education, 69, 219
Mercer University in Macon, evolution of, 218, 375
Methodist Episcopalian tradition, mission of, 116
Methodist tradition: and Georgia institutions, 330; and private universities, 189, 193–194, 196, 204–205

Metz, M. S., 105, 132

Michigan, University of: chair of education at, 244; impact of, 170, 257, 259

Middle Georgia College, evolution of, 338

Midwest, normal school evolution in, 140–143

Miller, J., 45, 228

Millersville State, evolution of, 292, 322

Mills, C. T., 100

Mills, S. T., 100, 105

Mills College: attributes of, 99–106; Children's School at, 103, 104–105, 128, 132; context of, 87, 390; Department of Child Development at, 103–104; Department of Education at, 102, 103, 104, 105; Department of Music at, 104; Department of Psychology at, 103; development of, 101–104; faculty at, 101, 102–103, 105–106, 127–129; founding of, 99–100; and Oakland Unified School District Teacher Training Center and Demonstration School, 105, 132–133; in sample, 10; School of Education at, 102; summer school at, 102; teacher education at, 105–106

Mills Seminary-College, evolution of, 100

Miner School, founding of, 144

Minimum Foundations Program, 368–369, 370, 372

Minnesota, normal school in, 141

Minnesota, University of, impact of, 170

Minority students, and urban problem, 35, 66–69

Miss Harrison's Kindergarten Training School, evolution of, 155–156. *See also* National College of Education

Mission: and change, 400–403; and ethical dimensions, 401–402; and excellence, 402; of liberal arts colleges, 110, 111; of normal schools, 154–155, 165, 168–169, 172, 173, 176, 178–179; and *praxis*, 402–403; of private institutions, 197, 211, 212, 218; of research universities, 238–249; and scholarly inquiry, 402. *See also* Institutional identity

Mitchell, E., 104, 132

Model schools, in normal schools, 157–158, 170

Monitorial plan, in teacher training schools, 137

Monroe, W. S., 78

Moore, E. C., 266

Morehouse College, evolution of, 363, 376

Morpeth, R. W., 281

Morrill Act of 1862; and Georgia institutions, 335, 336, 344; and liberal arts colleges, 119; and research institutions, 237, 238–240, 243, 245, 247, 397

Morrill Act of 1890, 344–345

Morris Brown College, evolution of, 344, 376

Mount Holyoke College, impact of, 99, 100

Mountain School, evolution of, 90. *See also* Berry College

Multiversity, research university as, 240

Muscogee Elementary School, 353

N

National Board for Professional Teaching Standards, 410

National Board scores (medical education), 394

National College of Education (NCE): and accreditation, 210; Baker Demonstration School of, 65; Children's School of, 210; and competency-based programs, 47; evolution of, 209–212; expansion of, 210; future for, 180; and knowledge-practice tension, 65; mission of, 211, 223; niche of, 166; pedagogical ideals of, 155–

156; programmatic approach of, 158; and Protestantism, 190; research emphasis of, 189; in sample, 11, 153, 188; School of Education of, 211, 212

National Commission on Teacher Education, 366

National Congress of Mothers, 209

National Council for Accreditation of Teacher Education (NCATE): and liberal arts colleges, 127, 131; and normal schools, 158, 160–161, 171; and program expansion, 59; and research universities, 238, 263, 275, 391

National Council of Teachers of Mathematics, 65

National Education Association, 169

National Kindergarten and Elementary College, evolution of, 210. See also National College of Education

National Kindergarten Association, 210

National Kindergarten College, evolution of, 210. See also National College of Education

National Labor Relations Board, 96

National School Boards Association, 234

National Science Foundation, 368

National Survey of Students in Teacher Education Programs, 66

National Teacher Education exam, 185

National Teacher Test, 370

National Teachers' Examination, 376

Neff, J., 137

Nelms, V., 218–219, 220, 233

Networks, for school-university collegiality, 66

Nevada at Reno, University of, impact of, 130

New England, normal schools in, 137–140

New Hampshire: normal school in, 149; rural schools in, 55–56

New Harmony Community School, founding of, 137

New York City, normal school in, 149

New York College for the Training of Teachers, evolution of, 147–148. See also Teachers College

New York state, teacher training schools in, 137, 140, 294, 296

New York State Normal College at Albany, admission to, 150

New York World's Fair, 250

Newell, M. A., 149, 181, 183, 184

Newman, J. H., 87, 129

Niches: of normal schools, 154, 161, 166–168, 172, 174, 175, 177–178; of private institution, 189; of research universities, 239–240, 277

Normal School Act of 1857 (Pennsylvania), 290–291, 292

Normal schools: and accreditation, 159–161, 166, 171; aspects of evolution for, 136–137; background on, 136–137; for black students, 144–147, 154; characteristics of, 153–154; and competition, 391; conclusions on, 178–181; constituencies of, 163–165, 170–171, 174–175, 177, 178–179; contributions of, 179; extent of, 143–144; external forces on, 158–162, 174, 390; and gender issues, 73–74; generalizations on, 153–168; graduate education at, 147–148, 150, 156–157, 171, 175; history of, 137–153; implications of, 179–180; and institutional identity, 21, 42–45, 69; internal forces on, 165–166, 171–172, 175; and knowledge-practice tension, 62; leadership at, 166, 169, 171, 173, 176; mission of, 154–155, 165, 168–169, 172, 173, 176, 178–179; model schools in, 157–158, 170; niches of, 154, 161, 166–168, 172, 174, 175, 177–178; normative issues in, 52–53; pedagogical ideals of, 155–156, 169–

Normal schools (*continued*)
170; as people's college, 143, 289; programmatic approaches of, 156–158, 169–170, 173–174, 176–177; research emphasis of, 387; services of, 164–165; and social forces, 161–162; and stability, 18; and status, 389; summer sessions of, 165, 170, 171; teachers colleges evolved from, 150–151, 155; university concepts for, 149–153; vignettes of, 168–178. *See also* Central State University; Chicago State University; Fitchburg State College; Fort Valley State University; Illinois State University; National College of Education; Northern Colorado, University of; Northern Iowa, University of; Public institutions; San Francisco State University; West Chester State University

North Central Association (NCA) of Colleges and Secondary Schools, 151, 158, 160

North Central Association of Colleges of Teacher Education, 210

North Carolina, normal schools in, 145

North Georgia Agricultural College, evolution of, 336

Northern Colorado, University of: and accreditation, 160–161, 171; constituencies of, 170–171; evolution of, 168–172; and internal forces, 165, 171–172; leadership at, 166, 169, 171; and military training, 171; mission of, 168–169, 172, 180; niche of, 172; pedagogical ideal at, 169; programmatic approaches of, 169–170; in sample, 11, 153

Northern Iowa, University of: and institutional identity, 42, 43–45; Price Laboratory School at, 44; in sample, 11, 153

Northwestern University, impact of, 205, 210

Nurss, J., 59–60

O

Oakes, J., 78

Oakland Unified School District Teacher Training Center and Demonstration School, 105, 132–133

Oberlin College, impact of, 99

Odgers, M. M., 121–122, 134

Oglethorpe Practice School, 350

Oklahoma: controls in, 274; institutional niche in, 154; normal schools in, 184; teacher education studied in, 5–6, 10, 11. *See also* Central State University; Oklahoma institutions

Oklahoma, University of, impact of, 274

Oklahoma Agricultural and Mechanical College, evolution of, 245–247. *See also* Oklahoma State University

Oklahoma Normal School: constituencies of, 163; model school at, 157

Oklahoma State University; College of Education at, 277; constituencies of, 252; external forces at, 272, 274, 275; and institutional identity, 44; internal forces at, 270–271; leadership of, 277; mission of, 245–247; preparatory department of, 246–247; in sample, 11, 237; School of Education at, 275, 277

Oliphant, J. O., 134, 135

Oregon, normal schools in, 184–185

Orr, D., 377, 378

Orr, G. J., 337, 338

Oskaloosa College, evolution of, 207. *See also* Drake University

Oswego, New York, normal school in, 140

Oxford University, impact of, 101

P

Paine College, evolution of, 374

Parent Teacher Association, 209

Parker, F., 340

Parsons, L. B., 109

Parsons Seminary, evolution of, 107, 109. *See also* Coe College
Payne, E. G., 379
Payne, W. H., 282
Peabody, G. F., 349
Peabody Education Fund, 336–337, 338, 339, 345, 353
Pedagogical ideals: of normal schools, 155–156, 169–170; in private institutions, 191–192, 200–201, 219–220
Peirce, C., 138, 163, 164
Pendley, E. H., 130, 131
Pennsylvania: aspects of teacher education in, 287–329; certification in, 290, 291; college status in, 302; community colleges in, 307–309; competition in, 309–320, 391; constituencies in, 311–313; control by, 295–296; corruption in, 294; curriculum in, 292–293, 294, 297–298; Department of Public Instruction in, 296, 300; education conference in, 124; external forces in, 390; history of teacher education in, 289–320; market forces in, 289, 309–320; normal schools in, 52–53, 161, 183, 289–302, 309–310, 312–317, 318–319; private institutions in, 289–292; professionalization in, 296–298; regulation in, 47, 123; summer programs in, 299–301; teacher education studied in, 5–6, 10, 11, 13; teachers' colleges in, 303–304; university status in, 304; women in, 313–316. *See also* Bucknell University; Pennsylvania institutions; Pittsburgh, University of; Temple University; West Chester institutions
Pennsylvania, University of: extension services of, 299; impact of, 297; niche of, 310, 311–313
Pennsylvania Association of Liberal Arts Colleges for the Advancement of Teacher Education, 318
Pennsylvania School Code of 1911, 295

Pennsylvania State Educational Association, 300
Pennsylvania State University: branch campuses of, 305–306; College of Education at, 306; commonwealth campuses of, 306–309; constituencies of, 251, 252, 311–313; extension services of, 299, 300–301; external forces at, 272; history of, 304–309, 323; impact of, 297; and institutional niche, 161, 288, 289, 316–320; internal forces at, 271; leadership of, 252; mission of, 245, 300; and normative issues, 54; in sample, 11, 237, 321; School of Education at, 54, 252, 271, 297, 300, 306, 316
Perkins, L. N., 321
Perlmann, J., 234
Pestalozzi, J. H., 140, 155, 346
Pestalozzi/Froebel College, acquisition of, 210. *See also* National College of Education
Phi Beta Kappa, 121
Phi Delta Kappa, 260
Philadelphia: competition in, 310–313, 326; kindergartens in, 311
Philadelphia Model School, early role of, 137, 181
Philadelphia Normal School, evolution of, 290, 310
Philips, G., 315
Phillips, D. E., 206
Phillips, L., 123
Pittsburgh, University of: branches of, 305, 308; constituencies of, 313; extension services of, 299, 301; impact of, 297, 330; niche of, 288, 305; and state support, 303, 320, 323
Platteville, Wisconsin, normal school at, 142
Plutarch, 395, 410
Plymouth, North Carolina, normal school at, 145
Plymouth State College (New Hampshire), and normative issues, 55
Populism, aspects of, 70–73

Possum Trot Church, 89, 91. *See also* Berry College
Possum Trot Elementary School, 93
Possum Trot School, 94, 98
Powell, A. G., 152, 184, 223, 227, 234
Practice, knowledge in tension with, 32–34, 61–66
Practitioners. *See* Student teaching
Praxis: concept of, 399; and mission, 402–403
Presbyterian tradition: and Coe College, 107–109; mission of, 116
Princeton University, impact of, 119
Private institutions: accreditation for, 210, 213, 215, 216, 219; attributes of, 187–235; background on, 187–188; characteristics of, 188–190; and competition, 391; conclusions on, 220–226; constituencies of, 190, 199, 207, 211, 213, 219; evolution of, 193–220; external forces on, 220–225; future for, 226; graduate education at, 190, 191–192, 195, 196, 201, 206, 208–209, 210, 211, 213, 215, 216–217, 221–222; history of teacher education in, 191–192; and institutional identity, 45–46; leadership of, 194–195, 198, 199, 205, 213, 216, 217, 218–219; mission of, 197, 211, 212, 218; national, 193–204; niche of, 189; pedagogy in, 191–192, 200–201, 219–220; programs at, 190, 215–216; religious affiliations of, 189–190, 193–194, 196, 200, 201, 203, 204–205, 207, 215, 218; research emphasis of, 24, 189, 196, 206, 209, 212, 221, 226, 387; in sample, 6–7, 11, 12; schools involved with, 193, 194–195, 198–199, 206–207, 208, 214, 222; service orientation of, 191–192, 196–197, 198, 201, 206, 216–217; status of teacher education in, 223–224, 389; summer schools of, 201, 205; and urban education, 190, 197, 198–199, 209, 211, 212, 215, 222–223. *See also* Boston College; Boston University; California Lutheran University; Denver University; Drake University; Emory University; Mercer University in Atlanta; National College of Education; Roosevelt University
Professional schools: in coalition with teacher education, 404; and external involvement, 407; in private institutions, 196, 200, 202, 205, 207; themes for, 392–395
Professionalism, and knowledge-practice tension, 32–34
Programs: fragmentation of, 27–29; issues of, 50–66; of normal schools, 156–158, 169–170, 173–174, 176–177; of private institutions, 190, 215–216; proliferation of, 56–61; of research universities, 253–262
Progressive movement: and normal schools, 140, 149, 156, 177; and Pennsylvania reforms, 288, 296–297; and private institutions, 209, 212, 214
Prophets, School for the, evolution of, 107, 108. *See also* Coe College
Public institutions: future of, 180–181; and normal school evolution, 136–186; and research emphasis, 24, 25–26; in sample, 6, 10–11, 12. *See also* Normal schools
Public Law, 94–142, 199
Pullin, D., 234
Punahou School, 100

Q

Quality Basic Education Act of 1985 (Georgia), 377

R

Rackley, J. R., 306
Rainey, H. P., 120–121
Ramsey, B. C., 378, 379, 380

Raths, J., 284
Reagan, R., 174
Redcay, E. E., 380
Reed, R., 321, 325
Regional institutions, in sample, 6.
See also Normal schools; Public
institutions
Reinhardt, A. H., 101–103, 132
Religious affiliations: for Georgia
institutions, 330–331, 334, 342,
350, 351, 362, 374, 375, 376; for
private institutions, 189–190,
193–194, 196, 203, 204–205, 207,
215, 218
Research emphasis: antiquity of,
395; aspects of, 23–27; impact of,
36–37; in liberal arts colleges, 96,
129; and loss of identity, 386–
388; and normal schools, 152; of
private institutions, 24, 189, 196,
206, 209, 212, 221, 226, 387; of
professional schools, 392
Research universities: accreditation
for, 238, 263, 275; aspects of
teacher education in, 236–284;
background on, 236–238; and
competition, 391; conclusions on,
278–279; constituencies of, 249–
253, 258; education faculty status at, 263, 389; external forces
on, 271–276; graduate education at, 237, 250, 258, 263, 268,
277; internal forces on, 262–271;
leadership for, 241–242, 243,
252, 276–278; missions of, 238–
249; niches of, 239–240, 277; and
practical studies, 239–240; programmatic development of, 253–
262; research emphasis in, 23–
24, 387; in sample, 6, 11, 12; service orientation of, 251–253;
summer courses from, 251–252,
254, 276. *See also* California at
Berkeley, University of; Georgia, University of; Georgia State
University; Illinois, University of;
Oklahoma State University;
Pennsylvania State University;
Temple University

Reward system, in teacher educa-
tion, 405
Rice University, impact of, 131
Riesman, D., 287, 320–321
Ringel, P. J., 79
Ritchey, C. J., 231
Robbins, J., 59
Robinson, D., 284
Rockefeller, J. D., 337, 351
Rogers, D. E., 410
Roosevelt F. D., 213
Roosevelt University: and accredi-
tation, 213; Auditorium Build-
ing of, 188, 213; College of Ed-
ucation of, 214, 215; constituency
of, 213; evolution of, 212–215;
leadership for, 213; Research and
Development Center of, 214; in
sample, 11, 188; school involve-
ment by, 214, 220; Teacher Corps
Center of, 215; and urban edu-
cation, 212, 213, 215, 223; and
YMCA, 190, 212–213
Rosenwald Fund, Julius, 349, 359,
360, 362, 364, 374, 380–381
Ross, E. D., 231, 232
Rothman, S. M., 231
Rudolph, F., 227
Rugg, H., 78
Rulon, P. R., 280
Rural schools, and normative is-
sues, 55–56
Rury, J. L., 234
Ryan Act of 1970 (California), 273

S

Salem, Massachusetts, normal school
at, 139
Salisbury, North Carolina, normal
school at, 145
San Francisco State Normal School,
evolution of, 42, 172–173
San Francisco State University:
constituencies of, 174–175; evolution of, 172–175; external
forces on, 174; Frederic Burk
School at, 158, 174; and institutional identity, 42–45, 49; internal forces on, 175; leadership at,

San Francisco State University (*cont.*) 166, 173; mission of, 172–173; niche of, 174, 175, 250, 268; pedagogical ideals at, 156; programmatic approach at, 157, 158, 162, 173–174; Ritual of Teachers Guild Service of, 74; in sample, 10–11, 153; School of Education at, 43, 174; and special education, 173–174

San Jose State University, niche of, 250, 268

Sanders, J. W., 230

Saphier, J., 80

Sarason, B., 3, 37

Sargent School of Physical Education, 58

Schön, D., 409

School involvement, by private institutions, 193, 194–195, 198–199, 206–207, 208, 214, 222

School reform, and evolution of teacher education, 3–4, 19–20, 29, 35–36

Schwab, J., 83

Schwebel, M., 235

Scott, F. W., 279

Scott, W. R., 409

Scranton, W., 303

Sears, B., 337

Seeley, H. H., 166

Sell, E. S., 378

Service orientation: of normal schools, 164–165; of private institutions, 191–192, 196–197, 198, 201, 206, 216–217; of research universities, 251–253

Shannon, D. A., 38, 227

Shatto, G. M., 96, 131

Shattuck, J. G., 206

Shettle, F., 229

Shibles, B., 229

Shippensburg Normal School, 322

Shufelt, L., 65

Silber, J., 69, 199

Sinclair, T. M., 110

Sirotnik, K. A., 39, 81, 234, 385, 411

Sisyphus, 386

Sizer, T., 66

Slater Fund, John F., 146, 345, 348, 349, 359, 374, 380

Sleeter, C. E., 78

Slippery Rock Normal School, 322

Sloyd courses, in normal schools, 156, 170

Smart, J. G., 71, 82

Smith, A. T., 328

Smith, H., 353

Smith, W., 227

Smith, W. W., 110

Smith-Hughes Act of 1917, 300, 348, 354

Smith-Lever Act of 1914, 354

Snyder, Z. X., 166, 169, 170, 185

Socialization, and fragmentation, 28–29

Soder, R., 34, 38, 385, 409, 410, 411

Solomon, B. M., 227

South, normal schools in, 144–147, 330–381

Southern Association of Colleges and Secondary Schools, 90, 91, 94

Southern California, University of, niche of, 264, 268

Southern College of Pharmacy, acquisition of by Mercer, 218

Southern Education Board, 351

Spalding, W., 270, 271

Sparling, E., 213

Special education programs: in normal schools, 156, 173–174; in private institutions, 198–199, 203

Spelman Seminary, evolution of, 344, 351, 363, 376

Spencer, H., 206

Spencer Foundation, 8, 214

Sperber, R., 69

Spring, J., 78

Sproul, R. G., 267

Sproul, W., 296

Stability and instability: aspects of, 18–20; issues of, 41–50

Stadtman, V. A., 131, 280, 282

Stanford, A., 315

Stanford University: chair of pedagogy at, 244; impact of, 170, 227, 264

State College of Agriculture (Georgia), evolution of, 335, 344, 345
State College of Industry for Colored Youth (Georgia), evolution of, 345, 365
State Female Normal School (Virginia), mission of, 144
State Normal School, evolution of, 331, 336, 339–340, 353, 354, 356. *See also* Georgia State Teachers College
State Teachers' Association (Georgia), 335
State Teachers' Society (Georgia), 339
States: bureaucracy and markets in, 287–329; competition and racism in, 330–381; evolution of teacher education in, 285–381; and knowledge-practice tension, 61; and liberal arts colleges, 128; and normal schools, 144–145, 155, 158–159, 174, 175; and stability, 42, 46–49. *See also* Certification
Status: antiquity of, 395–396; issues of, 41–50; and professional schools, 393; for teacher education, 388–389
Stepanek, C. C., 133
Stevens, S. K., 326
Stewart, J. P., 352, 353–354
Stone, J. C., 267, 283
Stowe, C., 138–139
Strategic action, and change, 403–406
Strauss, L., 411
Strayer, G. E., 381
Student teaching: and discontinuities, 31–32; issues of, 61–66; and knowledge-practice tension, 32–33; in normal schools, 157–158; in research universities, 258–259
Students, abilities and commitment of, 163–164. *See also* Constituencies
Sturzebecker, R. L., 302, 303, 322, 324

Su, Z., 37
Sullivan, H. B., 64, 198
Sullivan, L., 188
Summer sessions: in Georgia, 339, 349–350, 352–353, 357–358, 359, 364; at liberal arts colleges, 102, 124; at normal schools, 165, 170, 171; in Pennsylvania, 299–301; at private institutions, 201, 205; at research universities, 251–252, 254, 276
Sunday, B., 107
Suzzalo, H., 173
Swanson, A., 410
Sweden, sloyd courses from, 156, 170
Sykes, E., 303, 325

T

Talmadge, E., 357
Taylor, S. W., 117–118
Taylor, W. S., 321, 322, 323, 325, 326
Teacher Certification Test, 371
Teacher Corps, 215
Teacher education: administrative commitment to, 404–405; aspects of present from past of, 3–39; background on, 3–5; change in, 398–409; colonial, 137; and competition, 336, 375–377, 390–391, 394–396; conclusions on, 35–37; contemporary views of, 1–83; data gathering on, 7–9; discontinuities in, 29–32, 56–61; discussion of themes in, 391–398; diversity and commonality in, 15–17; ethical dimensions of, 401–402; evolution of, 85–381; excellence in, 402; exemplary programs in, 405; external forces on, 389–390; fragmentation in, 27–29, 50–66; future of, 383–411; gender issues in, 73–75; institutional identity sought in, 20–23; intellectual control of, 404; knowledge-practice tension in, 32–34, 61–66; in liberal arts col-

Teacher education (*continued*)
leges, 87–135; in normal schools, 136–186; pedagogical training by, 405; politics of, 385–411; populism and class in, 70–73; and *praxis*, 399, 402–403; in private universities, 187–235; professional schools in coalition with, 404; quality standards for, 405; research emphasis in, 23–27; in research universities, 236–284; reward system in, 405; sample in study of, 5–7, 10–11; and scholarly inquiry, 402; and school and community partnerships, 404; stability and instability in, 18–20, 41–50; state views of, 285–381; status declines for, 20–22, 44; status increases for, 388–389; and strategic action, 403–406; studying, 5–15; teaching methods in, 75–76; themes in, 18–35, 40–76, 386–398; and urban problem, 34–35

Teacher Proficiency Assessment Instrument, 371

Teachers College: history of, 38, 147; impact of, 210, 263, 265, 294, 297; status of, 44, 149, 227

Teachers College of the City of Boston, evolution of, 149

Teachers' institutes: and evolution of normal schools, 137–138, 143, 148, 151; in Georgia, 338; in Pennsylvania, 290

Teaching: methods issues in, 75–76; and research emphasis, 23–27

Temple University: constituencies for, 249, 251; deans at, 50; extension services of, 299–300, 301; external forces at, 272; internal forces at, 271; mission of, 248–249; niche of, 310–313; religious affiliation of, 249, 311; in sample, 11, 237, 321; and state support, 320, 323

Tennessee Supreme Court and religious control, 194

Texas, preparation hours in, 394

Theiss, L. E., 134, 135

Thomas, J. M., 271, 325

Thompson, J. G., 54, 166, 176, 177

Thorndike, E. L., 52

Thorne, B., 410

Tom, A. R., 81

Tompkins, A., 241

Townsend, M. E., 38, 227

Turner, F. J., 141

Tuskegee Institute: impact of, 345, 347, 348; as model, 145, 146

Tyack, D., 4, 38

U

Underwood, K., 12, 78, 136, 230, 231, 387, 389, 390, 391

United Kingdom, Lancasterian system from, 137

U.S. Army Air Force, 162

U.S. Department of Education, 128

U.S. Office of Education, 363

University Elementary School, 261

University High School (California), 259, 268

University High School (Georgia), 339

University High School (Illinois), 256

Urban education issue: aspects of, 34–35; diminishing commitments to, 66–69; and normal schools, 148–149; and private institutions, 190, 197, 198–199, 209, 211, 212, 215, 222–223; and research universities, 248

V

Values, and curriculum issues, 51–56

Van Til, W., 80

Vanderbilt University, and religious control, 194

Vassar College, impact of, 100, 103

Vermont, teacher training school in, 137

Veterans of Foreign Wars, 324

Veysey, L. R., 227, 287, 320

Vinovskis, M. A., 182, 183
Virginia, normal schools in, 144, 145
Virginia, University of, Rockfish Gap Report of 1818 from, 118
Virginia Normal and Collegiate Institute, mission of, 145
Vocationalism, and normative issues, 54

W

Wagoner, L. C., 103, 104
Walker, E., 252, 306–307, 308
Wallace, H., 107
Waltham, Massachusetts, extension program in, 57
Ward, J. C., 192, 195, 227, 228
Ware, E., 343, 344
Warren, W. F., 192, 227
Warren, W. M., 187, 227
Washburne, C., 173
Washington, B. T., 345, 348
Washington, D. C., normal schools in, 144
Washington, University of, and networks, 66
Wasserman, J., 142, 182
Watson, M., 132
Watters, R. K., 133
Wayland, F., 118, 119
Weber, S. E., 300
West Chester Academy, evolution of, 292
West Chester Normal School, evolution of, 52–53, 322
West Chester State Teachers College, evolution of, 302
West Chester University: constituencies of, 185, 304; deans at, 50; institutional niche of, 154, 289, 290, 325; mission of, 154; pedagogical ideals of, 155; programmatic approach of, 156–157; in sample, 11, 153, 321; and social forces, 161; and state support, 292, 302, 303; women at, 313–316, 327–328
Western Association of Schools and Colleges, 215, 216

Western College, absorbed by Coe College, 110
Westfield, Massachusetts, normal school at, 139–140
Wheeler, B. I., 258, 259, 261, 264, 265
White, E.-J. P., 133
White, J. B., 411
Whitewater, Wisconsin, normal school at, 142
Wilde, A., 49, 57, 79, 197, 229
Wilkes College, evolution of, 121
Willard, A. C., 242
Williams College, impact of, 100
Williston Jones School, evolution of, 107, 108. *See also* Coe College
Winona Normal School, students at, 141
Wisconsin, normal schools in, 142–143, 171, 289
Wisconsin, University of, and normal schools, 142
Wisniewski, R., 235
Women: and gender issues, 73–75; in Georgia, 331, 338–339, 340, 344, 351, 356; liberal arts college for, 99–106; in normal schools, 138, 139, 141, 144, 148, 149, 163, 164, 170–171, 174, 179; in Pennsylvania, 313–316; in private institutions, 190, 194, 196, 197, 200, 201–202, 203, 204, 207–208, 209–210, 211, 219; recruiting, 57, 79
Wood, F., 284
Wood, G., 107
Woodring, P., 182, 183, 184, 228
Woofter, T., 352, 353
World War I, and research universities, 265
World War II: and Georgia institutions, 366–367, 390; and normal schools, 161–162, 163, 165, 171, 173, 175, 178; and Pennsylvania institutions, 302, 315, 324; and private institutions, 198, 200, 205, 208; and research universities, 272
Wright, A. D., 380

Y

Yale University: impact of, 101, 119, 170, 202; Report of 1828 from, 118

Yeager, W. A., 323

Young Ladies' Seminary, evolution of, 99. *See also* Mills College

Young Men's Christian Association (YMCA), and private college, 190, 212–213

Z

Zelman, S., 234

Zimpher, N. L., 66, 81, 233–234